# Weeknight Meals
# Made Easy

# Weeknight Meals
# Made Easy

**Reader's Digest**

Montreal • New York

# Contents

# How to use this book

*Weeknight Meals Made Easy* is the answer to that everyday dilemma – what to serve for supper that's different, quick to prepare, healthy and, most importantly, will really get the taste buds tingling. Most of the recipes can be prepared, cooked and served in less than 30 minutes; others can be prepared quickly, then left to cook for 30 minutes or an hour while you get on with something else outside the kitchen – perhaps just relaxing with a glass of wine. All the recipes are nourishing, tasty and healthier than pre-made meals, which are usually heavy on salt, sugar and preservatives, but many of our quick dishes can be ready to eat in about the same amount of time it would take to heat up a TV dinner.

In the first chapter we explain how to make shopping, preparation and cooking quick and efficient, with suggestions about how you can stock up your pantry, fridge and freezer for the widest possible choice of meals. With our handy

checklists you can finish your shopping in record time and save money on unhealthy and pricey ready-made foods – choosing those convenience items, such as prepared vegetables, that will save you preparation time. Now you can cook a tasty, fresh, homemade meal every single day, no matter how busy you are.

### Equipment and quick techniques

When it comes to kitchen equipment, you don't need lots of gadgets but you do need a few good pots, pans and other essential items. On page 22 you will find a no-nonsense list of the equipment you need, as well as some items that make cooking easier but are not essential.

Some methods of cooking are more suitable for the quick cook than others, so we explain the six quickest and healthiest, such as stir-frying and grilling, on page 24. You will find lots of exciting dishes using these techniques in the

recipes that follow. And as it can be the simplest of kitchen chores that takes the longest time, we have given super-quick preparation techniques for vegetables and no-fuss shortcuts for cooking and preparation on pages 26-31.

### Ingredients and swaps

The recipes are mostly divided by main ingredient, so that you can select a variety of dishes for your week – the best way to aim for a balanced diet. You will also find chapters devoted to soups, light meals and vegetable-based meals. And for those days when you feel like something sweet to finish, or for a special occasion, we have the fastest-ever desserts. Many of the dishes can be prepared using pantry basics or with something you already have in the fridge or freezer – and there are lots of ingredient swaps, widening your choice even further. Some recipes are so easy to cook in bulk that we recommend cooking a double batch and then freezing one so that you have a meal ready to heat up for another day.

### Measuring and nutrition

When using the recipes, please note that eggs and vegetables (such as carrots, eggplants and onions) are medium-sized unless otherwise stated.

Each main recipe contains nutritional information, so that you can see at a glance how many calories or how much protein, fat or carbohydrate it contains – ideal if you're watching your weight or just keen to eat as healthily as possible. (A protein analysis is not given for desserts, however.) Optional ingredients or serving suggestions are not included in the analyses. Remember that if you choose a high-fat accompaniment, such as nan bread, this will greatly increase the calories and fat for your overall meal.

ⓥ **Suitable for vegetarians** Most cheeses are now suitable for vegetarians, but not all, as some cheeses are still made by traditional methods using animal rennet. Parmesan is one example, but you can choose Italian-style premium hard cheese instead. Always read the packaging carefully before buying cheese to serve to strict vegetarians.

# quick and easy cooking

# Smart Shopping for Easy Cooking

**The key to fast and healthy cooking is to be a smart shopper. The secret is knowing which convenience foods can save you time, without sacrificing flavour or quality. Keep your kitchen well stocked – having a wide range of ingredients close at hand when you want them will save you precious time when it comes to meal planning and preparation.**

## Take a list

A good shopping list will save you time and minimize stress and frustration. It will even save you money, as you will buy the items you actually need for your full week's meals rather than guessing and picking up things at random. Keep a notepad or board in the kitchen so that you can jot down items you run out of or need to buy as you think of them. Glance at the lists on pages 17, 19 and 21 from time to time to make sure your pantry, fridge and freezer are stocked with the basics, then add any fresh items you need after looking through your favourite recipes. You might find it helpful to jot down the ingredients you need for each recipe, then get organized and group similar items together on your list in the order of your store's layout, for a quick shopping trip.

## Shopping online

Online shopping is now offered by some major supermarkets, and this is becoming increasingly popular as websites get more sophisticated and easier to navigate. You can sometimes view items previously ordered, or repeat and add to a standard shopping list, making it even quicker. The items you order are delivered to your home at a time that suits you – which saves you the trouble of carrying your groceries home or driving to a faraway supermarket.

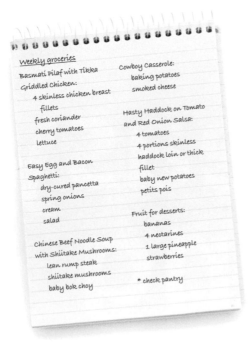

## Meat for fast meals

Many cuts of meat are sold ready-cubed, sliced or ground to reduce preparation time. There are also many quick-cook lean cuts that are ideal for speedy cooking methods such as stir-frying, grilling and griddling. Quick pork cuts are steaks, chops and tenderloin; snappy lamb cuts include leg steaks, cutlets and neck fillet; beef comes as stir-fry strips and minute steaks. For special occasions, venison steaks and veal escalopes are lean and tender cuts that can be grilled or pan-fried, and duck breast can be pan-fried or roasted. Liver is another great option. Ground beef, lamb, pork, chicken and turkey, or ground tofu for vegetarians, are must-haves for the freezer. Always go for lean meat, as it offers better value than economy packs, which tend to have a higher fat content.

If buying from a butcher or supermarket meat counter, ask the butcher to prepare cuts for you, by boning, trimming dicing, or cutting steaks to the exact size you want.

Bacon pieces and lardons, or strips or cubes of pancetta, are all perfect for quick meals. When buying sausages or chipolatas, choose the better-quality ones for a good flavour.

When it comes to poultry, chicken breast fillets and thighs are amazingly versatile – packs of individually wrapped chicken breast fillets are especially useful for the freezer and ready-roasted chicken from the deli counter, still hot and packed in a heat-sealed bag, makes an instant meal. Simply remove the skin and cut the meat into pieces to eat on its own with bread and a salad, or in a rice, grain or pasta dish.

## Great dairy basics

Cheeses are useful for making quick main meals, lunches and snacks, so it's worth having a selection. Choose a mature Cheddar to get the best flavour out of a small amount for adding to recipes. Strongly flavoured Parmesan works perfectly on pastas and most tomato-based dishes. Blue cheeses add flavour when they are melted over a chicken or steak. Mozzarella is good for pizzas and pasta, and soft cheeses are useful for spreads, dips and stuffings. Vacuum packs of ready-grated Cheddar cheese and mozzarella will save you time grating, but when it comes to Parmesan you will taste the difference if you grate your own rather than buying ready-grated. Parmesan shavings, however, make a good, authentic option.

Fresh cream (and in some cases, ricotta cheese or sour cream) is good for enriching soups, stews and sauces, and for creating dips and creamy desserts, making it a great fridge staple. Cream can be stirred directly into hot dishes and then simmered.

Low-fat yogurt and creamy, Greek-style yogurt are perfect for dips and cold dishes as well making cooling accompaniments for spicy dishes. Greek-style yogurt can also be used in much the same way as sour cream.

Tofu is a useful protein for vegetarian meals. Buy it plain or smoked in supermarkets, or try the variety of flavours found in health-food shops.

## Fast-cooking eggs

Eggs are a godsend for the quick cook. Eat them boiled, fried, scrambled, poached or in an omelette or frittata.

## Fish for swift suppers

Fish is ideal for busy people, as it is delicious, healthy and very quick to cook. If buying from a fresh-fish market, let the experts gut, fillet or skin the fish for you. Ready-prepared fish steaks, fillets and packs of shrimp are all handy for the freezer. Look out for frozen mixed seafood too, combining shrimp, mussels and squid rings, which can be used frozen or quickly thawed. They are ideal for whipping up a quick paella, risotto or a seafood salad.

Smoked salmon comes in vacuum packs, either sliced or in economical trimmings for everyday cooking. It goes well with egg dishes and will transform an omelette or scrambled eggs into something sensational. Keep a pack in the freezer. Other smoked fish such as trout, mackerel and haddock are great for sandwiches, salads or rice dishes.

## Quick vegetables

Many vegetables, especially baby varieties, are now sold washed, trimmed and peeled, all ready to cook. Baby corn, snow peas, sugar snap peas and fine green beans can be tossed straight into the pan, as can ready-cut broccoli, cauliflower florets and carrot sticks. Ready-washed baby leaf spinach for salads and spinach for cooking are a real boon for the busy cook, as are stir-fry packs of mixed vegetables. Frozen vegetables are packed with nutrients and perfect for quick meals. As well as basics like peas for accompaniments, look out for convenient wok vegetables and sliced peppers, and add protein to dishes with soy beans. Go for a variety of colours for appealing meals with maximum nutritional value.

## Salads in a hurry

Bags of mixed salad leaves provide an exciting selection that needs no preparation, although it is a good idea to give leaves a quick rinse, then spin dry before using.

## Make the most of the deli

Ham and other cold cuts are great for sandwiches and salads, and a pack of salami, snipped into rice and pasta dishes or scattered on top of a pizza, will enliven many meals. Chorizo, the Spanish paprika-flavoured pork sausage, is sold ready-cooked and sliced as a deli meat, or in large salami-type sausages for slicing and cooking. It's wonderful for adding a smoky, spicy flavour to dishes and it keeps well in the fridge. Sun-dried tomatoes, olives, dips and, of course, cheeses are also versatile deli items that will boost an impromptu meal.

## Keep cans on hand

Canned food is already cooked, so takes only minutes to heat up. It is canned immediately after harvesting, when flavour, vitamins and minerals are at their peak. No preservatives are needed and a good level of nutrients is maintained throughout the can's long shelf life. Pantry basics include an ever-increasing number of organic and healthy options such as low-salt, low-sugar or low-fat.

Stock up with canned fish for easy meals. Salmon, sardines mackerel and tuna all make quick lunches and sandwich fillings, and canned shellfish such as mussels, oysters and clams instantly perk up a fish pie or pasta sauce.

Canned fruit and vegetables are great alternatives for produce that is not in season, or that takes a while to prepare. Canned tomatoes are probably the most frequently used item in most kitchens. Buy them whole or chopped, plain or flavoured with herbs, garlic or chili peppers. Canned legumes are invaluable for vegetarian main meals.

Fruit, canned in juice rather than the less-healthy syrup, makes a useful standby when fresh fruit isn't available. Canned cream and custard are other items that you can use as the basis for quick desserts.

## Grab a jar

A couple of jars of your favourite pasta sauce are invaluable, either plain tomato that you can flavour yourself, or with added herbs, olives or peppers.

For instant desserts, bottled fruits in liqueur or fruit compotes are worth keeping in the pantry to serve with ice

cream or pancakes. A jar of ginger in syrup can jazz up a stir-fry or add an exotic flavour to a fruit salad.

## Fruit, nuts and seeds

As well as sultanas and raisins, choose ready-to-eat dried fruits, such as prunes, apricots and mangoes. They are soft and juicy and don't need soaking, so can be used straight from the package. A wide variety of unsalted nuts can be bought shelled, chopped or toasted – and don't forget seeds to add crunch and protein to salads and stir-fries.

## Pasta and rice

Keep packages of several different pasta shapes in your pantry. Dried pasta is quick to cook but fresh is faster still, although it needs to be stored in the fridge or freezer (and can be cooked from frozen). There are many varieties, including stuffed pasta. For fast lasagna choose fresh or no-pre-cook varieties. Gnocchi makes a good alternative to pasta and it, too, can be stored in the fridge or freezer and used straight from frozen.

Noodles are quick to cook, but speedier still are straight-to-wok noodles, ready-cooked in individual pouches to add directly to a stir-fry towards the end of cooking.

There's a wide range of different types of rice available, but a long-grain or basmati rice and a risotto are all you really need. If you have a microwave, stock up with flavoured rices that can be prepared in a few minutes.

## Wraps and pancakes

Tortillas, made from finely ground corn or wheat flour, are the base for Mexican-style dishes like fajitas and burritos, as well as wraps for sandwich fillings. You can buy plain and flavoured varieties, and they have a long shelf life.

Ready-made pancakes are good for sweet or savoury fillings and toppings. Store them in the fridge or freezer.

## Quick baking

Making pastry from scratch is enjoyable when you have time, but when you don't, ready-made pastry can produce delicious results. Fresh and frozen shortcrust and puff pastries are handy to keep in the fridge or freezer, although you need to allow a couple of hours thawing time before using frozen.

Ready-rolled pastries are quicker still, as the pastry comes in sheets, ready to use without further preparation, and they rise evenly when you bake them. Ideally, take ready-rolled pastry out of the fridge and leave it, still wrapped, for 20 minutes before unrolling it, to prevent it from cracking.

Bread freezes well. Partly-baked baguettes and ciabatta can be baked from frozen, and pita bread can be toasted from frozen. Pizza bases are a handy buy for the pantry, too. Simply add your favourite topping, and bake.

## Swift stocks

Many recipes call for stock, and your own homemade stock, once prepared, can be stored in the freezer. But there are also several good-quality alternatives, such as stock cubes, which are simply crumbled and added to boiling water, and light bouillon powder, which is available in organic and low-salt varieties. Concentrated bouillon is a liquid stock to be diluted.

Fresh stock is also now widely available from supermarket or butcher cold-display cases, alongside the respective meat, fish or poultry it's suited to. It is also handy for freezing. Although it is slightly more expensive than cubes or powders, the taste is generally good and very close to homemade.

## Spices

Ready-ground spices are ideal for the busy cook, but they lose their flavour once ground, so check the use-by dates on your jars. For a fresh flavour in convenient form, look out for chili, ginger and garlic pastes in jars and tubes. You can also buy oils and vinegars flavoured with herbs and spices.

## Herbs

Fresh herbs in packs are now easy to find, especially basil, coriander and parsley. You can also buy pot-grown herbs to keep on the kitchen windowsill and clip as needed, or you can grow some in the garden or in pots on the patio. If you keep only one fresh herb, make it parsley; but mint, chives, basil, coriander, tarragon, dill, thyme and rosemary can transform your cooking.

For when fresh herbs aren't available (and if you want a wider selection of flavours), keep a few dried ones as well. Those labelled freeze-dried or air-dried have the best flavour. A bouquet garni combines parsley, thyme and a bay leaf in a handy sachet, providing a mixed herb flavour all in one. Frozen herbs in little packets, such as coriander, are handy to keep in the freezer.

There are no hard-and-fast rules about which herbs to use with which food, but here are some perfect partners:

| | |
|---|---|
| **Lamb** | rosemary, mint |
| **Chicken** | parsley, thyme, tarragon |
| **Pork** | sage, marjoram, oregano |
| **Duck** | sage |
| **Fish** | parsley, dill, fennel, chives, bay leaves |
| **Tomatoes** | basil, chives, parsley |

## ...classic combinations

# The Well-Stocked Pantry

**Having the right ingredients on hand is the key to stress-free meals. There's nothing more annoying than deciding what you want to cook, then finding you've run out of an essential ingredient. Keep your pantry stocked with these basics and you'll always have the means to rustle up quick and healthy hassle-free meals.**

If you do run out of a particular ingredient, most items can be replaced by something similar, putting a slightly different spin on a recipe: couscous could be used as an alternative to bulgur wheat, and canned chickpeas in place of cannellini beans. Recipes can be endlessly varied and you'll find lots of ideas for switching things up in the recipe chapters.

## Fundamentals

**Oils and vinegars** Canola oil is economical and all-purpose, perfect for keeping on hand, but ideally have some extra-virgin olive oil for salad dressings as well. Extra virgin is the richest and finest olive oil for cooking and drizzling, but its lower smoke point means that it's not suitable for cooking at high temperatures, such as stir-frying. A light or mild olive oil is, however, good for general purposes, though it's slightly more expensive than canola.

Wine and cider vinegars are essential for salad dressings and sweet-and-sour-style dishes, but if you buy only one, red wine vinegar is the most versatile. Although expensive, balsamic is wonderfully dark and mellow, and you need only a few drops mixed with extra virgin olive oil to make a fine salad dressing.

**Stocks** Although you may have fresh or chilled stock in the fridge or freezer, you will also probably need some stock cubes or bouillon powder. Meat, fish, chicken and vegetable stocks are available, but vegetable stock can easily double for light poultry and fish dishes too. Beef stock is best used only for meat casseroles and making gravy, as cubes have a meaty taste and lend a deep brown colour. Look out also for organic or low-salt bouillon powders, which have a light and natural flavour.

**Seasonings** Always taste food *before* seasoning with salt and ground black pepper. Salt should be used sparingly to enhance the flavour of foods. Black peppercorns, which are best freshly ground in a pepper mill to retain their flavour, are more aromatic than white and can be used to season almost everything, unless black specks would spoil the appearance of the dish. Herbs and spices can reduce the need for seasoning.

## Packages of good stuff

**Pasta** A variety of different pastas is essential in every kitchen cupboard. Try to keep stock of several different varieties, such as spaghetti or tagliatelle, shapes such as bows (farfalle) and tubes (penne) and some lasagna.

**Rice** is so useful it is worth storing the three most versatile varieties. Long-grain can be used for countless dishes. Slender basmati rice has a fragrant nutty taste, and is the best choice to go with Indian dishes – it's also the quickest rice to

oils       vinegars       oats       noodles and pasta       rice and quinoa

cook. Risotto (the best-known variety is arborio), for making the Italian dish of the same name, is another useful staple for creating a variety of delicious fast meals. Cook 5 tbsp (75 mL) raw rice per person.

**Noodles** If you're fond of oriental and Asian dishes, noodles are the ultimate quick-cook food, as they unravel and soften in boiling water in just a few minutes, and they are packed in portion sizes for convenience. Straight-to-wok noodles need no pre-cooking and can make a stir-fry more filling.

**Flour** (self-raising and plain) is used for making batters, coating meat and fish and thickening sauces.

**Grains** Be adventurous and try grains such as couscous, bulgur wheat and quinoa (a small yellowy-brown grain with a nutty flavour). These lend themselves particularly well to warm and cold salads. Make sure the couscous you buy is the quick-cook variety, the type usually sold in supermarkets. Another grain to try is quick-cooking fine polenta, which can be soft like mashed potatoes or allowed to set, then grilled. It makes a pleasant change from pasta to serve with a sauce.

**Oats** are ideal for adding to sweet and savoury crumble toppings. They can also be used to thicken soups and make a good alternative to breadcrumbs for coatings.

---

**Tomatoes**, whole or chopped, for soups, casseroles, curries, pasta sauces and other dishes.

**Roasted peppers**, packed in oil with or without herbs. They are quick and easy to use when there's no time to roast your own peppers. The oil also makes a good flavouring to add to a dish.

**Bottled char-grilled artichokes** in olive oil. These are invaluable for jazzing up risotto-style dishes and for pizza toppings.

**Sun-dried tomatoes**, to provide an intense tomato flavour to soups and stews, dips and salads. For quick dishes, use sun-dried tomatoes in oil or soft sun-dried tomatoes in vacuum packs.

**Canned corn**, available without added sugar and salt, requires no cooking. Just use drained and rinsed straight from the can, warmed up or cold.

**Olives** can be tossed into pasta sauces, salads, casseroles or pizza toppings – in fact pretty much anything that has a Mediterranean flavour.

**Legumes** – beans, chickpeas and lentils – are the perfect nutritious choice for busy vegetarians. They add chunky texture to rice and grain-based dishes, are tasty in

casseroles, can be mashed to make dips like hummus and are also great in salads. Using cans avoids the long soaking and cooking times needed for dried beans and legumes. Keep a selection, such as cannellini, red kidney and butter beans – they are usually interchangeable in recipes. Red lentils and Puy lentils cook quite quickly from raw but you can also buy Puy lentils canned or in vacuum packs.

**Baked beans** – who could live without them? You'd be amazed at the range of meals you can get from this nutritious and popular convenience food. Look at the special feature on pages 156-7 for some ideas.

**Fish** is a fantastic pantry standby. Canned sardines, tuna, salmon, crab and anchovies are ideal for speedy, nutritious salads, pasta dishes, pizza toppings, fish cakes, egg dishes and baked-potato toppings.

**Fruit** is useful for making a quick dessert, or to add to a savoury dish, if you have run out of fresh.

**Custard** is an instant and versatile base for many desserts, and a healthier accompaniment than cream.

## ...don't be without these cans and jars

**canned legumes**

**canned tomatoes**

**canned coconut milk**

**canned fish**

**roasted peppers**

**Tortillas** are perfect for wrapping all kinds of salads or putting a different spin on last night's leftovers.

**Bread alternatives** Keep a good selection of rice cakes, oatcakes, crispbreads and crackers, as these are perfect for lunches or evening snacks, served with cheese, cold cuts or other deli foods you have in the fridge.

## Flavourings at your fingertips

**Herbs** are used in so many recipes that it's a good idea to keep a collection of the dried herbs you use the most frequently and like the best. This is most useful when fresh herbs are not available, especially during the winter months. Oregano, dill, bay leaves, tarragon, mint and thyme are some of the most commonly used dried herbs, although mixed herbs will cover many eventualities if you find you don't have a particular herb to hand. Remember that dried herbs stay fresh for only six months and are best stored in a dark pantry, not displayed on a shelf in the light. Parsley and coriander lose their flavour when dried and are useful as garnishes, so it's best to use them fresh.

**Spices** add depth, flavour and interest to your home-cooked dishes. The most useful spices to keep in the pantry are ground coriander, cumin, cayenne pepper, cinnamon, paprika, turmeric, chili powder and/or crushed chili flakes and cardamom pods. If you enjoy Thai flavourings, you may also want some dried lemongrass.

**Tomato paste** is essential for giving a tomato-flavour boost to numerous dishes. The flavour is intense, so you need only use a little. Keep a tube or jar in the fridge, once opened, and add to sauces, stocks, gravies, dressings and marinades.

**Tomato ketchup** adds a fruity sweetness to dishes and because it includes vinegar and sugar, it sometimes makes a better choice than tomato paste for giving an extra zing to the flavour.

**Tomato sauce**, made from ripe tomatoes with the seeds removed, is great for soups, pasta and even in drinks that need a tomato base. You can buy smooth or chunky versions.

**Pesto** is great for flavouring soups, pasta and rice dishes as well as stuffed vegetables, but also use it for making pesto bruschetta (spread on slices of toasted French bread or ciabatta), or a quick dip stirred into Greek yogourt with diced cucumber for a tasty twist on tzatziki.

**Mustard** goes especially well with pork and ham, and all cheese dishes. Dijon mustard has a clean, mild taste and makes a good, smooth all-rounder – great for marinades and dressings, perking up sauces or spreading on meat before cooking. A wholegrain mustard has a slightly more pungent flavour, rough texture and an attractive speckled appearance. English mustard is more fiery than French.

**Worcestershire sauce** gives a distinctive kick to gravy and red meat recipes. Also keep some Tabasco sauce and harissa paste if you like your food spicy.

**Soy sauce** is crucial to all oriental dishes. If you're frequently whipping up stir-fries, it's a good idea to invest in some toasted sesame oil too.

**Curry paste or powder** is essential for curries. Curry pastes are available in a variety of mixtures and strengths so you are sure to find one that has just the right combination of flavour and heat for your taste.

**Fish sauce**, also known as nam pla, is used for Southeast Asian cooking, much as the Chinese use soy sauce. It has a pungent aroma and should be used sparingly, but it adds a delicate flavour that is essential for authentic-tasting Thai curries and stir-fries.

**Fruit chutney**, such as mango, apricot or tomato, will transform cold cuts and curries. Go for a really good one.

**Spice pastes** are now available. A jar or tube of garlic, chili or ginger paste makes a good standby for when you run out of fresh and is very quick when you're cooking in a hurry. Keep them in the fridge once they have been opened.

**Condiments** such as cranberry sauce and redcurrant jelly, mint sauce, and grated and creamed horseradish are essential pantry standbys. They add the final touch to a roast and will last for some time in the fridge.

**dried herbs**    **dried spices and flavourings**    **curry powder and paste**    **fish sauce**

| Dry ingredients | Bottles and jars | Mayonnaise |
|---|---|---|
| Flour (plain and self-raising) | Oils (olive and canola) | Mustard (Dijon and/or whole-grain) |
| Cornstarch | Vinegar (red or white wine) | Crushed chili flakes |
| Sugar (white/superfine and brown) | Soy sauce | Preserves, spreads and syrups (jam, |
| Rice (long-grain, basmati and risotto) | Worcestershire sauce | marmalade, peanut butter, honey, |
| Pasta (various shapes) | Roasted peppers in oil | golden syrup, maple syrup) |
| Noodles | Artichoke hearts in oil | Coconut milk |
| Couscous (quick-cook) | Sun-dried tomatoes in oil | |
| Porridge oats | (or soft in vacuum packs) | **Cans** |
| Red split lentils | Tomato paste | Chopped tomatoes |
| Nuts | Olives | Baked beans |
| Seeds | Pesto | Corn |
| Dried fruit | Curry paste | Chickpeas, beans and Puy lentils |
| Stock cubes and/or bouillon powder | Tomato ketchup | Tuna and other fish |
| Seasonings, herbs and spices | Chutney | Canned fruit in juice |

## ...pantry

## Other useful ingredients

**Mayonnaise** is handy for dips, spreading in sandwiches and as an accompaniment. (Keep in the pantry until opened, then transfer to the fridge.)

**Nuts and seeds** Keep a small supply of nuts, such as cashew nuts, walnuts, flaked almonds and pine nuts, in your cupboard – they will be surprisingly useful, adding crunch to stir-fries, salads and noodle dishes. They are also a good protein to use for vegetarian cooking. Ground nuts have a much shorter life, so if possible grind whole nuts in a food processor or grinder when you need them. Keep some seeds in store too. Pumpkin and sunflower seeds add texture to salads, and sesame seeds add flavour to stir-fries. Store nuts and seeds in airtight containers and use within three months.

**Coconut milk** is an essential ingredient in many Thai curries and Korma-style Indian curries, so if you enjoy eating these, keep a can in the cupboard. You can also buy UHT cartons of

coconut cream, which is thicker than the milk and has a silky consistency. A pack of creamed coconut is another useful pantry ingredient, as it can be diluted with water to make coconut milk.

**Sugar and syrups** are essential ingredients for desserts and other sweet dishes, like glazes.

**Honey** can be used for sweetening both sweet and savoury dishes, lending a more distinctive flavour than sugar. You may like to buy a special flower honey for spreading on hot toast, but for cooking purposes, any clear honey is fine. It is useful for glazes, marinades, sweet-and-sour recipes, salad dressings or for sweetening sauces in place of using sugar.

**Maple syrup** is useful to keep as a quick topping for pancakes and ice cream (refrigerate once opened).

**Alcoholic drinks**, such as sherry, brandy and rum, as well as red and white wine, will add flavour to savoury and sweet food – and fun to the cooking!

tomato ketchup    pesto        mustards        mayonnaise        chutney        soy sauce    Worcestershire sauce

# Making the Most of Your Fridge

Some ingredients just have to be bought regularly – you can't stock up too far in advance on fresh foods like meat, fish, or fruit and vegetables, because they will deteriorate and lose their nutrients. Your best friend here is your fridge: With clever planning, refrigeration can prolong the life of fresh foods so that you can buy them with your groceries just once a week.

## The quick cook's fridge

A well-organized fridge is essential to fuss-free cooking. When you unpack your weekly groceries, it's worth taking the time to position items in your fridge according to where they will keep best and how often you need access to them. Put raw meat or fish on the bottom shelf, separated from cooked food to avoid the risk of contamination. Keep dairy products on one shelf, sauces on another, vegetables in the drawers and all the condiments together, with their labels showing.

## Dairy

**Milk and fruit juices or smoothies** are frequently used items, so store them in a handy position in the fridge – the door is a good place. Arrange it so that cartons with the earliest best-before dates are reached first.
**Butter and/or margarine** should also be stored by date.
**Cheeses** need to be stored in the warmest part of the fridge – at the top, in a door shelf if you have room. Keep them covered in a plastic container or wrapped in parchment paper or foil – avoid plastic wrap as it encourages dampness, and chemicals in the plastic may transfer to the cheese.
**Cream (or ricotta cheese, sour cream) and yogourts** Keep covered and use by the best-before date.
**Eggs** should be kept in their boxes near to the top of the fridge or in the egg holders in the door. As with milk, store eggs in date order.
**Tofu** should be stored with the cheese.

## Vegetables and salads

Keep a selection of fresh vegetables and salad stuff in the bottom of the fridge in the vegetable and salad drawers. If you find you are short of space, they can be stored in plastic bags in the main part of the fridge, but away from raw foods. Avoid the cold spots in the fridge; if ice crystals form in foods such as salad vegetables, they will be unusable and will have to be thrown away.
**Fresh herbs**, unless pot-grown or picked from the garden, should be stored in the salad drawer. Wrap fresh root ginger in plastic wrap (or freeze it; see page 20).

## Fish

It's best to eat fresh fish on the day you buy it, but if this is not possible, remove the packaging as soon as you get home, wipe the fish with a clean damp cloth, place on a plate and cover with plastic wrap. Store it at the bottom of the fridge, ideally for no more than 24 hours.

## Meats

It is essential to put fresh meats straight into the fridge as soon as you return from shopping. Keep them in their sealed packs or put unpacked meat on a plate and cover in plastic wrap. Make sure that raw meats are kept away from cooked food. **Bacon** should be stored with the raw meats. **Cold cuts**, like ham and salami, must be stored away from raw meats. Once opened, bacon and cold cuts should be placed in a sealed container and used within a few days.

## How long does fresh food keep?

Most items you buy from a supermarket for storage in the fridge will have a best-before date. If you are buying locally, ask your shopkeeper how long items can be kept before using. If you are unsure, here are some general guidelines.

## Raw food

**Fish** two days; **meat, sausages and poultry** three days; **bacon** one week; **green vegetables, salad and soft fruits** two to three days; **cheese, eggs and milk** up to one week.

## Cooked food

**Deli meats and fish** one week; **casseroles, curries and stews** two to three days; **cooked vegetables** one to two days; **cooked pasta or grains** one to two days. **Leftovers** can be covered and kept in the fridge for a day or two – it's often worth cooking a bit extra for another quick meal.

## Take special care with cooked rice

Rice may seem innocent but it is potentially dangerous, as harmful bacteria can form, so it can be kept in the fridge for only one or at most two days (see Rice safety, page 145).

## The correct container

Cans rust in the fridge, so transfer food from opened cans to sealed plastic containers before putting them away. Sauces in jars and tubes (mayonnaise, pesto, curry paste, horseradish, tomato paste and garlic paste) can be stored in the pantry until they are opened, but then need to be kept chilled and used by the best-before date.

## When not to use the fridge

Some foods should be stored at room temperature: tomatoes to develop their flavour; avocados to ripen properly; onions, potatoes and root vegetables (best stored in a vegetable rack in a cool, preferably dark, place); and most fruit, except berries (bananas will go black if stored in the fridge).

## Tips for safe storage

● Always store cooked food on a shelf above raw food to avoid the possibility of raw juices dripping on to it. Make sure that raw food is in a container that will keep drips from falling onto shelves below.

● Unless you are going to be using it within an hour, store strongly flavoured food in plastic containers so that the smell doesn't taint other foods.

● Avoid overpacking your fridge. Air needs to be allowed to circulate freely for the fridge to work efficiently.

● Don't open the fridge door more than necessary.

● Cover or tightly wrap any items that have been opened, and keep lids on jars and tops or corks on bottles. Arrange them so that their labels can be easily read, which will prompt you to use them and not forget they are there.

● Remember that best-before and use-by dates apply only when a product is sealed. Once opened, most packs of foods should be used within 2-3 days.

● Never put hot or warm food in the fridge, as it will raise the temperature. Allow cooked food to cool completely before storing it.

● Keep your fridge clean by mopping up spills immediately. Empty the fridge regularly and give it a good wipe with an antibacterial fridge cleaner or a weak solution of baking soda.

● Invest in a fridge thermometer so you can see if the temperature goes outside the recommended range of 0-5°C.

| In the fridge | | | Out of the fridge | For the fruit bowl |
|---|---|---|---|---|
| Milk | Yogourt | Leafy greens | Avocados | Lemons |
| Butter | Seasonal greens | Cucumber | Tomatoes | Oranges |
| Cheese | Stir-fry selection | Radishes | Garlic | Clementines |
| Eggs | Peppers | Scallions | Potatoes | Apples |
| Fruit juice | Carrots | Fresh herbs | Sweet potatoes | Bananas |
| Raw meats and fish | Celery | Berries | Onions | Kiwi fruit |
| Cooked meat and fish | Leeks | Grapes | Red onions | Pears |
| | Mushrooms | Smoothies | Squash | Plums |
| Bacon | Salad leaves | Chilled desserts | Pumpkin | Mango |

# in the fridge...or out of the fridge?

# Making the Most of Your Freezer

**A freezer is an essential piece of equipment for the quick cook, as most foods can be frozen. A freezer also lets you make the most of store bargains, big-batch-cooking and even homegrown and seasonal produce. It's just a question of labelling and organizing, so that you always know what's available.**

## Fish, poultry and meat

When buying fish, meat and poultry that you want to freeze, look out for "suitable for freezing" on the label, or buy ready-frozen produce. If buying from the counter, ask the butcher or fishmonger if the food has already been frozen, as previously frozen food is not suitable for refreezing. You can freeze food in its supermarket packaging for a month; for a longer period, open the pack and repack in a freezer bag, making sure you squeeze out all the air.

## Vegetables

Frozen vegetables are handy for the busy cook and can be bought in large, economical bags. Once opened, reseal with a clip or bag tie. Salad vegetables are not suitable for freezing.

---

Fresh vegetables are not usually suitable for freezing raw, but you can blanch them first, then freeze – perfect for a summer glut.
- Wash and prepare freshly picked vegetables in perfect condition and cut them into small pieces. Boil a pot of water (3 qt/3 L water for each 1 lb/500 g vegetables).
- Put the vegetables into the pot. Bring back to the boil and blanch until hot but not fully cooked. This will take about 3 minutes for broccoli, broad beans and French beans, and 2 minutes for sliced runner beans.
- Lift out with a slotted spoon and refresh under the cold tap until cold (or plunge into ice-cold water). Dry on a paper towel. Pack into containers, label and freeze.

### ...get ahead

---

## Bread and starchy foods

Loaves (sliced for convenience), pita and nan breads can all be frozen. Stale bread can be made into bread crumbs then frozen (see Good uses for bread, page 30). Bought and homemade pastry freezes well (see Quick pastry, page 31), and crumble mix can be frozen in bags. Stuffed pasta and gnocchi can be frozen and then cooked from frozen.

## Flavourings and quick additions

Grate cheese, or lemon, orange and lime zest, then bag them up for the freezer and use from frozen. Herbs can be simply washed, dried, put into a freezer bag and frozen; crumble them into dishes while cooking. Chilies can be cut in half lengthwise, seeds removed, and frozen, then chopped from frozen to use. Peel and freeze fresh root ginger, then grate straight into the cooking pan.

## Stock

Homemade or chilled stocks can be frozen for up to a month. Pour into freezer bags, leaving a little space for expansion (see Quick and easy stock, page 30).

## Cooked foods

Prepared meals such as pasta sauces, stews and soups are ideal for cooking in bulk and then freezing. Freeze in small batches or individual portions for up to three months, or one month if the food contains garlic, as the flavour deteriorates. To use, thaw, reheat thoroughly and simmer for 5 minutes.

## Sweet foods

Tubs of ice cream or frozen yogourt are handy for instant desserts, as are bags of frozen berries. You can freeze your

herbs                     soft fruit                     poultry

own raspberries: hull, rinse and dry perfect fruit, then open freeze on a baking tray. Pack into containers. (Strawberries can be frozen in the same way, although they are very soft when thawed and are best used in a coulis or purée.)

## Safe thawing

- Take large, dense items (meat, poultry and prepared meals) as well as fish, out of the freezer the night before and put them in the fridge, still wrapped, for thawing ready for cooking the next evening. Smaller items, such as chicken breast fillets, can be taken out of the freezer in the morning and thawed in the fridge for cooking that evening.
- Raw poultry and large joints of meat should never be cooked from frozen, as they may not cook right through.
- Thaw food in the fridge in a container that will catch any juices that drip.
- Prawns and seafood can be thawed instantly in a sieve, under cold running water, or can be cooked from frozen.

## Cooking from frozen

Vegetables, fresh pasta and shellfish can be dropped straight into the pan from frozen. Frozen herbs, ginger, chili and grated cheese can also be added frozen to dishes during cooking. Other larger foods can be cooked in the oven or on the stovetop from frozen but you should start cooking on a low temperature to thaw, then gradually increase the temperature to cook; soups, stews, casseroles and potato-topped pies such as shepherd's pie can all be cooked this way. Thin fish fillets like plaice or lemon sole can be cooked from frozen, and so can chipolatas. Always make sure that food is cooked through.

## Storage times in the freezer

- Butter and margarine – up to three months.
- Grated cheese – up to six months.
- Milk – up to one month. Thaw in the fridge and shake well. Milk products, such as cream, yogourt, egg sauces and custard, do not freeze successfully.
- Most bread (except crusty varieties) – up to three months.
- Lamb, beef, turkey and chicken – up to six months.

- Pork and fish – up to three months.
- Bacon – up to two months.
- Raw pastry – up to three months; thaw for 1 hour at room temperature.
- Fruit and vegetables, bought frozen or frozen at home (see box, opposite) – up to six months. Salad cannot be frozen and most fresh vegetables need to be blanched before freezing.
- Most herbs (although suitable only for using in cooked dishes, not as a garnish), excluding basil – up to three months.

## Tips for safe freezing

- Always cool then chill foods before you freeze them. Putting warm food in the freezer raises the freezer temperature and could cause other foods to start thawing.
- Never refreeze anything that has been frozen and thawed or is past its best. However, raw food that has been frozen and then cooked can be frozen again.
- Wrap foods carefully or put them in sealed containers, so that they don't get freezer burn (caused by the icy air drying the food). Freezer bags, ice cream tubs, yogourt tubs and foil dishes are all suitable.
- Freeze in sensible portion sizes. Spread chicken and fish fillets out on a baking tray and open freeze. Transfer the individual portions to a freezer bag, squeeze out the air and seal. You can then take out just what you need.
- Label your frozen food clearly using a permanent marker pen, with the date it was frozen.
- Keep a record of what's in the freezer and use before the use-by date, as although it doesn't necessarily become unsafe to eat, it does lose quality over time.

| | |
|---|---|
| Poultry | Pastry (shortcrust, puff) |
| Meat | Frozen vegetables |
| Ground meat or poultry | Frozen berries |
| Fish and shellfish | Ice cream |
| Sausages | Fresh or homemade stocks |
| Bread | |

### ...for the freezer

bread crumbs          grated cheese                    lasagna          soup          ice cream

# The **Well-Equipped Kitchen**

You don't need masses of kitchen equipment to help you cook quickly. Gadgets are cool and all, but if you rarely use them they will waste space in your cupboards and on work surfaces. Here's a list of essential equipment for a smooth-running kitchen. Buy the best you can afford – think quality not quantity – so it lasts longer.

## In your cupboards
- Nonstick, heavy-based frying pan with a lid. Choose one with a heatproof handle so it can be transferred to the oven or the grill.
- Nonstick wok with a lid, or a deep frying pan.
- Three heavy-based pots (small, medium and very large) with lids. Buy the best pots you can afford. Stainless-steel pots with an aluminum or copper base for effective heat transfer will last for many years.
- Cast-iron ridged griddle.
- Cast-iron flame-proof casserole. This invaluable item can be used on the stovetop, in the oven and for serving at the table. Although a little pricey, it will last a lifetime.
- Collapsible metal steamer, a steaming pan or steamer inserts that can be tiered on top of your pots.
- Wire cooling rack.
- Metal sieve and free-standing colander.
- Graters (a stainless-steel box grater plus a rotary hand-held grater for grating cheese).
- Set of mixing bowls – stylish mixing bowls can also double as salad and serving bowls.
- Salad spinner.
- Measuring cup.
- Citrus squeezer or juicer.
- Hand-held electric mixer, ideal for whipping cream, egg whites, sauces and batters and for making creamy mashed potatoes.
- Ovenproof casserole or gratin dish.

## On the shelf
- Set of weighing scales. Electronic digital scales are accurate and can switch from metric to imperial and back to zero instantly at the press of a button. An add-and-weigh feature allows you to measure out an entire recipe in one bowl. Traditional balance scales with metal weights are accurate too. Classic manual scales display dual measurements but may need adjusting to zero before using, and they are not always easy to read, especially for smaller quantities. Scales need to be kept handy, so if you're thinking of buying a new one, check out the space-saving, wall-mounted models that can be positioned right next to the work surface.

## On the work surface
- Salt and pepper mills.
- Knife block with a selection of good sharp knives, including a long serrated bread knife, a medium-sized cook's knife (7-in/18-cm blade) essential for chopping and slicing meat and vegetables, and a small cook's knife or curved paring knife (3-in/7.5-cm blade) for smaller jobs like paring or peeling. A top-quality knife makes food preparation easier, faster and safer – accidents happen when trying to hack through food using a semi-blunt knife. A stainless-steel blade is best, with a steel-lined handle. These knives are dishwasher-proof and do not rust. A good knife will last for many years, so think of it as an investment.
- Chopping boards – keep different coloured ones for raw and cooked food, and possibly a small one for flavourings. Plastic boards are best, as they are easy to keep clean.
- A roll of paper towels.

## In the top drawer
- Vegetable peeler.
- Garlic crusher.
- Can opener.

- Pair of sharp kitchen scissors.
- Set of measuring spoons.
- Corkscrew.
- Metal skewers, for kebabs and checking that roasts and bakes are cooked right through to the centre.
- Rolling pin.
- Knife sharpener or sharpening steel.
- Pizza wheel.

## In a large utensil pot (next to the stove)

- Selection of wooden or heatproof plastic spoons.
- Large metal spoon and ladle.
- Large draining spoon.
- Potato masher.
- Long-handled, slotted spatula.
- Nonstick plastic spatulas.
- Pair of tongs – handy for turning food in a frying pan, on a baking sheet or under the grill.

## In the oven drawer or a kitchen cupboard

- Roasting pan.
- Baking sheet. Buy one made from heavy-gauged aluminum, which won't warp or buckle and that has a tough, nonstick finish.
- Baking tray (with a raised edge) for foods that may spill.
- Bun tin or muffin pan.

## Wall-mounted

- Hand-held stick blender. This can be used as a mini food processor for quickly puréeing soups and smoothing any lumps in sauces in the pot, rather than having to transfer to a countertop processor or blender. Choose a wall-mounted version, which will be handy for immediate use rather than having to rummage in a cupboard to find it.

## Optional extras

- Pressure cooker. Less popular these days, but cooking in a pressurized container reduces cooking time dramatically and is particularly valuable for tougher cuts of meat and for poultry, soups, stocks, root vegetables and dried legumes. For foods that cook quickly, such as fish, fruit and green vegetables, there is little advantage in using a pressure cooker.
- Food processor. This machine will take many laborious food preparation chores off your hands. It will chop, mince, mix, purée, shred and grate, whip up cake mixtures and make pastry and dough, giving perfect results in seconds. Use it for grating cheese, chopping nuts, making bread crumbs, mixing smooth creamy sauces, dressings and dips and puréeing or blending soups. Find a space for your food processor on the countertop where it's always close at hand.
- Blender. Ideal for liquifying soups and sauces and for making smoothies and fruit purées. Can also be used on the pulse setting to make bread crumbs or to grind nuts. If you also have a hand blender and/or a food processor, you might find a blender becomes redundant.
- Electric grinder. As well as grinding coffee beans, this can be used to grind nuts and make bread crumbs; especially useful if you often prepare vegetarian dishes.

## Specialized equipment

Pasta machines, breadmakers and ice cream-making machines are great if you enjoy making such foods, and the results are rewarding, but otherwise they don't justify taking up cupboard space and are unlikely to be used often.

# The 6 Quickest Cooking Methods

**There are several different ways of cooking most foods, such as grilling or frying, steaming or microwaving. Here the focus is on six fast cooking methods that are also good for you and your family.**

## Grilling

This quick method of cooking is most suitable for tender cuts of meat and fish, and for shellfish. The grill — whether it is he one built into your stovetop, the broiler in your oven or outdoors on your barbecue — should be well heated before cooking begins. Some meats, such as sausages and bacon, contain sufficient fat for grilling, but leaner cuts such as skinless chicken breast fillets will need a light brushing of oil or other basting liquid, or they can be marinated for 30 minutes to 1 hour first to add moisture.

## Stir-frying

Lean cuts of meat and poultry are perfect for stir-frying, as are firm-textured fish and shellfish, vegetables, rice and noodles. Because cooking is so quick, the flavours, colours and nutrients are retained – and the method uses little oil, making dishes really healthy.

You need to use an oil that can withstand a high cooking temperature. A good choice is peanut, frequently recommended for Chinese cooking, but for a healthier alternative, turn to canola. Don't waste good-quality olive oil on stir-frying because it has a low smoke point and will burn. For the same reason, toasted sesame oil can be sprinkled over

a stir-fry towards the end of cooking, but should not be used at the outset.

Have all your ingredients prepared before you start cooking. If there's time, marinate meat and poultry first for 30 minutes or so, to help to tenderize and add extra flavour. Use a wok or large, deep-based frying pan and get it very hot before adding the oil to ensure an even heat. Add about 2 tbsp (25 mL) oil and swirl it around. When the oil is hot enough it will sizzle. It can spit, so use a long-handled spatula for stirring.

When you add the food, start with the ingredients that will take the longest to cook, such as carrots, and add the tender ones, such as bean sprouts, last. Keep the ingredients moving.

## Steaming

Food is steamed by setting it above simmering water. The natural flavour, colour, shape and texture, as well as water-soluble vitamins and minerals, are retained in the food, making steaming a healthy way to cook.

There are several ways of steaming, but the chief points to remember are that the pot containing the water must not be allowed to boil dry and the water must not stop boiling. Roughly sliced onions, chopped vegetables like celery or fennel, lemon slices, fresh herb sprigs or hot spices can be added to the boiling water so that their flavours waft upwards and seep into the foods as they cook.

Steaming is a moist method of cooking and is ideal for cooking delicate foods such as fish, chicken and vegetables, including new potatoes. Although food can be seasoned before steaming, never sprinkle salt over vegetables, as it will draw out the moisture and nutrients.

### En papillote

Parcels of sweet and savoury foods can be wrapped in squares of foil, greaseproof paper or baking parchment, then cooked in the microwave, oven or steamer, sealing in all the flavour and nutrients. It is a good way to cook fish or lean cuts of meat that might otherwise dry out in the heat of the oven or disintegrate under the grill. Serving individual portions still wrapped in their parcels is a fun way to present the food.

### Microwaving

A microwave is great when you are busy, as food can be prepared in a fraction of the time it would take to cook conventionally. It's also good for thawing food in minutes and reheating leftovers, as well as numerous little jobs, like softening butter, melting chocolate and heating liquids. Packs of baby leaf spinach and frozen peas can be cooked in their packs (pierce first with a sharp knife), which also saves on washing up. Cooking times vary depending on the power level and quantity of food in the oven, so it's best to follow the manufacturer's instructions. Always slightly undercook food, then stir (if appropriate) and allow to rest for a few minutes. Return to the microwave if it needs a little longer. Keep the dish covered to help the food cook more quickly and prevent it drying out or splashing the inside of the oven.

## Char-grilling

Also known as griddling, char-grilling is a method of cooking on a ridged (usually cast-iron) pan over high heat, searing the food quickly on the outside. It's fast and healthy, as it uses less oil than frying, and gives attractive markings to the food. Char-grilling is ideal for thin cuts of meat such as chops, steaks and poultry breast fillets as well as for seafood and thick slices of zucchini, eggplants and other summer vegetables. You can even char-grill halloumi cheese, which retains its shape and tastes excellent prepared this way.

When buying a ridged grill pan, choose one with deep ridges and grooves so that the food doesn't sit in the fat or juices that drip from it while cooking. Always make sure that the pan is really hot before using, otherwise the food will stick to the surface. To test, splash a few drops of water on the heated surface – they should splutter and disappear instantly. Brush the food (not the pan) lightly with oil. If it has been marinated, drain off the excess before placing it on the griddle. Cook the food on one side, then turn it over, using tongs. Don't turn food over too soon or it will stick – as the food chars it will come away from the griddle, naturally. For criss-cross lines, turn the food once by 90 degrees as it cooks. If you have time, allow meat to rest, covered on a warmed plate, for 3-5 minutes before serving; this gives the muscle fibres time to 'relax' so that the juices will be distributed evenly throughout the meat.

# Basic Food Preparation Know-how

**Don't be put off using vegetables that you are unfamiliar with, just because you are unsure how to use them. Preparation is simple when you know the basics.**

**Asparagus** Snap off any woody stems from the asparagus at the point where they break easily.

**Avocado** Cut in half lengthwise and slip out the stone using a teaspoon. Score a line down the centre of each half and peel the quarter of skin away from the top downwards. Squeeze over a little lemon juice to preserve the colour.

**Bok choy** Cut off the leafy stems from the main stalk and roughly chop or slice. The leaves cook faster than the stems, so if you prefer your leaves crunchy, cut them from the stems and add to the pan just before the stems are cooked. Very young bok choy can be halved or quartered.

**Butternut squash** Peel away the outer skin using a vegetable peeler, then trim the top and bottom. Cut the squash in half lengthwise using a sturdy knife. Scoop out the fibrous, seedy centre using a spoon, then chop the flesh into chunks.

**Cabbage** Remove the outer leaves. Cut the cabbage into quarters and cut out the core from each quarter. Cut the quarters into slices (for stir-frying) or separate the leaves.

**Celeriac** Remove the tough, knobbly skin using a vegetable peeler, then slice or dice using a sharp knife. Immerse the pieces in a bowl of acidulated water (water with a few drops of lemon juice or vinegar added) to prevent discoloration.

**Chili peppers** Using a small pointed knife, cut off the stalk. Scrape out any remaining pith and seeds. Slice widthwise. For the full heat, leave the seeds in, or for a milder flavour add the whole uncut chilli pepper to the dish, then remove before serving. Wash hands thoroughly after preparation.

**Fennel** Halve, quarter and thinly slice the bulb. Once sliced, put in acidulated water to prevent it from browning. Use the feathery fronds for garnishing.

**Garlic** A bulb, or head, of garlic has a cluster of cloves. Pull off a clove and peel away the papery skin. Crush the clove in a garlic crusher (or see Crushing garlic, page 28).

**Fresh ginger** Pare off the brown knobbly skin, then grate or finely chop. The unpeeled root will keep well for about one month, wrapped in plastic in the fridge, or peel and freeze for six months; you can then grate it from frozen.

**Jerusalem artichokes** Peel and put into cold water at once, with a little lemon juice to stop them going brown.

butternut squash

celeriac

fennel

**Leeks** Slice across the width and discard the root. Trim the dark green leaves, removing the outer layer. Cut lengthwise through the green part and wash thoroughly to remove any earth that may be trapped between the leaves. Slice or chop as required.

**Sugar snap or snow peas** These require no preparation, just "eat everything," as in their French name (*mange-tout*).

**Mushrooms** Simply wipe with a damp paper towel.

**Peppers** Cut in half lengthwise and remove the core and seeds, then slice or chop into pieces as required.

**Salad leaves** Rinse lettuce and other salad leaves (including prewashed leaves), then spin in a salad spinner to dry, or pat in a clean tea towel.

**Sweet potatoes** Either wash and bake whole or peel and cut into small pieces.

**Cube** Cut into bite-sized chunks.

**Dice** First cut into strips then cut across the strips to make small squares.

**Slice** To slice effectively, keep the tip of the blade on the cutting board, raising and lowering the knife handle to slice as you feed the vegetable under the blade. Be sure to keep the fingertips of your other hand tucked under and away from the knife blade.

**Shred** Finely slice into thin strips; for example, to prepare leafy vegetables for stir-frying.

## ...preparation terms

## Vegetable preparation shortcuts

Here's how to make short work of some of the more laborious tasks in vegetable preparation.

**Chopping onions** Leave the root end intact when peeling the onion, then cut in half lengthwise. Put each half cut-side down and make fine vertical cuts through to the root end, stopping just short of it. Cut across these slices so that the onion falls into dice.

**Skinning shallots and tomatoes** Place in a heatproof bowl and pour over boiling water. Leave for 1 minute, then drain and cover with cold water. The skins will now peel away easily with a small, sharp knife.

**Quick-trim vegetables** When trimming or slicing vegetables of a similar shape, such as green beans or scallions, line them up on a board, then trim or slice across the whole row.

## A quick freshen up

**Vegetables** All fresh fruit and vegetables (even bagged salads) should be washed before using, if they are not going to be peeled.

**Meat, poultry and fish** Always wash meat, poultry and fish before cooking. Pat dry with paper towel.

**Legumes** Canned legumes should be rinsed and drained well to remove the salt or sugar in the canning liquid.

Jerusalem artichoke

sweet potato

bok choy

# Time-Saving Techniques

**Whether it's a preparation or cooking shortcut, or cooking in bulk, there are many ways in which the busy cook can save time in the kitchen.**

## Scissor-snip herbs and vegetables

It's much quicker to scissor-snip fresh herbs than to chop them on a board with a knife. Either stuff the herbs into a mug or jug and snip down into them with sharp kitchen scissors, or snip them straight into the pan or mixing bowl, or over a finished dish as a garnish. Hold the bunch firmly and snip from the top, including the tender stems of herbs like coriander, chives, mint and parsley. Fresh basil is best roughly torn. As a guide, a 2/3 oz (25 g) bunch of parsley will give you about 4-5 tbsp (60-75 mL) of roughly chopped parsley.

Kitchen scissors are also useful for snipping scallions, trimming tough stalks off leafy vegetables, or topping and tailing snow peas, green beans, gooseberries and currants.

## Preparing bacon and ham

Scissors are also great for chopping and trimming bacon, ham and salami. Most bacon is now sold rindless, but a sharp pair of kitchen scissors makes it very quick to trim off excess fat before cooking, or for snipping into small pieces. Cooked bacon can also be scissor-cut to size, holding each strip in a pair of tongs if it's hot.

## Crushing garlic

To save cleaning a garlic press, try the chef's way to crush garlic – which also happens to be very quick. Lay the unpeeled clove on its side on a chopping board and crush it by pressing on it with the flat of a large knife blade. Remove the skin, then finely chop the garlic with a pinch of salt.

If you prefer, you can leave the garlic partly crushed and add it to the food as it cooks; you can then take out the piece of garlic at the end.

## Small is beautiful

The smaller the piece of food, the faster it will cook. Cut potatoes into smaller chunks if you are boiling them for mashing. Also, cut vegetables into small pieces if you are adding them to soups or for quick roasting.

Tender meats such as chicken breast fillets, or boned shoulder or leg of lamb, cut into bite-sized chunks, are great for kebabs. Chicken will take about 10-12 minutes, lamb about 20 minutes, under a hot grill.

## Squeeze in a squash

If you are using the oven for baking or roasting, you could put in a whole butternut squash to cook at the same time. Baking improves the flavour and saves time, as it removes the need for peeling the squash before cooking it. First prick the skin with a fork, then bake at 350°F (180°C) for 1 hour or until the flesh is tender when pierced. When it is cooked, halve and

remove the seeds. Scrape out the flesh to use in a soup or to serve as an accompanying vegetable – just season and add a drizzle of oil, or mash quickly with some butter.

## Mashed potatoes in no time

The easiest and quickest way to mash potatoes so that they're really soft and creamy is to beat them using a hand-held electric mixer, with a little warm milk or cream, some ground black pepper and a good knob of butter. To keep them light and fluffy while waiting to serve, cover them with a clean dish towel rather than the pot lid – this absorbs the steam rather than allowing it to condense and fall back into the pot. Alternatively, serve potatoes just roughly crushed with butter

snipping coriander

crushing garlic

and parsley, using a large fork to break down any large chunks of potato.

## Cook extra quantities

Soups, stews and casseroles freeze well, so if a recipe is suitable for freezing, simply double up the ingredients, then freeze half for an easy meal that just needs reheating another day. (Remove it from the freezer ahead of serving so that it has time to thaw. Overnight in the fridge is best for soups, sauces and casseroles with larger chunks of meat.) Leftover cooked pasta is great for salads or a baked pasta; any rice that you have left over can be stir-fried the next day; and cooked potatoes or vegetables are great for a tasty midweek hash.

## Pounding or flattening meat

Steaks and fillets of meat for grilling or frying cook faster and more evenly if they are uniformly flat with no thick areas. Place the meat between two layers of plastic wrap or parchment paper and pound with a meat mallet or rolling pin

to a regular thickness. Escalopes are already flattened out so that they cook quickly, and are excellent for a fast meal. Homemade burgers, too, should be fairly flat (about 4 in/10 cm in diameter and 3/4 in/2 cm thick is best) so that they cook right through without burning on the outside.

## Skinning chicken

If you have bought chicken breasts with the skin on and you want to remove it fast, grip the skin while holding the chicken with a sheet of paper towel, then pull firmly and the skin will come away easily. Sometimes getting the skin off a drumstick can be made easier if you use a sharp knife to cut the skin around the ankle first.

## Cook with the kettle

As soon as you start preparing a meal, put a full kettle on to boil. You will then have water ready for cooking vegetables or pasta, boiling eggs or soaking grains.

### Pasta

Pasta needs to be cooked in plenty of boiling water to give it room to move and prevent it from sticking together. It's far quicker to boil water in an electric kettle, then pour it into your pot, than to boil the water on the stove. Leave a little water in the pot when draining pasta, as it will stop it drying out and will help the sauce to coat the pasta.

For lasagnas, use fresh or no-precook lasagna noodles. Speed up cooking for no-precook lasagna by first plunging the sheets into a bowl of hot water. Add them individually to keep them from sticking. Leave for 2 minutes or so while you assemble the layers in the baking dish. The sheets will be moistened enough to ensure they soften and cook evenly.

### Noodles, couscous and bulgur wheat

These just need to be soaked in boiling water or stock to soften, before being tossed with other ingredients to make stir-fries or delicious salads. You'll need about 1²/₃ cup (400 mL) boiling water or stock to 8 oz (250 g) couscous or bulgur wheat, to serve four people. Cover and leave for 5 minutes or until the grain has absorbed all the liquid.

### Spinach

Spinach cooks very quickly and needs a minimum amount of water. First, wash thoroughly in a bowl of water to remove grit. Drain in a metal colander. If the spinach is tender and young, put the colander in the sink and pour over boiling water. Lay a small plate on top and press down firmly to squeeze out all the water, and the spinach will be ready to eat. Put larger washed leaves with tougher stems into a pot with no added water. Cover and cook for 1-2 minutes or until wilted. If bought ready-washed in a bag, pierce the bag a couple of times with a sharp knife, then pop it in the microwave. Cook for 3 minutes or until just wilted, then tip out of the bag and drain in a colander.

wilting spinach

pounding meat

## Quick tips for fruit

Fruit is the perfect snack or dessert, served on its own or with cream, ice cream or yogourt. Here are some quick and easy ways to prepare it.

### Strawberries

To take out the stalk and hull of a strawberry, push a sharp fine-pointed knife into the top of the strawberry just beneath the green calyx, and quickly turn the knife in a circle.

### Pineapple

A quick way to prepare pineapple into chunks or slices is to first cut off the top and base of the fruit. Stand the pineapple on its base and cut away all the skin, removing the eyes as you go. Now cut straight through the pineapple from top to bottom. Lay one half on the work surface cut-side up and cut into the flesh at the side of the central core at an angle. Cut the other side of the core in the same way, making a V-shape to remove the entire core from that half. Repeat for the other half. Cut the pineapple into slices or chunks.

### Get more juice from citrus

Lemons and limes can sometimes be a little dry. You'll find they are much juicier if you microwave them on High for 30 seconds first. Otherwise, roll them firmly in your hands.

### Pomegranate

To remove the seeds from the pith, slice off the crown of the pomegranate, then slice down through each of the white membranes inside the fruit. Pry the sections apart, then turn the fruit inside out and scoop the seeds into a bowl with any juice. Alternatively, split the pomegranate into its sections in a bowl of water. Push out the seeds with your fingers. They will fall to the bottom, while most of the debris will rise to the top and can be discarded. Strain out the water, and you're left with just the seeds.

### Mango

It can be messy and time-consuming to prepare a mango, but there is a quick way to do it. Slice down either side of the stone so you have three pieces. In each of the outer sections, score a lattice pattern into the flesh, taking care not to cut through the skin. Push the flesh inside out, then slice off the cubes into a dish. Peel the centre piece and cut the flesh away from the stone as neatly as you can.

## Good uses for bread

Don't throw away stale bread; instead, use it for bread crumbs or croutons that can stored for future use. To make your own bread crumbs, tear the bread into small pieces, then pop it in a food processor or blender and give it a quick whiz. Pack it into small freezer bags and label. The crumbs can be used straight from the freezer.

To make dry bread crumbs, break up the stale bread into small pieces and spread on a baking sheet. Put in a low oven for about 1 hour or until dried, then whiz in a food processor or blender. Store in an airtight jar for up to one week.

For croutons, cut the crusts off sliced bread and lightly brush each side with a little oil. Toast under the grill, then cut into squares and use to scatter over salads and soups. Store in an airtight container for two to three days.

## Quick and easy stock

Stock cubes and bouillon powder are quick to make up: simply dissolve in boiling water according to the instructions on the pack, to produce the desired strength. To give the flavour a boost, you might like to add a splash of wine, cider or dry sherry, Worcestershire sauce or some herbs. As stock cubes and powder are usually high in salt (although there are low-salt versions available) you may not need to add salt to your cooking – wait until the end of cooking and taste first, then add a little salt if necessary. You can also buy ready-made stock from the supermarket.

### Homemade stock

If you've had a roast chicken, don't simply throw out the carcass. Put it into a large pot, cover it with cold water and throw in some sliced onions and carrots, a dried bay leaf or bouquet garni and a sprig or two of fresh parsley. Bring to the boil, then simmer for about an hour with the lid on. Strain, allow to cool, then chill. Pour into a container, label and freeze. It will keep well for one month. For a vegetable stock, use roughly chopped vegetables such as onions, leeks and carrots, plus herbs.

Leftover gravy makes good stock, too. Freeze it in ice-cube trays, then tip the cubes into a plastic bag once frozen (to free-up the tray). Pop the frozen cubes into soups, stews and casseroles for an instant flavour boost – cubes will thaw more quickly than a larger amount of stock.

## Super-quick egg shelling

Tap the hard-boiled egg all over on a hard surface so that the whole shell is covered with cracks. Hold the egg under the flat of your hand and roll it around, pressing down to loosen the shell. Now tear off a section of shell – it should come away in a large strip with the inner membrane attached, so you can peel the whole shell away in just a few large pieces. Rinse the egg to remove any small pieces of shell. (Very fresh eggs, such as those bought direct from a farm, will not peel well. They need to be a few days old before they can be peeled easily.)

## Shake-and-go dressing

**A homemade French dressing (vinaigrette) takes moments to prepare and adds the finishing touch to salads. Serves 4.**

**4 tbsp (60 mL) extra virgin olive oil**
**1 tbsp (15 mL) wine vinegar**
**pinch of sugar or ½ tsp (2 mL) honey**
**½ tsp (2 mL) Dijon or whole-grain mustard**
**pinch of salt and ground black pepper**

Measure all the ingredients into a screw-top jar, then put the lid on firmly and shake well. You can save time by making double or triple the quantity and storing what you don't need in a jar. Keep the dressing in the fridge for up to one week. As the oil may solidify, remove from the fridge 30 minutes to 1 hour before using to allow it to return to room temperature. Shake well before using.

**Swaps** • For the vinegar, substitute lemon or orange juice, or add a dash of balsmic. • For extra flavour, add a crushed garlic clove, or 1 tbsp (15 mL) freshly chopped herbs, or 1 finely chopped red chili pepper or a dash of chili sauce.

## No-fuss dredging

When a recipe calls for pieces of meat or fish to be dredged in flour before cooking, put a couple of tablespoons of flour, with seasoning and dried herbs if you like, into a plastic bag or a bowl with a lid. Drop in the pieces of meat or fish, a few at a time, cover the bowl or hold the bag shut at the top, and give it a good shake until the pieces are evenly coated. Remove the floured pieces from the bag or bowl and put them aside while you do the rest.

## No-mess crumbs

To make crumbs or broken pieces from biscuits or chocolate, put in a plastic bag and bash against the countertop, or with a rolling pin.

## Quick pastry

You may prefer to use frozen or chilled ready-made pastry but it doesn't take long to make your own shortcrust if you have a food processor. Put 2 cups (500 mL) plain flour in the bowl of the processor with 3½ oz (100 g) chilled butter, cut into rough pieces. Mix briefly until the mixture resembles bread crumbs. Add 4 tbsp (60 mL) chilled water and mix again briefly to make a dough. (Alternatively, grate the block of butter into the flour and rub in using your fingers or a pastry cutter, until it resembles fine bread crumbs. Stir in the water using a fork, then gather the mixture together and knead briefly to make a dough.) Wrap in plastic and keep in the fridge for at least 20 minutes or until ready to use. Homemade pastry can be frozen for up to six months.

To make a crumble topping, leave out the water and add 4 tbsp (60 mL) raw cane sugar to the bread-crumb mixture.

## Cutting edge

Keep your knives and scissors sharp – it makes much faster work of cutting and chopping, and it's safer too; you are more likely to have an accident using a blunt knife than a sharp one.

## Coming to grips with cleaning up

While you wait for food to cook, wash all the preparation equipment, or put it into the dishwasher, so that you only have the pots and plates to deal with when you have finished your meal. If you keep your sink filled with warm soapy water, and put in cutlery and pans as you finish using them so that they have time to soak, it will make the task of washing up quicker.

# soups

# Chicken, Thyme and Mushroom Soup

Creamy chicken is enhanced by the warm flavours of sherry, thyme and Worcestershire sauce in this super-fast dish, made from fresh ingredients in under half an hour. Serve with chunks of toasted walnut bread.

**15** mins prep time

**15** mins cook time

### Serves 4

2 tbsp (25 mL) olive oil

7 oz (200 g) skinless chicken breast fillets, finely diced

1 red onion, chopped

1 garlic clove, chopped

2 celery sticks, chopped

½ lb (250 g) button mushrooms, roughly chopped

1 tbsp (15 mL) chopped fresh thyme or 1 tsp (5 mL) dried thyme, plus extra fresh thyme to garnish (optional)

1 tbsp (15 mL) dry sherry

1 tbsp (15 mL) Worcestershire sauce

3 cups (750 mL) chicken stock, made with stock cubes

4 tbsp (60 mL) sour cream

**Each serving provides** • 161 cals • 14 g protein • 9 g fat of which 2.5 g saturates • 5 g carbohydrate

**Swap** For chicken, use **rabbit**.

### Autumn mushroom and artichoke soup

Omit the chicken. Fry the onion, garlic and celery in the oil with **2 peeled and chopped Jerusalem artichokes**. Stir in **7 oz (200 g) chopped, mixed mushrooms** with **1 tbsp (15 mL) chopped fresh sage or 1 tsp (5 mL) dried**. Add ⅔ cup (150 mL) dry cider and **2 cups (500 mL) vegetable stock**, made with a stock cube. Season to taste and simmer for 5 minutes, then purée. Accompany with Chili Bean Wraps (page 53).

## ...another idea

**1 Fry the vegetables and chicken** Heat the oil in a large pot and fry the chicken for 5 minutes or until golden brown all over. Remove from the pot with a slotted spoon and set aside. Add the onion, garlic and celery to the pot and cook for 5 minutes.

**2 Add the flavourings** Add the chopped mushrooms, thyme, sherry and Worcestershire sauce. Season lightly and cook the vegetables for 2-3 minutes, stirring occasionally.

**3 Purée the soup** Tip the mixture into a food processor or blender and add half the stock. Process until smooth, then return to the pot and add the remaining stock. Return the chicken to the pot and heat until boiling. Simmer for 3 minutes. Stir in 2 tbsp (25 mL) sour cream and return to the boil.

**4 Serve** Ladle into bowls and swirl a small spoonful of the remaining sour cream on to each, with a sprinkling of fresh thyme, if using.

# Creamy Butternut Squash Soup

Vibrant orange and velvety smooth, this intensely flavoured soup is an absolute treat. The sharp flavour of the blue cheese perfectly balances out the sweet taste of the soup.

**50**mins
prep/cook
time

### Serves 4

**1 butternut squash, about 1⅔ lb (800 g), peeled, seeded and cut into chunks**

**1 large carrot, peeled and thickly sliced**

**1 red pepper, seeded and chopped**

**1 large onion, thinly sliced**

**3 cloves garlic, crushed**

**salt and freshly ground black pepper**

**⅓ cup (75 mL) cream cheese**

**1 tbsp (15 mL) fresh chives, finely snipped**

**1 tbsp (15 mL) fresh flat-leaf parsley, chopped**

**blue cheese, crumbled, to garnish**

**sprigs of fresh flat-leaf parsley, to garnish**

Each serving provides • 169.5 cals • 7 g protein • 8 g fat of which 5 g saturates • 18 g carbohydrate

Swap For the cream cheese, use **cream cheese with herbs.**

**1 Cook the vegetables** Bring 4 cups (1 L) of water to the boil in a large pot. Add the squash, carrot, red pepper, onion, garlic and a pinch of salt, then cover and cook gently for 30 minutes, or until the vegetables are tender.

**2 Purée the soup** Take the pot off the heat and let the mixture cool slightly. Tip the cooled mixture into a blender or food processor and purée until smooth. Add the cream cheese and blend again.

**3 Finish and serve** Return the soup to the pot, stir in the herbs and reheat gently. Season with salt and pepper to taste. Serve the soup with little pieces of the blue cheese scattered over the top and garnished with springs of parsley.

---

If you prefer not to add blue cheese, add fresh **Parmesan** and a touch of **nutmeg** to enrich the flavour.

**...cooking tip**

# Celeriac and Pear Soup
## with Sausage Bites

This tangy, thick, winter soup with its delicate celery-like flavour and chunks of sausage takes no time to prepare. Serve with cornbread for a substantial meal.

**30 mins prep/cook time**

**Serves 4**

1 tbsp (15 mL) olive oil

1 tbsp (15 mL) butter

1 celeriac, about 1¼ lb (620 g), peeled and chopped

1 large onion, chopped

2 pears, preferably Bartlett, peeled and roughly chopped

juice of ½ lemon

4 cups (1 L) chicken stock, made with stock cubes

8 small, spicy pork sausages, about 12 oz (375 g) total weight

2 tbsp (25 mL) chopped fresh flat-leaf parsley

½ tsp (2 mL) paprika

**Each serving provides** • 361 cals • 15 g protein • 23 g fat of which 8 g saturates • 25 g carbohydrate

**1** **Cook the vegetables and fruit** Heat the oil and butter in a large pot and stir in the celeriac, onion and pears. Add the lemon juice. Cover and cook over a low heat, shaking the pot occasionally, for about 10 minutes. Add 1 cup (250 mL) stock and cook for 5 more minutes or until the vegetables are softened.

**2** **Cook the sausages** Preheat the broiler to hot. While the vegetables and fruit are cooking, broil the sausages, turning occasionally, for about 10 minutes or until golden brown. Drain on paper towels and keep hot.

**3** **Purée the soup** Tip the vegetables and fruit into a food processor or blender, add the remaining stock and process until smooth. Season, then return to the pot and heat gently until boiling.

**4** **Complete the dish** Slice the sausages into bite-sized chunks using a sharp knife, or snip into chunks using scissors. Add to the soup with the parsley. Ladle into bowls, sprinkle with paprika and serve.

**Swaps** • For celeriac, use **turnips**, plus **2 chopped celery sticks**. • For a vegetarian soup, use **vegetable stock** and replace the chipolatas with **vegetarian sausages**.

The soup (without the sausages) can be made in advance and puréed at step 3, then cooled and stored in the fridge for up to three days. It also freezes well.

**...get ahead**

At step 1 the vegetables and pears can be cooked with the oil, butter and lemon juice in a covered dish in the microwave. Cook on High for about 2 minutes or until softened.

**...speed it up**

# Ham 'n' Pea Soup

Peas and ham are perfect partners and make classic comfort food. Here they are brought snappily up to date with a swirl of soft cheese and a little nutmeg. Serve with soda bread or toasted whole-grain "soldiers."

**Serves 4**

2 tbsp (25 mL) olive oil

1 large onion, chopped

2¾ cups (675 mL) frozen peas

3 cups (750 mL) ham or chicken stock, made with stock cubes

7 oz (200 g) cooked ham, in one piece, diced

3½ oz (100 g) reduced-fat soft cheese

½ tsp (2 mL) freshly grated nutmeg

**Each serving provides** • 228 cals • 20 g protein • 10.5 g fat of which 3 g saturates • 16 g carbohydrate

**Swaps** • For meat stock, use **vegetable stock**.

**1** **Fry the onion** Heat the oil in a large pot and fry the onion gently for 5-6 minutes to soften.

**2** **Cook the soup** Stir in the peas and stock, and bring to the boil. Reduce the heat, cover and simmer for 5 minutes. Season lightly.

**3** **Purée the soup** Put the soup in a food processor or blender and process to a fairly rough purée. Add the ham and return to the pot. Heat until boiling.

**4** **Finish and serve** Add the soft cheese and stir gently until just melted. Ladle the soup into bowls and sprinkle with nutmeg.

Prepare to the end of step 3, cool quickly and pour into a freezerproof container. Freeze for up to one month. **...keep it**

# Roasted **Tomato**, Pepper and **Chorizo Soup**

**Bursting with rich Mediterranean flavours, this soup is a great choice for a fast, satisfying supper. Serve with crunchy baguette, or make it a more substantial meal with Ricotta and Pesto Bites (page 53).**

**Serves 4**

**1 red onion, with skin, quartered**

**2 long sweet red peppers, halved lengthwise**

**4 plum tomatoes, halved**

**2 garlic cloves, unpeeled**

**2 cups (500 mL) chicken stock, made with stock cubes**

**19 oz (540 mL) can red kidney beans, drained and rinsed**

**3½ oz (100 g) chorizo, chopped**

**2 tsp (10 mL) balsamic vinegar**

**⅓ cup (75 mL) fresh basil, torn**

**Each serving provides** • 194 cals • 11 g protein • 7 g fat of which 3 g saturates • 23 g carbohydrate

The soup can be made up to two days in advance. Prepare to the end of step 3, then cool, cover and store in the fridge. To use, continue the recipe.

## ...get ahead

Grill the onions and garlic as in steps 1 and 2. Use a 12 oz (370 mL) jar of roasted red peppers and add a 19 oz (540 mL) can tomatoes to save time on peeling the fresh ones. Chop and purée with the roasted onion and garlic at step 3.

## ...speed it up

**1 Prepare the vegetables for broiling** Preheat the broiler to high. Arrange the onion, peppers and tomatoes on a baking sheet, cut sides down, with the garlic cloves.

**2 Cook and skin the vegetables** cook the vegetables for 6-8 minutes or until the skins are beginning to blacken. Remove the skins from the onion, pepper and tomatoes, and squeeze the garlic flesh from the skins.

**3 Purée the vegetables** Chop half the vegetables into small chunks and put the remainder into a food processor or blender with the garlic flesh and stock. Process until smooth, then add to a pot with the chopped vegetables. Season the soup with a little salt and ground black pepper.

**4 Add the beans and chorizo** Bring the soup to the boil, stirring occasionally. Add the beans, chorizo and balsamic vinegar, cover and simmer gently for 2-3 minutes. Toss the basil into the soup and serve.

**Swaps** • For chorizo, use diced **lean salami or chopped frankfurters.** • For a vegetarian soup, use **vegetable stock** and omit the chorizo. Add a **19 oz (540 mL) can drained chickpeas** with the red kidney beans.

15 mins prep time   15 mins cook time

### Roasted cherry tomato soup

Replace the plum tomatoes in the basic recipe with **11 oz (350 g) cherry tomatoes**: grill the tomatoes until the skins split, with **1 halved unpeeled red onion**, **1 halved red pepper** and **2 garlic cloves**, as for the basic recipe. Purée the tomatoes whole with their skins, with the stock and garlic. Peel and chop the vegetables, then add to a pot with the puréed tomatoes. Omit the beans and balsamic vinegar, but include the **chorizo, or a 6-oz (170-g) can tuna**, drained and flaked. Add **2 tbsp (25 mL) green pesto** with the basil leaves. Simmer for 2-3 minutes. Finish the soup by sprinkling with ⅔ **cup (150 mL) crumbled feta cheese** and **2 oz (60 g) pine nuts**. Serve with Chili Bean Wraps (page 53).

## ...another idea

# Garden **Vegetable** Broth
## with Parma Ham

Seasonal vegetables are cooked in beef consommé with delicate Parma ham to make a fresh, nourishing and fuss-free soup. Accompany with Cheddar Chutney Pitas (page 53).

**10** mins prep time  **20** mins cook time

**Serves 4**

2 x 14-oz (398-mL) cans beef consommé

1 onion, finely chopped

1 celery stick, finely chopped

½ fennel bulb, finely chopped

1 small kohlrabi or turnip, peeled and finely chopped

1 waxy potato, peeled and finely chopped

1 bay leaf

2⅔ oz (75 g) lean Parma ham, torn into strips

4 savoy cabbage leaves, cored and finely shredded

**Each serving provides** • 124 cals
• 13 g protein • 3 g fat of which 1 g saturates • 12 g carbohydrate

**1 Heat the vegetables with the consommé** Heat the consommé and 6¾ tbsp (100 mL) water in a large pot until boiling, then add the onion, celery, fennel, kohlrabi or turnip and potato. Return to the boil.

**2 Cook the soup** Add the bay leaf, then reduce the heat, cover and simmer for about 10 minutes or until the vegetables are almost tender.

**3 Add the ham and cabbage** Add the Parma ham to the pot with the shredded cabbage. Return to the boil, cover and simmer for 5 more minutes or until the cabbage is tender. Adjust the seasoning if necessary. Discard the bay leaf. Ladle into large bowls and serve.

**Swaps** • Vary the vegetables according to what is in season. • For a vegetarian soup, use **4 cups (1 L) vegetable stock**, omit the ham and add a **14-oz (398-mL) can Puy lentils or cannellini beans**, drained and rinsed, at step 3.

Make double the quantity of the basic vegetable soup (prepare up to the end of step 2). Freeze half and use within three months or chill for another day. If you like, make the second half into a minestrone soup (see right).

## ...get ahead

### Zippy minestrone
To the basic vegetable soup (at the end of step 2), add **2 oz (60 g) short-cut macaroni or soup pasta shapes**. Bring to the boil and simmer for 5 minutes, then add **3½ oz (100 g) chopped fine green beans, 2 chopped plum tomatoes** and a **8 oz (225 mL) can borlotti beans**, drained and rinsed, at step 3 with the ham and cabbage. Simmer for a further 5 minutes or until the pasta is tender. Serve topped with **grated Parmesan cheese** and a swirl of **good olive oil** and accompanied by Tapenade Toasts (page 53).

## ...another idea

# Caramelized Onion and Ale Soup
## with Beef Ribbons

Sweet, golden-cooked onions add richness to brown ale and beef stock for this satisfying soup topped with tender strips of seared steak. Ready in no time, it's perfect with crusty French baguettes.

**10** mins prep time **20** mins cook time

**Serves 4**

2 tbsp (25 mL) butter

2 tbsp (25 mL) olive oil

1 lb (500 g) onions, thinly sliced

2 tsp (10 mL) white/superfine sugar

⅔ lb (300 g) tenderloin steak, cut into ¾-in (2-cm) thick slices

1 garlic clove, crushed

1 cup (250 mL) brown ale

1 bay leaf

3 cups (750 mL) beef stock, made with stock cubes

2 tbsp (25 mL) chopped fresh flat-leaf parsley

**Each serving provides** • 283 cals • 18 g protein • 17 g fat of which 7 g saturates • 14 g carbohydrate

**Swaps** • For ale, use **extra stock** with 2 tbsp (25 mL) Worcestershire sauce or soy sauce. • For bay leaf, use a sprig of **fresh thyme**.

**1 Caramelize the onions** In a large, heavy-based pot, heat the butter and 1½ tbsp (20 mL) oil, then stir in the onions and sugar. Cover the pot with a lid and cook, stirring occasionally, over a medium heat, for 10 minutes. Remove the lid, turn up the heat a little and cook, stirring frequently, for a further 5 minutes or until the onions are softened and golden brown.

**2 Cook the steak** While the onions are caramelizing, heat a heavy frying pan until very hot. Brush the steak slices with the remaining oil and season lightly. Fry for about 3 minutes on each side, turning once, until golden brown but still pink inside. Remove from the heat and cover with a sheet of foil to keep warm.

**3 Add the flavourings and stock** Add the garlic, ale and bay leaf to the onions. Bring to the boil, then simmer, uncovered, for 5 minutes. Add the stock, season, then return to the boil.

**4 Slice the steak** Slice the steak pieces into thin ribbon strips, adding any juices to the soup. Discard the bay leaf. Ladle the soup into wide bowls and place a pile of meat strips in the centre of each. Sprinkle with parsley and serve.

If you have some **leftover roast beef or lamb** you can use it instead of the steak. Slice into thin ribbons and add to the soup for the last 2-3 minutes of cooking to heat through.

**...use it up**

The basic onion soup can be made up to two days in advance. Cool quickly, cover and store in the fridge. The steak can be cooked at the time of serving.

**...get ahead**

# Green Gazpacho
## with Hot-Smoked Salmon

Aromatic hot-smoked salmon has a ham-like texture and contrasts deliciously well with the chilled gazpacho. Preparation takes moments and can be done in advance. Serve with Melba toast.

**10** mins prep time

**Serves 4**

1 large green pepper, chopped

1 cucumber, trimmed and chopped

1 onion, chopped

1 ripe avocado, halved, stoned and peeled

1 garlic clove, chopped

6 tbsp (90 mL) fresh flat-leaf parsley

2½ cups (625 mL) vegetable stock, made with stock cubes

3 tbsp (45 mL) white balsamic vinegar or white wine vinegar

3 tbsp (45 mL) extra virgin olive oil

8 oz (250 g) hot-smoked salmon, cut into strips

Each serving provides • 259 cals • 17 g protein • 18.5 g fat of which 3 g saturates • 6 g carbohydrate

**1 Prepare the soup** Put the pepper, cucumber, onion, avocado, garlic, parsley, stock, vinegar and oil in a food processor or blender. Season, then process until smooth.

**2 Chill and serve** Keep covered in the refrigerator until needed, then ladle into serving bowls and add strips of salmon to each bowl.

Swaps • For hot-smoked salmon, use **ordinary smoked salmon, smoked trout or flaked crabmeat**, either fresh or canned. • For a vegetarian soup, omit the salmon and top with **4 chopped hard-boiled eggs** and **4½ oz (125 g) grated Gruyère cheese or crumbled feta cheese**.

### Red-hot gazpacho

Put **1 slice of white bread** into a food processor and add **1 chopped red pepper**, **1 chopped red onion**, a **19 oz (540 mL) can plum tomatoes with garlic**, **1 peeled and chopped cucumber**, **1 red chili pepper** (seeded if you prefer a mild flavour), **1¼ cups (300 mL) vegetable stock**, made with stock cubes, **3 tbsp (45 mL) olive oil**, **3 tbsp (45 mL) red wine vinegar** and **2 tbsp (25 mL) chopped fresh mint**. Season. Process until smooth, then ladle into bowls. Add a few ice cubes to each bowl and top with torn **fresh basil leaves** and **ready-made garlic croutons**. Add a **6-oz (170-g) can tuna**, drained and flaked.

## ...another idea

# Speedy Two-Fish Chowder

Fish and baby new potatoes cook quickly and make an ideal fast-meal combination. Fennel and chili impart sharpness and spice for a hearty meal. Serve with bread sticks.

**10** mins prep time

**20** mins cook time

### Serves 4

1 tbsp (15 mL) olive oil

5 oz (150 g) leeks, trimmed and sliced

2½ oz (70 g) pancetta or bacon, diced

14 oz (400 mL) fish stock, made with stock cubes

19 oz (540 mL) can chopped tomatoes

¼ tsp (1 mL) chili powder

1 tsp (5 mL) fennel seeds

7 oz (200 g) prewashed baby new potatoes, halved

7 oz (200 g) monkfish fillet, cut into bite-sized chunks (black membrane removed)

6 oz (175 g) skinless smoked haddock fillet, cut into bite-sized chunks

**Each serving provides** • 216 cals • 23 g protein • 9 g fat of which 2 g saturates • 12 g carbohydrate

**1 Cook the leeks and pancetta** Heat the olive oil in a large pot and add the leeks and pancetta or bacon. Stir over a medium heat for 3-4 minutes.

**2 Add the stock and flavourings** Add the fish stock, tomatoes, chili and fennel seeds. Bring to the boil. Add the potatoes and season, then cover and boil for about 5 minutes.

**3 Cook the fish** Stir in the chunks of monkfish and smoked haddock. Return to the boil, then reduce the heat. Cover and simmer very gently for 6-8 minutes or until the fish flakes easily and the potatoes are tender. Ladle into wide bowls to serve.

**Swaps** • For potatoes, use **3½ oz (100 g) tiny soup pasta shapes**, such as conchigliette (shells), stelline (stars) or broken-up pieces of vermicelli. • For fish, use a **14 oz (400 g) pack of frozen cooked seafood mix**. Add from frozen and increase the cooking time by 1 minute. • For canned tomatoes and chili, use a **19 oz (540 mL) can chopped tomatoes with chili**.

---

• Buy a pack of **pre-diced pancetta** to cut down on preparation time.
• Buy **pre-cooked new potatoes**, and if they are available in a herb butter this will make your soup even more flavourful. Add them when the fish has been cooking for about 3 minutes.

**...speed it up**

---

**Louisiana seafood chowder**
Gently fry **1 chopped onion, 1 chopped celery stick** and **1 chopped green pepper** in **1 tbsp (15 mL) sunflower oil** for 5 minutes or until softened. Add a **19 oz (540 mL) can chopped tomatoes with garlic**, **14 oz (400 mL) fish stock**, made with stock cubes, and **1 tsp (5 mL) Tabasco sauce**. Bring to the boil, stir in **3½ oz (100 g) long-grain rice**, then reduce the heat, cover and simmer for 10 minutes. Add **11 oz (350 g) fresh or frozen mixed seafood** (such as cubed white fish and small peeled prawns) and **3½ oz (100 g) canned and drained, or frozen, sweetcorn**. Season. Bring to the boil, then simmer for 4-5 minutes or until the rice is tender and the fish flakes easily.

**...another idea**

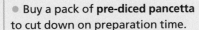

# 5 quick and easy pantry soups

Keep your pantry stocked with dried red lentils and cans of tomatoes, corn, potatoes, beans and legumes to take the time and effort out of cooking, and a nourishing bowl of soup will be just minutes away – the perfect comfort food. All recipes serve 4.

## thai cream of **tuna** soup

Combine **1 cup (250 mL) coconut milk** with **14 oz (400 mL) chicken or fish stock**, made with stock cubes, **3 tbsp (45 mL) dried onions** and about **2 tsp (10 mL) Thai green curry paste**. Heat in a pot until boiling, then simmer for 4 minutes. Add a drained and flaked **6-oz (170-g) can tuna** and **3½ oz (100 g) frozen peas**. Season lightly. Return to the boil and simmer for 1 minute. Serve with bread.

**Each serving provides** • 236 cals
• 14 g protein • 15 g fat of which
8 g saturates • 11 g carbohydrate

Thai curry pastes can vary in strength, so go easy when you're adding it, as it can be quite fiery. Try adding just 1 tsp (5 mL) first, then add more to taste.

**...cooking tip**

## **corn** chowder

Fry **1 chopped onion** in **2 tbsp (25 mL) olive oil** in a pot for about 5 minutes to soften. Add a **14 oz (398 mL) can creamed corn**, **10½ oz (300 g) can new potatoes**, drained and diced, **1¼ cups (300 mL) chicken stock**, made with stock cubes, and **⅔ cup (150 mL) 1% milk**. Season. Cover and simmer for 5 minutes, then add **3 oz (90 g) diced Parma ham or grilled bacon**. Ladle into bowls, add a dollop of **sour cream** to each and sprinkle with **smoked paprika** to serve.

**Each serving provides** • 353 cals
• 12 g protein • 16 g fat of which
6 g saturates • 44 g carbohydrate

If you only have ordinary corn, you can just put it into a blender and mix for 2 minutes.

**...cooking tip**

# chickpea and bacon soup

In a large pot, fry **1 chopped onion** with **4 strips bacon**, diced, stirring, for 7-8 minutes or until the onions are golden and the bacon is cooked. Add **14 oz (400 mL) ham stock**, made with stock cubes, **1¼ cups (300 mL) tomato paste or ground tomatoes with herbs**, and a **14-oz (398-mL) can chickpeas**, drained and rinsed. Season lightly. For a spicy flavour, add **1 tsp (5 mL) crushed chili flakes** and **1 tsp (5 mL) crushed garlic** from a jar or tube (or use 1 crushed garlic clove). Simmer for 10 minutes, and serve with crusty bread.

**Each serving provides** • 170 cals
• 9.5 g protein • 8 g fat of which
2 g saturates • 16 g carbohydrate

**10** mins prep time   **20** mins cook time

# lentil potage

In a large pot, put **3¼ cups (800 mL) vegetable stock**, made with stock cubes, and add **7 oz (200 g) red lentils**, an **8-oz (250-g) package of diced vegetables**, fresh or frozen, **1 tsp (5 mL) dried herbes de Provence** and **¾ cup (175 mL) dry white wine**. Bring to the boil and season. Cover and simmer for 20 minutes or until the vegetables are tender. Purée in a food processor or blender until smooth. Return to the pot and heat until just boiling, then ladle into bowls. Top each serving with **1 tbsp (15 mL) sour cream**, sprinkle with a little **paprika** and add a small **sprig of rosemary** to garnish, if you like. Serve with whole-grain bread. ⓥ

**Each serving provides** • 274 cals
• 13 g protein • 7 g fat of which
4 g saturates • 35 g carbohydrate

**5** mins prep time   **20** mins cook time

# tomato bisque

In a food processor or blender, process **2 x 14-oz (398-mL) cans chopped tomatoes with herbs** with **1 cup (250 mL) sour cream** and **2 tbsp (25 mL) brandy**. Heat in a pot until boiling. Add **7 oz (200 g) cooked, peeled jumbo shrimp**, thawed if frozen, and seasoning. Return to the boil, and cook for 1 minute or until heated through, then add **2 tbsp (25 mL) chopped fresh parsley**. Serve with crisp, ready-made croutons or toast.

**Each serving provides** • 288 cals
• 14.5 g protein • 21 g fat of which
14 g saturates • 7 g carbohydrate

**5** mins prep time   **5** mins cook time

> If you prefer not to add brandy, add a **squeeze of lime juice or 1 tbsp (15 mL) sun-dried tomato paste** to enrich the flavour.
>
> **...cooking tip**

# Jumbo **Shrimp,** Scallion and **Egg Ribbon Soup**

An aromatic soup influenced by recipes from Southeast Asia, where eggs are often lightly cooked in a broth. Serve with crackers or crusty bread for a speedy, light meal.

**10** mins prep time

**10** mins cook time

**Serves 4**

4 cups (1 L) fish or chicken stock, made with stock cubes

1 lemon grass stalk, crushed

¾-in. (2-cm) piece of fresh ginger, peeled and thinly sliced

1 bunch of scallions, sliced

3½ oz (100 g) Thai fragrant rice, or long-grain or basmati rice

2 tbsp (25 mL) rice vinegar or white wine vinegar

6 oz (175 g) cooked, peeled jumbo shrimp

7 oz (200 g) bean sprouts

3 eggs, lightly beaten

4 tsp (20 mL) chili oil

**Each serving provides** • 257 cals • 20 g protein • 9 g fat of which 2 g saturates • 24 g carbohydrate

**1** **Flavour the stock** Put the stock in a large pot, add the lemon grass, ginger and scallions, and bring to the boil.

**2** **Cook the rice** Stir in the rice and return to the boil, then reduce the heat. Cover and simmer gently for 8 minutes.

**3** **Add the jumbo shrimp** Season, then add the vinegar, jumbo shrimp and bean sprouts. Return to the boil and simmer for 1 minute.

**4** **Cook the eggs** Pour the eggs into the simmering soup in a continuous drizzle. They should set into ribbons within a few seconds. Immediately, remove the pot from the heat and ladle into bowls. Drizzle each serving with chili oil and serve immediately.

**Swaps** • For jumbo shrimp, use cooked, shelled **crayfish tails**.
• For a vegetarian soup, use **vegetable stock** and replace the jumbo shrimp with cubes of **smoked or plain tofu**. • For a less spicy soup, use **toasted sesame oil instead of chili oil.**

Ready-crushed lemon grass, and crushed ginger (sold in jars) can be used to save preparation time – about 1½ tsp (7 mL) of each should give a good flavour.

## ...speed it up

Crush the lemon grass with a rolling pin or the flat edge of a knife to release its delicate lemon flavour before adding it to the stock.

## ...cooking tip

# Seafood Noodle Bowl

Spiked with fresh ginger, this fabulously fast seafood bowl makes a warming and complete lunch dish. You can vary the seafood depending on availability and your preference.

**Serves 4**

- 3 cups (750 mL) fish or chicken stock, made with stock cubes
- 1 bunch of scallions, chopped
- ¾-in. (2-cm) piece of fresh root ginger, peeled and grated
- 1 lemon grass stalk, finely chopped (optional)
- 2 tsp (10 mL) soy sauce
- 7½ oz (220 g) white fish fillet, such as haddock or pollock, cut into ¾-in. (2-cm) chunks
- 4 oz (125 g) scallops, cut into bite-sized pieces
- 6 oz (175 g) cooked, peeled jumbo shrimp
- 7 oz (200 g) bok choy, thinly sliced
- 2 x 5-oz (150-g) packages straight-to-wok medium noodles

**Each serving provides** • 266 cals • 32 g protein • 3 g fat of which 0.3 g saturates • 29 g carbohydrate

**1** **Heat the stock and flavourings** Put the stock, scallions, ginger, lemon grass, if using, and soy sauce in a large pot and bring to the boil. Season.

**2** **Cook the fish** Add the white fish chunks and return to the boil. Add the scallops and simmer gently for 1 minute.

**3** **Add the remaining ingredients** Stir in the jumbo shrimp, bok choy and noodles, then heat until boiling. Ladle into bowls and serve immediately.

**Swaps** • For haddock or pollock, use **monkfish, sea bass, hake or halibut**. • For jumbo shrimp and scallops, use cooked and shelled **cockles and mussels.**

**10** mins prep time

**8** mins cook time

## Chicken and spinach noodle bowl

Bring to the boil **3 cups (750 mL) chicken stock**, made with stock cubes, with the scallions, ginger, lemon grass, soy sauce and seasoning, as for per basic recipe. Add **1 lb (500 g) skinless chicken breast fillet**, thinly sliced, instead of the seafood. Return to the boil and simmer for 5-6 minutes, then stir in **7 oz (200 g) baby spinach leaves** instead of the bok choy. Add the noodles and heat through.

## ...another idea

- Frozen fish is a great freezer standby. Many fish fillets or shellfish come in resealable packs, so it's easy to remove just what you need without thawing large amounts. Thaw larger pieces of fish for about 30 minutes and then cut into chunks. You can put frozen fish in small pieces, or frozen shellfish, straight into the pot – just add 4-6 minutes to the cooking time.
- If you have time, set the stock aside with the flavourings, to allow them to infuse before completing the soup.

## ...get ahead

# Asian Chili Crabmeat Soup

Rich, creamy and filling, this effortless Southeast Asian-style soup combines the superb flavour of fresh crabmeat with coconut milk, chili and lime. Accompany with bread and a salad, if you like.

**10** mins prep time

**15** mins cook time

### Serves 4

- 12 oz (375 g) fresh crabmeat (white and brown)
- 6 shallots, roughly chopped
- 1 garlic clove, chopped
- 3⅓ cup (800 mL) hot fish stock, made with stock cubes
- 2½ oz (70 g) basmati rice
- 1½ tsp (7 mL) crushed chili flakes
- 2 tsp (10 mL) fish sauce
- 1 cup (250 mL) coconut milk
- juice of 1 lime
- 3 tbsp (45 mL) coriander leaves mixed with 2 scallions, thinly sliced diagonally, to garnish

**Each serving provides** • 204 cals • 19 g protein • 5 g fat of which 1 g saturates • 19 g carbohydrate

**To serve** If you have time, serve the soup with a dish of **coarsely shredded or thinly sliced vegetables** (such as carrot, celery, onion and cucumber) – just as they are or sprinkled with rice vinegar or white wine vinegar.

**1 Process the crab and vegetables** Put the brown crabmeat, shallots, garlic and fish stock into a food processor or blender and process until smooth.

**2 Cook the soup** Tip the mixture into a pot and add the rice and crushed chili flakes. Bring to the boil, then reduce the heat. Cover and simmer, stirring occasionally, for about 10 minutes or until the rice is just tender.

**3 Add the flavourings** Stir in the fish sauce, coconut milk and lime juice. Add the white crabmeat and heat through gently. Season lightly. Ladle into bowls, then sprinkle with coriander and scallions. Serve immediately.

- Buy ready-dressed crab from the fishmonger or supermarket and use within a day of purchase.
- Avoid using frozen or canned crabmeat for this recipe as it has less flavour than fresh.

## ...shopping tips

# Smoked **Haddock** and **Cannellini Bean Soup**

Zucchini, celery and dill combine to add depth to this swiftly prepared Italian-style dish using fresh and pantry ingredients. Serve with crusty bread.

**10** mins prep time

**12** mins cook time

**Serves 4**

**1 tbsp (15 mL) olive oil**

**1 onion, chopped**

**1 celery stick, chopped**

**2 small zucchini, chopped**

**2½ cups (625 mL) fish or chicken stock, made with stock cubes**

**6 oz (175g) smoked haddock fillet, skinned and diced**

**2 x 14-oz (398-mL) cans cannellini beans, drained and rinsed**

**1 tbsp (15 mL) chopped fresh dill**

**Each serving provides** • 190 cals • 19 g protein • 2 g fat of which 0.2 g saturates • 24 g carbohydrate

**Swaps** • For the haddock, use **5 oz (150 g) cooked, peeled shrimp.** • For the beans, use **½ lb (250 g) frozen or drained, canned corn**.

**1** **Fry the vegetables** In a saucepan, heat the oil and fry the onion, celery and zucchini for 4-5 minutes or until softened but not browned.

**2** **Cook the fish** Add the stock and bring to the boil, then stir in the haddock fillet and seasoning. Cover and simmer gently for 4-5 minutes or until the fish flakes easily.

**3** **Finish the soup** Add the beans and dill. Stir, then heat until almost boiling. Serve in wide bowls.

## Bean and halloumi soup Ⓥ

For a vegetarian version, omit the fish in the basic recipe and use **2½ cups (625 mL) vegetable stock**, made with stock cubes, for the base. Fry **1 small fennel bulb**, diced, with the vegetables instead of the zucchini, and simmer in the stock with the other vegetables, seasoning until tender at step 2. Mash the cannellini beans lightly with a fork before adding to the soup for a creamier, slightly thicker texture. Finally, stir in **6 oz (175 g) diced halloumi cheese** and heat until boiling. (Alternatively, cut the halloumi into cubes and thread on to short bamboo skewers that have been soaked in water for 15 minutes. Brush with oil and grill until golden, then rest on the rim of the soup bowls to serve.)

## ...another idea

# Spicy Lentil Soup

A warming, chunky soup is given an Eastern touch with a kick of curry and the sweetness of coconut. Serve with mini nan breads or parathas on the side.

**30 mins** prep/cook time

**Serves 4** Ⓥ

2 tbsp (25 mL) canola oil

1 onion, chopped

1 garlic clove, crushed

1 celery stick, chopped

1 carrot, peeled and chopped

1 tbsp (15 mL) medium Madras curry paste

3½ oz (100 g) red split lentils

3 plum tomatoes, fresh or canned, chopped

2¼ cups (550 mL) vegetable stock, made with stock cubes

4 tbsp (60 mL) coconut cream

4 tbsp (60 mL) plain low-fat yogourt

2 tbsp (25 mL) roughly chopped fresh coriander

**Each serving provides** • 311 cals • 11 g protein • 19 g fat of which 10 g saturates • 26 g carbohydrate

**1 Fry the vegetables** Heat the oil in a large pot and fry the onion, garlic, celery and carrot over a medium heat, stirring occasionally, for about 5 minutes.

**2 Add the flavourings and lentils** Stir in the curry paste and cook for 1 minute, then add the lentils, tomatoes and stock. Season and bring to the boil.

**3 Finish the soup** Reduce the heat and simmer gently for about 15 minutes or until the lentils and vegetables are tender. Stir in the coconut cream. Ladle into bowls and serve each with a drizzle of yogourt and scattered with chopped fresh coriander.

**Swap** For a Moroccan flavour, replace the curry paste with **3 tsp (15 mL) harissa paste**, and serve with **flatbreads**.

Instead of the dried red lentils, use a **14-oz (398-mL) can brown, green or Puy lentils**, rinsed and drained. Simmer the vegetables, tomatoes and stock for about 5 minutes at step 3, then add the canned lentils and heat through for 2 minutes before adding the coconut cream.

**...speed it up**

# 5 quick and easy
## bready bites
### to enjoy with soups

To make a soup into a complete meal, sometimes you need a little more than just a hunk of bread. Be inventive, adding flavours and textures to complement and contrast with your soup. Here are just a few trouble-free accompaniments that can be prepared while the soup cooks, using a variety of breads. All recipes serve 4.

## hummus and
## pepper slices

Brush **4 large, diagonally cut slices of ciabatta bread** with **olive oil** on both sides and rub the surfaces with a cut **garlic clove**. Toast on a hot ridged griddle until golden, turning once. Spread about **3½ oz (100 g) hummus** over the toasts. Thinly slice **2 red peppers** from a jar of roasted peppers and arrange on top of the toasts. Serve with Spiced Beet and Apple Soup (page 54). Ⓥ

**Each serving provides** • 224 cals • 6 g protein • 13 g fat of which 1 g saturates • 22 g carbohydrate

**5** mins prep time   **4** mins cook time

# tapenade toasts

Lightly toast **8 diagonally cut slices of French baguette** until golden, then spread with **3 tbsp (45 mL) black olive tapenade** from a jar. Serve the toasts with Speedy Two-Fish Chowder, instead of the bread sticks (page 43), Zippy Minestrone (page 40) or Carrot, Orange and Feta Soup (page 60). Ⓥ

**Each serving provides** • 232 cals • 7.5 g protein
• 3 g fat of which 0.5 g saturates • 45 g carbohydrate

**5** mins prep time  **4** mins cook time

# ricotta and pesto bites

Lightly stir **2 tbsp (25 mL) red pesto** into **5 oz (150 g) ricotta cheese** to give a marbled effect and spoon rough heaps of the mixture on to **4 pumpernickel slices**. Cut each slice into four triangles and sprinkle with torn **basil leaves**. Serve with Roasted Tomato, Pepper and Chorizo Soup (page 39) or Minted Asparagus and Garden Pea Soup (page 58). Ⓥ

**Each serving provides** • 194 cals • 9 g protein
• 11 g fat of which 4 g saturates • 16 g carbohydrate

**8** mins prep time

# cheddar chutney pitas

Warm **4 pita breads** under a medium-hot broiler for 1 minute on each side (just to make the pita breads easier to open – take care not to toast them). Cut a slit along one edge of each and make a pocket. Spread each inside with 1 tbsp **(15 mL) sweet chutney**, such as onion and tomato. Grate **5 oz (150 g) mature cheddar cheese** and divide among the pita breads, tucking it inside the pocket. Toast under a hot broiler, turning once, until the cheese is hot and bubbling. Serve with Garden Vegetable Broth with Parma Ham (page 40). Ⓥ

**Each serving provides** • 448 cals • 18 g protein
• 14 g fat of which 8 g saturates • 65 g carbohydrate

**5** mins prep time  **4** mins cook time

# chili bean wraps

Gently warm a **14-oz (398-mL) can red kidney beans in chili sauce**. Meanwhile, warm **4 soft flour tortilla wraps** under the grill for 10 seconds on each side or in the microwave for 10 seconds. Shred **4 romaine lettuce leaves** and arrange over the tortillas. Top with the beans and **2 thinly sliced scallions**. Roll up the tortillas and slice each in half. Serve with Roasted Cherry Tomato Soup (page 39). Ⓥ

**Each serving provides** • 233 cals • 9 g protein
• 1 g fat of which 0.1 g saturates • 49 g carbohydrate

**10** mins prep time  **4** mins cook time

# Spiced Beet
## and Apple Soup

Mildly spiced and a stunning colour, this impressive soup is quick to rustle up. If you have a hungry family to feed, try serving with Hummus and Pepper Slices (page 52).

**15** mins prep time    **15** mins cook time

**Serves 4** Ⓥ

1 tbsp (15 mL) butter

1 tbsp (15 mL) olive oil

½ lb (250 mL) raw beets, peeled and roughly chopped

2 dessert apples, peeled, cored and cut into chunks

1 large red onion, cut into small chunks

1 tbsp (15 mL) mild curry powder

2 eggs

2 cups (500 mL) vegetable stock, made with stock cubes

4 tbsp (60 mL) low-fat sour cream

**Each serving provides** • 194 cals • 6.5 g protein • 12 g fat of which 5 g saturates • 16 g carbohydrate

**Swap** For the curry powder, use 2 tsp (10 mL) grated horseradish from a jar, or 1 tsp (5 mL) crushed chili flakes or wasabi paste.

If you prefer, buy **ready-cooked beets** (without vinegar) to save time. Or cook the beets in the microwave first: Put the trimmed, unpeeled beets in a covered dish with 2-3 tbsp (25-45 mL) water and microwave on High for 8-10 minutes or until tender. Drain and rub in a cloth to remove the skin, then chop and use for the soup.

## ...speed it up

**1 Fry the vegetables and apples** Melt the butter and oil in a large pot and stir in the beets, apples and onion. Cover and cook over a medium heat, shaking the pot occasionally to prevent sticking, for 10 minutes. Stir in the curry powder and cook for a further 5 minutes over a gentle heat.

**2 Hard-boil the eggs** While the vegetables are frying, hard-boil the eggs in a pot of boiling water for 10 minutes, then put them into a bowl of cold water to cool. Peel them and chop roughly.

**3 Purée the soup** Add half the stock to the vegetables, tip into a food processor or blender and process until smooth. Pour back into the pot.

**4 The final touches** Stir the remaining stock into the purée. Season and heat gently until boiling. Ladle into bowls, swirl 1 tbsp (15 mL) sour cream into each and scatter with the chopped hard-boiled eggs.

The soup can be cooked, puréed and mixed with the remaining stock and sour cream, then stored in the fridge for two days. The eggs can be hard-boiled and stored in their shells in the fridge.

## ...get ahead

# Sweet Potato
## and Bean Soup

Orange-fleshed sweet potato and flavourful leeks make a hearty and creamy base for lima beans. Serve with crusty bread rolls for a brisk winter warmer.

**30** mins prep/cook time

**Serves 4** Ⓥ

2 tbsp (25 mL) butter

2 leeks, sliced

14 oz (400 g) sweet potatoes, peeled and thinly sliced

½ tsp (2 mL) ground cumin

4 cups (1 L) vegetable stock, made with stock cubes

4 tbsp (60 mL) sour cream

2 tbsp (25 mL) chopped fresh coriander

7 oz (200 g) canned lima beans, drained and rinsed

juice of ½ lemon

**Each serving provides** • 283 cals • 5 g protein • 18 g fat of which 12 g saturates • 27 g carbohydrate

> The basic soup can be made in advance to the end of step 3, then cooled and stored in the fridge for up to two days. To use, gently reheat and complete the recipe.
>
> **...get ahead**

**1** **Fry the vegetables** Melt the butter in a large pot, add the leeks and sweet potatoes, then cook over a low heat for 3 minutes, stirring occasionally, until they begin to soften. Add the cumin and cook for 2 more minutes.

**2** **Cook until tender** Add the stock and bring to the boil. Reduce the heat, cover and cook gently for 12 minutes or until the vegetables are tender. While the soup is simmering, mix together the sour cream and chopped coriander for the garnish. Set aside.

**3** **Add the beans and purée the soup** Add the lima beans to the soup. Ladle into a blender or food processor and purée until smooth. Return to the pot. Bring back to the boil and simmer gently until piping hot. Season and add the lemon juice.

**4** **Finish the soup** Ladle the soup into four bowls and swirl a large spoonful of coriander cream on top of each. Serve immediately.

**Swaps** • Omit the beans. After puréeing the soup, stir in a drained **6-oz (170-g) can white crabmeat** and **2 tbsp (25 mL) dry sherry**. • Use **7 oz (200 g) ordinary potatoes** with **7 oz (200 g) sweet potatoes**.

# Watercress and Onion Cream with Cashews

The peppery flavour of watercress comes through beautifully in this nutritious soup – ideal healthy food in a hurry. Serve with crusty bread or a microwaved "baked" potato.

**10** mins prep time  **15** mins cook time

Serves 4 Ⓥ

1 tbsp (15 mL)  olive oil

1 large onion, chopped

¾ lb (375 g) baking potatoes, peeled and chopped

3 oz (90 g) cashews

3⅓ oz (100 g) watercress

2 cups (500 mL) vegetable stock, made with stock cubes

½ cup (125 mL) 1% milk

2 oz (60 g) Gruyère cheese, coarsely grated

**Each serving provides** • 327 cals • 13 g protein • 19.5 g fat of which 6 g saturates • 27 g carbohydrate

**Swap** For watercress, use **spinach or arugula leaves**.

**1 Cook the onion and potato** Heat the olive oil in a large, heavy-based pot and add the onion and potatoes. Cover and cook on a medium heat, stirring occasionally, for about 10 minutes or until softened. Meanwhile, put the cashews in a dry frying pan and toast over a medium-high heat, tossing regularly, for 2-3 minutes or until golden brown. Roughly chop the nuts.

**2 Add the watercress and stock** Add the watercress, including the stalks, to the onion and potato and stir over the heat for 2-3 minutes or until wilted. Add the stock and season. Cook for a few minutes if the potato is not quite tender. Tip into a food processor or blender and process to a smooth purée. Return to the pot.

**3 Enrich the soup** Add the milk and bring the soup just to the boil. Ladle into bowls and sprinkle over the cashews and cheese.

### Chunky mussel and arugula soup

Heat a **1-lb (500-g) vacuum pack of mussels** for 5 minutes or according to the pack instructions. Omit the cashews, watercress and cheese from the basic recipe. Cook the onion and potatoes as step 1 and add the stock. Purée the soup. Add the milk and bring to the boil. Add the mussels and their juices to the soup and simmer for 5 minutes. Season, then stir in **3 tbsp (45 mL) double cream** and a **3-oz (90-g) bag of arugula leaves**, roughly chopped. Serve immediately.

## ...another idea

# Cauliflower
## and Blue Cheese Soup

With a chunky texture and a rich, blue cheese flavour, this winter vegetable soup couldn't be simpler to prepare. Serve with Hummus and Pepper Slices (page 52) for a substantial meal in a flash.

**10** mins prep time

**15** mins cook time

### Serves 4 Ⓥ

1 small cauliflower, divided into small florets

2 small leeks, diced

1 small potato, peeled and chopped

4 cups (1L) vegetable stock, made with stock cubes

¼ lb (125 g) Gorgonzola cheese, roughly chopped

**Each serving provides** • 187 cals • 11 g protein • 12 g fat of which 7 g saturates • 9.5 g carbohydrate

**1 Cook the vegetables** Put the cauliflower, leeks and potato into a pot and add the stock and seasoning. Bring to the boil, then reduce the heat. Cover and simmer gently for about 14 minutes or until tender.

**2 Purée the vegetables** Transfer half the soup to a food processor or blender and purée until smooth. Return to the pot. (Alternatively, use a hand-held blender straight in the pot to process the soup lightly, leaving a chunky appearance.)

**3 Finish the soup** Heat the soup gently until boiling, then remove from the heat. Add the cheese and stir lightly. Ladle into bowls and serve immediately.

**Swaps** • For Gorgonzola, try **Roquefort or Dolcelatte**. • For cauliflower, use **broccoli**.

If you have some **leftover mashed potato**, add this at the end of cooking instead of using raw potato. Reduce the cooking time for the onion at step 1 to 5 minutes.

**...speed it up**

# Minted Asparagus and Garden Pea Soup

Fresh asparagus is the ideal vegetable partner for peas in this perky soup topped with quark, baking cheese or fromage frais and toasted pine nuts. Serve with Ricotta and Pesto Bites (page 53).

**15** mins prep time

**15** mins cook time

Serves 4 Ⓥ

8 oz (250 g) asparagus spears

1 tbsp (15 mL) olive oil

2 shallots, chopped

6 oz (175 g) potatoes, peeled and chopped

5 oz (150 g) frozen peas

2⅔ cups (650 mL) vegetable stock, made with stock cubes

small sprig of fresh mint

4 tbsp (60 mL) Greek-style yogurt

1½ oz (40 g) toasted pine nuts

Each serving provides • 219 cals • 9 g protein • 14 g fat of which 3.5 g saturates • 15 g carbohydrate

**1** **Prepare the asparagus** Snap off any woody ends from the asparagus stalks at the point where they break easily. Cut off the tender tips and reserve. Roughly chop the remainder.

**2** **Fry the vegetables** Heat the olive oil in a large, heavy pot and add the shallots, chopped asparagus and potatoes. Cover and cook over a medium heat, stirring occasionally, for 6-8 minutes or until tender.

**3** **Add the peas, and purée** Reserve a handful of peas and add the remainder to the pot with the stock and mint sprig. Cook for a few minutes if the potato is not quite tender. Season, then tip into a food processor or blender and process to a smooth purée. Return to the pot.

**4** **Add the asparagus tips** Blanch the asparagus tips and reserved peas in a pot of boiling water for 2 minutes. Drain. Bring the soup to the boil, then stir in the blanched asparagus tips and peas. Ladle into bowls. Swirl a spoonful of fromage frais on to each and scatter the pine nuts over the top.

Instead of the potatoes, add about **4 oz (125 g) leftover mashed potato** to the soup for the last few minutes of cooking. Or use quick instant mash, adding just enough to thicken the soup. Reduce the cooking time to 3-4 minutes at step 2.

**...speed it up**

# Miso **Noodle** Soup
## with Tofu

**Lightning-quick to prepare, miso makes a nutritious base for a light Japanese-style broth with tofu, mushrooms and watercress. Serve with bread.**

**10** mins prep time   **10** mins cook time

Serves 4 Ⓥ

**4 x ⅔-oz (18-g) packets miso soup powder**

**4 cups (1 L) boiling water**

**6 oz (175 g) button mushrooms, sliced**

**6 scallions, sliced**

**4 oz (125 g) rice noodles**

**3 oz (90 g) watercress, with stalks, roughly chopped**

**6 oz (175 g) tofu, cut into small cubes**

Each serving provides • 165 cals • 7 g protein • 3 g fat of which 0.4 g saturates • 27 g carbohydrate

For a really speedy soup, buy a **14-oz (400-g) pack of pre-sliced stir-fry vegetables** and add them to the hot miso soup at step 1 instead of the mushrooms and onions. Simmer until the vegetables are almost tender, then add the noodles and, after 4 minutes, the tofu. Omit the watercress.

**...speed it up**

**1 Make the miso base** Dissolve the miso soup powder in the boiling water in a pot. Bring to the boil and add the mushrooms and scallions.

**2 Add the noodles** Cover and simmer for 2-3 minutes to soften the vegetables, then stir in the noodles and simmer gently for 4 minutes.

**3 Add the tofu** Stir in the watercress and tofu, then return to the boil. Season if necessary and serve immediately.

**Swaps** • For miso soup, use a **14 oz (398 mL) can beef consommé** and take it up to 4 cups (1 L) with boiling water (or use 2 cans if you like). • Add **smoked tofu** instead of plain.

# Carrot, Orange and Feta Soup

Fragrant orange, sweet carrot and tangy feta cheese combine in this simple, warming soup. Accompany with Tapenade Toasts (page 53) for a touch of luxury.

**15** mins prep time

**15** mins cook time

**Serves 4** Ⓥ

1 tbsp (15 mL) olive oil

1 onion, finely chopped

4 carrots, peeled and finely chopped

1 garlic clove, crushed

2½ cups (600 mL) vegetable stock, made with stock cubes

juice of 1 small orange

2 tbsp (25 mL) chopped fresh tarragon, plus leaves, to garnish

3½ oz (100 g) feta cheese, crumbled

**Each serving provides** • 140k cals • 5 g protein • 8.5 g fat of which 4 g saturates • 11 g carbohydrate

**1 Fry the vegetables** Heat the oil in a large pot and fry the onion, carrots and garlic over a medium heat for about 5 minutes, to soften but not brown.

**2 Add the stock and flavourings** Add the stock, orange juice and half the tarragon, and bring to the boil. Reduce the heat, cover and simmer gently for 6-8 minutes or until tender.

**3 Process the soup** Reserve about a quarter of the diced vegetables and tip the remainder into a food processor or blender. Process until almost smooth – it's best to leave some texture and not process to a completely smooth purée. Season.

**4 Complete the soup** Return the purée to the pot with the reserved diced vegetables and heat until boiling. Ladle into bowls and add some crumbled feta cheese to each. Sprinkle with the reserved chopped tarragon and the leaves, and serve immediately.

**Parsnip, lemon and thyme soup** Ⓥ
Make the soup with **4 parsnips** instead of carrots, and fry them with the onion and garlic at step 1. Replace the orange juice with the **juice of ½ lemon**, and the tarragon with **chopped fresh thyme leaves**. Cook up to step 3, then tip the whole quantity into the food processor or blender and process until smooth. Season, then return to the pot and stir in **3½ oz (100 g) reduced-fat soft cheese** until melted. Omit the feta cheese. Sprinkle with **chopped thyme** to serve.

## ...another idea

The soup can be made in advance and chilled for up to three days. Add the feta just before serving. Or you can freeze it. Prepare to the beginning of step 4, add the diced vegetables and then cool quickly. Pour into a freezerproof container and freeze for up to a month.

## ...get ahead

If time is short, you can omit the processing at step 3 – the soup can be served as a simpler, country-style chunky version.

## ...speed it up

# light
# meals

# Roasted Artichoke
## and Pepper Bruschetta

Make high-speed bruschetta by using tapenade to give the ciabatta toasts a rich flavour of olives, olive oil and garlic, then top with artichokes and crispy, cooked salami.

**Serves 4**

1 ciabatta, about ½ lb (250 g)

1 red pepper, thinly sliced

2 tbsp (25 mL) olive oil (from the jar of artichokes)

12 slices Milano salami, about 2½ oz (70 g) in total

4 tbsp (60 mL) tapenade

1 jar char-grilled or roasted artichokes in olive oil, about 10 oz (300 g), drained and sliced

**Each serving provides** • 391 cals • 12 g protein • 22 g fat of which 4 g saturates • 37 g carbohydrate

**1** **Toast the bread** Preheat the broiler to medium-hot and line the bottom of a broiling pan with foil. Cut the ciabatta into 12 slices on the diagonal, each ¼ in. (1.5 cm) thick. Put on the broiling pan rack and cook for about 1 minute on each side or until golden.

**2** **Prepare the topping** While the bread is toasting, toss the red pepper slices in the oil. Carefully remove the broiling pan rack with the toast still on it and set aside. Put the pepper slices in a single layer to one side of the foil-lined pan and cook for 3 minutes. Add the salami slices to the other side and broil for a further 2-3 minutes or until the peppers are lightly singed and the salami slices start to crisp.

**3** **Assemble the bruschetta** While the salami is cooking, stir the contents of the tapenade jar to blend in the oil, then thinly spread the toasts with tapenade. Place a few pepper and artichoke slices on each piece, then top with the crispy salami. Return to the broiler for 1 minute to heat through. Serve at once.

**Shopping tip** Tapenade is a purée of capers, black olives, anchovies and garlic in olive oil. You can make it yourself, if you like (see page 173).

**10** mins prep time

**10** mins cook time

Slice a **large baguette** on the diagonal into ¼ in. (1.5 cm) slices and put on a baking sheet. Mix **3 tbsp (45 mL) olive oil** with **2 tsp (10 mL) dried Italian herbs** and lightly brush over the bread. Bake at 400°F (200°C), for 15 minutes or until golden. Leave to cool on the baking sheet, then pack into plastic bags and freeze for up to 1 month. Take out a few slices as required. Warm them under a medium-hot grill for 1 minute and use to make bruschetta or mini pizzas.

## ...get ahead

**Pear and gorgonzola bruschetta** Ⓥ
Rub the toasted bread at the end of step 1 with **2 cut garlic cloves**. Drizzle with **2 tbsp (25 mL) walnut oil**. Sauté **2 cored and sliced pears** in **1 tbsp (15 mL) butter** until tender and beginning to brown. Put on the toasts. Add **5 oz (150 g) diced Gorgonzola cheese**. Grill until bubbling.

## ...another idea

# Snappy English Muffins

For a children's favourite, this pantry trio of baked beans, bacon and cheese makes a great topping on toasted English muffins for a no-hassle snack or light meal.

**15** mins prep time

**10** mins cook time

**Serves 4**

**4 whole wheat or white English muffins**

**1 tbsp (15 mL) softened butter**

**14 oz (398 mL) can baked beans**

**8 slices white cheddar cheese (8 oz /250 g total weight)**

**12 cherry tomatoes, or baby plum tomatoes, halved**

**4 slices back (Canadian) bacon, cut into strips**

**Each serving provides** • 514 cals • 29 g protein • 26 g fat of which 14 g saturates • 46 g carbohydrate

**1 Toast the English muffins** Preheat the broiler to medium-hot and line the grill pan with foil. Split the English muffins in half horizontally. Put the muffin halves on a baking sheet under the broiler, cut side down, and toast the base of the muffins for about 1 minute. Turn over and thinly spread the cut sides with butter (this helps to prevent the beans from soaking into the muffins). Grill, cut side up, for about 1½ minutes or until lightly browned.

**2 Prepare the beans and cheese** Tip the beans into a sieve over the sink and drain off some of the tomato sauce. Gently heat them in a small pan until steaming hot. Divide the beans among the toasted English muffins, then top each with a slice of cheese (make sure the surfaces of the muffins are completely covered with beans or cheese, as any exposed parts will burn).

**3 Complete the topping** Put 3 halved cherry tomatoes, cut side up, on top of each slice of cheese, then scatter with the bacon strips. Season with a little ground black pepper, if you like. Return the muffins to the broiler and cook for 3-5 minutes or until the bacon is cooked and the cheese is melted and bubbling. Serve at once, or if serving to young children, allow to cool for a minute first.

**Swaps** For beans, cheese, tomatoes and bacon, use a drained **6-oz (170-g) can tuna** mashed with **2 tbsp (25 mL) lemon mayonnaise** and seasoning. Top with **tomato** slices and **Gruyère or Emmental cheese**.

**Smoked turkey English muffins**
Mix the softened butter with **2 tsp (10 mL) yellow mustard** and spread over the cut sides of the muffin halves. Toast under a medium-hot broiler for 2 minutes or until lightly browned. Sprinkle with **3½ oz (100 g) coarsely grated Monterey Jack or Cheddar cheese** and press down gently. Top with **4 smoked turkey slices**, about 3½ oz (100 g) in total, snipped into strips. Broil for 2 minutes or until sizzling. Dot **2 tsp (10 mL) cranberry jelly** on top of each muffin half. Cook for a further 30 seconds or until just beginning to melt. (Split bagels also work well in this recipe.)

## ...another idea

# Greek Style Pizza

Red onions, cherry tomatoes, olives and tangy feta cheese give a Mediterranean feel to this express pizza. Toss together an arugula or baby leaf salad to accompany.

**10** mins prep time

**10** mins cook time

### Serves 4 ⓥ

2 tbsp (25 mL) olive oil (from the jar of sun-dried tomatoes)

1 tsp (5 mL) balsamic vinegar

1 small red onion, thinly sliced

1 large, thin and crispy ready-made pizza base, about ½ lb (250 g), or 2 x 5-oz (150-g) pizza bases

3 tbsp (45 mL) sun-dried tomato paste

8 cherry tomatoes, halved

1¾ oz (50 g) sun-dried tomatoes in oil, cut into thin slices

12 stoned black or green olives

5 oz (150 g) feta cheese, crumbled

**Each serving provides** • 429 cals • 13 g protein • 24 g fat of which 7 g saturates • 44 g carbohydrate

**1 Marinate the onions** Preheat the oven to 425°F (220°C). Whisk 1 tbsp (15 mL) oil and the vinegar in a bowl, add the onion rings and toss to coat. Leave while you prepare the remaining ingredients (the marinade helps to soften the onion and mellows the flavour a little).

**2 Add the pizza topping** Spread the pizza base with the sun-dried tomato paste. Arrange the onion rings and cherry tomatoes on top, then scatter with the sun-dried tomato slices, olives and feta cheese. Drizzle the remaining oil over the pizza.

**3 Bake the pizza** Put the pizza directly on to the top shelf of the oven, putting a baking sheet on the shelf below to catch any drips. Bake for 10 minutes or until the base is crisp and the topping lightly browned. Season with ground black pepper. Cut into wedges and serve.

**Cooking tip** Add flavour by using **sun-dried tomato paste with the addition of herbs and spices** such as hot chilies, garlic, oregano and capers.

### Chicken, dolcelatte and spinach
Spread the base with **3 tbsp (45 mL) red pesto**. Top with **10 oz (300 g) lightly cooked spinach, 7 oz (200 g) bought cooked sliced chicken breast** and **3½ oz (100 g) roasted red peppers in oil**, well-drained and sliced. Scatter **2⅔ oz (75 g) diced Dolcelatte or Gorgonzola** cheese on top. Bake.

### Eggplant and red onion ⓥ
Spread **3 tbsp (45 mL) red pepper pesto** over the base. Brush **1 small eggplant**, thinly sliced, with **olive or chili oil**. Put on a baking tray and bake for 15 minutes, turning once, then sprinkle with **1 tsp (5 mL) balsamic vinegar**. Brush **1 thinly sliced red onion** with oil and add to the tray for the last 5 minutes. Top the pizza with the eggplant and onion, and bake. Scatter with **2⅔ oz (75 g) pine nuts** and serve.

### Spicy lamb
Spread the base with **3 tbsp (45 mL) sun-dried tomato paste**. Stir-fry **½ lb (250 g) lean ground lamb** with **1 zucchini**, cut into ½ in. (1 cm) dice, until the meat is lightly browned, then add **2 crushed garlic cloves** and **1 tsp (5 mL) ground cumin**. Stir-fry for 1 minute. Season, then pour on to the pizza and scatter with **2⅔ oz (75 g) grated or diced mozzarella**. Bake.

### Tuna and tomato
Spread the base with **3 tbsp (45 mL) sun-dried tomato paste**. Top with **2 large tomatoes**, thinly sliced, and a **6-oz (170-g) can tuna**, drained and flaked. Add **12 stoned black olives** and **3½ oz (100 g) cubed mozzarella**. Bake.

## ...more ideas

● Packs of **one-step bread dough** have a long shelf life and are useful to keep in the pantry for making pizzas. Roll out the pre-made dough to a 10-in. (25-cm) circle on a baking sheet lined with baking parchment, add your topping and bake. ● Save time by using a bought **margherita pizza** as a base. Top as the basic recipe, but omit the sun-dried tomato paste and reduce the feta cheese to 2⅔ oz (75 g).

● You can make a **quick pizza base** in about 5 minutes: Put 8 oz (250 g) self-raising flour, ½ tsp (2 mL) baking powder and ¼ tsp (1 mL) salt in a bowl. Stir, then make a hollow in the centre and pour in ⅔ cup (150 mL) semi-skimmed milk and 1 tbsp (15 mL) olive oil. Mix to a soft dough and roll out. Top as before but bake for 12-15 minutes.

## ...tips for pizza bases

# Stuffed Mushrooms
## with Grilled Polenta

**For an impressive lunch to share with friends, whip up some mushrooms filled with goat's cheese, walnuts and tarragon, and serve with ready-made polenta and a crisp salad.**

**15** mins prep time

**15** mins cook time

Serves 4 Ⓥ

**4 large, flat mushrooms, about 14 oz (400 g) in total**

**2½ tbsp (30 mL) olive oil**

**2⅔ oz (75 g) walnut pieces, broken if large**

**5 oz (150 g) medium-fat mild goat cheese**

**2 tbsp (25 mL) chopped fresh tarragon**

**1 lb (500 g) pack ready-made polenta, cut across into 8 slices, each about ¾ in. (2 cm) thick**

**2 tbsp (25 mL) walnut oil**

**1 tsp (5 mL) red wine vinegar**

Each serving provides • 788 cals
• 19 g protein • 35 g fat of which
7.5 g saturates • 99 g carbohydrate

**1 Prepare the mushrooms** Preheat the broiler to medium-hot and line the bottom of a broiling pan with foil. Wipe the mushrooms and remove the stalks (use these for another dish or to flavour stock). Brush the gill side with 1 tbsp (15 mL) olive oil and season. Broil gill side up for 6 minutes, then turn over, brush with ½ tbsp (7 mL) olive oil and cook for a further 5 minutes or until softened and golden.

**2 Make the filling** While the mushrooms are cooking, put the walnuts on a piece of foil and broil for 2 minutes or until golden (take care not to burn them). Mix these with the goat cheese and 1 tbsp (15 mL) of the tarragon. Remove the mushrooms from the pan.

**3 Cook the polenta and warm the mushrooms** Lightly brush the polenta slices on both sides with the remaining olive oil. Add to the broiling pan and cook for 5 minutes or until lightly browned. Meanwhile, divide the goat cheese mixture among the mushrooms. Turn the polenta slices over and add the filled mushrooms to the pan. broil for a further 3 minutes or until the mushroom filling begins to colour and the polenta is lightly browned.

**4 Serve the polenta and mushrooms** Whisk together the walnut oil and red wine vinegar, then stir in the remaining tarragon. Transfer the mushrooms to warmed serving plates and add 2 slices of broiled polenta to each. Drizzle the polenta with the tarragon dressing.

Cooking tip You can use your own polenta for this recipe (see Cooking tip, page 151).

# Mediterranean Tarts

These vibrant tarts, topped with pesto, tomatoes, olives and ricotta, are easy to make with ready-rolled puff pastry. Serve with a salad of radicchio leaves or some coleslaw.

**30**mins prep/cook time

**Serves 4 Ⓥ**

¾ lb (375 g) pack ready-rolled puff pastry

4 tbsp (60 mL) green pesto

2 large tomatoes, thinly sliced

½ lb (250 g) ricotta cheese

8 stoned black olives, halved

2 oz (60 g) grated Parmesan or Italian-style hard cheese

basil leaves, to garnish (optional)

**Each serving provides** • 639 cals • 22 g protein • 46 g fat of which 10 g saturates • 39 g carbohydrate

**To serve** Make a simple salad with torn **radicchio leaves** and tossed with a **walnut oil** and **balsamic vinegar** dressing (see page 31).

**1 Turn on the oven** Preheat the oven to 425°F (220°C). Remove the pack of pastry from the fridge and, if time allows, leave it, still wrapped, at room temperature for 20 minutes (this makes it easier to unroll without cracking, but isn't essential).

**2 Make the pastry bases** Carefully unroll the pastry, then cut into four even-sized rectangles, each about 7 x 4⅓ in. (18 x 11 cm). Put them on a baking sheet and prick them all over with a fork. Bake for 12 minutes, turning the baking sheet around if they are cooking or browning unevenly.

**3 Add the topping** Spread each with 1 tbsp (15 mL) pesto, then divide the tomato slices evenly among them. Dot the ricotta cheese over the tops in small blobs, then scatter with the olives. Sprinkle with Parmesan and ground black pepper.

**4 Complete the cooking** Return the tarts to the oven to bake for 5-10 minutes or until the pastry bases are well browned and crisp, and the topping slightly melted and coloured. Serve garnished with basil, if you like.

**Swaps** Vary the toppings using ingredients you already have, or try these: • **Cream cheese** topped with **scrunched smoked salmon** trimmings. Bake, then scatter with **arugula**. • Brush the **young asparagus** with **olive oil** and bake (while the pastry bases are cooking, on the shelf below) for 12 minutes. Spread **green pesto** over each tart. Top with the asparagus and scatter with shaved **Parmesan cheese**. Bake for 2 minutes.

# 5 great meals with flatbreads and wraps

Flatbreads and wraps come in all shapes, sizes and flavours. They make great light lunches, portable feasts and super-quick suppers, and many will keep for a week or two, or can be frozen. Here are some quick-prep ideas to get you started. All recipes serve 4.

## moroccan wraps

Finely **dice ½ small cucumber** and **3 ripe tomatoes** and slice **2 scallions**. Put them all in a sieve, sprinkle with **¼ tsp (1 mL) salt** and leave them to drain for 5 minutes. Transfer to a bowl and mix in **2 tbsp (25 mL) roughly chopped fresh mint**. Drain and rinse a **14 oz (398 mL) can chickpeas** and tip them into a bowl. Mash roughly with a fork, then add **½ tsp (2 mL) ground cumin**, **1 crushed garlic clove**, **2 tbsp (25 mL) extra virgin olive oil**, **1 tbsp (15 mL) lemon juice** and **1 tbsp (15 mL) tahini**. Mash again until fairly smooth. Season to taste with ground black pepper. Spread **4 soft flour tortilla wraps** (buy spinach-flavoured ones, if available) with the chickpea mixture, leaving a 1-in. (2.5-cm) border. Spoon the cucumber and tomato mixture down the centre of each, then roll up tightly to enclose the filling. Ⓥ

**25 mins prep time**

**Each serving provides** • 323 cals • 11 g protein • 12 g fat of which 2 g saturates • 45 g carbohydrate

Tortillas are more pliable for folding if warmed. The simplest way is one at a time on a plate in the microwave on high for 15 seconds, or microwave a stack of 4 tortillas together for 1 minute. Alternatively, preheat the oven to 325°F (160°C). Wrap the stack of tortillas in foil and warm for 10 minutes, or according to the pack instructions.

### ...ways to warm wraps

# grilled **tofu** and **pepper** wraps

Toss **¾ lb (375 g) tofu pieces** in **3 tbsp (45 mL) red pesto**, then thread onto skewers with **2 diced peppers**, preferably 1 yellow and 1 green (the skewers make the pieces easier to turn, but are not essential). Cook under a medium-hot broiler for 8-10 minutes, turning several times, until the peppers are slightly charred and tender. Remove the pieces from the skewers. Warm **4 large soft flour tortilla wraps** (see left), then spread **8 oz (250 g) tzatziki** over them, leaving a 1-in. (2.5-cm) border. Divide the tofu and pepper filling among them, spooning it on to one half of the tortilla. Fold the uncovered tortilla over the filling, then carefully fold again into a fan shape. Ⓥ

**Each serving provides**
- 380 cals • 23 g protein
- 16 g fat of which 5 g saturates
- 39 g carbohydrate

# **tuna** and **cheese** melt flatbreads

Drain **2 x 6-oz (170-g) cans tuna** and mash the fish with **3 tbsp (45 mL) mayonnaise, 1 tbsp (15 mL) lemon juice** and **2 tsp (10 mL) tomato paste.** Season. Warm **2 large flatbreads or focaccias** (such as garlic and rosemary or pesto and sweet pepper) under a medium-hot grill for 1 minute, then spoon and spread the tuna mixture over the tops. Scatter with **1 small finely sliced red onion** (if time allows, marinate this in **1 tbsp/15 mL French dressing** for a few minutes to mellow the flavour), then divide **6 large slices of Emmenthal, Gruyère or Lancashire cheese** (buy packs ready-sliced) between them. Cook under a medium-hot grill for 3 minutes or until the cheese is lightly browned and bubbling. Cut each flatbread into four wedges and serve two per person.

**Each serving provides**
- 651 cals • 47 g protein
- 35 g fat of which 14 g saturates
- 38 g carbohydrate

# **californian** wraps

Take **4 large soft flour tortilla wraps** and lay out on a clean and dry, flat surface. Spread each with **2 tbsp (25 mL) yogurt-dill spread** (mix 5 oz/150 g plain yogurt with 1 tbsp/15 mL chopped fresh dill and some ground black pepper). Divide **7 oz (200 g) thinly sliced firm goat cheese** down the centre of the wraps. Top with **¼ romaine lettuce**, finely shredded, and **1¾ oz (50 g) arugula leaves**. Scatter **1 tbsp (15 mL) sunflower seeds or toasted mixed seeds** over each. Fold in the sides of each wrap to meet the filling, then roll up. Cut in half diagonally to serve. Ⓥ

**Each serving provides** • 353 cals • 17 g protein
- 16 g fat of which 9 g saturates
- 37 g carbohydrate

# **pita** pocket toasties

Warm **4 large, oval pita breads**, preferably whole-grain, under a medium-heat broiler for 1 minute on each side, or in a toaster for 20 seconds (just to make the pitas easier to open – take care not to toast them). Cut each in half widthwise and open up each half to make a pocket. Thinly spread inside with softened butter or margarine, if you like. Divide **3½ oz (100 g) sliced Gruyère cheese** and **3½ oz (100 g) dry-cure or honey-roast ham** (fat trimmed) among the pita breads and add **1 tsp (5 mL) chutney or relish** to each. (Make sure that the cheese and ham are tucked inside the pocket or they may catch and burn.) Grill the pita breads for 1½ minutes on each side or until the pita is lightly toasted.

**Each serving provides** • 400 cals • 21 g protein
- 11 g fat of which 6 g saturates • 58 g carbohydrate

# Smoked Trout
## and Watercress Open Sandwich

Peppery watercress and lemon mayonnaise, silky smoked trout and quail (or small) eggs – it's a beautifully sophisticated combination that's fast to prepare and tastes wonderful.

**20** mins prep time

**2** mins cook time

**Serves 4**

**12 quail eggs or 8 small-sized eggs**

**1¾ oz (50 g) watercress**

**4 tbsp (60 mL) mayonnaise**

**1 tbsp (15 mL) lemon juice**

**8 thick slices rye bread**

**3 skinless smoked trout fillets, about 2⅔ oz (75 g) each, flaked**

**Each serving provides** • 349 cals • 21 g protein • 20 g fat of which 4 g saturates • 23 g carbohydrate

**1** **Boil the eggs** Simmer the quail eggs in boiling water for 1½–2 minutes, depending on whether you prefer them slightly soft or medium boiled. Plunge into cold water and leave to cool.

**2** **Make the watercress mayonnaise** While the eggs are cooking, set aside a few watercress sprigs for garnishing, then roughly chop the rest, discarding any very thick stems. Mix the chopped watercress, mayonnaise and lemon juice together.

**3** **Assemble the sandwiches** Spread the watercress mixture evenly over one side of each slice of rye bread, then top with flakes of smoked trout. Carefully peel the shells off the eggs, then cut each in half and arrange three quail's egg halves (or two egg halves) on top of each open sandwich. Season with a little ground black pepper and garnish with the reserved sprigs of watercress.

# Honey-Baked Ham and Apple Croissants

For a brilliant brunch or picnic, grab sweet, crunchy carrot and apple and combine with smoke-flavoured ham to make a speedy filling for croissants.

**20 mins prep time**

**Serves 4**

4 large croissants
1 tbsp (15 mL) mayonnaise
4 tbsp (60 mL) sour cream
1 large carrot, coarsely grated
1 sweet apple, quartered, cored and chopped
2 scallions, finely chopped
1 oz (30 g) radishes, sliced
1¾ oz (50 g) pecan nuts
4 large slices of honey-baked ham, trimmed of fat and cut in half widthwise

**Each serving provides** • 422 cals • 13 g protein • 27 g fat of which 9 g saturates • 33 g carbohydrate

**1 Prepare the croissants** Using a serrated knife, cut the croissants open horizontally, keeping the top halves still attached along one side like a hinge.

**2 Make the filling** Blend the mayonnaise and sour cream together in a bowl. Add the carrot, apple, scallions, radishes and pecan nuts. Season and mix together well.

**3 Fill the croissants** Spoon the mixture on to the bottom half of each croissant, then top with the ham. Close the croissants and serve at once.

**Swaps** Fill croissants with your favourite ingredients, or try these ideas. (For the best results, first warm the croissants under the broiler or in the oven.) • **Canned salmon** mixed with a little **mayonnaise**, topped with sliced **cheddar cheese**. • **Lettuce**, chopped ripe **tomatoes** and **stoned black olives**, topped with hard-boiled **egg** and **anchovies**. • Cooked **turkey breast** with **lettuce** and a little **mayonnaise**. • **Mushrooms** fried with crushed **garlic**, **thyme** and **mascarpone**.

## Shrimp and egg mayonnaise

Cover the bread with shredded leaves from **1 Little Gem lettuce**. Mix **1 tbsp (15 mL) mayonnaise, 2 tbsp (25 mL) sour cream, 1 tsp (5 mL) tomato paste** and **12 oz (375 g) cooked, peeled jumbo shrimp**. Spoon over the lettuce. Stir **3 chopped hard-boiled eggs** with **2 tbsp (25 mL) mayonnaise** and seasoning, and put on top.

## Chicken and avocado

Spread the bread with **tarragon mayonnaise** (stir 1 tbsp/15 mL chopped fresh tarragon into 4 tbsp/60 mL mayonnaise). Put **4 arugula leaves** on each slice. Top with **3 cooked chicken breast fillets**, sliced, and **1 ripe avocado**, sliced and tossed in **2 tsp (10 mL) lemon juice**.

## Smoked pork and sauerkraut

Spread the bread with **mustard butter** (mix 1 tbsp/15 mL softened butter with 2 tsp/10 mL German mustard) and then spread with **4 tbsp (60 mL) bought apple sauce**. Top with **7½ oz (220 g) sliced smoked pork loin** and **5 oz (150 g) well-drained sauerkraut**.

## Scrambled egg, bacon and tomato brioche

Lightly toast 8 slices from a **brioche loaf**, then butter one side. Beat **6 eggs** with seasoning and **2 tbsp (25 mL) 2% milk or 10% cream**. Melt **1 tbsp (15 mL) butter** in a pan. Add **2 chopped tomatoes**, then add the eggs and stir over a gentle heat until they start to thicken. Remove from the heat and allow to finish cooking in the residual heat. Spoon onto the toast and top with **8 strips cooked bacon**.

## ...more ideas

Make the salad mixture up to 4 hours in advance and keep covered in the fridge until you are ready to fill the croissants.

## ...get ahead

# Chili Beef Tortillas

Tender minute steak is quick-cooking and inexpensive, and it goes superbly well with chili vegetables and smooth avocado in tortilla wraps, for a spicy light meal.

**20** mins prep time

**10** mins cook time

### Serves 4

- **12 thin slices minute (flash-fry or sandwich) steaks, about 11 oz (350 g) in total**
- **1 tsp (5 mL) paprika**
- **1 tsp (5 mL) ground cumin**
- **3 tbsp (45 mL) canola oil**
- **1 red onion, thinly sliced**
- **1 yellow pepper, sliced**
- **2 chili peppers, preferably 1 red and 1 green, seeded and finely sliced**
- **4 x 8-in. (20-cm) soft flour tortilla wraps**
- **1 ripe avocado, thinly sliced**

**Each serving provides** • 397 cals • 24 g protein • 21 g fat of which 5 g saturates • 30 g carbohydrate

**1 Cook the beef** Lightly dust the beef with the paprika, cumin and a little seasoning. Heat 1 tbsp (15 mL) oil in a large nonstick frying pan with a lid. Add the beef (you'll need to cook it in batches, adding a little more oil each time) and cook over a medium-high heat, turning once, until browned and cooked to your liking (about 30 seconds each side for rare, 45 seconds for medium, and 1 minute for well-done). Remove from the pan and put on a board to rest.

**2 Cook the vegetables** Add the remaining oil to the pan. Add the onion and cook, stirring, for 2 minutes or until beginning to soften. Add the pepper and chilies, and cook for a further 3 minutes or until the vegetables are tender. Lightly season. Meanwhile, cut the beef into ½-in. (1-cm) strips. Scatter the strips over the vegetables in the pan (the steam will reheat the beef). Remove from the heat and cover with the lid to keep the filling warm.

**3 Warm and fill the tortillas** In another pan, heat the tortillas one at a time for about 30 seconds on each side (or all together in a microwave). Spoon the beef mixture down the centre of each tortilla and add the avocado slices. Roll up and serve.

## Steak sandwich

Split **4 ciabatta rolls** in half lengthwise, keeping one side attached. Warm or toast them under a medium-heat broiler for 1 minute. Cook the minute steaks as in step 1. Spread **5 tbsp (75 mL) whole-grain mustard mayonnaise** over the bottom halves of the rolls. Top with **4 large sliced tomatoes**. Cut the steak into slices and add to the rolls. Mix **1 tbsp (15 mL) olive oil** with **1 tsp (5 mL) lemon juice** and the juices from the meat in a bowl. Add **1½ oz (40 g) watercress** and toss to coat. Scatter over the steaks.

**...another idea**

### Serves 4

- **1½ cups (375 mL) bulgur wheat**
- **4½ cups (1.13 L) boiling vegetable stock, made with stock cubes**
- **1 eggplant, cut into ½-in. (1-cm) slices**
- **2 zucchini, cut into ½-in. (1-cm) slices**
- **1 large yellow pepper, thickly sliced**
- **3 tbsp (45 mL) olive oil**
- **3 tsp (15 mL) red wine vinegar**
- **14 oz (400 g) flame-grilled chicken pieces (quartered if breast fillets)**
- **14 oz (398 mL) can black-eyed beans, drained and rinsed**
- **2 tbsp (25 mL) chopped fresh parsley**
- **2 tbsp (25 mL) butter**
- **2 tbsp (25 mL) chopped fresh mint, plus leaves, to garnish**

**Each serving provides** • 484 cals • 28 g protein • 17 g fat of which 5 g saturates • 56 g carbohydrate

**Addition** For a spicy dressing, stir a finely chopped, seeded **red chili pepper** into the melted butter or whisk in ¼ **tsp (1 mL) chili paste**.

**10** mins prep/plus soaking

**20** mins cook time

The salad can be prepared to the end of step 3 up to 12 hours in advance and kept covered in the fridge. If possible, remove the salad from the fridge about an hour before you need it, then drizzle over the mint butter dressing just before serving.

**...get ahead**

# Flame-Grilled Chicken
## and Vegetable Salad with
## Mint Butter Dressing

**Char-grilled Mediterranean vegetables and ready-cooked chicken combine with no-cook bulgur wheat to make an attractive salad drizzled with an aromatic dressing for a delightfully easy meal.**

**1 Prepare the bulgur wheat** Put the bulgur wheat in a large bowl, pour over the stock and stir well. Cover with a pan lid or baking sheet and leave to soak for 20-25 minutes or until tender and most of the stock has been absorbed.

**2 Char-grill the vegetables** While the bulgur wheat is soaking, preheat the grill to medium-hot and line the grill pan with foil. Arrange the vegetables on the grill rack and brush with 1 tbsp (15 mL) oil. Grill for 15-20 minutes or until tender and beginning to char, turning over halfway through and brushing the other side with 1 tbsp (15 mL) oil. Check the vegetables regularly and remove them as they are cooked.

**3 Assemble the salad** Drain the bulgur wheat. Whisk the remaining oil and 1 tsp (5 mL) vinegar in the bowl, then add the chicken, beans and parsley. Return the bulgur wheat to the bowl. Cut the eggplant slices into halves, or quarters if large, and add to the bowl with the zucchini and pepper slices. Mix everything together well. Season.

**4 Make the dressing** Heat the butter and remaining vinegar in a small pan. Stir in the mint. Spoon the bulgur wheat salad on to plates and drizzle over the mint dressing. Garnish with mint leaves.

# 5 great meals with a **bag** of **salad**

There's a huge variety of ready-to-eat prepared salad leaves at the supermarket, from the everyday to the colourful and exotic. Rather than just serving them on the side, let them take the leading role. Here you'll find ideas for all budgets, seasons and occasions – all made in record time. All recipes serve 4.

## smoked **mackerel** salad

Add **3 eggs** to a pot of boiling water and cook for 10 minutes. Drain the eggs and put them into a bowl of cold water to cool. Arrange a **7-oz (200-g) bag of crispy leaf salad** on a serving platter or four individual plates. Top with **¾ lb (375 g) smoked mackerel**, skinned and broken into large flakes, and **1 chopped red apple** tossed in **2 tsp (10 mL) lemon juice**. Peel and quarter the eggs and add to the salad. Mix **6 tbsp (90 mL) good-quality mayonnaise or salad cream** with **2 tsp (10 mL) lemon juice** and drizzle over the salad. Grind over a little black pepper. Serve with triangles of whole-grain bread and butter.

**Each serving provides** • 474 cals • 23 g protein • 39 g fat of which 8 g saturates • 8 g carbohydrate

**Shopping tip** Choose an English-style salad mix, with **shredded lettuce leaves**, **grated carrot** and **raw beet**, or a combination of slightly bitter leaves such as **frisée**, **chicory** and **radicchio**.

**20** mins prep time

Although most bags of salad leaves are "ready-to-use," if you have time it's best to freshen them up by rinsing them thoroughly with cold water, then draining well or using a salad spinner.

...taste tip

# barbecued chicken and bacon salad

Dry-fry (don't add oil) a **7-oz (200-g) pack of thick-sliced bacon** until crisp and golden. Remove from the pan with a slotted spoon and put on a plate lined with paper towel. Scissor-snip **2 slices white bread** into small squares. Add to the hot fat in the pan, adding **1-2 tbsp (15-25 mL) olive oil** if necessary, and fry over a medium-high heat until golden. Drain these croutons on paper towel. Whisk together **2 tbsp (25 mL) olive oil** and **2 tsp (10 mL) balsamic vinegar** in a serving bowl. Add **8 oz (250 g) barbecue-style chicken breast slices**, cut into thin strips, and toss to coat in the dressing. Add a **4¾-oz (135-g) bag of watercress, baby spinach and arugula leaf salad**, and toss again. Scatter with the lardons and croutons. Serve with bread, if you like.

**Each serving provides** • 316 cals • 28 g protein • 19 g fat of which 5 g saturates • 9 g carbohydrate

**3** mins prep time   **12** mins cook time

# stir-fried teriyaki steak salad

Slice a **thick-cut lean sirloin steak**, about 10 oz (300 g), trimmed of fat, into thin strips across the grain. If time allows, toss with **1 tbsp (15 mL) teriyaki marinade** and leave in the fridge for 2 hours. Mix a **5-oz (150-g) baby leaf and arugula salad** with **1 finely sliced yellow pepper**. Divide among four serving plates. Heat a heavy-based nonstick frying pan until hot, add **1 tbsp (15 mL) olive oil** and swirl to coat the base. Add the beef and stir-fry for 1 minute or until browned on the outside, but still pink inside. Add **3 tbsp (45 mL) teriyaki marinade** and **1 tbsp (15 mL) water**. Quickly swirl around in the pan to coat the meat, then spoon on to the salad. Serve at once, with bread.

**Each serving provides** • 163 cals • 19 g protein • 6.5 g fat of which 2 g saturates • 5 g carbohydrate

**Shopping tip** Teriyaki marinade, made with soy sauce, rice wine and vinegar, can be bought from supermarkets. It has a very intense flavour, so don't be tempted to add more to this dish. If the pan is very hot and too much of the sauce evaporates and becomes very thick, add an extra 1-2 spoonfuls of water.

**10** mins prep time   **2** mins cook time

# fried cod and romaine

Mix **1 tbsp (15 mL) extra virgin olive oil**, **1 tbsp (15 mL) fresh or bottled lime juice** or **2 tsp (10 mL) lemon juice** and **1 tsp (5 mL) paprika** and brush over **14 oz (400 g) skinless cod fillet or cod steaks (or any kind of firm white fish)**. Cook under a medium-hot grill for 6-7 minutes or until the fish flakes easily (there's no need to turn it over). Meanwhile, whisk **4 tbsp (60 mL) extra virgin olive oil**, **1 tbsp (15 mL) vinegar** from a jar of capers, **½ tsp (2 mL) Dijon mustard**, coarsely ground sea salt and black pepper together. Stir in **1 tbsp (15 mL) drained capers**. Flake the fish into large chunks. Add to a **5-oz (150-g) bag of torn romaine lettuce** (or any other crispy leaf) in a serving bowl. Drizzle over the dressing and gently mix together. Serve with crusty bread.

**Each serving provides**
• 213 cals • 19 g protein
• 15 g fat of which 2 g saturates
• 1 g carbohydrate

**7** mins prep time   **7** mins cook time

# curried chickpea salad

In a salad bowl, mix a **5-oz (150-g) bag of crispy lettuce leaves**, such as frisée, baby spinach and mâche or lamb's lettuce, with **1 large avocado**, cubed and tossed in **1 tsp (5 mL) lemon juice**, **10 oz (300 g) halved cherry tomatoes** and a **2-in. (5-cm) piece of cucumber**, diced. In a large nonstick pan, cook **1 red onion**, thinly sliced, in **1½ tbsp (20 mL) olive oil** for 5 minutes or until tender and beginning to brown. Stir in **½ tsp (2 mL) ground cumin**, **1 tsp (5 mL) ground coriander**, a **pinch of ground turmeric** and a drained and rinsed **14-oz (398-mL) can chickpeas**. Cook, stirring all the time, for 1-2 minutes or until the spices give off a rich aroma. Remove from the heat and stir in **2 tsp (10 mL) lemon juice**. Cool for 2 minutes, then add to the salad and toss together until well mixed. Make a simple minted yogurt dressing by stirring **2 tsp (10 mL) mint sauce** into **½ cup (125 mL) plain yogurt**. Drizzle over the salad. Serve with warmed nan bread. Ⓥ

**Each serving provides** • 257 cals • 9 g protein • 16 g fat of which 3 g saturates • 20 g carbohydrate

**10** mins prep time   **12** mins cook time

# Greek **Salad**
## with Tahini Dressing

Throw together ripe plum tomatoes, crisp salad vegetables, feta cheese and kalamata olives, then drizzle with a nutty tahini dressing and serve with fresh crusty bread.

**20** mins prep time

Serves 4 Ⓥ

7 oz (200 g) feta cheese

1 small romaine lettuce, torn into bite-sized pieces

½ cucumber, halved lengthwise and sliced

12 oz (375 g) large plum or other well-flavoured ripe tomatoes, sliced

1 small red onion, halved and thinly sliced

20 stoned kalamata olives, or other stoned black olives

4 tbsp (60 mL) extra virgin olive oil

1 tbsp (15 mL) tahini

1 tbsp (15 mL) lemon juice

4 large sprigs of fresh flat-leaf parsley

**Each serving provides** • 337 cals • 12 g protein • 29 g fat of which 10 g saturates • 6 g carbohydrate

**1 Briefly soak the feta cheese** Remove the feta cheese from its package, drain off any liquid and put into a small bowl of cold water. Leave to soak for a few minutes while preparing the rest of the salad (this will remove excess saltiness from the cheese).

**2 Prepare the salad** Divide the lettuce among four individual serving plates, then top with cucumber, tomato and red onion slices. Scatter with the olives.

**3 Make the dressing** Whisk the oil, tahini, lemon juice and a little ground black pepper in a bowl or shake together in a screw-top jar. Scissor-snip the parsley into the dressing.

**4 Complete the salad** Drain the feta cheese and crumble into small pieces. Scatter about two-thirds over the salads. Drizzle the dressing over the salads, then scatter with the remaining feta. Serve at room temperature.

**Shopping tips** • Tahini is a sesame seed paste that is used in Middle Eastern cooking. It has a good nutty flavour and is one of the essential ingredients in hummus. • In Greece, wild purslane, which has a mild taste and crunchy texture, is often used instead of Romaine lettuce. Arugula leaves, although more peppery in flavour, make another good substitute.

# Vegetarian **Couscous** Salad

**North African harissa paste adds fire to this swift salad of stir-fried smoked tofu with sun-dried tomatoes, sultanas and almonds in fluffy couscous.**

**15** mins prep time

**5** mins cook time

Serves 4 Ⓥ

3 tbsp (45 mL) oil (from the jar of sun-dried tomatoes)

7½ oz (220 g) pack smoked tofu, cut into ¾ in. (2 cm) cubes

1 tbsp (15 mL) olive oil

4 scallions, sliced

1 garlic clove, crushed

2 cups (500 mL) vegetable stock, made with a stock cube

1½ cups (375 mL) couscous

2⅔ oz (75 g) sultanas or raisins

a pinch of ground cinnamon

6 sun-dried tomatoes in oil

2 tsp (10 mL) red wine vinegar

2 tsp (10 mL) harissa paste

1¾ oz (50 g) toasted flaked almonds

chopped fresh parsley, to garnish

**Each serving provides** • 528 cals • 16.5 g protein • 23 g fat of which 3 g saturates • 64 g carbohydrate

**1 Stir-fry the tofu** Heat 1 tbsp (15 mL) of the sun-dried tomato oil in a frying pan, add the tofu cubes and stir-fry for about 2 minutes or until golden brown. Remove from the pan and set aside on kitchen paper.

**2 Prepare the couscous** Heat the olive oil in the pan, add the scallions and garlic, and stir-fry over a medium heat for 2 minutes. Pour in the stock and bring to the boil. Remove from the heat and stir in the couscous, sultanas and cinnamon. Cover the pan and leave for 3 minutes, then stir in the tofu. Re-cover the pan and leave for a further 2 minutes.

**3 Make a dressing** While the couscous is soaking, snip the sun-dried tomatoes into small pieces with kitchen scissors. Make a spicy dressing by whisking together the remaining sun-dried tomato oil, red wine vinegar, harissa paste, tomatoes and a little ground black pepper.

**4 Dress the couscous** Drizzle the dressing over the hot couscous, then mix and fluff up with a fork. Spoon on to warmed plates and scatter with the almonds and chopped parsley.

# Italian **Tomato** and **Bread Salad**

In a modern twist on the Italian bread salad *panzanella*, bread is roasted then flavoured with the juices from ripe tomatoes, fresh basil and piquant capers – for the easiest summer food.

**10** mins prep time

**20** mins cook time

**Serves 4** (V)

¾ small loaf of country-style bread, 1-2 days old, cut or torn into bite-sized chunks

1 yellow pepper, cut into chunks

5 tbsp (75 mL) extra virgin olive oil

2 tbsp (25 mL) red wine vinegar

½ tsp (2 mL) white (superfine) sugar

1 small red onion, halved and thinly sliced

1 lb (500 g) juicy ripe plum tomatoes, roughly chopped

2 tbsp (25 mL) capers, drained

1 small bunch of fresh basil, about ¾ oz (20 g), torn

20 mini mozzarella cheeses, 7½ oz (220 g) total weight

**Each serving provides** • 487 cals • 19 g protein • 27 g fat of which 10 g saturates • 43 g carbohydrate

**Swaps** For mozzarella, use a drained **6-oz (170-g) can tuna in olive oil, flaked, or skinless boneless sardines**.

**1 Roast the bread and pepper** Preheat the oven to 375°F (190°C). Spread the bread out over two-thirds of a large roasting pan. Toss the yellow pepper chunks in 1 tbsp (15 mL) oil and put in a single layer on the remaining third of the pan. Roast in the oven for 20 minutes or until golden. Remove and leave to cool for a few minutes.

**2 Prepare the dressing and vegetables** While the bread and peppers are roasting, put the remaining oil in a large serving bowl and whisk in the vinegar, superfine sugar and a little ground black pepper. Add the onion slices and toss well to coat in the dressing, then add the tomatoes and capers, and mix together.

**3 Assemble the salad** Add the bread and yellow peppers to the bowl. Scatter with the torn basil, then mix well. Cover and chill until you are ready to serve. Drain the mini mozzarella cheeses and arrange over the top of the salad before serving.

**Shopping tips** • If you can't find mini mozzarella, buy two 4-oz (125-g) packs mozzarella and cut into pieces. • You can buy the 50 per cent less fat mozzarella, if you prefer.

**Cooking tip** The salad can be chilled for several hours, or even overnight.

For an even faster *panzanella*, cut the bread into thick slices and dunk quickly in cold water, then squeeze gently to remove the excess. Tear into pieces, dropping them into a bowl. Top with the vegetables and capers. Whisk the dressing in a small bowl as step 2 and drizzle over the salad. Put a plate on top and press the salad gently to flavour the bread with some of the juices from the tomatoes. Chill in the fridge for 15 minutes, then gently toss. Scatter with the basil and mini mozzarella.

**...speed it up**

# Chef's Salad

Take fresh salad ingredients, ham and some piquant Gouda cheese, and drizzle with a smooth anchovy-flavoured dressing for an appetizing salad that's great for a fast, healthy meal. Serve with crusty bread.

**20 mins prep time**

**1 Make the dressing** Put the anchovy fillets, garlic, mustard, oil and lemon juice into a food processor or blender. Blend together until the dressing is smooth, then add the cream and blend again for just a few seconds.

**2 Prepare the salad** Put the lettuce, tomatoes, avocado, cucumber, cheese and ham into a large bowl and gently mix together. Alternatively, arrange the ingredients on four individual plates.

**3 Finish the salad** Lightly drizzle the anchovy dressing over the salad, season with black pepper and serve at once.

**Serves 4**

1½ oz (40 g) anchovy fillets in olive oil, drained and roughly chopped

1 garlic clove, roughly chopped

½ tsp (2 mL) Dijon mustard

4 tbsp (60 mL) extra virgin olive oil

1 tbsp (15 mL) lemon juice

2 tbsp (25 mL) thick cream

1 romaine lettuce, torn into bite-sized pieces

4 tomatoes, cut into wedges

1 avocado, diced

¼ cucumber, diced

3½ oz (100 g) Gouda cheese, diced

3½ oz (100 g) roast ham, diced

Each serving provides • 422 cals • 17 g protein • 37 g fat of which 14 g saturates • 5.5 g carbohydrate

**Vegetarian salad**
Instead of the ham add **2 hard-boiled eggs**, cut into wedges. Make a creamy dressing by whisking together **1 tsp (5 mL) Dijon mustard**, a **pinch of superfine sugar**, **1 tbsp (15 mL) white wine vinegar**, **4 tbsp (60 mL) olive oil** and **2 tbsp (25 mL) sour cream**.

## ...another idea

- Make a topping using **garlic croutons** or crumbled pieces of **cooked crispy bacon**. • Or make Parmesan wafers: sprinkle 1¾ oz (50 g) grated Parmesan cheese over baking parchment set on a baking sheet. Bake at 350°F (160°C) for 15 minutes or until the Parmesan is melted, crisp and pale golden. Cool, then break into pieces and use to top the salad.

## ...topping ideas

# Bacon and Potato Salad

Make quick work of a potato salad by using halved tiny new potatoes, then toss them while still warm in a creamy mayonnaise, sour cream and lemon juice dressing. Delicious.

**Serves 4**

2 lb (1 kg) pre-washed baby new potatoes, halved

5 strips bacon, chopped

4 medium eggs, hard-boiled and quartered

¼ cup (50 mL) dill pickles, chopped

3 tbsp (45 mL) fresh flat-leaf parsley, chopped

⅔ cup (150 mL) good-quality mayonnaise

4 tbsp (60 mL) sour cream

1 tbsp (15 mL) lemon juice

1 tsp (5 mL) ground paprika

2 tbsp (25 mL) fresh dill, chopped

**Each serving provides** • 556 cals • 25 g protein • 32 g fat of which 10 g saturates • 43 g carbohydrate

**Swaps** For bacon, use **pancetta** or a **1½-oz (40-g) can marinated anchovies.**

**1** **Cook the potatoes** Fill a large pot halfway with water, add the potatoes and bring to the boil. Reduce heat and simmer 10 to 12 minutes or until just tender. Drain.

**2** **Cook the bacon** fry the bacon in a lightly oiled frying pan over high heat until crisp. Drain on paper towels.

**3** **Assemble the pieces** Place the warm potatoes in a large serving bowl. Add the eggs, cucumbers and parsley, and toss gently. Combine the mayonnaise, sour cream, lemon juice and paprika in a small bowl Add to salad and toss gently

**4** **Finishing touches** Divide into four bowls, sprinkle the bacon and dill on top and serve immediately.

Both the bacon and eggs can be cooked ahead of time and used cold. Only the potatoes must be served warm.

**...get ahead**

# Summer Beef Salad

Griddling lean, tender steak gives it a smoky flavour that enhances a refreshing salad of crisp vegetables in a walnut and balsamic dressing. Enjoy with warm, crusty French bread.

**Serves 4**

½ tsp (2 mL) salt

1 small red onion, halved and thinly sliced

3½ oz (100 g) radishes, sliced

1 thick-cut lean rump steak, about 12 oz (375 g), trimmed of fat

1 tbsp (15 mL) olive oil

¼ tsp (1 mL) dried mixed herbs

2 tbsp (25 mL) walnut oil

1 tbsp (15 mL) balsamic vinegar

4 celery sticks, sliced on the diagonal

4 oz (125 g) bag of arugula or mixed lettuce leaves such as oakleaf, romaine

**Each serving provides** • 207 cals • 20 g protein • 12 g fat of which 2 g saturates • 4 g carbohydrate

1 **Soak the onion and radishes** Stir the salt into a bowl of cold water until dissolved. Add the onion and radish slices and leave to soak while cooking the steak (this will take away some of the heat and sharpness and prevent the radishes from discolouring).

2 **Cook the steak** Heat a ridged griddle or a nonstick frying pan until hot. Pat the steak dry with kitchen paper. Rub the steak on both sides with 2 tsp (10 mL) of the olive oil, then season with the herbs and some ground black pepper. Cook the steak for 2½–3½ minutes on each side, depending on whether you like it medium-rare or medium. Transfer the steak to a board and leave it to rest for a few minutes.

3 **Make the dressing and slice the steak** Whisk the remaining olive oil, the walnut oil and vinegar together. Cut the steak into slices about ¼ in. (5 mm) thick. Pour any juices that have collected into the dressing.

4 **Prepare the salad** Drain the onion and radishes well, put into a large bowl, then add the dressing with the celery and slices of beef. Gently toss everything together. Divide the arugula or salad leaves among four individual plates, then spoon over the beef mixture. Serve immediately.

Swaps • For arugula or mixed leaves, use **chicory** leaves and thinly sliced **fennel**. • For the radishes, use sliced **red apple**.

Instead of the dressing in the basic recipe, make a horseradish dressing for the beef salad: Whisk together **4 tbsp (60 mL) light olive oil**, the **juice of 1 small lemon** and **2 tsp (10 mL) horseradish relish**.

**...or try this**

# Warm **Fava Bean** and **Feta** Salad

**Combine the flavours of feta cheese, fava beans, ripe plum tomatoes and olives, and enjoy this salad served warm with bread.**

Serves 4 Ⓥ

**1 lb (500 g) shelled fresh or frozen fava beans**

**2 tbsp (25 mL) olive oil**

**7½ oz (220 g) small plum tomatoes, cut into wedges**

**2 garlic cloves, crushed**

**7 oz (200 g) feta cheese, cubed**

**2 tbsp (25 mL) chopped fresh parsley**

**12 stoned kalamata olives, or other stoned black olives**

**1 tbsp (15 mL) lemon juice**

Each serving provides • 278 cals • 16 g protein • 19 g fat of which 9 g saturates • 11 g carbohydrate

1 **Cook the beans and tomatoes** Cook the fava beans in boiling water until just tender, then drain well. Meanwhile, heat the olive oil in a large nonstick frying pan, add the tomatoes and garlic, and gently cook for 2-3 minutes or until softened. Remove the pan from the heat.

2 **Combine the salad ingredients** Add the feta cheese to the frying pan, with the beans, parsley, olives, lemon juice and a few grinds of ground black pepper. Stir together, then serve warm.

# 5 great meals with noodles

With a pack of dried quick-cook noodles in the pantry, speedy meals are just a few moments away. Partner the noodles with other ingredients from your pantry, a selection of prepared goodies from the deli or simple stir-fry sauces for the ultimate fast food. All recipes serve 4.

## mascarpone **mushroom** noodles

Dry-fry **1¾ oz (50 g) pine nuts** in a large nonstick frying pan over a medium heat for 2 minutes or until golden. Remove from the pan and set aside. Measure **1 tbsp (15 mL) canola oil** and **1 tbsp (15 mL) vegetable stock** or water into the pan. Add **4 sliced scallions** and **¾ lb (375 g) thickly sliced mushrooms**. Cook gently for 7-8 minutes until the mushrooms are tender and the juices very concentrated. Meanwhile, cook **½ lb (250 g) fine dried Chinese egg noodles** in boiling vegetable stock for 3 minutes or until just tender, then drain well. Stir **1 tsp (5 mL) chopped fresh thyme** and **4 tbsp (60 mL) mascarpone** into the mushrooms. Season. Add the noodles to the frying pan and mix well. Scatter with the toasted pine nuts and serve. Ⓥ

**Each serving provides** • 504 cals • 13 g protein
• 31 g fat of which 11 g saturates • 47 g carbohydrate

**10** mins prep time  **12** mins cook time

Most noodles usually take about 4 minutes to cook, and some need only to be soaked in hot water. To cook noodles, heat plenty of boiling water to a rolling boil. Add the noodles and, when the water returns to the boil, time according to the package instructions. Move the noodles gently once or twice with a fork during cooking to separate them. Drain.

## ...perfect noodles

## chili **tomato** and **egg** noodles

Cook **½ lb (250 g) fine Chinese egg noodles** in a large pot of boiling vegetable stock or water for 3 minutes or until tender. Meanwhile, lightly beat **3 eggs** with **2 tsp (10 mL) 1% milk**, **¼ tsp (1 mL) crushed dried chilies** and seasoning. Heat **2 tsp (10 mL) canola oil** in an 8-in. (20-cm) nonstick frying pan over a medium heat. Pour in half the egg mixture, tipping the pan to spread out the egg in a thin, even layer. Cook for 1 minute or until set and lightly browned underneath. Slide the omelette out of the pan onto a plate. Repeat with the remaining egg mixture, then cut both omelettes into fine strips. Drain the noodles well, return to the pot and cover with a lid to keep warm. Dice **4 large ripe tomatoes**. Add **2 tbsp (25 mL) canola oil** and **2 tsp (10 mL) red wine vinegar** to the frying pan. Add the tomatoes and heat until the mixture bubbles. Add this mixture and half the omelette strips to the noodles and gently toss together. Pile the noodles onto warmed serving plates and top with the remaining omelette strips. Ⓥ

**Each serving provides** • 400 cals • 14 g protein
• 18 g fat of which 4 g saturates • 50 g carbohydrate

**5** mins prep time  **8** mins cook time

# shredded chicken salad with peanut dressing

Drop **3½ oz (100 g) broccoli**, cut into small florets, and **1 orange pepper** and **1 yellow pepper**, cut into strips, into a large pot of boiling water. Add **½ lb (250 g) medium Chinese egg noodles**. Bring back to the boil, then remove from the heat, cover with a lid and leave for 4 minutes. Reserve 5 tbsp (75 mL) of the cooking liquid. Tip the noodles into a colander and drain. Gently cool the noodles and vegetables with cold running water and drain again. Transfer to a serving bowl. Whisk together **4 tbsp (60 mL) crunchy peanut butter** with the reserved cooking liquid, the juice of **1 small lemon**, **2 tbsp (25 mL) soy sauce** and **a pinch of superfine sugar**. Shred **2 cooked chicken breast fillets** and add to the noodles and vegetables with **3½ oz (100 g) bok choy**, shredded, and half the peanut dressing. Gently toss together to mix. Drizzle over the remaining dressing.

**Each serving provides** • 503 cals • 35 g protein
• 18 g fat of which 4 g saturates
• 53 g carbohydrate

**15** mins prep time  **6** mins cook time

# sausage and noodle sauté

Heat **1 tbsp (15 mL) canola oil** in a large nonstick frying pan and add **1 sliced onion** and **½ lb (250 g) mini chipolata or spicy pork sausages**. Fry, stirring frequently, for 10 minutes or until golden brown. Meanwhile, cook **½ lb (250 g) fine dried Chinese egg noodles** in boiling **vegetable stock** or lightly salted water for 3 minutes or until just tender. Add **3½ oz (100 g) frozen peas** for the last minute of cooking (turning the heat up as you add them so that the stock rapidly returns to the boil). Reserve 3 tbsp (45 mL) of the stock, and then tip the noodles and peas into a colander to drain. Cover the colander with the pan lid to keep warm. Add **2 large carrots**, coarsely grated, **1 crushed garlic clove** and the reserved stock to the frying pan and cook for 1-2 minutes or until the vegetables are almost tender and the stock has evaporated. Add the noodles and peas, and cook for a final minute, stirring most of the time until everything is piping hot. Serve with sweet chili sauce or tomato ketchup.

**Each serving provides** • 461 cals • 17.5 g protein
• 19 g fat of which 6 g saturates
• 59 g carbohydrate

**8** mins prep time  **15** mins cook time

# crispy bacon and noodle stir-fry

Dry-fry **6 bacon strips**, scissor-snipped into ¾-in. (2-cm) pieces, in a large nonstick frying pan for 3-4 minutes or until lightly browned and crispy. Remove with a slotted spoon. Add **2 tsp (10 mL) canola oil** to the pan. Heat for a few seconds, then stir in **1 red onion**, cut into very thin wedges. Stir-fry for 2 minutes, then add **2 zucchini**, sliced on the diagonal, and **1 crushed garlic clove**. Cook for a further 4-5 minutes or until tender. Meanwhile, cook **½ lb (250 g) fine dried Chinese egg noodles** in boiling water for 3 minutes or until just tender, then drain well. Sprinkle the zucchini with **2 tsp (10 mL) balsamic vinegar** and cook for a few more seconds. Add the noodles to the frying pan and gently toss together over a low heat to mix. Spoon on to warmed plates and serve sprinkled with the crispy bacon.

**Each serving provides**
• 377 cals • 14 g protein
• 15 g fat of which 4.5 g saturates
• 49 g carbohydrate

**10** mins prep time  **15** mins cook time

# Eggs *en Cocotte* with Ham and Cheese

Bake eggs in ramekin dishes, with a creamy ham layer beneath, for a fast and simple lunch or supper that's light and tasty. It just needs toasted whole-grain bread or baked finger toasts to accompany.

**10 mins prep time**

**15 mins cook time**

### Serves 4

1 tsp (5 mL) unsalted butter, softened

4 oz (125 g) thickly sliced ham, fat removed, diced

5½ tbsp (80 mL) heavy cream

4 eggs

1 oz (30 g) mature cheddar cheese, finely grated

**Each serving provides** • 368 cals • 16 g protein • 34 g fat of which 18 g saturates • 1 g carbohydrate

**To serve** For finger toast, lightly spread **6 slices thick-cut bread** with softened **butter or sunflower margarine**. Trim off the crusts, then cut each slice into three long fingers and put on a baking sheet. Bake at the same time as the eggs until light golden and crisp.

**1 Prepare the ramekins** Preheat the oven to 325°F (160°C). Butter four ramekin dishes.

**2 Add the ham, eggs and cheese** Divide the ham among the ramekins, then spoon 1 tsp (5 mL) of cream into each one. Break an egg into each ramekin. Spoon 1 tbsp (15 mL) cream over each egg, then season. Sprinkle the cheese over the tops.

**3 Bake the eggs** Put the ramekins in a small roasting pan and pour in enough hot water to come halfway up the sides of the dishes. Transfer the pan to the oven and bake for 10-15 minutes, depending on how well you like your eggs cooked. Serve hot.

**Swaps** • For ham, use a mix of steamed **baby spinach leaves** with **1 oz (30 g) mascarpone cheese** and **freshly grated nutmeg**. Top with **Parmesan cheese** instead of cheddar. • Or use **sliced button mushrooms** sautéed in **butter** with **crushed garlic** mixed with a spoonful of **sour cream** • Or use **6 oz (175 g) finely sliced leeks** cooked in **butter** then add a little **heavy cream** and **chopped fresh tarragon**.

### Serves 6

1¼ cups (300 mL) 1% milk

¾ cup (175 mL) sour cream

1 tsp (5 mL) lemon juice

2 eggs

4 scallions, roughly chopped

2 large sprigs of fresh dill

2 cups (500 mL) self-raising flour

4 oz (125 g) smoked salmon trimmings, cut into fine strips

canola or light olive oil

1 jar black lumpfish roe, about 1¾ oz (50 g) (optional)

sprigs of fresh dill or snipped chives, to garnish

**Each serving provides** • 417 cals • 22 g protein • 15 g fat of which 7 g saturates • 53 g carbohydrate

**To serve** For a cucumber and avocado salsa, toss **2 chopped ripe avocados** in a bowl with the juice of **1 small lime**. Add **½ cucumber**, finely chopped, **3 tbsp (45 mL) chopped fresh coriander** and a **chopped fresh red chili pepper or a pinch of mild chili seasoning**, or to taste.

**10 mins prep time**

**15 mins cook time**

### Chickpea and corn pancakes Ⓥ

In a blender, combine **6 oz (175 g) chickpea flour, 1 cup (250 mL) fine cornmeal, 4 tsp (20 mL) baking powder, 1 tsp (5 mL) curry powder** and **½ tsp (2 mL) each salt and white (superfine) sugar**. Add **2 eggs, 2 cups (500 mL) 1% milk** and **¼ cup (50 mL) cooled melted butter**. Blend until smooth. Stir in **⅓ cup (75 mL) corn**, well-drained or thawed if frozen. Cook the pancakes as the basic recipe and serve with bought or homemade cucumber raita.

## ...another idea

# Smoked **Salmon** Pancakes

Smart and delicate, these quick and easy mini pancakes are flavoured with scallions and dill, then topped with sour cream. Serve with a fresh-tasting salsa for the perfect final touch.

**1 Make the batter** Measure the milk in a large jug, then whisk in 2 tbsp (25 mL) of the sour cream and the lemon juice using a fork. Pour half the mixture into a blender. Crack the eggs into the blender and add the scallions. Blend for 1 minute. Add the dill and flour, and blend for a further minute or until the batter is fairly smooth with tiny pieces of scallion and chopped dill. Add the remaining milk mixture and blend again. Stir in 1¾ oz (50 g) smoked salmon trimmings and season with ground black pepper.

**2 Cook the pancakes** Preheat the oven to 300°F (150°C). Heat a heavy nonstick frying pan until it is medium hot, then add a little oil and swirl it around to coat the pan. Spoon in about 2 tbsp (25 mL) of the batter to make a pancake about 3½ in. (9 cm) in diameter. Make two or three more (depending on how many you can fit in the pan), spacing them slightly apart. Cook for 1 minute or until small bubbles appear all over the surface of the pancakes and the tops are dry. Turn the pancakes over and cook the other sides for about 1 minute. Take out of the pan and keep warm in the oven on a baking sheet while you cook the remaining batter – there will be enough to make 18 pancakes.

**3 Serve the pancakes** Put a heaped teaspoon of sour cream in the middle of each pancake, then top with slivers of the remaining smoked salmon and garnish with lumpfish roe, if using, and dill or chives. Arrange on a large, warm platter or individual plates and serve.

**Swaps** • For smoked salmon, use skinned and flaked **smoked mackerel fillets** and add a little **mild horseradish sauce** to the sour cream for topping; garnish with **watercress**. • For scallions, dill and salmon, coarsely grate **1 carrot**, **1 zucchini** and **1⅔ oz (75 g) Gruyère cheese**, and reduce the milk to 1 cup (250 mL). Serve with Greek-style yogurt and a sliced tomato and red onion salad.

# Stir-fried Sesame Jumbo **Shrimp**

For a really special meal that's simplicity itself, this oriental-style platter of jumbo shrimp in a fragrant lemon-grass sauce is hard to beat. Serve with quick-cook noodles and vegetables.

**10** mins prep time  **3** mins cook time

### Serves 4

**40 peeled raw jumbo shrimp, about 12 oz (375 g), thawed if frozen**

**1 tbsp (15 mL) toasted sesame oil**

**1½ tbsp (20 mL) dark soy sauce**

**1 tbsp (15 mL) canola oil**

**1 medium-hot red chili pepper, seeded and finely chopped**

**1 garlic clove, crushed**

**1 lemon-grass stalk, outer leaves removed, the core finely chopped**

**2 tsp (10 mL) ginger paste or grated fresh ginger**

**1 tsp (5 mL) light brown sugar**

**1 tbsp (15 mL) sesame seeds**

**2 tbsp (25 mL) chopped fresh coriander**

**sweet chili dipping sauce, to serve**

**Each serving provides** • 145 cals • 17 g protein • 8 g fat of which 1 g saturates • 2 g carbohydrate

### Quick-cook noodles and vegetables

Heat **1 tbsp (15 mL) canola oil** in a large nonstick pan over a medium heat. Add **3½ oz (100 g) whole baby corn** and **1 sliced red pepper** and cook for 2-3 minutes or until lightly coloured. Crush **1 garlic clove** into the pan and stir for a few more seconds, then pour in **2 cups (500 mL) vegetable stock**. Add **7½ oz (220 g) fine egg noodles**. Cover and cook for 2 minutes, then stir in **3½ oz (100 g) shredded bok choy**. Cook for a further minute or until everything is tender.

### ...to serve

1 **Coat the jumbo shrimp** Pat the shrimp dry on paper towels, then put them in a bowl with the sesame oil and soy sauce, and toss together to coat. Tip them into a sieve placed over another bowl to catch the marinade (there will not be much).

2 **Start cooking the jumbo shrimp** Heat a wok or large nonstick frying pan until very hot, then add the canola oil and swirl to coat the base of the pan. Add the jumbo shrimp and stir-fry for 1½ minutes.

3 **Complete cooking** Add the chili pepper, garlic, lemon grass and ginger to the pan and stir-fry for a further 30-60 seconds or until the shrimp have turned pink and are just cooked through (take care not to overcook or they will be tough). Remove from the heat and stir in the reserved marinade, the sugar, sesame seeds and coriander. Serve with sweet chili dipping sauce.

**Swaps** Instead of all the oils and flavourings, use **2 tbsp (25 mL) canola oil** and cook **2 tbsp (25 mL) Thai red curry paste** in it for 30 seconds, stirring, before adding the shrimp. Stir-fry for 1½ minutes, as step 2, then stir in **2 tbsp (25 mL) coconut milk**. Cook a further 30-60 seconds, until shrimp are cooked.

# Glazed Chicken
## and Green Vegetables

A healthy stir-fry of crisp, fresh vegetables accompanies tender chicken in a Chinese-style sticky glaze for a meal that cooks in moments. Rice or quick-cook noodles make a good accompaniment.

**20** mins prep time  **8** mins cook time

### Serves 4

- **2 tbsp (25 mL) hoisin sauce**
- **2 tbsp (25 mL) sherry or white wine vinegar**
- **2 tbsp (25 mL) dark soy sauce**
- **1 tbsp (15 mL) clear honey**
- **2 tsp (10 mL) toasted sesame oil**
- **10 oz (300 g) skinless chicken breast fillets, cut into thick strips**
- **1½ tbsp (20 mL) canola oil**
- **7 oz (200 g) broccoli, cut into small florets**
- **1 leek, finely sliced**
- **3½ oz (100 g) snow peas**

**Each serving provides** • 222 cals • 23 g protein • 7 g fat of which 1 g saturates • 16 g carbohydrate

**1 Cook the chicken** Preheat the grill to medium-hot and line the grill pan with a piece of lightly oiled foil. Mix together the hoisin sauce, sherry or vinegar, soy sauce, honey and sesame oil. Put the chicken fillets or strips into the grill pan in a single layer and brush two thirds of the hoisin glaze over them. Cook for 3-4 minutes, turning over halfway through the cooking time (the chicken should be just cooked through; cut a piece in half to check).

**2 Stir-fry the vegetables** While the chicken is cooking, heat the canola oil in a wok or large, heavy-based nonstick frying pan. Add the broccoli and stir-fry for 2 minutes. Add the leek and stir-fry for 1 minute, then stir in the snow peas and stir-fry all the vegetables for a further 2 minutes.

**3 Add the glaze** Blend the remaining glaze with 4 tbsp (60 mL) water and add to the wok with the chicken. Cook for a further 2-3 minutes, stirring frequently, until the vegetables are tender and everything is hot.

**Shopping tip** Hoisin sauce is a sweet and thick Chinese sauce made from fermented soya beans and flavoured with garlic, spices and chili. It's readily available in most supermarkets.

### Glazed chicken salad pitas

Cook the chicken as in step 1, basting with the remaining glaze after turning, then leave it to cool for a few minutes. Warm **4 large whole-grain or sesame-seed pita breads** under the grill for about 1 minute on each side, then split the breads in half widthwise and gently open up each half to make pockets. Shred or tear **½ romaine lettuce or 1 heart of romaine lettuce** into small pieces, and thinly slice **2 plum tomatoes**. Half-fill the pita bread pockets with the lettuce and tomatoes, then drizzle 1 tbsp (15 mL) **plain yogurt** into each. Add the glazed chicken strips and serve.

Instead of using individual vegetables, buy a bag of ready-prepared stir-fry vegetables. These are usually sliced so that all the vegetables take the same time to cook, and can be added in one go. Rinse before using.

**...speed it up**

**...another idea**

# eggs and cheese

# Country Frittata

Creamy butternut squash works especially well with the distinctive flavour of leeks in this simple and speedy egg dish. Serve with a spinach salad and boiled new potatoes.

**10** mins prep time

**20** mins cook time

Serves 4 (V)

2 tbsp (25 mL) olive oil

3 leeks, sliced into rings

½ butternut squash, about 1 lb (500 g), peeled and cut into small cubes

2 tbsp (25 mL) pine nuts

8 eggs

½ cup (125 mL) 10% cream

3 tbsp (45 mL) grated Parmesan, or Italian-style hard cheese

2 fresh sage leaves or a small bunch of fresh chives, about ¾ oz (20 g), chopped

**Each serving provides** • 424 cals • 22 g protein • 33 g fat of which 10 g saturates • 12 g carbohydrate

**1 Cook the leeks and squash** Heat the olive oil in a heavy cast-iron or nonstick frying pan (10-12 in./25-30 cm diameter) that can be used safely under the broiler (wrap a wooden handle with foil). Add the leeks and squash to the pan and stir well. Cook over a medium heat for 10 minutes or until just soft, stirring frequently. Stir in the pine nuts.

**2 Prepare the eggs** While the vegetables are cooking, break the eggs into a large bowl. Add the cream, Parmesan and herbs. Season and mix thoroughly with a fork. Stir in the cooked vegetables, then tip the whole mixture back into the pan. Turn down the heat and cook gently for 4-5 minutes or until almost set. Meanwhile, preheat the broiler to high.

**3 Brown the top** Slide the pan under the broiler and cook the frittata for 2-3 minutes or until puffed and golden brown. Eat hot or warm, cut into wedges.

**Swaps** Try different combinations of vegetables instead of the butternut squash and leek filling. Here are some ideas.
• **7 oz (200 g) sliced mushrooms** and **3½ oz (100 g) thawed frozen peas or cooked green beans**, halved. Cook for 5 minutes at step 1. • Or try **1¾ oz (50 g) thickly sliced soft sun-dried tomatoes** and **3 thinly sliced peppers**. Cook the vegetables for 5 minutes at step 1, then add **2 crushed garlic cloves** to the egg and Parmesan mixture.

**To serve** Make a crunchy salad of **ready-prepared baby spinach leaves** and **croutons**. Toss with a tangy dressing (see page 31 for a basic dressing) flavoured with a little **whole-grain mustard** and **honey**.

# Provençale **Piperade**

**Pep up this attractive traditional dish of softly scrambled eggs and sautéed peppers with some chili, then serve with garlic bread and a crisp, green salad for a fast and easy meal.**

**10 mins prep time**

**20 mins cook time**

**Serves 4** Ⓥ
2 tbsp (25 mL) olive oil
2 red peppers, sliced
2 yellow peppers, sliced
1 onion, thinly sliced
2 garlic cloves, crushed
¼ tsp (1 mL) crushed chili flakes, or to taste
1¾ oz (50 g) soft sun-dried tomatoes, roughly chopped
8 eggs
small bunch of fresh basil leaves, about ¾ oz (20 g), torn

**Each serving provides** • 307 cals • 18.5 g protein • 19.5 g fat of which 4.5 g saturates • 16.5 g carbohydrate

**1 Cook the vegetables** Heat the olive oil in a large nonstick frying pan or sauté pan. Add the sliced peppers, onion, garlic and chili flakes, and cook over a medium heat for 10 minutes, stirring frequently, until softened but not browned.

**2 Cook the tomatoes** Add the tomatoes to the vegetables in the pan. Season, then cook over a medium heat for 7-8 minutes, stirring frequently, until the mixture is very soft and thick, and most of the liquid has evaporated.

**3 Cook the eggs** Break the eggs into a bowl and add the torn basil leaves. Beat lightly with a fork. Pour the eggs into the pan and stir over a low heat for about 2 minutes or until the mixture has thickened and looks like soft scrambled eggs. Serve immediately.

**To serve** For quick, homemade garlic bread cut a slightly stale **ciabatta loaf or small baguette** into thick diagonal slices. Mix **1 crushed garlic clove** into **3 tbsp (45 mL) olive oil**, then lightly brush on both sides of each slice. Cook on a heated ridged griddle or under a hot broiler for 1 minute on each side or until lightly browned.

# Salmon and Artichoke
## Open Omelette

For a quick trick with eggs, top with smoked salmon, aromatic dill and sour cream to transform a simple omelette into a substantial and luxurious dish. Serve with crusty whole-grain bread and a crisp salad.

**15** mins prep time

**5** mins cook time

**Serves 4**

**8 eggs**

**¼ lb (125 g) smoked salmon slices**

**1 tbsp (15 mL) chopped fresh dill**

**3 tbsp (45 mL) sour cream**

**1½ tbsp (20 mL) butter**

**14 oz (398 mL) can baby artichokes, rinsed, drained and sliced into quarters**

Each serving provides • 321 cal • 25 g protein • 23 g fat of which 9 g saturates • 4.5 g carbohydrate

Swap For artichokes, use **1 tbsp (15 mL) capers**, rinsed and drained.

**1 Mix the eggs** Break the eggs into a large bowl and add 3 tbsp (45 mL) water and seasoning. Beat thoroughly with a fork until combined but not foamy.

**2 Prepare the topping** Using scissors, snip the slices of smoked salmon into ribbons roughly 4 x 1¼ in. (10 x 3 cm). Stir the dill into the sour cream. Set aside until needed. Preheat the grill to high.

**3 Cook the omelette** Heat the butter in a large, nonstick heavy-based frying pan (about 10 in./25 cm) that can go under the grill safely (wrap a wooden handle with foil). As soon as the butter starts to look foamy pour in the beaten egg. Cook over a high heat for about 30 seconds or until the egg starts to set underneath. Using the back of a fork gently stir the mixture so that the liquid egg runs under the set mixture. Leave to cook for 30 seconds without stirring so that the omelette starts to brown underneath.

**4 Add the topping** When the omelette looks almost set but is still quite moist on top, quickly top with the smoked salmon strips and scatter the artichoke quarters over. Remove the pan from the heat and slide under the grill to cook for 1 minute or until lightly browned on top.

**5 Add the sour cream** Remove the pan from the grill. Spoon dollops of sour cream on to the omelette, which will melt to make a light sauce. Serve immediately, cut into wedges.

### Mix 'n' match omelette
Instead of the basic toppings you can use leftovers from the fridge, such as cooked **peas**, **ham** and **mushrooms**. Add to the plain omelette at step 4 and cook under the grill for 3 minutes or until heated through. Top with the sour cream or **ready-made croutons** to give a crunchy topping.

### Vegetarian omelette ⓥ
Instead of the basic toppings, put **1 tbsp (15 mL) oil** in a pan and cook **2 thinly sliced small zucchini** and **1 thinly sliced small red onion** for 3-4 minutes to soften. Add to the plain omelette at step 4 and top with **¼ lb (125 g) goat cheese**, cut into slices or crumbled into large chunks. Continue as step 4. Omit the sour cream.

## ...topping swaps

**Picnic omelette with feta and peppers** Ⓥ
Omelettes are excellent for picnics and packed lunches. Combine **8 eggs** with **4 tbsp (60 mL) 10% cream** and seasoning. Heat **2 tbsp (25 mL) olive oil** in a 10-in. (25-cm) ovenproof cast-iron frying pan or a small roasting pan (about 9 x 10 in./20 x 25 cm), then pour in the egg. Top with a **10-oz (290-g) jar roasted red peppers**, drained, and a **7-oz (200-g) jar feta in oil and herbs**, drained, or **3½ oz (100 g) good-quality feta cheese**, diced. Bake at 400°F (200°C), 10 minutes or until just set (the mixture will continue cooking after it comes out of the oven). Leave to cool, then cut into wedges or squares. Eat within one day.

**Tomato, noodle and spinach omelette** Ⓥ
If you have any **leftover noodles or pasta** (with or without sauce), use 7½ oz (225 g) and chop up any large strands. Add to the eggs with **4 oz (125 g) cooked spinach** (either leftover or bagged and steamed in the microwave), **2 tbsp (25 mL) chopped fresh parsley** and a **pinch of freshly grated nutmeg**. Cook the omelette as for the basic recipe, then add **4 oz (125 g) halved cherry tomatoes** before sliding under the grill at step 4.

**...more ideas**

# 5 super-quick ways with eggs

The ultimate super-food, eggs are easily stored in the fridge, ready to be combined with fresh or pantry ingredients for any number of meals in just a few minutes. All recipes serve 4.

## smoky **haddock** scramble

Cook **½ lb (250 g) smoked haddock** in a deep frying pan with just enough **1% milk** to cover for 8 minutes or until it flakes when lifted with a knife tip (or cook in a dish in the microwave). Drain and reserve the milk. Leave to cool a little, then flake the fish, discarding the skin. Break **8 eggs** into a medium-sized bowl and whisk briefly, then whisk in 6¾ tbsp (100 mL) of the reserved milk, **1 tbsp (15 mL) snipped fresh chives** and plenty of freshly ground black pepper. Melt **2 tsp (10 mL) butter** in a medium-sized nonstick frying pan over a low heat. Add the egg mixture and cook gently, stirring constantly with a wooden spoon until the eggs just start to set. Stir in the flaked fish and serve with plenty of hot toast.

**Each serving provides** • 256 cals • 28 g protein • 16 g fat of which 5 g saturates • 1 g carbohydrate

**Swaps** For haddock, use **fresh salmon fillet**. Or use thickly sliced **chorizo** cooked briefly on a heated ridged griddle or nonstick frying pan, then set on top of the scrambled eggs.

**10** mins prep time

**15** mins cook time

# soufflé cheese omelette

Separate **8 eggs** and put the yolks in a large bowl. Beat thoroughly with plenty of ground black pepper and **¼ lb (125 g) finely grated well-flavoured mature cheese such as Gruyère or cheddar**. In another bowl whisk the egg whites until stiff, then fold them into the yolk mixture as gently as possible. Heat **1½ tbsp (20 mL) butter** in a large (10-in./25-cm), fairly deep nonstick frying pan until foaming, then carefully pour in the egg mixture. Cook over a low heat without stirring for about 5 minutes or until the edges start to turn golden and puff up. Meanwhile, preheat the grill to high. Slide the pan under the grill (cover a wooden handle with foil) and cook for 3-4 minutes or until set. Cut into four wedges and serve with crusty bread and a salad. It is also good served with a plate of thinly sliced Parma ham or cooked ham or cold chicken legs and a salad.

**Each serving provides**
• 296 cals • 20 g protein
• 25 g fat of which 12 g saturates • 0 g carbohydrate

# pasta with poached eggs

Cook **1 lb (500 g) fresh egg tagliatelle** in salted boiling water following the directions on the pack. Drain, reserving about 6¾ tbsp (100 mL) of the cooking water, and return the pasta to the warm cooking pot. Add **2 tbsp (25 mL) olive oil**, **4 tbsp (60 mL) grated Parmesan cheese** and seasoning. Stir in half the reserved cooking water, toss gently and keep warm. While the pasta is cooking, poach **4 eggs** for 2 minutes or until the whites are firm but the yolks are still runny (see step 4, Eggs Benedict, page 100). Toss the pasta again, adding a little extra reserved cooking liquid if it seems a little dry, then divide among four pasta plates or bowls. Put the eggs on top of the pasta. Add **1 tsp (5 mL) salmon caviar or chopped fresh herbs** to the top of each egg, if you like, and serve immediately with steamed green beans.

**Each serving provides** • 521 cals • 25 g protein • 18 g fat of which 4.5 g saturates • 70 g carbohydrate

# egg foo yong

Cook **1⅓ cups (325 mL) long-grain rice** in boiling water for 12-15 minutes or until just tender. Drain in a colander, then rinse with cold water and leave to drain thoroughly. Heat **2 tbsp (25 mL) olive oil** in a large nonstick frying pan over a medium heat. Beat **8 eggs** with **1 tbsp (15 mL) soy sauce** and pour into the pan. Cook, stirring gently, until the eggs begin to set, then stir in the drained rice, **¼ lb (125 g) cherry tomatoes**, halved, and **4 scallions**, finely sliced. Cook, stirring constantly, until the rice is piping hot and the eggs have set. Serve sprinkled with sesame seeds.

**Each serving provides** • 415 cals • 16 g protein • 16 g fat of which 3.5 g saturates • 56 g carbohydrate

**Swaps** For tomatoes, use quickly cooked **frozen peas** or **asparagus tips**, or add some **cooked shrimp, shredded ham** or **sautéed mushrooms**.

# egg, avocado and tomato salad

Boil **6 eggs** for 10 minutes. Drain, then put them into a bowl of cold water to cool. Combine a **¼-lb (125-g) bag of colourful mixed salad leaves** with **½ lb (250 g) halved cherry tomatoes**, **½ lb (250 g) halved yellow teardrop tomatoes** and **2 avocados**, peeled and diced. Peel and roughly chop the eggs, and add to the salad. Mix a **small bunch of basil leaves**, about ¾ oz (20 g), torn or shredded, with **3 tbsp (45 mL) olive oil**, **2 tsp (10 mL) balsamic vinegar** and seasoning. Pour this dressing over the salad and toss gently. Serve immediately with warm ciabatta.

**Each serving provides** • 346 cals • 14 g protein • 30 g fat of which 6.5 g saturates • 6 g carbohydrate

# Eggs Benedict

Poached eggs taste special jazzed up with ham and asparagus and topped with a quick version of hollandaise sauce. Accompany with steamed spinach or green beans.

**15** mins prep time

**8** mins cook time

**Serves 4**

**4½ oz (125 g) asparagus tips**

**6¾ tbsp (100 mL) unsalted butter**

**5 eggs**

**1 tbsp (15 mL) lemon juice**

**2 tbsp (25 mL) sour cream**

**4 whole-wheat English muffins, split in half**

**8 thin slices cooked ham or Parma ham, about 7 oz (200 g) total**

**2 tsp (10 mL) vinegar**

**Each serving provides** • 539 cals • 28 g protein • 34 g fat of which 18 g saturates • 32 g carbohydrate

---

Cook the asparagus tips in the microwave, in a suitable covered dish with 2 tbsp (25 mL) water, for 2 minutes on High.

## ...speed it up

**1 Cook the asparagus** Preheat the broiler to high. Drop the asparagus tips into a small pot of boiling water and cook for 2 minutes or until just tender. Alternatively, steam for 2 minutes. Drain, then cover and keep warm. Fill a heavy-based frying pan to a depth of 1 in. (2.5 cm) with boiling water and bring back to the boil, then reduce the heat to a simmer.

**2 Prepare the sauce** Melt the butter in a small pan until hot. Break 1 egg into a food processor or blender. Add the lemon juice and seasoning. Process until just combined. While the motor is running, pour the hot butter through the hole in the blender's lid in a thin, steady stream to make a thick sauce. Briefly work in the sour cream. Cover the sauce to keep it warm until needed.

**3 Prepare the muffins** Toast the muffins under the grill. Put a split muffin on each serving plate and top each half with a slice of ham. Arrange the asparagus on one half of each muffin. Keep warm.

**4 Poach the eggs** Break one of the remaining eggs into a teacup. Add the vinegar to the frying pan of boiling water. Carefully pour the egg towards the side of the pan. Repeat with the other eggs, so that they are evenly spaced. With two spoons quickly gather the whites up around each yolk. Cover the pan with a lid or foil and cook for 4-5 minutes or until the white is set but the yolk is still soft.

**5 Complete the dish** Lift the eggs out of the water with a slotted spoon and set on the ham-topped muffin halves. Spoon the warm sauce over the asparagus and eggs, and serve immediately.

**Swaps** • For ham, use **7 oz (200 g) thinly sliced smoked salmon or cold cooked salmon, white crabmeat or cooked, peeled jumbo shrimp**. • For muffins, use **4 potatoes**. Prick in several places with a sharp knife, then microwave on high for 8 minutes. Turn over and microwave for a further 1-2 minutes or until tender. Leave to rest for 2 minutes. Halve and make a small indentation in the cooked potato flesh to hold the poached eggs.

Poach the eggs ahead of time and transfer them to a bowl of cold water. They can be kept in the fridge for up to 4 hours. When ready to serve transfer the eggs to a bowl of boiling water for 1 minute to reheat. Alternatively, hard-boil the eggs, shell them and keep in a bowl of cool water. When ready to serve cut the eggs in half and arrange on top of the ham.

## ...get ahead

# Tunisian Ratatouille with Eggs

Warm North African spices add a tangy flavour to eggs nestled in a bed of colourful Mediterranean vegetables. Crusty bread is all you need to complete this delicious and easy meal.

**Serves 4** (V)

2 tbsp (25 mL) olive oil
2 onions, thinly sliced
3 green peppers, sliced
3 zucchini, thinly sliced
3 garlic cloves, crushed
1 tsp (5 mL) mild paprika
1 tsp (5 mL) ground cumin
good pinch of cayenne, or to taste
14 oz (398 mL) can chopped
   tomatoes
8 eggs

**Each serving provides** • 303 cals
• 20 g protein • 20 g fat of which
4.5 g saturates • 14 g carbohydrate

**Swaps** For peppers and tomatoes, use
10 oz (300 g) prepared **spinach or
curly kale** and **2 leeks**, thinly sliced.

Instead of adding the eggs, this
ratatouille can be served with **grilled
sausages, chops, lentils or beans,
such as cannellini.**

## ...or try this

- For a real taste of North Africa,
  replace the paprika, cumin and
  cayenne with **2 tsp (10 mL) ras-el-
  hanout spice mix** (a Moroccan mix
  flavoured with rose petals) or
  replace the mild paprika with
  **smoked hot paprika.**
- Before adding the eggs at step 3,
  stir in **4 cooked and sliced spicy
  sausages** (such as merguez).

## ...spice it up

**1 Cook the vegetables** Heat the oil in a very large, deep frying pan or sauté pan that can be used under the grill (cover a wooden handle with foil). Add the onions and cook gently for 5 minutes, then add the peppers, zucchini and garlic, and stir well. Cover and cook over a medium heat for 5 minutes, stirring frequently, until just tender and beginning to colour.

**2 Add the spices and tomatoes** Stir in the paprika and cumin with cayenne and seasoning to taste. Stir in the tomatoes. Cover and cook gently for 5 minutes. Meanwhile, preheat the grill to high.

**3 Cook the eggs** Make eight small hollows in the mixture and crack an egg into each. Cook gently over a low heat for 2 minutes. Slide the pan under the grill and cook for 2-3 minutes or until the eggs are just set. Serve immediately.

**Addition** When you add the tomatoes, stir in **8 oz (225 mL) canned lima beans**, drained and rinsed, **or cooked new potatoes.**

**Cooking tip** If more convenient, make the ratatouille in a flame-proof and ovenproof dish and do the final cooking with the eggs in the oven at 375°F (190°C), for about 10 minutes.

# Egg and Lentil Curry

Effortless to prepare using a great pantry standby – ready-cooked Puy lentils – this hearty medium-hot curry is a speedy way to feed a hungry family. Delicious with warmed nan and a grated carrot salad.

**Serves 4** Ⓥ

6 eggs

2 tbsp (25 mL) olive oil

1 onion, finely chopped

4 garlic cloves, crushed

2-in. (5-cm) piece fresh root ginger, peeled and grated

2 beefsteak or other large tomatoes, roughly chopped

1 tbsp (15 mL) garam masala

¼ tsp (1 mL) crushed chili flakes

2 x 14-oz (398-mL) cans Puy lentils, drained

4 tbsp (60 mL) vegetable stock or water

**30** mins prep/cook time

**Each serving provides**
- 592 cals • 43 g protein
- 18.5 g fat of which 4 g saturates
- 68 g carbohydrate

**Swap** For tomatoes, use ½ lb (250 g) ready-prepared baby leaf spinach or sliced mushrooms.

**1 Hard-boil the eggs** Add the eggs to a pot of boiling water and cook for 10 minutes. Drain the eggs, put them into a bowl of cold water to cool, and set aside.

**2 Cook the sauce** While the eggs are boiling, heat the oil in a heavy frying pan and add the onion. Cover and cook over a low heat for 4 minutes or until softened but not browned. Stir in the garlic and ginger, and cook for 1 minute, then stir in the tomatoes and the spices. Cook gently, covered, for a further 5 minutes.

**3 Add the lentils** Stir in the drained lentils and the stock or water, and cook gently for 5 minutes more. While the lentils are cooking, peel and halve the eggs.

**4 Serve the dish** Season the lentils. Spoon into a serving bowl and arrange the eggs on top.

**Addition** Chop a **large bunch of fresh coriander** and stir into the lentils just before serving, if you like.

## Egg and vegetable curry Ⓥ

Hard-boil the eggs, and prepare the vegetable mixture as for the basic recipe, but at step 3 replace the lentils with the florets from **½ cauliflower, 1 diced eggplant** and **3½ oz (100 g) prepared green beans, halved, or okra,** plus **6¾ tbsp (100 mL) vegetable stock or water**, or enough to moisten the mixture and prevent it from sticking. Cover the pan and cook gently, stirring occasionally, for 15 minutes or until the vegetables are just tender. Spoon into a serving dish, then dollop with **4 tbsp (60 mL) Greek-style yogurt** before adding the eggs at step 4. (A pack of frozen mixed vegetables can be used for this curry, if you like.)

**...another idea**

---

**Serves 4** Ⓥ

2 tsp (10 mL) soft butter

1 lb (500 g) young spinach

1 slice white bread, crusts removed

⅔ cup (150 mL) sour cream

5 eggs, separated

½ cup (125 mL) grated Parmesan, or Italian-style hard cheese

freshly grated nutmeg, to taste

**Each serving provides** • 294 cals
• 19 g protein • 21 g fat of which 10 g saturates • 9 g carbohydrate

**15** mins prep time  **15** mins cook time

**Bolognese soufflés**

Spoon 1-2 tbsp (15-25 mL) warmed leftover **Family Shepherd's Pie filling or Bolognese Sauce** (pages 230 and 120) into the base of each dish. Top with the soufflé mix used for the basic recipe at step 4, and bake.

**...another idea**

Supermarket bags of ready-washed and prepared young and tender spinach are one of the most useful time-savers. There's no waste and the spinach can be cooked in the bag. You will need 2 x 8-oz (250 g) bags for this recipe. Cook the spinach according to the pack instructions: pierce the bags and steam for 1 minute or cook in the microwave (usually for about 3 minutes).

**...speed it up**

# Spinach and Parmesan Soufflés

Sour cream and bread crumbs make a creamy base for Parmesan
cheese and spinach in this stress-free version of a traditional soufflé.
Serve with new potatoes and steamed baby vegetables.

**1 Cook the spinach** Preheat the oven to 425°F (220°C).
Lightly butter the inside of four 1-cup (250-mL) ovenproof
dishes. Tip the washed spinach into a dry pot with only the
moisture left on the leaves and stir over a low heat for about
2 minutes or until wilted. Leave to drain while making the
bread crumbs.

**2 Make the soufflé base** Tear the bread into small
pieces and process in a food processor or blender to make
fine crumbs. Squeeze as much liquid as possible out of
the drained spinach, then add to the crumbs with half the
sour cream and process to make a coarse purée. Add the
remaining sour cream and process for a few more seconds
until just combined.

**3 Finish the base** Add the egg yolks to the food processor
or blender with 3 tbsp (45 mL) of the grated Parmesan
cheese. Season and add plenty of nutmeg, then process again
to make a smooth purée.

**4 Lighten the mixture** Whisk the egg whites in a large
bowl until stiff. Tip the spinach mixture on to the egg whites
and carefully fold together using a large metal spoon. Sprinkle
half the remaining Parmesan inside the prepared dishes and
set them on a baking sheet. Spoon the soufflé mixture into the
dishes. Sprinkle with the remaining Parmesan, then bake for
15 minutes or until puffed and golden brown. Serve at once.

*Additions* • Finely chop ¼ **lb (125 g) cooked ham or crispy
cooked bacon or a few drained canned anchovies** and add
to the base mixture before folding into the egg whites at step 4.
• Put a little **cooked flaked smoked fish** – smoked haddock,
trout or herring – in the base of each dish before spooning in
the soufflé mix at step 4. • Put **diced smoked tofu** into the
base of each dish, then top with the soufflé mix at step 4.

# Chunky Vegetable Fricassee

Fresh-tasting chunks of vegetables in a cheese custard, topped with nuts and crushed bread sticks, make a simple but filling vegetarian dish. Accompany with tagliatelle or a warmed baguette.

**10** mins prep time  **18** mins cook time

**Serves 4** Ⓥ

1½-lb (750-g) bag prepared fresh or frozen mixed vegetables

¼ lb (125 g) mature cheddar cheese, grated

1 cup (125 mL) sour cream

2 eggs, beaten

4 bread sticks, crushed

2 tbsp (25 mL) chopped hazelnuts

**Each serving provides** • 412 cals • 21 g protein • 26 g fat of which 13.5 g saturates • 23 g carbohydrate

**Swaps** For mixed vegetables, use small cooked **new potatoes** plus your favourite vegetables, such as **baby leeks**, **zucchini** and **carrots**, as well as **green beans** or fava beans.

**Additions** Serve with **8 pieces of cooked back (Canadian) bacon or bacon strips**, for non-vegetarians, if you like.

**1 Cook the vegetables** Preheat the oven to 425°F (220°C). Add the vegetables to a pot of boiling water, bring back to the boil and cook for 3 minutes or until just tender (or use a steamer if you prefer). Drain.

**2 Make the cheese sauce** Reserve 2 tbsp (25 mL) of the cheese for the topping and stir the remainder into the sour cream. Mix in the eggs. Season to taste with plenty of ground black pepper. Mix in the cooked vegetables, then transfer to a warm, greased, shallow ovenproof dish.

**3 Make the topping** Mix the bread sticks with the reserved grated cheese and the chopped nuts, then scatter over the vegetables.

**4 Bake and serve** Bake on the top shelf of the oven for 12-15 minutes or until golden and slightly puffed.

**Cooking tips** • The cheese sauce for Cauliflower and Broccoli with Gorgonzola (see page 107) can be made in quantity and frozen, and is excellent for this recipe. You will need half a batch (1 cup/250 mL) instead of the sour cream and cheese. At step 2, mix the eggs into the pre-made cheese sauce. Use 2 tbsp (25 mL) grated cheese for the topping. • If you have time, prepare a selection of your own favourite vegetables instead of using the bags of mixed vegetables. • If you have a microwave, "baked" potatoes would go well with the fricassee (see page 270).

• For a speedy all-in-one sauce, mix **2 tbsp (25 mL) cornstarch** with **2 tbsp (25 mL) 1% milk**, then stir in **1 cup (250 mL) hot milk** (add a bit more if it's too thick). Return the mixture to the pot and bring to the boil, stirring constantly, then simmer gently for 2 minutes. Remove from the heat and stir in **1½ tbsp (20 mL) butter**, **¼ lb (125 g) grated cheese** and seasoning to taste. • Keep a **2-cup (500-mL) jar pre-made béchamel sauce** in the pantry for times when you need a speedy sauce. You will need half the jar for this recipe and add **¼ lb (125 g) grated cheese**.

## ...more quick cheese sauce ideas

# Quickie **Quiche**

With pre-rolled shortcrust pastry you can whip up a tasty, homemade quiche in no time, then leave it to bake. A colourful salad and boiled new potatoes go with it perfectly.

**20** mins prep time

**30** mins cook time

**Serves 4**

¾ lb (375 g) **pre-rolled shortcrust pastry**

3½ oz (100 g) **ham, sliced medium-thick and cut into small pieces**

4 **scallions, sliced into rounds**

2 **eggs**

⅔ cup (150 mL) **1% milk**

4 tbsp (60 mL) **whipping cream (or use extra milk)**

3½ oz (100 g) **extra-mature cheddar cheese, grated**

**Each serving provides** • 435 cals • 15 g protein • 29 g fat of which 11.5 g saturates • 31 g carbohydrate

**To serve** Halved **baby tomatoes** and **prepared watercress** make a colourful and healthy combination for a salad to serve with the quiche. **Pre-washed baby new potatoes** make a quick accompaniment.

### Zucchini, leek and goat cheese quiche ⓥ

Cut **1 large zucchini** into very small dice. Trim and thinly slice **1 leek**. Heat **1½ tbsp (20 mL) butter** in a medium pan and gently cook the zucchini and leek for 5 minutes or until barely tender. Remove from the pan and leave to cool a little. Crumble or slice **¼ lb (125 g) goat cheese**. Use this filling to replace the filling in the basic recipe. Arrange the vegetables in the base of the pastry case. Scatter with the goat cheese, then pour over the egg and milk mixture as in step 3, and bake.

## ...another idea

**1** **Line the pan with pastry** If time allows, leave the pastry, still wrapped, at room temperature for 20 minutes (this makes it easier to unroll without cracking). Preheat the oven to 400°F (200°C), and put a baking sheet inside to heat. Lift the roll of pastry over an 8-in. (20-cm) flan pan and gently unroll it. Carefully press the pastry onto the base and sides of the pan. Neatly trim the overhanging pastry with a sharp knife. Use a piece of baking parchment to line the pastry base roughly and cover it with baking beans or scrunched up foil. Put on the baking sheet and bake for 10 minutes. Remove the paper and beans or foil and bake for a further 5 minutes.

**2** **Prepare the filling** While the pastry is baking, mix the ham with the onions. Break the eggs into a bowl with the milk and cream, or extra milk, and seasoning. Whisk lightly.

**3** **Fill the pastry case** Sprinkle half the cheese over the base of the pastry case, then top with the onion and ham. Scatter the remaining cheese on top. Return the flan to the baking sheet and pour the egg mixture over the filling. Bake for 30 minutes or until golden and just firm to the touch.

# Cauliflower and Broccoli
## with Gorgonzola

Add strongly flavoured Gorgonzola to perk up cauliflower and broccoli florets, then serve with noodles or mixed wild rice for a sophisticated take on cauliflower cheese.

**Serves 4** Ⓥ

⅔ lb (300 g) cauliflower, divided into florets

½ lb (250 g) broccoli, divided into florets

3 tbsp (45 mL) unsalted butter

1 small onion, finely chopped

2½ tbsp (35 mL) plain flour

1¼ cups (300 mL) 1% milk

5 oz (150 g) Gorgonzola piccante cheese, roughly chopped or crumbled

2 tomatoes, sliced

**Each serving provides**
- 352 cals • 17 g protein
- 23.5 g fat of which 14 g saturates • 19 g carbohydrate

**30 mins prep/cook time**

**1** **Cook the vegetables** Drop the cauliflower and broccoli into a pot of boiling water and cook for 3-4 minutes or until just tender. Drain, reserving the cooking water for the sauce, and set aside.

**2** **Make the sauce** Melt the butter in the same pot, stir in the onion and cook gently for 5 minutes without browning. Stir in the flour with a wooden spoon, then gradually add the milk and ⅔ cup (150 mL) of the reserved cooking water. Bring to the boil, stirring constantly, then simmer for 2 minutes to make a smooth, light sauce. Remove from the heat.

**3** **Add the cheese and vegetables** Preheat the grill to high. Stir two thirds of the cheese into the sauce. Season, then gently fold in the cooked cauliflower and broccoli. Spoon into a warm, shallow ovenproof dish.

**4** **Top and grill** Arrange the tomato slices on top, then scatter with the remaining cheese. Grill for 4-5 minutes or until browned and bubbling.

**Swap** For Gorgonzola, use diced **Gruyère cheese** and increase the cooking water added at step 2 to ¾ cup (175 mL) or more.

### Traditional cauliflower cheese Ⓥ
Use **1 lb (500 g) cauliflower** (or 1 very large cauliflower) and omit the broccoli. Increase the cooking water added at step 2 to ¾ cup (175 mL) or more. Instead of Gorgonzola use **extra-mature cheddar cheese**. Add **1 tsp (5 mL) Dijon mustard** with the seasoning at step 3.

## ...another idea

Make the cheese sauce with milk (2 cups/500 mL), then leave to cool and freeze. If you like, make the sauce in bulk by doubling or tripling the quantities and then dividing into approximately 1- or 2-cup (250- or 500-mL) batches. Pour each batch into a freezerproof container and freeze for up to four weeks. The sauce can also be frozen in ice-cube trays (one 1-cup/ 250-mL batch will fill a tray). The cubes thaw quickly and are useful if you want to use just a small amount of sauce for one portion or part of a batch.

## ...get ahead

# 5 super-quick ways with cheese

Don't get stuck in a rut when it comes to using cheese in cooking – a different variety can add a new slant to your weeknight meals. Cheese dishes can be the fastest around and it's amazing what you can make using ingredients you already have on hand. All recipes serve 4.

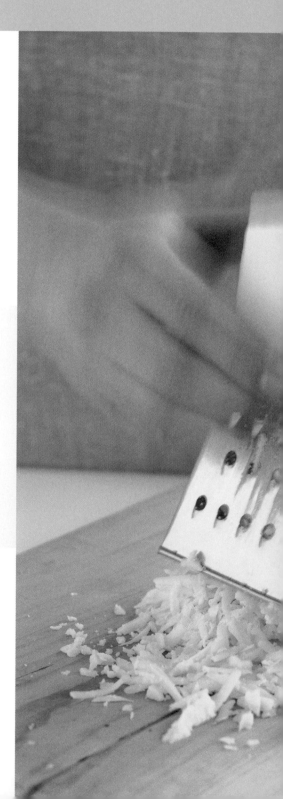

## fontina on toasted ciabatta with ham

Drain a **12-oz (375-mL) jar roasted red peppers** and cut into slices. Mix with a **bag of salad leaves** and add **2 tbsp (25 mL) olive oil, 2 tbsp (25 mL) lemon juice, 1 crushed garlic clove** and a **small bunch of flat-leaf parsley**, roughly chopped. Season to taste and toss gently. Slice **½ lb (250 g) fontina or dolcelatte cheese** and arrange or spread on thick slices of toasted **ciabatta**. Serve with **7 oz (200 g) cured ham** and the salad in its tangy dressing.

**Each serving provides** • 495 cals • 20 g protein • 31 g fat of which 14 g saturates • 35 g carbohydrate

**10** mins prep time   **2** mins cook time

## feta and chickpea salad

Drain **½ lb (250 g) feta cheese** and cut into ¾-in. (2-cm) cubes. Put into a bowl and scatter with **½ tsp (2 mL) dried oregano or herbes de Provence**, plenty of ground black pepper, a **pinch of crushed chili flakes, 1 tbsp (15 mL) lemon juice** and **3 tbsp (45 mL) olive oil**. Mix gently and let marinate while you prepare the rest of the salad. Put a drained **14-oz (398-mL) can chickpeas** into a salad bowl. Add **3½ oz (100 g) sun-dried tomatoes**, roughly chopped, and a **2⅔-oz (75-mL) bag of watercress**. Add the marinated feta mixture and toss. Ⓥ

**Each serving provides** • 428 cals • 15.5 g protein • 36 g fat of which 12 g saturates • 12 g carbohydrate

**10** mins prep time

• Blue-veined cheeses usually have a strong flavour; try crumbly French **roquefort**, English **Blue Stilton**, Italian **gorgonzola** and creamy **dolcelatte**. • Soft cheeses with a white floury crust are French **Brie** and **Camembert**; their flavours can range from mild to piquant. • **Parmesan** is a strong, hard Italian cheese that is used in small amounts to flavour a dish. • Delicately flavoured Italian **mozzarella** cheese melts well and is often used for toppings, but is also good uncooked in salads. • The distinctive flavour of **smoked cheeses** makes them useful in bakes or cold dishes.

## ...a few cheeses to try

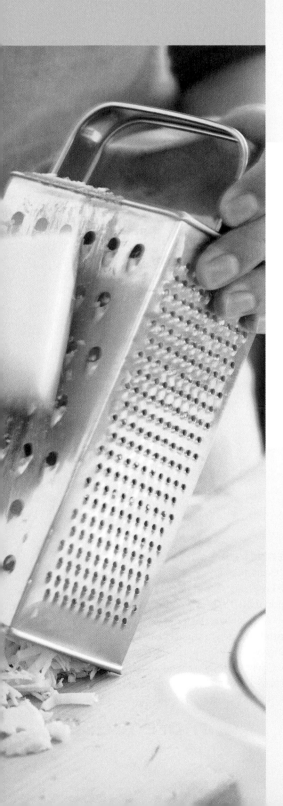

# pasta with **parmesan** and **zucchini**

Cook **14 oz (400 g) dried egg pasta** (or use 1 lb/500 g quick-cooking fresh egg pasta) according to the package instructions, then drain. Meanwhile, heat **2 tbsp (25 mL) olive oil** in a heavy frying pan, add **1 small, finely chopped red onion** and gently cook for 3 minutes. Stir in **4 zucchini**, coarsely grated (easily done in a food processor), with **2 crushed garlic cloves**. Cook over a medium-high heat for 2 minutes, stirring frequently. Add the pasta plus ⅔ **cup (150 mL) 10% cream**, if you like. Toss gently and season. Turn into a serving dish and scatter with ½ **cup (125 mL) grated Parmesan or Italian-style hard cheese**. Serve with a salad of sliced tomatoes in a simple dressing (see page 31). Ⓥ

**Each serving provides** • 541 cals • 20 g protein • 18 g fat of which 8 g saturates • 78 g carbohydrate

**10** mins prep time    **10** mins cook time

# old-fashioned **welsh rarebit**

Grate ½ **lb (250 g) well-flavoured mature Cheddar cheese** (you can also use a good Double Gloucester or Shropshire) and put into a heavy-based medium-sized pot (preferably nonstick) with **1 tbsp (15 mL) butter**, **1 tsp (5 mL) mustard** (English, whole-grain or Dijon), plenty of ground black pepper and **4 tbsp (60 mL) ale or 1% milk**. Set over a low heat and melt gently, stirring, until smooth and thick. Spoon onto **4 thick slices of toast** and grill until browned and bubbling. Serve with grilled mushrooms and a leaf salad for a light lunch or snack. Ⓥ

**Each serving provides** • 384 cals • 21 g protein • 25 g fat of which 15 g saturates • 20 g carbohydrate

**5** mins prep time    **6** mins cook time

# speedy **macaroni**

Cook **1 lb (500 g) fresh egg macaroni or ridged or quick-cook macaroni** in boiling water for 4 minutes or according to the instructions on the package. Add ½ **lb (250 g) frozen peas** to the pot for the final 3 minutes of the cooking time. Drain, reserving about 5 tbsp (75 mL) of the pasta cooking water. Tip the pasta into a warmed serving bowl. Combine the cooking liquid with the **grated zest of 1 lemon** and the squeezed **juice of ½ lemon**, plus seasoning. Pour over the pasta and peas. Crumble or dice ¼ **lb (125 g) creamy goat cheese** and add to the bowl. Toss gently to combine the ingredients, then serve with a tomato and leaf salad. Ⓥ

**Each serving provides** • 489 cals • 22 g protein • 10 g fat of which 6 g saturates • 82 g carbohydrate

**10** mins prep time    **5** mins cook time

# Mid-week Moussaka

Here's an easy take on a Greek moussaka, using diced eggplant instead of fried eggplant slices. Cover with cooked potatoes and a traditional egg and cheese topping and leave in the oven. Serve with a salad.

**30** mins prep time

**20** mins in oven

**Serves 4**

2 lb (1 kg) baby new potatoes, halved

2 tbsp (25 mL) olive oil

2 onions, finely chopped

1 lb (500 g) lean ground lamb

2 eggplants, roughly chopped

¼ tsp (1 mL) ground cinnamon

14 oz (398 mL) can chopped tomatoes

½ cup (125 mL) well-flavoured lamb or vegetable stock, made with a stock cube

½ tsp (2 mL) dried mixed herbs

1 tbsp (15 mL) cornstarch

1 cup (250 mL) milk

1 egg, beaten

½ tsp (2 mL) mustard powder or dried mustard (optional)

⅔ cup (150 mL) cheddar cheese, grated

**Each serving provides** • 507 cals
• 33.5 g protein • 17.5 g fat of which
2 g saturates • 57.5 g carbohydrate

**1 Fry the onions and lamb** Cook the potatoes in a pot of slightly salted boiling water until tender. Drain. Meanwhile, heat the oil in a heavy nonstick frying pan or sauté pan and stir in the onions and lamb. Cook over a medium heat, stirring frequently, for 5 minutes or until the onions are softened and the lamb is lightly browned.

**2 Add the eggplant** Stir in the eggplant, then cook over a fairly high heat for 3 minutes.

**3 Season and simmer** Add the cinnamon and season, then add the chopped tomatoes, stock and herbs. Stir well, then cover and simmer for 15 minutes or until cooked through and tender. Meanwhile, preheat the oven to 400°F (200°C).

**4 Make the topping** While the meat mixture is cooking, put the cornflour in a small pot and add 2 tbsp (25 mL) milk. Stir until blended using a wooden spoon, then stir in the remaining milk. Bring to the boil over a medium heat, stirring until thickened. Cook, stirring, for 3 minutes. Remove from the heat and stir to cool a little. Beat in the egg and season with mustard, if using, and salt and pepper.

**5 Assemble the dish** Spoon the meat and eggplant mixture into a warm, shallow ovenproof dish and spread evenly. Lay the potato halves over the top, flat side up. Pour over the topping and sprinkle with grated cheese. Bake near the top of the oven for 20 minutes or until golden.

### Spicy South African bobotie

Omit the potatoes. Soak a **thick slice of white bread** in **6¾ oz (200 mL) 1% milk**, then squeeze it out well (reserve the milk). At step 2 omit the eggplant, and tear the bread into the browned meat mixture. Stir in **1 tbsp (15 mL) medium curry powder**, or to taste, **3 tbsp (45 mL) mango or apricot chutney** and **1 tbsp (15 mL) raisins**. Season and add a little lemon juice if you like, then turn the mixture into a greased baking dish. Omit the egg and cheese topping. Mix the reserved milk with **1 beaten egg** and spoon over the meat. Bake at 350°F (180°C), for 30 minutes or until golden.

### Lamb with fennel and coriander

Omit the potatoes. Cook the lamb with the onions and tomatoes as for the basic recipe, but omit the eggplant. Replace the cinnamon with **1 tsp (5 mL) ground coriander**. Spoon half the lamb sauce into a baking dish. Slice **2 large (or 3 medium) fennel bulbs** lengthwise, then quarter the slices. Cook in boiling water for 5 minutes, drain and arrange on top of the lamb. Cover with the remaining lamb mixture. Omit the egg and cheese topping. Cover the dish with a lid or foil and bake at 350°F (180°C), for 30 minutes.

## ...more ideas

# Potato and Camembert Bake

To speed up cooking this bistro dish – based on the *tartiflette*, from Savoy in France –
use tiny new potatoes, then serve with gherkins, radishes and a dressed green salad.

**Serves 4**

1½ lb (750 g) pre-washed baby
new potatoes

4 lean slices back (Canadian) bacon
or bacon slices

4 scallions, cut into rounds

½ round of Camembert, Reblochon
de Savoie or raclette cheese, ½ lb
(250 g)

½ cup (125 mL) 10% cream

**Each serving provides** • 404 cals
• 23 g protein • 22 g fat of which
13 g saturates • 31 g carbohydrate

**30** mins
prep/cook
time

**1 Cook the potatoes** Preheat the oven to 440°F (230°C). Cook the potatoes in a pot of boiling water for 12-15 minutes or until tender. Drain thoroughly and tip into a greased, shallow ovenproof dish.

**2 Fry the bacon** While the potatoes are cooking, snip the bacon into thin strips using kitchen scissors. Put into a cold, nonstick frying pan and cook over a high heat for 1 minute or until crispy. Remove from the pan with a slotted spoon. Mix the scallions with the cooked bacon.

**3 Prepare the cheese** Cut the semicircle of cheese in half horizontally to make two semicircles (if using raclette, remove the hard rind first). Score the rind in a criss-cross pattern to help the cheese to melt.

**4 Layer the ingredients** Scatter the bacon and onions over the potatoes. Season with plenty of ground black pepper, then pour over the cream. Set the cheese on top, rind side uppermost, then bake for 7-10 minutes or until melting and bubbling. Serve piping hot.

**Swaps** • Omit the bacon and serve with **sliced salami, cured or smoked ham or cold sausages**. • For the bacon, use **¼ lb (125 g) button or exotic mushrooms**, sliced and fried in **1 tbsp (15 mL) oil**. • For the potatoes, use **1½ lb (750 g) cooked beets** (without vinegar), peeled and thickly sliced. Arrange in a greased baking dish, scatter with diced **cooked ham or bacon**, add the cream and top with **½ lb (250 g) blue Brie**, cut into slices. Bake as the basic recipe.

# Cheddar and Broccoli Strata

This savoury casserole is made up of layers of bread and vegetables and a cheesy egg custard topping. Served with a quick homemade tomato sauce (see page 122), it is a tasty and nutritious dish, especially when served with a nice, leafy salad.

**50** mins prep time

**60** mins cook time

1 tbsp (15 mL) butter

4 shallots, finely chopped

½ lb (250 g) broccoli florets

6 oz (175 g) green beans, halved

2 cups (500 mL) frozen corn

9 slices bread, halved and crusts removed

4 eggs

2 ⅓ cups (575 mL) 2% milk

2 tbsp (25 mL) fresh chives, snipped

2 tbsp (25 mL) fresh parsley, chopped

¾ cup (175 mL) cheddar cheese, grated

salt and freshly ground black pepper

**Each serving provides** • 439 cals • 23 g protein • 17 g fat of which 7 g saturates • 53 g carbohydrate

**1 Cook the vegetables** Melt the butter in a frying pan. Add the shallots and cook gently for about 7 minutes, or until softened. Meanwhile, cook the broccoli and green beans in a pot of boiling water for 4 minutes, or until just tender. drain well, then stir the shallots in with the corn in a bowl and season to taste.

**2 build the layers** Arrange six of the halved bread slices side-by-side in a lightly greased, deep overproof dish. Top with half the broccoli mixture, repeat with another layer of bread and another layer of the broccoli mixture, then top with a final layer of bread.

**3 make the topping.** Whisk together the eggs, milk, chives and parsley, then season with salt and pepper. Pour the mixture over the layered bread and vegetables, then sprinkle the cheese on top. Set aside for 30 minutes, to allow the bread to soak up some of the liquid. Preheat the oven to 350°F (180°C).

**4 Cook and serve** Bake the casserole for 1 hour or until set, puffy and golden brown. Spoon the strata onto serving plates and top with a homemade tomato sauce (see p 122).

**Swaps** • For the green beans , use **baby corn** • For the frozen corn, use **frozen peas** • For the white bread, use **whole-grain bread**.

# Cheesy Ham and Potato Gratin

Use a thickly sliced ham to give this straightforward and comforting bake of waxy potatoes and Gruyère cheese the best flavour. Layer the prepared ingredients, then sit back and relax while it cooks. Serve with a green salad.

**20** mins prep time  **30** mins cook time

Serves 4

1⅔ lb (800 g) waxy potatoes, peeled and thinly sliced

⅔ lb (300 g) sour cream

⅔ cup (150 mL) 1% milk

2 garlic cloves, thinly sliced

6 oz (175 g) thickly sliced lean ham, cut into small dice

3½ oz (100 g) Gruyère or Emmenthal cheese, grated

**Each serving provides** • 414 cals • 26 g protein • 18 g fat of which 10.5 g saturates • 40 g carbohydrate

**1 Cook the potatoes** Preheat the oven to 375°F (190°C). Cook the sliced potatoes in a pot of boiling water for 2-3 minutes or until just tender, then drain thoroughly. Mix the sour cream with the milk.

**2 Layer the potatoes** Layer the potatoes over the base of a greased, shallow ovenproof dish. Scatter with a little of the garlic and diced ham, then season lightly. Arrange another layer of potatoes on top, followed by more ham, garlic and seasoning. Continue layering in this way, finishing with a layer of potatoes.

**3 Top and bake** Pour over the milk mixture. Scatter the cheese evenly over the top. Cook in the oven for 30 minutes or until golden and bubbling.

**Swaps** • For diced ham, use **crispy cooked bacon or cooked and flaked smoked haddock**. • For Gruyère cheese, use a well-flavoured **goat cheese or mature cheddar cheese**. • For a vegetarian dish replace the ham with **grated or diced cheese or cooked mushrooms**. Try using one type of diced cheese inside and a different one grated on top, such as diced Stilton and grated cheddar.

**Cooking tip** You can use any odd-shaped pieces of leftover cooked ham or bacon in this dish.

# pasta and noodles

# Spaghetti with **Artichokes** and **Fava Beans**

For fast food Mediterranean-style, use a tasty combination of spring vegetables and sun-dried tomatoes tossed in pesto. It's a simple pasta dish that can be made at any time of the year.

**10** mins prep time

**10** mins cook time

Serves 4 Ⓥ

14 oz (400 g) spaghetti

½ lb (250 g) frozen fava, or small broad beans

14-oz (398-mL) can artichoke hearts, drained

½ cup (125 mL) sun-dried tomatoes, roughly chopped

4 tbsp (60 mL) good-quality pesto

grated Parmesan, or Italian-style hard cheese, to serve

**Each serving provides** • 594 cals • 22 g protein • 21 g fat of which 4 g saturates • 83 g carbohydrate

**1 Cook the spaghetti and beans** Cook the spaghetti in a pot of salted boiling water for 10 minutes, or according to the pack instructions, until al dente. Add the fava beans to the pot for the final 5 minutes of cooking.

**2 Add the vegetables to the pasta** While the pasta is cooking, cut each artichoke heart into six pieces. Drain the pasta and beans, reserving about 6¾ tbsp (100 mL) of the cooking liquid. Turn the pasta and beans into a warmed serving bowl. Add the artichoke hearts and tomatoes.

**3 Serve** Combine the pesto with the reserved water and spoon over the pasta. Season with plenty of black pepper, then toss gently to combine all the ingredients. Serve immediately with a bowl of grated Parmesan cheese.

**Swap** If you have time to prepare them, you can use **fresh fava beans** for this recipe. You will need 2 lb (1 kg) fresh beans in their pods.

**Addition** Add **5 oz (150 g) chopped lean ham or Parma ham**, or a **6-oz (170-g) can tuna**, drained and flaked, at the end of step 2.

Serves 4 Ⓥ

11 oz (350 g) penne

2 lb (1 kg) butternut squash, peeled and cut into ¾-in. (2-cm) cubes

1 tbsp (15 mL) olive oil

¼ tsp (1 mL) crushed chili flakes, or to taste

¼ tsp (1 mL) cumin seeds, or to taste

5 oz (150 g) soft goat cheese, crumbled

½ cup (250 mL) grated Parmesan or Italian-style hard cheese

**Each serving provides** • 526 cals • 25 g protein • 18 g fat of which 9.5 g saturates • 70 g carbohydrate

**15** mins prep time

**15** mins cook time

## Tagliatelle with pancetta and pumpkin

Peel and cube **2 lb (1 kg) pumpkin or butternut squash**. Put into a roasting pan with **1 large red onion**, cut into rings, and a **5-oz (150-g) pack pre-cut pancetta strips or cubes, or thick bacon**. Drizzle over **2 tbsp (25 mL) olive oil** and roast at 440°F (230°C) for 17 minutes, stirring occasionally. Add **2 tbsp (25 mL) pine nuts** and **2 chopped garlic cloves**, and roast for a further 3 minutes. Meanwhile, cook **11 oz (350 g) tagliatelle verde** according to the pack instructions, and drain. Toss with the roasted vegetable mix and season to taste. Serve with a bowl of grated Parmesan cheese.

**Swap** For pancetta or bacon, use **3 spicy or Toulouse sausages** cut into ¾-in. (2-cm) chunks.

## ...another idea

# Chili Penne with Butternut Squash

**Spice up butternut squash with cumin and chili, then toss in crumbled goat cheese to create a creamy, flavourful sauce for pasta that takes moments to prepare. Serve with a mixed-leaf salad.**

**1 Cook the pasta** Cook the penne and squash in a large pot of salted boiling water for 12 minutes or until the squash is soft and the pasta is al dente. Reserve 6¾ tbsp (100 mL) of the cooking water, then drain thoroughly.

**2 Fry the flavourings** Pour the olive oil into the warm pasta pot set over a low heat, and stir in the crushed chili flakes and the cumin seeds. Cook for 1 minute, then remove the pot from the heat.

**3 Assemble and serve** Return the pasta and squash to the pot and add the reserved cooking liquid. Combine gently. Add the goat cheese, season to taste and toss thoroughly. Turn into a warm serving bowl and top with the Parmesan cheese. Serve immediately.

**Shopping tip** Butternut squash will keep uncut for several weeks as long as the skin is not damaged. Store in a cool, dark place and check its condition regularly.

# Spicy **Napolitana** Spaghetti

Make a colourful and delicious pasta sauce using pantry treasures – canned chopped tomatoes, a jar of red peppers and a jar of stuffed green olives. Just add spaghetti and a leaf salad to serve.

**5**
mins prep
time

**25**
mins cook
time

**Serves 4** Ⓥ

**2 tbsp (25 mL) olive oil**

**1 large onion, finely chopped**

**a good pinch of superfine sugar**

**2 x 14-oz (398-mL) cans tomatoes**

**¼ tsp (1 mL) crushed chili flakes, or to taste**

**14 oz (400 g) spaghetti**

**16 oz (450-g) jar roasted red or mixed peppers, drained and cut into slices**

**¾ cup (175 mL) stuffed green olives, rinsed, drained and halved**

**grated Parmesan, or Italian-style hard cheese, to serve**

**Each serving provides** • 517 cals • 16 g protein • 14 g fat of which 2 g saturates • 88 g carbohydrate

**Swaps** For the peppers, use **7 oz (200 g) frozen fava beans**, boiled for 4 minutes or according to the package instructions, **or a 9-oz (280-g) can or jar artichoke hearts**, drained and cut into quarters.

**1 Fry the onion** Heat the oil in a medium-sized pot, add the onion and sugar, then cook gently for 5 minutes or until just softened. Meanwhile, tip the tomatoes into a food processor or blender and process to make a purée.

**2 Add the tomatoes and chili** Add the puréed tomatoes and crushed chili flakes to the onion in the pot and season lightly with salt and plenty of pepper (the olives will add more salt to the dish). Bring to the boil, then cook, stirring occasionally, over a medium heat so that the sauce boils gently for 20 minutes.

**3 Cook the spaghetti** While the sauce is cooking, cook the spaghetti in a pot of salted boiling water for 10 minutes, or according to the pack instructions, until al dente.

**4 Serve** Drain the pasta and turn into a warmed serving bowl. Spoon over the sauce, add the peppers and olives, and toss gently to combine. Serve immediately with grated Parmesan cheese.

**Shopping tips** • You could use olives stuffed with pimento, almonds or anchovies, or use plain stoned olives. • This makes a good meal for vegetarians when served with a vegetarian Italian-style hard cheese.

---

**If you're really short of time, ready-made pasta sauces can be a useful standby. Here's how to make them more exciting:**

• Put the contents of a **3-cup (750-mL) jar pasta sauce** in a pot and stir in **¼ lb (125 g) sliced peeled chorizo (or garlic sausage) your choice of spicy sausage**, plus a **14-oz (398-mL) can drained cannellini beans or 7½ oz (220 g) cooked whole green beans** (fresh or frozen). Heat according to the jar instructions.

• Cut **7 oz (200 g) thinly sliced cured ham or Parma ham**, into strips. Pot-fry then stir in a **3-cup (750-mL) jar spicy pasta sauce**, a **9-oz (280-g) jar or can artichoke hearts**, drained and quartered, and a **9-oz (280-g) jar roasted red peppers**, drained and sliced. Heat according to the jar instructions.

• Cut **½ lb (250 g) pork or lamb** into strips (either raw or cooked leftovers), then stir-fry in **1 tbsp (15 mL) oil** for 7 minutes for raw meat or 4 minutes for cooked. Add **1 crushed garlic clove** and **1 zucchini** cut into thick sticks, then stir in a **3-cup (750-mL) jar pasta sauce** and heat according to the jar instructions until piping hot.

• Put the contents of a **3-cup (750-mL) jar pasta sauce** into a pot and add **2 x 7½-oz (220-g) packs frozen cooked seafood mix**. Heat according to the jar instructions.

• Stir-fry a **7½-oz (220-g) pack sliced mushrooms and zucchini sticks** (or diced eggplant) and **1 chopped garlic clove**, then stir in a **3-cup (750-mL) jar pasta sauce** and heat through according to the jar instructions.

## ...magic meals with ready-made sauces

# Quick Spaghetti **Bolognese**

This fast-track version of everyone's favourite pasta sauce is bursting with flavour and it's ready to eat in very little time. Serve with a crunchy, colourful salad, if you like.

**10** mins prep time  **18** mins cook time

**Serves 4**

2 tbsp (25 mL) olive oil

1 lb (500 g) lean ground beef

1 large onion, finely chopped

1 carrot, peeled and finely chopped

2 celery sticks, finely chopped

4 garlic cloves, crushed

14 oz (398 mL) can chopped tomatoes

14 oz (398 mL) can tomato sauce

good pinch of dried oregano, or to taste

14 oz (400 g) spaghetti

grated Parmesan cheese, to serve

**Each serving provides** • 685 cals • 43 g protein • 20 g fat of which 6 g saturates • 89 g carbohydrate

---

Cool unused sauce quickly then chill and store in the fridge for up to two days or pour into a suitable freezerproof container and freeze for up to one month. To use, thaw, reheat and simmer for 10 minutes.

## ...keep it

**1 Fry the meat** Heat a wok or large, deep frying pan with the olive oil. Crumble the beef into the pan and stir-fry over a high heat for 2 minutes to break up the meat and brown it.

**2 Add the vegetables** Add the onion, carrot, celery and garlic. Stir over a medium heat for 1 minute, then add the chopped tomatoes and the tomato sauce. Stir well, then add the oregano and seasoning. Cook over a medium heat so that the sauce boils gently, stirring occasionally, for 15 minutes or until thick.

**3 Cook the spaghetti** While the sauce is cooking, cook the spaghetti in a pot of salted boiling water for 10 minutes, or according to the pack instructions, until al dente. Drain and turn into a warmed serving bowl.

**4 Serve** Taste the sauce and adjust the seasoning, then pour over the hot pasta. Toss gently and serve immediately with grated Parmesan cheese.

**Swap** For a richer sauce, replace 3½ oz (100 g) of the ground beef with **3½ oz (100 g) chicken or turkey livers**, roughly chopped. Stir in a **small carton of 10% cream** after the sauce has been cooking for 5 minutes.

### Macaroni Bolognese

Make up a double batch of Bolognese sauce and save one portion to make a simple *pasticcio* (a macaroni and mince bake). Cook **14 oz (400 g) macaroni or 1 lb (500 g) fresh egg macaroni**, according to the pack instructions. Drain and mix with the meat sauce, **2 tbsp (25 mL) grated Parmesan cheese** and **3½ oz (100 g) ricotta cheese**. Tip into a greased baking dish, then top with **½ cup (125 mL) diced mozzarella** and **2 tbsp (25 mL) grated Parmesan cheese**. Bake at 400°F (200°C), for 20 minutes or until bubbling and browned.

### Pork and chorizo pasta sauce

Replace the minced beef with **lean minced pork or veal**. Thickly slice **½ cup (125 mL) chorizo** and cut the slices into quarters. While the meat sauce is cooking, fry the chorizo in a small pan without any additional fat for 2 minutes and serve on top of the dressed pasta.

## ...more ideas

# Egg and Bacon Spaghetti

A few simple ingredients are all you need to create this swift version of the Italian classic, spaghetti carbonara. Creamy eggs softly scramble in the hot pasta with pancetta and fresh scallions for extra flavour.

**Serves 4**

**14 oz (400 g) spaghetti**

**3½ oz (100 g) frozen peas**

**3½ oz (100 g) dry-cured pancetta or bacon strips, cut into ½-in. (1-cm) pieces**

**6 scallions, sliced**

**½ cup (125 mL) grated Parmesan cheese, plus extra to garnish**

**4 eggs**

**6¾ tbsp (100 mL) ricotta cheese**

**Each serving provides** • 628 cals • 32 g protein • 23 g fat of which 9.5 g saturates • 78 g carbohydrate

---

• A pack of **pre-cut pancetta** saves time, or add strips of **cooked crispy bacon** (you will need about 6) at step 4. • **Quick-cook spaghetti** takes just 5 minutes.

## ...speed it up

---

**1 Cook the spaghetti and peas** Cook the pasta in a pot of salted boiling water for 10 minutes, or according to the package instructions, until al dente. Add the peas to the pot for the final 3 minutes of cooking, returning the water to the boil.

**2 Fry the pancetta** While the pasta is cooking, put the pancetta or bacon pieces into a frying pan and fry without fat over a medium heat, stirring occasionally, for 4-5 minutes or until lightly browned and crispy. If necessary, drain off the excess fat from the pan, leaving about 1 tsp (5 mL). Add the scallions to the pan and cook gently for 1 minute or until just soft.

**3 Mix the cheese and eggs** Put the Parmesan cheese into a bowl with the eggs and ricotta cheese. Season with ground black pepper and beat together with a fork.

**4 Add the egg mixture** Drain the spaghetti and peas, and return them to the hot, empty pot with the pancetta or bacon and scallions. Off the heat, add the egg mixture and toss thoroughly so that the eggs thicken in the residual heat to make a creamy sauce to coat the pasta. Turn into a serving bowl and serve sprinkled with more Parmesan cheese.

**Swaps** • Instead of using eggs, ricotta cheese and Parmesan cheese, make a smooth, creamy sauce by heating **¼ lb (125 g) soft goat cheese with garlic and herbs** with **6¾ tbsp (100 mL) 3.25% milk** in a small pot, stirring constantly. Toss through the cooked spaghetti with the pancetta or bacon, scallions and peas, and serve immediately. • Instead of frying pancetta or bacon and scallions, use **¼ lb (125 g) smoked salmon**, cut into thin strips (or use trimmings), and add **2 tbsp (25 mL) snipped fresh chives**.

**10** mins prep time

**12** mins cook time

# 5 quickest-ever sauces for pasta and noodles

Pasta and noodle dishes are all-time favourites, and a filling and nourishing meal can be put together in the time it takes for the pasta to cook – ideal for meals in a hurry. Try these recipes as they are, or embellish them with your favourite ingredients or leftovers. All recipes serve 4.

Keep these pasta basics in your pantry and fridge for quick and tasty meals in moments:
- dried pasta
- extra virgin olive oil
- garlic
- a hunk of Parmesan cheese, grana padano, or vegetarian Italian-style hard cheese

## ...get ahead

## fresh **tomato** and **chili** sauce

Cook ¾ **lb (375 g) spaghetti** in a pot of salted boiling water for 10 minutes, or according to the pack instructions, until al dente. Drain, then toss with **8 large ripe tomatoes**, roughly chopped, **2 crushed garlic cloves**, **2 tbsp (25 mL) chopped flat-leaf parsley** and **2 tbsp (25 mL) olive oil**. Season to taste with ground black pepper and **crushed chili flakes**, then serve with **grated Parmesan cheese, grana padano or Italian-style hard cheese**. Ⓥ

**Each serving provides** • 402 cals
- 13 g protein • 8 g fat of which
2 g saturates • 74 g carbohydrate

**10** mins prep time   **10** mins cook time

## pesto pasta

Cook ¾ **lb (375 g) tagliatelle** in a pot of salted boiling water for 8 minutes, or according to the pack instructions, until al dente. Drain, reserving 6 ¾ tbsp (100 mL) of the cooking liquid. Mix the reserved cooking water with **4 tbsp (60 mL) good-quality pesto** and toss with the pasta. Top with **7 oz (200 g) flaked hot-smoked salmon**, season with ground black pepper and serve with **grated Parmesan cheese or grana padano**.

**Each serving provides** • 541 cals
- 28 g protein • 21 g fat of which
5 g saturates • 65 g carbohydrate

**5** mins prep time   **10** mins cook time

# anchovy and cherry tomato sauce

Cook ¾ lb (375 g) farfalle in a pot of salted boiling water for 10 minutes, or according to the pack instructions, until al dente. Drain. Meanwhile, drain **1 can anchovy fillets** and tip into a nonstick frying pan. Gently sauté for 3-4 minutes with **2 chopped garlic cloves** and **½ lb (250 g) halved cherry tomatoes**, stirring and crushing the anchovies occasionally. Season with plenty of ground black pepper or **crushed chili flakes** and **2 tbsp (25 mL) chopped fresh parsley**, then toss with the hot pasta.

**Each serving provides** • 336 cals
• 14 g protein • 3 g fat of which
0.5 g saturates • 67 g carbohydrate

# pancetta and balsamic vinegar sauce

Cook ¾ **lb (375 g) linguine** in a pot of salted boiling water for 6 minutes, or according to the pack instructions, until al dente. Drain, reserving 6¾ tbsp (100 mL) of the cooking liquid. Meanwhile, heat **1 tbsp (15 mL) olive oil** in a large frying pan and cook **¼ lb (125 g) pancetta strips, or chopped bacon**, until crispy. Add **1 tbsp (15 mL) balsamic vinegar** and stir vigorously to deglaze the pan. Toss the pasta with the bacon mixture, the reserved cooking liquid and **¼ lb (125 g) arugula**. Season with plenty of ground black pepper.

**Each serving provides** • 435 cals
• 17 g protein • 13 g fat of which
4 g saturates • 65 g carbohydrate

# five-spice noodles

Heat a wok or frying pan with **2 tbsp (25 mL) canola oil**. Add **2 chopped garlic cloves, 1 large onion**, finely sliced and **2 tsp (10 mL) grated fresh ginger**. Stir-fry for 2 minutes. Stir in **1 lb (500 g) stir-fry vegetables** and stir-fry for 5 minutes. Season the vegetables with **2 tbsp (25 mL) soy sauce** and **½ tsp (2 mL) five-spice powder**, then stir in ⅔ **lb (300 g) straight-to-wok Chinese noodles** and cook for 2 minutes or according to the pack instructions. When thoroughly heated through, top with **¼ lb (125 g) roasted peanuts or cashew nuts**. Ⓥ

**Each serving provides** • 423 cals
• 14 g protein • 23 g fat of which
3.5 g saturates • 42 g carbohydrate

# Farfalle with **Broccoli**
## and Anchovies

Broccoli florets, anchovy fillets and parsley are perked up with just enough chili to give this fast-and-fresh pasta mixture some fire. It's delicious served with a refreshing salad of sliced tomatoes and finely sliced leek or onion.

**10** mins prep time  **15** mins cook time

**14 oz (400 g) farfalle or garganelli**

**⅔ lb (300 g) broccoli florets**

**1¾ oz (50 g) can anchovy fillets, drained**

**2 tbsp (25 mL) 1% milk**

**2 tbsp (25 mL) olive oil**

**4 large garlic cloves, crushed**

**small bunch of fresh flat-leaf parsley, leaves chopped**

**¼ tsp (1 mL) crushed chili flakes**

**1½ tbsp (20 mL) unsalted butter**

**grated Parmesan cheese, to serve (optional)**

Each serving provides • 417 cals • 18 g protein • 14 g fat of which 4 g saturates • 58 g carbohydrate

**1** **Cook the pasta and broccoli** Cook the pasta in a pot of salted boiling water for 12 minutes, or according to the pack instructions, until al dente. Remove any thick stalks from the broccoli florets, then slice in half or quarters to make small florets. Add to the pasta for the final minute of cooking. Reserve about 6¾ tbsp (100 mL) of cooking water, then drain the pasta and broccoli thoroughly.

**2** **Remove the salt from the anchovies** While the pasta is cooking, soak the anchovies in the milk for 5 minutes to remove some of the salt. Drain, then chop.

**3** **Cook the flavourings** Heat the olive oil in the warm pasta pan and add the chopped anchovies, garlic, parsley and crushed chili flakes. Stir over a medium heat for 2 minutes.

**4** **Assemble and serve** Add the pasta and broccoli to the pan with the reserved cooking water. Toss gently and season with plenty of ground black pepper. Add the butter and toss until melted. Turn into warmed serving bowls and serve immediately with Parmesan cheese, if you like.

Additions • Add **1 tbsp (15 mL) capers or ½ cup (125 mL) chopped soft sun-dried tomatoes** to the pan with the chopped anchovies and flavourings at step 3. • Add **½ lb (250 g) cooked, peeled jumbo shrimp** to the pan with the anchovies and flavourings at step 3. Cook for 3 minutes if fresh, 4 minutes if frozen.

# Mariners' Lasagna

**Use ricotta cheese instead of a traditional white sauce to make a quick lasagna. Layer the tuna, tomato and spinach filling, then relax while it cooks in the oven. Serve with a salad.**

**20** mins prep time  **30** mins cook time

**8 oz (250-g) package fresh egg lasagna**

**2 x 6-oz (170-g) cans tuna, drained**

**14 oz (398 mL) can tomato sauce**

**9 stoned black olives, roughly chopped**

**7½ oz (220 g) baby spinach**

**¼ lb (250 g) ricotta cheese**

**4 tbsp (60 mL) 1% milk**

**2 tbsp (25 mL) grated Parmesan cheese**

Each serving provides • 526 cals • 45 g protein • 21 g fat of which 7 g saturates • 43 g carbohydrate

**1** **Prepare the pasta** Preheat the oven to 400°F (200°C) and grease a lasagna dish or shallow ovenproof dish. Prepare the pasta according to the package instructions. Or put the sheets into a heatproof bowl, pour over enough boiling water to cover and leave for 5 minutes to soften. Drain thoroughly.

**2** **Make the tuna sauce** While the lasagna is softening, flake the tuna, then put it into a sauté pan that has a lid and add the tomato sauce. Heat gently. Stir in the olives and spinach, then season to taste with plenty of black pepper. Cover and simmer gently for 5 minutes to wilt the spinach.

**3** **Assemble the lasagna** Spoon a third of the tuna sauce into the lasagna dish. Cover with a layer of the lasagna sheets, slightly overlapping them if necessary. Spread half the remaining tuna mixture on top and cover with lasagna sheets, then repeat.

**4** **Make the topping** Mix the ricotta cheese with the milk and season to taste. Spoon over the top of the lasagna, then sprinkle with the Parmesan cheese. Bake in the hot oven for 30 minutes or until piping hot. Serve immediately.

Swaps • For fresh spinach, use **14 oz (400 g) Swiss chard, thinly sliced, or arugula**. • For tuna, use **canned salmon, mackerel fillets or sardines**.

# Garlic **Seafood** Pasta

Take an all-in-one seafood mix and cook with a garlicky sauce of wine, ricotta cheese and tomatoes to make a gutsy and glamorous dish that's completely straightforward to prepare.

**15** mins prep time

**15** mins cook time

**Serves 4**
**14 oz (400 g) linguine**
**2 tbsp (25 mL) olive oil**
**3 garlic cloves, crushed**
**4 tbsp (60 mL) dry white wine or vermouth**
**½ lb (250 g) cherry tomatoes, quartered**
**2 x 7½-oz (220-g) packs ready-to-eat or frozen cooked seafood mix**
**3 tbsp (45 mL) ricotta cheese**
**1 oz (30 g) fresh flat-leaf parsley, roughly chopped**

**Each serving provides** • 447 cals • 28 g protein • 12 g fat of which 3 g saturates • 59 g carbohydrate

**1 Cook the pasta** Cook the linguine in a pot of salted boiling water for 6-7 minutes, or according to the pack instructions, until al dente.

**2 Cook the seafood** While the pasta is cooking, heat the oil in a frying pan or sauté pan. Add the garlic, then stir in the wine or vermouth. Simmer gently for 1 minute, then stir in the tomatoes. Add the seafood and return to a simmer. Cook, stirring occasionally, for 3 minutes if using fresh, or 4 minutes if using frozen, until the tomatoes have started to soften and the seafood is thoroughly heated. Stir in the ricotta cheese, heat gently and season to taste.

**3 Serve** Drain the pasta and turn into a warmed serving bowl. Spoon the sauce over the pasta. Add the parsley and gently toss until thoroughly combined. Serve immediately.

**Shopping tip** Packages of frozen cooked mixed seafood make a good standby for meals such as this. They usually contain a good combination of cooked prawns, mussels, calamari and crayfish tails or scallops. Here, you can use them straight from the freezer, or use a pack of fresh seafood, if you prefer.

### Seafood and chili noodles
Stir-fry **2 x 7½-oz (220-g) packs ready-to-eat or frozen cooked seafood mix** in **2 tbsp (25 mL) olive oil** for 1 minute, then add **7 oz (200 g) frozen soybeans** and cook for 1 minute. Add **3 scallions**, cut into short pieces, **2 chopped garlic cloves**, **1 fresh red chili pepper**, seeded and finely chopped, and a **1¼-in. (3-cm) piece fresh ginger**, peeled and grated. Cook for 2 minutes, then stir in **1 tbsp (15 mL) soy sauce** and **6¾ tbsp (100 mL) vegetable stock**. Cook for 2 minutes or until the vegetables are just tender. Meanwhile, cook **14 oz (400 g) Chinese egg noodles** for 4 minutes or according to the pack instructions. Drain and toss with the sauce. (Or use **3 x 5-oz (150-g) packs straight-to-wok noodles** added to the sauce. Stir-fry for 1-2 minutes or until hot.)

## ...another idea

# Pappardelle with **Chicken** and **Cherry Tomatoes**

Bite-sized pieces of chicken cook in record time and go beautifully with sweet cherry tomatoes and pappardelle, a wide ribbon pasta, tossed with peppery arugula for a fresh flourish.

**Serves 4**

2 tbsp (25 mL) olive oil

1 red onion, halved and thinly sliced

2 garlic cloves, crushed

4 skinless chicken breast fillets, about 1 lb (500 g) total weight, cut into ¾-in. (2-cm) cubes

14 oz (400 g) cherry tomatoes, halved

14 oz (400 g) pappardelle

5 oz (150 g) arugula

**Each serving provides** • 481 cals
• 40 g protein • 10 g fat of which
2 g saturates • 62 g carbohydrate

**1** **Cook the sauce** Heat the olive oil in a frying pan or sauté pan with a lid. Add the onion and garlic, and cook gently for 2 minutes. Add the chicken and stir-fry over a medium heat until lightly coloured. Reduce the heat slightly and stir in the tomatoes. Cover the pan and cook, stirring occasionally, for 8-10 minutes or until the tomatoes have become very soft and the chicken is cooked through.

**2** **Cook the pasta** While the sauce is simmering, cook the pasta in a pot of salted boiling water for 8-10 minutes, or according to the pack instructions, until al dente. Drain.

**3** **Serve** Stir the arugula into the sauce and season to taste. Tip the pasta into a warmed serving bowl. Spoon over the sauce and toss gently to combine thoroughly. Serve immediately.

# Spicy **Sausages** with **Farfalle**

On a freezing day you can't beat this rich, warming and hearty combination of quick-cook ingredients. Choose your favourite spicy sausages, such as Toulouse or pork with chili, to go with the sauce.

**Serves 4**

4 large or 6 medium spicy pork sausages, about 14 oz (400 g) total weight

2 tbsp (25 mL) olive oil

1 onion, chopped

2 garlic cloves, crushed

¼ lb (125 g) chestnut or large, flat mushrooms, halved

14 oz (398 mL) can chopped tomatoes

14 oz (400 g) farfalle

9 oz (280 g) jar roasted mixed peppers, drained and cut into thick strips

¼ tsp (1 mL) crushed chili flakes, or to taste

**Each serving provides** • 622 cals
• 27 g protein • 29 g fat of which
8 g saturates • 69 g carbohydrate

**1** **Make the sauce** Cut each sausage into five pieces. Heat the oil in a frying pan or sauté pan that has a lid. Add the sausages and fry, stirring frequently, for 4 minutes or until lightly browned. Add the onion and garlic to the pan, and cook for 1 minute, then add the halved mushrooms. Stir-fry for 2 minutes, then stir in the tomatoes. Bring to the boil, cover and simmer gently for 5-10 minutes.

**2** **Cook the pasta** While the sauce is simmering, cook the pasta in a pot of salted boiling water for 12 minutes, or according to the pack instructions, until al dente.

**3** **Add the peppers and chili** Add the peppers to the sauce with the crushed chili flakes and plenty of black pepper, and heat through for 1 minute.

**4** **Serve** Drain the pasta and turn into a warmed serving bowl. Taste the sauce and adjust the seasoning, then pour over the pasta and toss gently to combine. Serve immediately.

# Chicken, Baby Corn
## and Snow Peas with Noodles

**Boost your daily vegetable intake using bright, fresh baby corn, snow peas and red and yellow peppers in a healthy meal that's as colourful as it is tasty – and it cooks in a flash.**

**15** mins prep time

**12** mins cook time

**Serves 4**

7-8 oz (200-250 g) medium egg noodles

2 tsp (10 mL) toasted sesame oil

¾ lb (375 g) skinless chicken breast fillets, cut into thin slices

1 egg white

2 tsp (10 mL) cornstarch

1 tbsp (15 mL) canola oil

3 scallions, cut diagonally into ¾-in. (2-cm) pieces

½ lb (250 g) baby corn, halved lengthwise

½ lb (250 g) snow peas, halved lengthways

1 red pepper, cut into strips

1 yellow pepper, cut into strips

5 tbsp (75 mL) yellow bean sauce

⅔ cup (150 mL) vegetable or chicken stock, made with a stock cube

**Each serving provides** • 484 cals • 37 g protein • 11 g fat of which 1 g saturates • 63 g carbohydrate

**1 Cook the noodles** Boil the noodles in a pot of salted water for 4 minutes, or according to the pack instructions, until just tender. Drain thoroughly and toss with 1 tsp (5 mL) sesame oil. Set aside until needed.

**2 Marinate the chicken** While the noodles are cooking, mix the chicken in a bowl with the egg white, cornstarch and remaining sesame oil. Leave to marinate until needed.

**3 Stir-fry the chicken and vegetables** Heat a wok or large frying pan with the canola oil. When very hot add the chicken and stir-fry for 2 minutes or until lightly coloured.
Add the vegetables and stir-fry for 3-4 minutes or until just softened, then add the yellow bean sauce and stock, and mix thoroughly. Reduce the heat so that the liquid simmers gently, then cook for about 2 minutes or until the vegetables are just tender and the chicken thoroughly cooked.

**4 Add the noodles** Stir the cooked noodles into the chicken and vegetables, and toss to combine all the ingredients. As soon as the noodles are hot, turn into a warmed serving bowl and serve immediately.

**Swap** For chicken, use **peeled raw jumbo shrimp**, added with the yellow bean sauce at step 3. Cook for 3 minutes if fresh, 4 minutes if frozen, or until they turn pink.

• Replace the peppers with a pack of pre-sliced peppers, or use prepared stir-fry vegetables to cut down on preparation time if you prefer. • Buy straight-to-wok noodles that don't need boiling first.
• For extra speed, look out for thin strips of chicken breast or chicken mini fillets, which don't need slicing.

**...speed it up**

# Pad Thai Noodles with Chicken

Stir-frying is a super-quick cooking method that seals in all the flavours of the ingredients. Here, tender chicken and lightly scrambled eggs are cooked with chili, fish sauce and lots of garlic.

**10** mins prep time  **10** mins cook time

**Serves 4**

- **7-8 oz (200-250 g) dried medium rice noodles**
- **2 tbsp (25 mL) canola oil**
- **2-4 garlic cloves, crushed**
- **1 small onion, finely chopped**
- **1 red or green Thai chili pepper, seeded and finely chopped**
- **¾ lb (375 g) skinless chicken breast fillets, cut into thin slices**
- **2 eggs, beaten**
- **7 oz (200 g) bean sprouts**
- **1 tbsp (15 mL) soy sauce, or to taste**
- **2 tbsp (25 mL) fish sauce, or to taste**
- **1 tbsp (15 mL) lime juice, plus lime halves to serve (optional)**
- **crushed chili flakes, to taste (optional)**
- **1 bunch of fresh chives, snipped**
- **¼ cup (50 mL) roasted peanut halves**

Each serving provides • 484 cals
• 32 g protein • 14 g fat of which
3 g saturates • 56 g carbohydrate

**1 Prepare the noodles** Soak the rice noodles in a bowl of hot water for 10 minutes or according to the pack instructions. Stir gently with a fork or chopsticks to separate. Drain thoroughly and set aside until needed.

**2 Cook the chicken** While the noodles are soaking, heat a wok or large frying pan with the oil. When very hot add the crushed garlic, onion and chili pepper, and stir-fry for 1 minute. Add the chicken slices to the wok and stir-fry for 2 minutes or until lightly coloured.

**3 Cook the eggs** Push the chicken to one side of the wok to make room for the eggs. Pour the eggs into the wok and stir gently until lightly scrambled. Add the drained noodles and 3 tbsp (45 mL) water. Add the bean sprouts, soy sauce, fish sauce and lime juice, and stir-fry with the noodles, chicken and eggs for 2 minutes.

**4 Adjust the seasoning** Remove the wok from the heat. Taste, then add black pepper or more fish sauce or soy sauce if necessary. If you like, add some crushed chili flakes. Turn into a warmed serving dish and garnish with the chives and peanuts. Serve immediately, with lime halves to garnish, if using.

**Swaps** For chicken, use thin strips of lean **pork**. Cook the pork strips for 5 minutes. Or use **½ lb (250 g) raw jumbo shrimp**, adding them with the fish sauce at step 3. Cook for 3 minutes if fresh and 4 minutes if frozen, or until they turn pink.

# 5 quick and easy pasta and noodle salads

A pasta or noodle salad makes a good, quick one-pot meal, and the sky's the limit when it comes to what to add. You can rustle one up in a jiffy with ingredients you already have in your pantry or fridge. For the best flavour, add a dressing to pasta while it's still hot, then serve warm. Or prepare ahead to serve cold, if you have time. All recipes serve 4.

## italian summer salad

Cook **8 oz (250 g) dried pasta**, such as penne, in a pot of salted boiling water for 10 minutes, or according to the pack instructions, until al dente. Drain, put into a large bowl and toss while hot with a dressing made from **2 tbsp (25 mL) extra virgin olive oil, 1 tbsp (15 mL) lemon juice, 1 crushed garlic clove** and **1 small bunch of fresh basil**, finely chopped. Season and set aside. Halve **7 oz (200 g) red and yellow cherry tomatoes** and cube **5 oz (150 g) fresh mozzarella**. Slice **7 oz (200 g) roasted red peppers** from a jar into strips. Add the vegetables and mozzarella to the pasta and toss together. Ⓥ

**Each serving provides** • 395 cals
• 15 g protein • 16 g fat of which
6 g saturates • 50 g carbohydrate

**8** mins prep time

**10** mins cook time

• Tossing hot pasta in a dressing helps the flavours to be absorbed.
• The best pasta shapes to use for salads are spirals (fusilli), bows (farfalle), small tubes (penne), shells (conchiglie) and wheels (trulli). Or use Chinese egg noodles.
• For a good balance of tastes and textures remember to match the quantity of pasta to prepared vegetables and seafood, chopped meats or vegetarian alternatives.

## ...cooking tips

# bright **pepper** and **salami** salad

Cook **8 oz (250 g) dried pasta**, such as fusilli, in a pot of salted boiling water for 10 minutes, or according to the pack instructions, until al dente. Drain, put into a large bowl and toss while hot with **3 tbsp (45 mL) prepared vinaigrette** (page 31). Season, then set aside. Thinly slice **1 green, 1 red and 1 yellow pepper** and **1 small red onion**. Cut **3½ oz (100 g) good-quality salami** into thin strips. Add to the pasta with **3½ oz (100 g) arugula** and toss gently.

**Each serving provides** • 435 cals
• 14 g protein • 19.5 g fat of which
5 g saturates • 54 g carbohydrate

# **trout** and **cucumber** salad

Cook **8 oz (250 g) dried pasta**, such as farfalle, in a pot of salted boiling water for 8 minutes, or according to the pack instructions, until al dente. Drain, put into a large bowl and toss while hot in a green vinaigrette made with **3 tbsp (45 mL) olive oil**, the grated zest and juice of **1 small lemon** and **3 tbsp (45 mL) chopped watercress or fresh flat-leaf parsley**. Season, then set aside. Flake the flesh from a **7½-oz (220-g) pack pre-cooked trout fillets** and dice **½ small cucumber**. Toss with the dressed pasta and **1 tbsp (15 mL) drained capers**.

**Each serving provides** • 366 cals
• 20 g protein • 12 g fat of which
2 g saturates • 47 g carbohydrate

# easy pasta **niçoise** salad

Boil **1 egg** for 10 minutes. Drain and cool in cold water, then peel and quarter. Meanwhile, cook **8 oz (250 g) dried pasta**, such as conchiglie, in salted boiling water for 10 minutes, or according to the pack instructions. Drain, put into a large bowl and toss with **3 tbsp (45 mL) vinaigrette** (page 31). Season. Drain and flake a **6-oz (170-g) can tuna**. Chop **3 tbsp (45 mL) stoned olives**. Add to the pasta with **1 large carrot**, grated, and **3½ oz (100 g) cooked green beans**. Toss, then garnish with the egg.

**Each serving provides**
• 407 cals • 20 g protein
• 15.5 g fat of which
2.5 g saturates • 50 g carbohydrate

**10** mins prep time   **10** mins cook time

> If you have time to spare, leave the salad to cool, then chill in the fridge for up to 4 hours before serving.
>
> **...get ahead**

# **chicken** and sugar snap pea noodle salad

Steam or boil **7 oz (200 g) sugar snap peas** for 4 minutes. Meanwhile, cook **7 oz (200 g) dried medium egg noodles** for 3 minutes or according to the pack instructions. Drain and toss the pasta in a dressing made from **1 tbsp (15 mL) tahini**, **2 tbsp (25 mL) canola oil**, **2 tbsp (25 mL) lemon juice**, **1 tbsp (15 mL) soy sauce**, **1 tsp (5 mL) toasted sesame oil**, **1 crushed garlic clove** and **2 tsp (10 mL) grated fresh ginger**. Cool the noodles for 15 minutes, then toss with **½ lb (250 g) cold cooked chicken**, cut into thin strips, and the sugar snap peas.

**Each serving provides** • 411 cals
• 27 g protein • 17 g fat of which
3 g saturates • 39 g carbohydrate

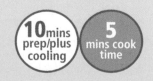

# Oriental Noodles
## with Plum and Ginger Duck

If you enjoy Chinese food you'll love this speedy dish, which is healthy as well as tasty. Lean duck meat and crunchy sugar snap peas go well with oriental spices and quick-cooked noodles for superb fast food.

### Serves 4

2 large or 3 medium skinless duck breast fillets, about 14 oz (400 g) total weight

2 tbsp (25 mL) soy sauce

2 tbsp (25 mL) rice wine or dry sherry

a pinch of five-spice powder

2 tbsp (25 mL) olive oil

3 scallions, cut into ¾-in. (2-cm) pieces

1¼-in. (3-cm) piece fresh ginger, peeled and grated

⅔ lb (300 g) sugar snap peas

5 tbsp (75 mL) plum sauce

⅔ cup (150 mL) chicken or vegetable stock, made with a stock cube

12 oz (375 g) instant egg or rice noodles

1 oz (30 g) fresh coriander

Each serving provides • 634 cals • 35 g protein • 20 g fat of which 4 g saturates • 82 g carbohydrate

Swap For duck, use **stroganoff strips**: ready-cut strips of lean beef or venison that are ideal for stir-fry dishes.

1 **Marinate the duck** Slice the duck breasts crosswise fairly thinly. Combine the soy sauce, rice wine or dry sherry and five-spice powder in a bowl. Add the duck and toss gently so that the slices are thoroughly coated in the marinade.

2 **Cook the duck** Heat a wok or frying pan with the oil, remove the duck from the marinade and stir-fry over a high heat for 1 minute. Reserve the marinade. Stir in the scallions and ginger, followed by the sugar snap peas. Stir-fry for 1 minute, then add the reserved marinade, the plum sauce and stock. Stir well and leave to cook over a medium heat for 3-4 minutes.

3 **Cook the noodles** While the sauce is cooking, add the noodles to boiling water and cook for 3-4 minutes or according to the pack instructions.

4 **Assemble and serve** Drain the noodles and add to the wok. Toss gently to combine all the ingredients. Turn into a warmed serving bowl and garnish with sprigs of coriander.

Shopping tip If you like to cook Chinese dishes regularly, you will find rice wine is a useful ingredient to keep in the pantry. Sherry is a good alternative and has other culinary uses too, so this might be the most practical option.

**15** mins prep time

**15** mins cook time

## Special Pork Chow Mein

Stir-fried vegetables contrast perfectly with toasted cashew nuts, succulent pork strips and soft noodles for this filling meal. It's ready in minutes, and lower in salt and oil than ready-prepared and take-out versions of this popular dish.

**10** mins prep time

**10** mins cook time

Serves 4

2 tbsp (25 mL) canola oil

3½ oz (100 g) cashew nuts

4 garlic cloves, crushed

2-in. (5-cm) piece fresh ginger, peeled and finely chopped

1 lb (500 g) stir-fry vegetables

½ lb (250 g) cooked pork, such as char sui, cut into strips

10 oz (300 g) straight-to-wok egg noodles

2 tbsp (25 mL) soy sauce

1 tbsp Chinese rice wine or dry sherry

2 tsp (10 mL) toasted sesame oil

Each serving provides

• 653 cals • 37 g protein

• 27 g fat of which 4 g saturates

• 70 g carbohydrate

1 **Fry the cashew nuts** Heat a wok or large frying pan over a medium heat with 1 tbsp (15 mL) oil. Add the cashew nuts and stir-fry for 2 minutes or until golden. Transfer to a plate, and wipe the wok clean.

2 **Stir-fry the vegetables and pork** Heat the remaining oil in the wok or frying pan over a medium heat and stir-fry the garlic and ginger for 10 seconds. Increase the heat and add the vegetable mixture. Stir-fry for 1 minute. Stir in the strips of cooked pork and stir-fry for a further 3 minutes to heat the meat through.

3 **Cook the noodles** Add the noodles, soy sauce and rice wine or sherry to the wok or pan, and add seasoning. Stir-fry for 3 minutes or until piping hot, then add the sesame oil and toss well to mix. Turn into a warmed serving bowl, scatter with the nuts and serve immediately.

Shopping tip Look out for packs of prepared stir-fry vegetables that contain bok choy, water chestnuts, peppers, bamboo shoots, broccoli and carrots for this dish.

### Noodles with chicken and oyster mushrooms

Thinly slice **3 skinless chicken breast fillets**, about ⅔ lb (300 g) in total, and toss in a mixture of **2 tbsp (25 mL) each soy sauce and rice wine or dry sherry** and **1 tsp (5 mL) grated fresh ginger** (if there's time, chill and marinate in the mixture for up to 8 hours). Heat a wok or frying pan with **2 tbsp (25 mL) canola oil**, then stir-fry **2 thinly sliced garlic cloves** and **1 mild red chili pepper**, seeded and cut into rings. After 1 minute add the chicken and marinade, and stir-fry for 3 minutes. Add **6 oz (175 g) sliced oyster mushrooms, 4 tbsp (60 mL) plum sauce** and **6¾ tbsp (100 mL) chicken or vegetable stock**. Cook for 3-4 minutes, then stir in **12 oz (375 g) straight-to-wok noodles**.

### ...another idea

### Vegetarian chow mein Ⓥ

Heat a wok or frying pan with **2 tbsp (25 mL) canola oil** and stir-fry **2-3 chopped garlic cloves** and a **2-in. (5-cm) piece fresh ginger**, peeled and chopped. After 10 seconds add **1 red onion**, cut into thin wedges, and **1 large diced eggplant**. Stir-fry for about 4 minutes or until starting to soften. Add **1 large zucchini**, thinly sliced, and **5 oz (150 g) sliced chestnut mushrooms**. Stir-fry for 4 minutes or until softened, then add **7 oz (200 g) diced smoked tofu** and **16 oz (500 g) straight-to-wok egg noodles**, with **3 tbsp (45 mL) black bean stir-fry sauce**. Stir-fry for 3 minutes or until the noodles are piping hot, then serve.

### ...another idea

# Singapore Noodles
## with Jumbo Shrimp

This is a fiery combination of seafood, bean sprouts and noodles stirred in a creamy coconut sauce. A Thai curry paste makes short work of a curry that supplies an authentic flavour without lots of preparation.

**10** mins prep time  **12** mins cook time

**Serves 4**

1 tbsp (15 mL) canola oil

1 onion, finely chopped

3 garlic cloves, crushed

1 tbsp (15 mL) laksa paste or yellow Thai curry paste, or to taste

1⅔ cups (400 mL) coconut milk

1 cup (250 mL) vegetable or fish stock, made with a stock cube

7-8 oz (200-250 g) rice noodles

7 oz (200 g) peeled raw jumbo shrimp

4 scallions, roughly chopped

⅔ lb (300 g) bean sprouts

2 limes

**Each serving provides** • 367 cals • 16 g protein • 5 g fat of which 1 g saturates • 63 g carbohydrate

**1** **Make the sauce** Heat a wok or frying pan with the oil, add the onion and garlic, and cook for 2 minutes, stirring frequently. Add the laksa or curry paste and fry for another 2 minutes, then stir in the coconut milk and stock. Bring to the boil, then simmer for 5 minutes.

**2** **Soak the noodles** While the sauce is cooking, put the noodles into a large heatproof bowl, pour over enough boiling water to cover and leave to soak for 5 minutes or according to the pack instructions. Separate the noodles gently using a fork or chopsticks.

**3** **Complete the sauce** Add the jumbo shrimp to the sauce in the wok or frying pan and cook, stirring frequently, for 3 minutes or until the jumbo shrimp have turned pink. Stir in the scallions and bean sprouts. Squeeze the juice of one of the limes into the sauce. Taste and season. Quarter the other lime.

**4** **Serve** Drain the noodles and divide among four serving bowls. Ladle over the prawn laksa and serve immediately, garnished with lime wedges.

**Shopping tip** You can use fresh or frozen jumbo shrimp for this recipe. There's no need to thaw them if frozen; cook for 4 minutes at step 3.

**Thai noodles with monkfish**
Heat a wok or frying pan with **1 tbsp (15 mL) canola oil**. Add **1½ tbsp (20 mL) Thai green curry paste** and stir-fry for 2 minutes. Stir in **1⅔ cups (400 mL) coconut milk** and **1 cup (250 mL) vegetable stock**, made with a stock cube. Bring to the boil and simmer for 5 minutes. Add **½ lb (250 g) halved green beans** and simmer for 5 minutes. Add **⅔ lb (300 g) diced monkfish** and simmer for 5 minutes or until cooked through. Taste and season. Meanwhile, cook **11 oz (350 g) fresh Chinese or Thai egg noodles** in boiling water for 1 minute, or according to the pack instructions. Drain and divide among four serving bowls. Ladle over the sauce and serve.

## ...another idea

# Chinese Beef Noodle Soup
## with Shiitake Mushrooms

Lean steak is flash-fried then added to a full-flavoured beef stock with oriental vegetables and nests of fine egg noodles in this attractive noodle-bar favourite.

**10** mins prep time

**10** mins cook time

**Serves 4**

2 tbsp (25 mL) soy sauce

1 tbsp (15 mL) toasted sesame oil

2 tbsp (25 mL) Chinese rice wine or dry sherry

⅔ lb (300 g) lean rump steak, sliced into very thin strips

4 cups (1 L) beef stock, made with stock cubes

4 scallions, sliced

5 oz (150 g) shiitake mushrooms, thickly sliced

7 oz (200 g) baby bok choy, leaves halved

7-8 oz (200-250 g) instant fine egg noodles

1 tbsp (15 mL) canola oil

**Each serving provides** • 430 cals • 26 g protein • 15 g fat of which 4 g saturates • 51 g carbohydrate

**1** **Make the marinade** Combine the soy sauce, sesame oil and Chinese rice wine or sherry in a bowl. Add the strips of beef and toss until well mixed. Leave to marinate until needed.

**2** **Cook the vegetables in the stock** Heat the stock in a large pot or flame-proof casserole. Add the scallions, sliced mushrooms and halved bok choy, and simmer for 2 minutes.

**3** **Add the noodles** Add the nests of noodles to the pan of vegetables and cook for 2-4 minutes or until tender.

**4** **Stir-fry the beef** While the noodles are cooking, heat a wok or frying pan with the oil and stir-fry the beef for 2 minutes or until browned. Tip the contents of the pan into the simmering stock. Bring back to the boil. Taste and season with black pepper, then ladle into four serving bowls and serve.

**Swap** For beef, use **chicken breast fillets**. Replace the stock with **chicken stock**.

**Shopping tip** Dried shiitake mushrooms are useful to keep in the pantry, but you will need time to soak them before they can be added to a recipe. Soak in water for about 3 minutes, then rinse to remove any grit. Soak in warm water for a further 30 minutes to soften. Cut off the stalks and discard, then continue as for fresh shiitake. (The soaking liquid can be strained and added to the stock.)

# rice, beans and grains

# Basmati Pilaf
## with Tikka Griddled Chicken

Fluffy grains of basmati rice cooked with garlic and spices and some cherry tomatoes taste great in a dish with quick marinated griddled chicken breast. Just serve with a green salad or some cooling raita.

**10** mins prep time

**20** mins cook time

**To serve** If you like, make a quick raita while the rice and chicken are cooking. Finely chop **½ cucumber** and mix with **⅔ cup (150 mL) plain yogurt**, **1 tbsp (15 mL) chopped fresh mint** and **¼ tsp (1 mL) ground cumin**.

**Serves 4**

- **4 small skinless chicken breast fillets**, about ¼ lb (125 g) each
- **1 fat garlic clove**, chopped
- **1 tbsp (15 mL) tikka spice mix** or mild curry powder
- **2 tbsp (25 mL) vegetable oil**
- **1 onion**, sliced
- **1⅓ cups (325 mL) basmati rice**, rinsed
- **2½ cups (625 mL) hot vegetable or chicken stock**, made with stock cubes
- **⅓ cup (75 mL) raisins**, packed
- **1 tbsp (15 mL) chopped fresh coriander**
- **3½ oz (100 g) cherry tomatoes**, halved
- **3 tbsp (45 mL) toasted pine nuts**
- **lemon wedges**, to serve

**Each serving provides** • 510 cals • 37 g protein • 12 g fat of which 1 g saturates • 63 g carbohydrate

**1 Marinate the chicken** Cut each chicken breast fillet into 3-4 strips and mix with half the garlic and half the tikka spice mix or curry powder. Leave to marinate while you cook the pilaf, turning the chicken strips in the marinade after about 10 minutes.

**2 Flavour the rice** Heat the vegetable oil in a large nonstick pot, add the sliced onion and the remaining garlic, and cook gently for 3 minutes. Stir in the basmati rice, then sprinkle in the remaining spice powder. Mix well. Preheat the grill or a ridged griddle.

**3 Cook the pilaf** Pour the hot stock into the rice with ½ tsp (2 mL) salt and the raisins. Bring to the boil, then reduce the heat to a low simmer. Cover and cook for 10 minutes without lifting the lid. The liquid should have been absorbed and small steam holes should have appeared. If necessary, cover and cook for a further 2 minutes. Add the coriander and tomatoes, stir through to reheat briefly then remove the pan from the heat and leave for 5 minutes. Add the pine nuts and fork through the rice gently.

**4 Cook the chicken** While the rice is cooking, grill or griddle the chicken strips for 6-8 minutes or until just firm, turning once. Spoon the pilaf into a serving dish and put the chicken on top. Serve with lemon wedges.

**Swaps** For chicken breasts, use **salmon fillets** (left whole) or **lamb cutlets**. Make a ginger marinade for salmon or lamb by blending **1 tsp (5 mL) fresh ginger, grated (or 1 tsp/ 5 mL ginger paste)** into the tikka spice mix.

### All-in-one beef pilaf

Omit the chicken. Cook ⅔ **lb (300 g) lean ground beef** with the onion, all the garlic and **1 tsp (5 mL) grated fresh ginger** until crumbly. Add the rice, as step 2, with **2 pinches of saffron threads**, all the spice mix or curry powder and **1 sliced and seeded green chili pepper**. Increase the hot stock to 3 cups (750 mL), add the raisins and cook as step 3, then fork through the pine nuts and serve.

## ...another idea

# Oven-Baked **Mushroom Pilaf**
## with Sausages

In this robust rice dish, a mix of red kidney beans, continental sausage and mushrooms is quickly prepared, then left to bake in the oven. This hearty dish needs just a salad to accompany it.

**20** mins prep time

**20** mins cook time

**Serves 4**

2 tbsp (25 mL) olive oil

1 celery stick, sliced

1 onion, chopped

½ lb (250 g) cup mushrooms, sliced

1⅓ cups (325 mL) basmati rice, rinsed

3¼ cup (800 mL) hot vegetable stock, made with stock cubes

14-oz (398-mL) can red kidney beans, or borlotti or flageolet beans, drained and rinsed

½ lb (250 g) Polish sausage or German Bockwurst, cut into short lengths

3 strips of orange zest

2 bay leaves

⅔ oz (10 g) fresh parsley

**Each serving provides** • 540 cals
• 20 g protein • 23 g fat of which
6 g saturates • 65 g carbohydrate

**1 Fry the vegetables** Preheat the oven to 375°F (190°C). Heat the oil in a large flameproof casserole or pot and cook the celery and onion in the oil for 2 minutes. Add the mushrooms and cook for 3 minutes.

**2 Add the rice** Mix the rice into the casserole or pot. Stir in the hot stock, beans, sausage, ½ tsp (2 mL) salt, the orange zest, bay leaves and ground black pepper. Bring to the boil.

**3 Bake the pilaf** Cover the casserole (if cooked in a pot, transfer the mixture to a warm casserole, and cover). Bake for 20 minutes or until the rice is tender. Add the parsley and fork through the mixture, then serve.

**Swaps** • Try some of the more **unusual cultivated or exotic mushrooms** in the pilaf. • For extra flavour, replace ⅔ cup (150 mL) of the vegetable stock with **dry cider or white wine**.

**Shopping tip** Rice sold as "easy-cook" surprisingly takes longer to cook than basmati rice and loses much of its natural aroma. So if you find plain boiled rice tricky to cook, make a pilaf or a stir-fry (page 148) to be sure of perfect fluffy grains.

# Seafood and Bacon Paella

Throw this gorgeous paella together for a quick meal that's absolutely bursting with flavour. Just add a tossed, crisp green salad or steamed green vegetables.

**30 mins** prep/cook time

### Serves 4

**2 tbsp (25 mL) olive oil**

**1 large onion, chopped**

**1 green pepper, chopped**

**2 large garlic cloves, chopped**

**7 oz (200 g) bacon, chopped**

**1 large tomato, chopped**

**1⅓ cups (325 mL) paella rice**

**½ tsp (2 mL) saffron threads, crushed**

**5 cups (1.25 L) hot chicken or fish stock, made with stock cubes**

**14 oz (400 g) frozen cooked seafood mix**

**lime wedges, to serve (optional)**

Each serving provides • 521 cals • 29 g protein • 15 g fat of which 5 g saturates • 73 g carbohydrate

**1 Fry the vegetables** Heat the oil in a large, nonstick frying pan. Add the onion, pepper, garlic and bacon pieces, and cook over a gentle heat for 5 minutes. Add the tomato and cook for 2 minutes.

**2 Add the rice and saffron** Add the rice and stir to coat in the oil. Add the saffron threads and heat for a few seconds, then pour in the hot stock. Bring to the boil, then stir lightly and simmer for 5 minutes.

**3 Add the seafood** Mix in the frozen seafood, return to a gentle simmer and cook for up to 10 minutes or until the rice is tender and the liquid absorbed, stirring the pan occasionally. Serve with lime wedges, if you like.

**Swaps** • For seafood mix, use your own choice of seafood such as prepared **mussels, raw shrimp and squid**.
• Or use **½ lb (250 g) stir-fry chicken strips**, fried with the vegetables at step 1.

**Shopping tip** If you can't find paella rice, **Italian arborio** rice works well in this recipe.

### Golden chickpea paella Ⓥ

Cook a mixture of chopped vegetables in the oil at step 1, such as **1 fennel bulb or 3 celery sticks**, **1 yellow pepper**, and **1 onion**, and **1 crushed garlic clove**. Omit the bacon. Add the tomato, rice and saffron as for the basic recipe and **1 tsp (5 mL) ground paprika**. Add **1 chopped zucchini**, **3½ cups (875 mL) hot vegetable stock**, made with stock cubes, and **½ cup (125 mL) white wine**, and cook for 5 minutes as step 2. Add a **14-oz (398-mL) can chickpeas**, drained and rinsed, instead of seafood, and simmer for 10 minutes as step 3.

### Chorizo and pork paella

Replace the chopped bacon with **5 oz (150 g) sliced chorizo** and use **½ lb (250 g) stir-fry pork strips** instead of the seafood. Fry the pork and chorizo with the vegetables at step 1 or until the chorizo is crisp and the pork lightly browned. Instead of the green pepper and saffron add **1 tsp (5 mL) paprika**, if you like (the chorizo may be sufficiently spicy). Stir in **¼ lb (125 g ) frozen peas** 5 minutes before the end of cooking.

A traditional paella is cooked in a large, wide, open pan, which is shaken occasionally during cooking and not stirred. It's easy to cook in a frying pan, but you will need to stir the mixture occasionally.

**...cooking tip**

**...more ideas**

# Thai **Coconut Rice**
## with Lime and Coriander **Shrimp**

Delicately flavoured Thai rice goes perfectly with jumbo shrimp, coriander and chili for this fast, exotic dish. Lightly steamed vegetables are all you need to eat with it.

**10** mins prep time

**20** mins cook time

**To serve** Packs of **prepared mixed vegetables** such as snow peas, baby corn and asparagus tips make perfect accompaniments to main dishes – they just need to be quickly steamed, microwaved or boiled.

**Serves 4**

**2 tbsp (25 mL) vegetable oil**

**1 large shallot or small onion, chopped**

**2 garlic cloves, crushed**

**1 large red chili pepper, seeded and sliced**

**1²/₃ cup (400 mL) Thai fragrant rice or long-grain rice**

**2¹/₃ cup (600 mL) hot vegetable or chicken stock, made with stock cubes**

**¾ cup (175 mL) coconut cream**

**½ cucumber, halved lengthwise and sliced**

**14 oz (400 g) raw, peeled jumbo shrimp**

**1 tsp (5 mL) ground cumin**

**juice of 1 lime**

**½ oz (15 g) sprigs of fresh coriander**

**lime wedges, to serve**

**Each serving provides** • 632 cals • 26 g protein • 25 g fat of which 16 g saturates • 81 g carbohydrate

**1** **Flavour the rice** Heat 1 tbsp (15 mL) oil in a large nonstick pot. Add the shallot or onion, garlic and chili, and cook for 3 minutes or until softened. Stir in the rice, stock and coconut cream. Season lightly.

**2** **Cook the rice** Bring the rice mixture to the boil. Stir once, then lower the heat to a gentle simmer. Cover and cook for 10 minutes without lifting the lid, or according to the package instructions. The liquid should have been absorbed and small steam holes should have appeared. If necessary, cover and cook the rice mixture for a further 2 minutes. Add the cucumber slices and cook, covered, for a further minute, then remove the pot from the heat and leave for 5 minutes.

**3** **Cook the Shrimp** While the rice is standing, heat the remaining oil in a wok or large pan and stir-fry the shrimp for 3 minutes or until they turn pink. Stir in the cumin and cook for a few seconds, then add the lime juice.

**4** **Garnish and serve** Reserve a few whole coriander sprigs and roughly chop the remainder (including the stalks). Add to the shrimp and stir. Divide the rice among four plates and top with the shrimp. Garnish with the coriander sprigs and serve with the lime wedges.

**Shopping tip** You can use cooked jumbo shrimp if you prefer. Heat them through for 1-2 minutes.

# Indonesian Spicy Rice Salad

**Sprouted beans and unsalted nuts give lots of crunchy texture to this piquant salad. It's super-easy to make with brown basmati rice and salad vegetables on a bed of torn Chinese leaves or baby spinach.**

**Serves 4** Ⓥ

1⅓ cups (325 mL) brown basmati rice, rinsed

2 tbsp (25 mL) olive oil

2 tbsp (25 mL) lime or lemon juice

1 large garlic clove, crushed

1 large fresh red chili pepper, seeded and thinly sliced

2 tbsp (25 mL) soy sauce

2 tsp (10 mL) clear honey, or to taste

2 tbsp (25 mL) rice vinegar or white wine vinegar

4 scallions, thinly sliced

2 celery sticks, thinly sliced

½ lb (250 g) sprouted beans or bean sprouts

3½ oz (100 g) unsalted cashew nuts or peanuts

Bok choy and baby spinach, to serve

Each serving provides • 462 cals • 11 g protein • 20 g fat of which 4 g saturates • 63 g carbohydrate

**30** mins prep/cook time

**1** **Cook the rice** Add the rice to a large pot of lightly salted boiling water. Stir, then simmer for 25 minutes.

**2** **Make the dressing** While the rice is cooking, put the oil, lime or lemon juice, garlic, chili pepper, soy sauce, honey and vinegar into a large salad bowl. Season with ground black pepper and whisk to blend.

**3** **Add the vegetables** Add the vegetables to the bowl together with the nuts. Toss well.

**4** **Mix in the rice** When the rice is just tender, drain in a colander, and rinse under cold running water until warm. Drain well, then add to the salad bowl and toss to mix. Serve in shallow bowls lined with torn bok choy and spinach.

**Addition** Add strips of **rare roast beef or lamb** left over from a Sunday roast just before serving the salad.

For a spicy chili flavour without the bother of chopping, simply add a whole chili pepper, slit lengthwise, seeds removed. Discard before serving. Or use ½-1 tsp (2-5 mL) crushed chili flakes.

**...speed it up**

● Never keep rice warm once it is cooked, as bacteria can develop. Cook and serve it immediately, then quickly cool any that is left over if you want to keep it.

● You can cook rice ahead of time or make up a double batch to use later, but remember that it must be used within two days. Although you can freeze rice, the texture becomes a little brittle when thawed. Frozen rice must be used within three months.

**...rice safety**

# 5 irresistible risottos

Keep a package of risotto rice in the pantry and you'll never be stuck for a quick, satisfying meal. A creamy risotto is straightforward to make and simply delicious. Follow the basic recipe for a classic Risotto Milanese, or add extra ingredients for endless variations. All recipes serve 4.

● The secret of a perfect risotto is to have your stock simmering in a pot while you cook the rice. This way the temperature of the rice never drops. ● Adding the stock gradually ensures that each ladleful will be fully absorbed, preventing mushy rice. ● The rice is cooked when it is tender and creamy but with the very slightest bite at the centre of each grain.

## ...perfect risotto

## risotto milanese

4 cups (1 L) hot vegetable stock, made with stock cubes
3½ tbsp (50 mL) butter
1 tbsp (15 mL) olive oil
1 onion, chopped
1 garlic clove, crushed
1½ cup (325 mL) arborio rice
⅔ cup (125 mL) dry white wine
1 tbsp (25 mL) chopped fresh parsley, or snipped chives
½ cup (125 mL) Parmesan or Italian-style hard cheese shavings

**Each serving provides** • 483 cals
• 12 g protein • 18 g fat of which
9 g saturates • 60 g carbohydrate

**5** mins prep time    **25** mins cook time

**1 Fry the onion and garlic** Heat the stock in a small pot and keep it gently simmering. Heat the butter and olive oil in a large pot. Add the onion and garlic, and cook over a medium heat for 4-5 minutes, stirring, until softened.

**2 Add the rice** Using a wooden spoon, stir in the rice and coat it with the buttery onions. Add the wine and simmer until almost evaporated. Stir in a ladleful of hot stock. Cook, stirring occasionally, until it has been absorbed into the rice.

**3 Complete the risotto** Continue adding the hot stock a ladleful at a time, stirring occasionally, for about 20 minutes or until the risotto is tender and creamy. Stir in the herbs, then season to taste. Serve with Parmesan cheese shavings scattered over the top. Ⓥ

## chicken and spinach

Complete step 1. Stir in the rice as step 2, then add the wine and simmer until almost evaporated. Gradually add **3⅔ cups (900 mL) chicken stock**, made with stock cubes, as step 3. Five minutes before the rice will be ready, increase the heat and stir in **7½ oz (220 g) baby spinach leaves**. Lower the heat when the risotto starts to bubble again. Two minutes before the end of cooking time, stir in **9 oz (280 g) cooked chicken** and **2 tbsp (25 mL) mascarpone cheese**. When the risotto is tender and creamy, stir in **2 tbsp (25 mL) chopped parsley**, seasoning and a little freshly grated nutmeg. Scatter with Parmesan cheese.

**Each serving provides** • 667 cals • 35 g protein
• 28 g fat of which 15 g saturates • 61 g carbohydrate

**5** mins prep time    **25** mins cook time

Leftover risotto can be made into risotto cakes for an instant meal. Cool the risotto quickly, then chill and use within one day. Take about 4 tbsp (60 mL) of the mixture for each cake. Roll into balls, and coat in fresh white bread crumbs, then flatten into small rounds.
Fry in a little butter or oil until golden. Serve with grilled meats or fish and a green salad.

...get ahead

## mushroom and smoked bacon

Make the basic risotto milanese. Meanwhile, dry-fry **6 strips bacon or pancetta** in a nonstick frying pan until browned and crisp. Transfer to a plate lined with paper towels, then, once cool, tear and crumble into small pieces. Wipe the pan, removing any bits of bacon, but leaving a little of the fat. Add **2 tsp (10 mL) olive oil** and **10 oz (300 g) sliced chestnut mushrooms** and stir-fry over a high heat for 4-5 minutes or until tender. When the risotto is cooked, stir in the mushrooms with their juices and half of the bacon. Spoon onto warmed plates and scatter with the remaining bacon and the **Parmesan cheese**.

**Each serving provides** • 596 cals • 18 g protein • 28 g fat of which 12 g saturates • 60 g carbohydrate

**5** mins prep time

**25** mins cook time

## shrimp, sun-dried tomatoes and peas

Complete steps 1 and 2, but chop **6-8 soft sun-dried tomatoes** and add them to the risotto when you first add the stock at step 2. Follow step 3, but stir in **½ lb (250 g) cooked, peeled shrimps** and **7 oz (200 g) peas** (thawed, if frozen, by putting them into a colander and pouring boiling water over), for the last 2 minutes of cooking.

**Each serving provides** • 607 cals • 36 g protein • 19 g fat of which 9 g saturates • 65 g carbohydrate

**5** mins prep time

**25** mins cook time

## fresh green vegetables

Complete step 1. Meanwhile, snap off any woody stems from **7½ oz (220 g) asparagus spears** at the point where they break easily. Slice the stalks. Follow step 2, but add the stalks to the risotto when you start to add the stock. Follow step 3, but after 12 minutes of cooking, add the asparagus tips and **1 zucchini**, thinly sliced. Add **¼ lb (125 g) baby fava beans or frozen soya beans** (thawed by putting them into a colander and pouring boiling water over) with the last measure of stock. You could also add drained and quartered **artichoke hearts** with the beans or peas, if you like. Serve with Parmesan or Italian style hard cheese. Ⓥ

**Each serving provides** • 515 cals • 15 g protein • 19 g fat of which 9 g saturates • 64 g carbohydrate

**5** mins prep time

**25** mins cook time

Traditionally, a risotto is cooked in a pot or deep pan on the stovetop, but if it's more convenient, it can be left to cook in a covered dish in the oven. Preheat the oven to 400°F (200°C). Make the vegetable stock using boiling water. Cook the onion and garlic in the butter and oil in a flameproof casserole or pot, as for the basic recipe. Add the rice and wine, and bring to the boil. Pour in the hot vegetable stock and stir the mixture again. Transfer to a warm casserole, if cooked in a pot. Cover with a tight-fitting lid and bake for 25 minutes or until the rice is tender and creamy. Stir in the herbs and scatter with Parmesan or Italian-style hard cheese before serving.

...oven method

# Glorious Vegetable and **Cashew** Stir-Fry **Rice**

Basmati rice cooks so quickly that it can be boiled and then added to a speedy stir-fry. Nuts and seeds make this a complete meal, but it's also a great side dish for grilled meats or fish.

**Serves 4** Ⓥ

1⅓ cups (325 mL) basmati rice, rinsed

2 tbsp (25 mL) soy sauce

1 tbsp (15 mL) dry sherry

2 tsp (10 mL) toasted sesame oil

2 tbsp (25 mL) canola oil

7½ oz (220 g) carrots, peeled, halved lengthwise and thinly sliced

⅔ lb (300 g) leeks, thinly sliced

5 oz (150 g) Savoy cabbage, thinly sliced

1 large garlic clove, crushed

1 large fresh red chili pepper, seeded and sliced

4 tbsp (60 mL) cashew nuts

4 tbsp (60 mL) mixed toasted seeds

**Each serving provides** • 561 cals • 15 g protein • 27 g fat of which 4 g saturates • 64 g carbohydrate

**1 Cook the rice and make the sauce**
Add the rice to a pot of boiling water and boil for 10 minutes or until the grains are tender. Drain. Meanwhile, mix together the soy sauce, sherry and sesame oil in a small bowl and set this mixture aside.

**2 Cook the vegetables** While the rice is cooking, heat a wok or large frying pan with the canola oil and stir-fry the carrots and leeks for 2-3 minutes or until softened. Add the cabbage, garlic and chili pepper, and stir-fry for 2-3 minutes. Stir in the soy sauce mixture and the cashew nuts. Season to taste.

**3 Add the rice and serve** Mix the hot rice into the wok or pan. Sprinkle with the seeds and fork through.

**Swaps** You can vary the vegetables as you like depending on what is available. Try strips of **zucchini, eggplant, peppers,** or **fennel.** Or use **2 x ⅔-lb (300-g) packs stir-fry vegetables.**

# Lebanese **Bulgur** Wheat and **Feta Salad**

Bulgur wheat makes a tasty base for a fast salad. Here it is combined with herbs, olives, some al dente vegetables and crumbly feta cheese, all tossed in a spicy dressing. Great with iceberg lettuce and chunks of sesame-seed bread.

**Serves 4** Ⓥ

1½ cups (375 mL) bulgur wheat

2½ cups (625 mL) boiling water

¼ lb (125 g) green beans, halved

2 tbsp (25 mL) olive oil

juice of 1 lemon

1 tsp (5 mL) each ground cinnamon, cumin and coriander

1 oz (30 g) chives, snipped

⅓ oz (10 g) fresh coriander, chopped

⅓ oz (10 g) fresh mint, chopped

12 pitted black olives, sliced

3 tbsp (45 mL) sliced marinated or roasted peppers

1 large tomato, chopped, or ½ lb (250 g) cherry tomatoes, halved

5 oz (150 g) feta cheese, crumbled

**Each serving provides**
• 359 cals • 12 g protein
• 16 g fat of which 6 g saturates
• 42 g carbohydrate

**1 Prepare the bulgur wheat**
Tip the bulgur wheat into a large heatproof bowl and cover with the boiling water. Stir in 1 tsp (5 mL) salt and leave to stand for 15-20 minutes or until absorbed, then use a fork to fluff up the grains.

**2 Cook the beans** While the bulgur wheat is soaking, blanch the green beans in a small pot of boiling water for 1-2 minutes, or in a covered bowl with 1 tbsp (15 mL) water in the microwave for 3 minutes on High. Drain, rinse under cold running water and drain again.

**3 Make the dressing** Mix together the oil, lemon juice, spices and a little salt and ground black pepper. Stir into the bulgur.

**4 Assemble the salad** Mix the green beans into the bulgur wheat with the chives, herbs, olives, peppers and chopped tomato or cherry tomatoes. Add the feta cheese and gently fork through the salad.

**Swap** For green beans, use **broccoli florets or frozen soy beans,** but cook for 3-4 minutes at step 2.

**Warm chicken and almond salad**
Instead of the olives, peppers, tomato and feta cheese, use **1 coarsely grated carrot** and **¼ cucumber,** chopped. While the bulgur wheat is soaking at step 1, heat a wok or frying pan with **1 tbsp (15 mL) olive oil** and stir-fry **14 oz (400 g) skinless chicken breast fillet,** cut into strips, with **1 crushed garlic clove** and **1 tsp (5 mL) grated fresh ginger** for 7-8 minutes or until just cooked through. Season, remove from the heat and mix in **3 tbsp (45 mL) Greek-style yogurt** and **3 tbsp (45 mL) toasted flaked almonds.** Serve the salad with the chicken on top, garnished with more flaked almonds.

## ...another idea

# Lamb with Apricot
## and Pine Nut Couscous

Hot chili, aromatic cumin and lemon-flavoured pan-fried lamb accompany
a light and fluffy couscous in this super-fast dish. It's perfect served with
steamed whole green beans or small zucchini.

**10**mins
prep/plus
soaking

**10**
mins cook
time

**Serves 4**
1⅛ cups (275 mL) couscous
1¾ oz (50 g) ready-to-eat dried
   apricots, chopped
2¼ cups (550 mL) boiling stock,
   made with stock cubes
2 tbsp (25 mL) olive oil
14 oz (400 g) lamb stir-fry strips
   or leg steaks, thinly sliced
2 large garlic cloves, crushed
1 large fresh red chili peppers,
   seeded and thinly sliced
1 tsp (5 mL) ground cumin
1 tsp (5 mL) paprika, plus extra
   for dusting
juice of 1 lemon
4 tbsp (60 mL) sour cream
4 tbsp (60 mL) toasted pine
   nuts, plus extra to serve
2 tbsp (25 mL) chopped fresh
   coriander

**Each serving provides**
• 465 cals • 26 g protein
• 26 g fat of which 3 g saturates
• 32 g carbohydrate

You can soak a 1-lb (500-g) pack of
couscous using 3¼ cups (800 mL)
boiling water or stock, and chill or
freeze half the quantity. Frozen
couscous must be eaten within
three months. Reheat the couscous
in the microwave for 4-5 minutes
on high until light and fluffy,
forking through the grains once.

### ...get ahead

**1 Soak the couscous** Put the couscous and apricots into
a heatproof bowl and mix in 1⅔ cup (400 mL) stock,
1 tbsp (15 mL) oil and 1 tsp (5 mL) salt. Set aside so that
the liquid can be absorbed while you prepare the lamb.

**2 Cook the lamb** When the grains have been soaking
for 10 minutes, heat the remaining oil in a large nonstick
frying pan and stir-fry the lamb strips with the garlic, chili
pepper, cumin and paprika for about 7 minutes or until
nicely browned and just tender. Add the remaining stock
and bring to the boil, stirring to loosen the residue on the
base of the pan. Season and squeeze over the lemon
juice, then mix in the sour cream.

**3 Assemble the couscous** Fork through the couscous
quite briskly to separate the grains. Mix in the pine nuts
and coriander, then divide among four plates. Top with
the creamy lamb and garnish with more pine nuts and
a light dusting of paprika.

### Curried vegetables and couscous
This is a great way to use up leftover vegetables and meat
from a roast dinner. Cut all the lean **meat from a cooked
joint** into small dice. Cut any **leftover vegetables** (roast
potatoes, carrots, parsnips) into small chunks (allow about
3½ oz/100 g per person). Soak the couscous and apricots as
step 1. Heat a wok with **1 tbsp (15 mL) olive oil** and add the
meat with **1 crushed garlic clove**, a ¾-in. (2-cm) piece
**fresh ginger**, peeled and grated and **1 large red chili
pepper**, seeded and chopped. Sprinkle in **1 tbsp (15 mL)
mild curry powder or curry paste**. Stir-fry for 2-3 minutes,
then toss in the vegetables and cook until hot. Season, then
mix into the couscous.

### Moroccan couscous Ⓥ
Soak the couscous as step 1 but omit the apricots.
Meanwhile, cook **1 sliced onion** in **2 tbsp (25 mL) olive
oil** with **2 crushed garlic cloves** and a ¾-in. (2-cm) piece
**fresh ginger**, peeled and grated, for 5 minutes. Mix in
**2 tsp (10 mL) harissa paste**, or to taste. Season, then add
**2 x 14-oz (398-mL) cans chickpeas**, drained and rinsed.
Add a **9-oz (280-g) jar of roasted red peppers or
marinated eggplant**. Stir lightly and cook for 3 minutes.
Mix into the couscous.

### ...more ideas

# Italian Cheese **Polenta**
## with Quick Ratatouille

If you need comfort food fast, make a spicy ratatouille and serve it with delicious creamy polenta flavoured with fontina or dolcelatte cheese.

**Serves 4** ⓥ

**2 tbsp (25 mL) olive oil**

**1 red onion, cut into thin wedges**

**2 garlic cloves, crushed**

**1 red or yellow pepper, sliced**

**1 medium-large zucchini, cut into small chunks**

**1 small eggplant, cut into small chunks**

**1 large red chili pepper, seeded and sliced**

**4 cups (1 L) boiling water**

**7 oz (200 g) polenta**

**5 oz (150 g) fontina or dolcelatte cheese, cubed**

**14 oz (398 mL) can chopped tomatoes with basil**

**½ oz (15 g) fresh basil leaves, torn, plus extra to garnish (optional)**

**Each serving provides** • 424 cals • 14 g protein • 19 g fat of which 9 g saturates • 49 g carbohydrate

### Polenta toast with sautéed mushrooms ⓥ

Make grilled polenta (see Cooking tip). Meanwhile, slice **½ lb (250 g) chestnut or large, flat mushrooms** and **3½ oz (100 g) oyster or shiitake mushrooms**, or use other mushrooms in season. Pan-fry in a large frying pan with **1 tbsp (15 mL) each olive oil and butter**, stirring frequently, until the mushrooms begin to wilt. Add **1 crushed garlic clove, 2 sprigs of fresh thyme and 2 tbsp (25 mL) dry sherry or vermouth**. Season and add **2 tbsp (25 mL) ricotta or mascarpone**. Pile on to the grilled polenta and sprinkle with **grated Parmesan cheese**.

## ...another idea

**1 Make the ratatouille** Heat the oil in large pot over a medium heat and add the onion, garlic, pepper, zucchini, eggplant and chili pepper. Cover the pot and cook, stirring occasionally, for 10 minutes or until the vegetables begin to soften. Add salt and ground black pepper.

**2 Make the polenta** While the ratatouille is cooking, put the boiling water in a large nonstick pot, bring back to the boil and add 1 tsp (5 mL) salt. Pour the polenta into the water in a steady stream with one hand, while you stir with a wooden spoon in the other hand.

**3 Add the cheese** Lower the heat and continue stirring briskly until the polenta begins to thicken and bubble slowly. It should be free from lumps. Half-cover the pot with a lid and cook for 5 minutes, stirring often. Remove from the heat and mix in the cheese. Season with ground black pepper, then cover and set aside.

**4 Add the tomatoes** Stir the tomatoes into the ratatouille and cook for a further 10 minutes or until the vegetables are tender. Add the torn basil. Spoon the polenta onto plates and put the ratatouille on top, with the garnish if using.

**Swap** For fontina or dolcelatte cheese, use **½ cup (125 mL) grated Parmesan, Italian-style hard cheese or grana padano**.

**Cooking tip** Make double the quantity of polenta, then use half with the ratatouille and pour the remainder into a baking tray, spreading it level. Cool until set, then cover and chill. Next day, cut into wedges or squares. Brush with 2 tbsp (25 mL) oil or melted butter, then broil at a high temperature until browned and crisp. Serve with a vegetable or meat sauce.

**30** mins prep/cook time

# Summer Couscous Salad

Toss light and fluffy couscous in a little vinaigrette with grilled vegetables, tender fava beans or peas and chicken and you'll have a wonderfully easy warm salad ready in no time. Serve with a leaf salad.

**10** mins prep/plus soaking    **15** mins cook time

**Serves 4**

1 cup (250 mL) couscous

1⅔ cups (400 mL) boiling water or stock, made with stock cubes

2 green or red peppers, quartered

1 zucchini, quartered lengthwise

5 oz (150 g) frozen fava beans or 3½ oz (100 g) frozen peas

5 tbsp (75 mL) vinaigrette, preferably homemade (page 31)

1-2 tbsp (15-25 mL) lemon juice, to taste

1 cinnamon stick, bruised

4 tbsp (60 mL) toasted flaked almonds, plus extra to serve

14 oz (400 g) cooked chicken, chopped

½ oz (15 g) fresh parsley or coriander, chopped

**Each serving provides** • 473 cals • 39 g protein • 21.5 g fat of which 3 g saturates • 32 g carbohydrate

**1 Soak the couscous** Preheat the grill to high. Mix the couscous with the boiling water or stock and 1 tsp (5 mL) salt, then leave to soak while you cook the vegetables.

**2 Grill the vegetables** While the couscous is soaking, grill the peppers and zucchini for 15 minutes or until browned and just tender, turning them as necessary. Cut into small pieces.

**3 Cook the fava beans** While the peppers are grilling, cook the fava beans or peas in a pot of boiling water for 3 minutes, then drain and rinse under cold running water. Pat dry. If you have time, slip the beans from their skins.

**4 Assemble the salad** Fork through the couscous quite briskly to separate the grains. Add the vinaigrette, lemon juice, cinnamon stick, flaked almonds, the grilled vegetables and chicken. Season, then add the chopped herbs and combine well. Serve, garnished with pieces of lemon, if you like.

**Swap** For a vegetarian version, instead of chicken, use a **14-oz (398-mL) can black, kidney or other beans**, drained and rinsed. Toss them quickly in **2 tbsp (25 mL) vinaigrette dressing or 1 tbsp (15 mL) olive oil and 1 tbsp (15 mL) lemon juice**, then season with black pepper.

**Harissa seafood couscous**
Make the basic recipe, but omit the chicken. Spread ½-1 tsp (2-5 mL) harissa paste over **4 x ¼-lb (125-g) fillets of red mullet or snapper**. Drizzle with a little **extra virgin olive oil** and **lemon juice**, and grill under a medium-high heat for 8-10 minutes or until cooked through. Season the fish. Tip the roasted vegetable couscous salad onto a large serving platter and lay the fillets on top.

**Cooking tip** Harissa paste is an aromatic spice blend. As the strengths of different brands vary, it's wise to add ½ tsp (2 mL) at first.

...another idea

# Quinoa with
## Balsamic Vegetable
# Kebabs

The miracle grain of the Incas, quinoa (pronounced *keen-wa*) makes a colourful and nourishing dish served pilaf-style. Accompany it with quickie vegetable kebabs, drizzled with balsamic vinegar.

**10** mins prep time

**20** mins cook time

**Serves 4** ⓥ

⅔ cup (150 mL) quinoa, rinsed

1⅔ cups (400 mL) hot vegetable stock, made with a stock cube

2 x ½-lb (250-g) packages roasting vegetables, such as wedges of red onion, pepper strips, and chunks of zucchini and squash

2 tbsp (25 mL) sunflower oil

2-3 sprigs of fresh thyme

7 oz (200 g) can corn, drained

1 tbsp (15 mL) butter

¼ lb (125g) frozen peas or sliced green beans

½ lb (250 g) marinated tofu, cut into bite-sized cubes

1 tsp (5 mL) mild chili powder or a few shakes of Tabasco sauce, to taste

3 tbsp (45 mL) chopped fresh parsley

2 tbsp (25 mL) balsamic vinegar

**Each serving provides** • 341 cals • 15 g protein • 15 g fat of which 3 g saturates • 39 g carbohydrate

Quinoa can be cooked, cooled and stored in the freezer for up to three months. To use, microwave from frozen on high for 5 minutes, forking through the grains once.

## ...keep it

**1** **Cook the quinoa** Preheat the oven to 400°F (200°C). Place the quinoa and stock in a large pot, and add ½ tsp (2 mL) salt and ground black pepper. Bring to the boil, then cover and simmer gently for 10 minutes.

**2** **Make the kebabs** While the quinoa is cooking, push the roasting vegetables onto eight metal skewers, brush with the oil and scatter with some leaves from the thyme sprigs. (The kebabs can also be cooked on wooden skewers, but soak them for 15-30 minutes beforehand so that they do not burn in the oven.) Place in a shallow roasting pan and season. Roast for 10-12 minutes or until the vegetables begin to soften.

**3** **Flavour the quinoa** Stir the corn into the pan of quinoa and add the butter, peas or beans and the tofu. Add the chili powder or Tabasco sauce to taste. Cover again and cook gently for a further 5 minutes. Remove from the heat and leave to stand for 5 minutes. Add the parsley and fork through.

**4** **Serve** Drizzle the balsamic vinegar over the kebabs and return them to the oven to roast for a further 5 minutes or until just tender. Serve with the quinoa.

**Cooking tips** • Always rinse quinoa thoroughly before using, as it has a natural coating, called saponin, which can give the grain a bitter taste. • Quinoa is a complete protein and you can make it into an even more nourishing meal by serving with a little additional protein and some vegetables.

# Buckwheat
# Cauliflower Cheese

Kasha, or buckwheat, is one the fastest grains to cook. It's a non-wheat grain that has a nutty texture and mildly aromatic flavour which goes very well with vegetables and a creamy cheese sauce.

**15** mins prep time   **15** mins cook time

### Serves 4 ⓥ

1 cup (250 mL) buckwheat groats

1⅔ cups (400 mL) boiling water or stock, made with a stock cube

1⅔-cup (400-mL) mixture of half water and half 1% milk

1 cauliflower, cut into small florets

1 large leek, thinly sliced

3½ oz (100 g) baby leaf spinach

2½ tbsp (30 mL) cornstarch

1 tbsp (15 mL) butter

¼ lb (125 g) aged cheddar cheese, grated

12 cherry tomatoes, halved

**Each serving provides** • 468 cals • 20 g protein • 19 g fat of which 11 g saturates • 58 g carbohydrate

**Addition** Add some **crispy pancetta strips, or cut up and dry-fry a package of bacon** until crisp. Scatter over the vegetables before covering with the sauce.

**1** **Cook the buckwheat** Put the buckwheat and the water or stock into a large pot and add ½ tsp (2 mL) salt and ground black pepper. Bring to the boil, then cover and simmer gently for 10 minutes or until the liquid has been absorbed. Remove from the heat and allow to stand, still covered, for 5 minutes, then fork through the grains.

**2** **Cook the vegetables** While the buckwheat is cooking, put the milk and water into a pot and add a little salt. Add the cauliflower and leek, and cook for 7 minutes or until just tender. Transfer the vegetables with a slotted spoon into a large, shallow, warm ovenproof dish. Mix the buckwheat grains and spinach leaves into the vegetables.

**3** **Make the sauce** Preheat the grill to high. Blend the cornstarch with 3 tbsp (45 mL) cold water to make a paste and stir briskly into the hot milk mixture. Stir over a medium heat until the sauce starts to thicken. Add the butter and simmer for 1 minute, then remove from the heat and stir in two thirds of the cheese until melted. Check the seasoning and pour over the vegetables and grains, mixing in lightly.

**4** **Top the dish** Dot the surface with the tomato halves and scatter with the remaining cheese. Grill until the top is browned and bubbling. Serve hot.

**Cooking tip** Cooled, cooked buckwheat can also be used as the base for a salad. Stir in chopped vegetables and toss with vinaigrette (page 31).

> Buckwheat can be cooked, cooled quickly and frozen for up to one month. To use, reheat in the microwave, partially covered in a bowl, for 4-5 minutes on high, forking through the grains once. To use in a salad, leave to thaw at room temperature for 2-3 hours or thaw in the microwave on high for 3-4 minutes.
>
> **...keep it**

# 5 great meals with a can of **baked beans**

Baked beans are incredibly versatile – and not just for breakfast, brunch or a snack. As long as you have a can in the pantry, you can always create a tasty meal. Try these quick ideas for easy, nutritious, bean-based meals that the whole family will love. All recipes serve 4.

## bean, **cheddar** and potato bake

Preheat the oven to 400°F (200°C). Chop **1 onion** and **2 carrots**, and fry with **1 lb (500 g) lean ground beef**, stirring until lightly browned. Add **1¼ cups (300 mL) beef stock, 1 tbsp (15 mL) Worcestershire sauce** and a **bay leaf or bouquet garni**. Cook gently for 15 minutes. Meanwhile, slice **1⅓ lb (600 g) new potatoes**, then parboil for 8 minutes or until tender. Drain. Remove the bay leaf or bouquet garni, and stir a **14-oz (398-mL) can baked beans** into the ground meat. Warm through. Spoon half the meat and bean mixture into an ovenproof dish and top with half the potato slices. Repeat with the remaining ground meat and potato slices. Sprinkle **½ cup (125 mL) grated mature cheddar cheese** over the top, then bake for 20 minutes or until golden and bubbling.

**Each serving provides** • 437 cals • 39 g protein • 12 g fat of which 5.5 g saturates • 47 g carbohydrate

**25** mins prep time  **20** mins cook time

## **chorizo** and **bean** casserole

Chop **1 onion, 2 carrots, 2 celery sticks, 1 yellow pepper** and **2⅔ oz (75 g) chorizo**. Heat **1 tbsp (15 mL) oil** in a large flameproof casserole or heavy-based pot and cook the vegetables and chorizo for 5 minutes, stirring occasionally, until softened and lightly browned. Add **1⅔ cup (400 mL) chicken stock**, made with a stock cube, a **14-oz (398-mL) can baked beans, 1½ oz (40 g) chopped sun-dried tomatoes, 1 tsp (5 mL) dried thyme** and **1 tsp (5 mL) paprika**. Bring to the boil. Reduce the heat, cover and simmer for 13 minutes. Stir in an **11-oz (350-g) package hot dogs**, cut into bite-sized pieces and return to the boil. Simmer for 2 minutes. Combine **3 oz (90 g) fresh white bread crumbs** with **1 tbsp (15 mL) chopped parsley** and **1 tbsp (15 mL) oil** in a bowl. If using a pan, transfer the bean mixture to a warmed ovenproof dish. Scatter the bread crumbs over the top of the dish or casserole and pop under a hot broiler for 4-5 minutes to crisp and brown before serving.

**Each serving provides** • 506 cals • 22 g protein • 30 g fat of which 10 g saturates • 39 g carbohydrate

**5** mins prep time  **25** mins cook time

# tex-mex **bean burritos**

Heat **1 tbsp (15 mL) canola oil** in a pot. Add **1 chopped onion**, **1 crushed garlic clove**, **1 green chili pepper**, seeded and finely chopped, and **1 chopped red pepper**. Fry for 4-5 minutes or until softened. Stir in a **14-oz (398-mL) can baked beans**, sprinkle with **½ tsp (2 mL) dried oregano** and warm through. Crush the mixture lightly with a fork or potato masher. Heat **8 soft flour tortilla wraps**, one at a time, in a frying pan for about 30 seconds on each side, or in the microwave according to the package instructions. Put bowls containing **1 shredded romaine lettuce**, **1½ cups (375 mL) grated cheddar cheese**, **⅔ cup (150 mL) plain yogurt** and a **ready-made tomato salsa** on the table with the tortillas and the warm bean mixture. To serve, each diner spoons the beans into the middle of a tortilla and tops with the filling ingredients. Roll up the tortilla and eat immediately. Ⓥ

**Each serving provides** • 498 cals • 22 g protein
• 16 g fat of which 7.5 g saturates • 72 g carbohydrate

**15** mins prep time    **10** mins cook time

# curried **veggies** with chapattis

Lightly fry **1 chopped onion** in **1 tbsp (15 mL) oil** in a pan for 4-5 minutes or until softened. Stir in **1 tbsp (15 mL) mild curry powder or paste** and cook for 1 minute. Add **11 oz (350 g) mixed cooked vegetables**, chopped into small pieces (either leftovers or use frozen mixed vegetables, cooked for 3 minutes). Add a **14-oz (398-mL) can baked beans** and **1 tbsp (15 mL) sultanas**. Warm through gently. Warm **8 large or 12 small chapattis** in the microwave according to the pack instructions. Serve the curry immediately with the chapattis, **Greek-style yogurt and/or mango chutney**. Ⓥ

**Each serving provides** • 399 cals • 17 g protein
• 5 g fat of which 0.5 g saturates • 76 g carbohydrate

**10** mins prep time    **10** mins cook time

# baked bean **soup**

Heat **1 tbsp (15 mL) canola oil** in a large pan. Chop and lightly fry **1 onion**, **1 carrot**, **2 celery sticks** and **2 chopped slices of back (Canadian) bacon or bacon strips** for 10 minutes. Add a **14-oz (398-mL) can baked beans** with **1¼ cups (300 mL) each of vegetable stock and tomato juice**. Add a splash of **Worcestershire sauce** and a pinch each of **paprika** and **mixed herbs**, then cover and cook gently for 10 minutes or until the vegetables are tender. Serve hot with crusty rolls or French bread.

**Each serving provides** • 162 cals • 9 g protein
• 4.5 g fat of which 1 g saturates • 23 g carbohydrate

**Cooking tip** To serve to young children, whirl in a blender and thin with a little more water, if you like.

**10** mins prep time    **20** mins cook time

# Bacon and Bean Stew

Butternut squash, green beans and corn make a superb combination in this fast and tasty stew, based on a Native American dish. Serve with crusty bread.

**10** mins prep time

**20** mins cook time

**Serves 4**

2 tbsp (25 mL) olive oil

1 red onion, roughly chopped

1 garlic clove, crushed

2 lb (1 kg) butternut squash, peeled and cut into ¾-in. (2-cm) cubes

14 oz (398 mL) can chopped tomatoes

1¼ cups (300 mL) ham or vegetable stock, made with stock cubes

6-8 sun-dried tomatoes, roughly chopped

4 slices back (Canadian) bacon

1⅓ cups (325 mL) frozen corn

1⅓ cups (325 mL) frozen green beans

2 tbsp (25 mL) chopped fresh parsley

**Each serving provides** • 426 cals • 27 g protein • 19 g fat of which 4 g saturates • 39 g carbohydrate

**1 Fry the flavourings and squash** Heat the oil in a large flameproof casserole or pot. Add the onion, garlic and squash, and cook gently for 5 minutes or until softened.

**2 Add the tomatoes** Stir in the canned tomatoes, stock and sun-dried tomatoes. Bring to the boil, then reduce the heat. Cover and cook gently for 10 minutes. Preheat the grill to medium-high.

**3 Cook the bacon** While the vegetables are cooking, fry the bacon on both sides until crisp.

**4 Add the corn and beans** When the tomatoes and squash have been cooking for 10 minutes, stir the corn and green beans into the vegetable stew. Bring back to the boil, then cover and cook gently for a further 5 minutes or until all the vegetables are cooked. Season.

**5 Serve** Lay the bacon over the top of the vegetable stew, sprinkle with parsley and serve immediately.

**Cooking tip** If you use jarred sun-dried tomatoes in oil, you could replace the olive oil with the oil in the jar.

---

● If you have some stew left over, turn it into a delicious soup for another meal by adding extra stock. Mix the stew in a blender or food processor for a smooth consistency – or just do it partially to leave it slightly chunky. Serve sprinkled with grated cheese.

● This is suitable for freezing for one month. To use, thaw, reheat and simmer for 3 minutes.

**...keep it**

# Spicy Three-Bean Salad

Canned legumes are a fantastic convenience food and can be transformed into a healthy meal in moments. Here they are tossed in a spicy dressing with fresh green beans and mozzarella. Enjoy with warm garlic bread.

20 mins prep time · 5 mins cook time

**Serves 4** Ⓥ

- ¼ lb (125 g) green beans, halved
- 2 tbsp (25 mL) olive oil
- 2 tbsp (25 mL) white wine vinegar
- 1 tsp (5 mL) mild curry powder or smoked paprika
- 1 garlic clove, crushed
- 14 oz (398 mL) can cannellini or red kidney beans, drained and rinsed
- 14-oz (398-mL) can flageolet beans or black-eyed peas, drained and rinsed
- 6 scallions, chopped
- 5 oz (150 g) firm mozzarella, cut into cubes or sticks
- 2 large or 4 medium vine-ripened tomatoes, thinly sliced
- 4 tbsp (60 mL) roughly chopped fresh flat-leaf parsley or coriander

**Each serving provides** • 286 cals • 17.5 g protein • 14.5 g fat of which 6 g saturates • 21 g carbohydrate

**Swap** For mozzarella, use cubes of **feta, Stilton or cheddar cheese**.

**1 Cook the beans** Cook the green beans in a pot of boiling salted water for 3-5 minutes, then drain and rinse under cold running water. Drain again and tip into a large bowl.

**2 Make the dressing** Put the oil into a screw-top jar with the vinegar, curry powder or paprika and the garlic. Add ½ tsp (2 mL) sea salt and ground black pepper, and shake well to blend.

**3 Finish the salad** Tip the canned beans into the bowl together with the scallions and mozzarella. Toss with the dressing.

**4 Serve** Lay the tomato slices on a large serving plate and spoon the dressed beans and mozzarella on top. Scatter with the parsley or coriander. If you have time, chill before serving.

**Addition** Add an **avocado**, halved, peeled and pitted, then cut into chunky pieces.

# Chinese Shrimp and Bean Sprouts

Here's perfect fast-food for busy people who need lots of energy: jumbo shrimp mixed with nutritious bean sprouts and vegetables in a colourful, multi-textured noodle dish.

**10** mins prep time

**10** mins cook time

**Serves 4**

7 oz (200 g) egg noodles

2 tsp (10 mL) toasted sesame oil

3 tbsp (45 mL) canola oil

small bunch of scallions, chopped

2 large garlic cloves, crushed

1 large fresh green chili pepper, halved, seeded and thinly sliced

½ lb (250 g) package stir-fry vegetables

1¼ cups (300 mL) chicken or vegetable stock, made with stock cubes

5 oz (150 g) button mushrooms, sliced

5 oz (150 g) fresh lentil or mung bean sprouts, or other sprouted beans

2 tbsp (25 mL) soy sauce

⅔ lb (300 g) cooked, peeled jumbo shrimp

3 eggs, beaten

Each serving provides • 476 cals • 32 g protein • 20 g fat of which 4 g saturates • 43 g carbohydrate

**1 Prepare the noodles** Soak or cook the noodles according to the package instructions. Drain, then toss with the sesame oil and set aside.

**2 Cook the vegetables** Heat a wok or large pot with 4 tsp (20 mL) of the vegetable oil and stir-fry the scallions, garlic, chili pepper and packaged vegetables for 3 minutes. Stir in the stock and bring to the boil. Add the mushrooms and lentil or mung bean sprouts. Cook for another 2-3 minutes.

**3 Add the jumbo shrimp** Stir in the soy sauce, then add the jumbo shrimp and cook for 1-2 minutes if fresh, 3 minutes if frozen. Toss in the noodles and reheat thoroughly.

**4 Cook the eggs** Heat the remaining oil in a small pan. Season the eggs and pour into the pan. Fry, gently stirring to scramble the eggs slightly, until lightly set into large, soft curds. Mix into the noodles and serve immediately.

**Swap** For a vegetarian version, omit the jumbo shrimp and add **3½ oz (100 g) roughly chopped cashew nuts**.

# Lemony Puy Lentils
## with Curry-Dusted Scallops

**Dainty dark-green Puy lentils are regarded as the best-tasting lentils, and they cook the fastest, too. For a mid-week treat serve them with fresh scallops, jazzed up with a little curry, and rice or bread.**

**30 mins prep/cook time**

### Serves 4

**7 oz (200 g) Puy lentils**

**1⅔ cups (400 mL) boiling water or stock, made with a stock cube**

**1 small carrot, peeled and chopped**

**½ small fennel bulb, thinly sliced**

**1 shallot, sliced**

**1 tsp (5 mL) mild curry powder**

**14 oz (400 g) fresh scallops, rinsed and dried with paper towel**

**2 tbsp (25 mL) extra virgin olive oil**

**1 tsp (5 mL) grated lemon zest**

**2 tbsp (25 mL) lemon juice**

**3 tbsp (45 mL) fresh parsley, chopped**

**7 oz (200 g) bag of salad (such as spinach, arugula and watercress)**

**Each serving provides** • 340 cals • 37 g protein • 9 g fat of which 1 g saturates • 30 g carbohydrate

Cook the lentils as for step 1 above, then add 3 tbsp (45 mL) vinaigrette (page 31) and let cool. Serve as a salad mixed with cold cooked rice, chopped vegetables or pasta.

**...or try this**

**1 Cook the lentils** Put the lentils into a pot with the boiling water or stock, the carrot, fennel and shallot. Bring back to the boil, then cover and simmer gently for 12-15 minutes or until the lentils are just tender and most of the liquid has been absorbed. Drain the lentils, leaving just enough liquid to moisten.

**2 Prepare the scallops** While the lentils are cooking, put the curry powder and a little fine sea salt onto a plate and roll the scallops in the mixture to coat lightly.

**3 Dress the lentils** Season the lentils and mix with half the oil. Mix in the lemon zest and juice, and the parsley. Divide the lentils among four warmed plates and scatter the salad leaves on top.

**4 Cook the scallops** Heat the remaining olive oil in a large nonstick frying pan and add the scallops in a circle in the pan. Cook for 1-2 minutes, then turn the scallops over in the same order in which you placed them (to ensure even cooking). Cook for 1 minute, then immediately remove and place on top of the lentils. Serve.

**Shopping tip** Puy lentils come from a defined area in France and have their own *appellation contrôlée*. Canadian *lentilles vertes* (green lentils) are similar. This recipe would also work well with the slightly larger green or brown continental lentils, which are much cheaper but take a little longer to cook (up to 25 minutes, depending on size). All lentils can be cooked without pre-soaking.

# Cassoulet of Cannellini Beans, Duck and Toulouse Sausage

A traditional French cassoulet would take several hours to cook, but you can make this shortcut version using canned beans and succulent, quick-browned duck breasts, then leave it to bubble on the stovetop. Serve with crusty garlic bread and steamed Savoy cabbage.

**15** mins prep time

**25** mins cook time

### Serves 4

2 tbsp (25 mL) olive oil

3 fresh Toulouse or spicy sausages

2 skinless duck breast fillets, cut into bite-sized chunks

¼ lb (125 g) chopped bacon

1 onion, chopped

3 garlic cloves, crushed

14 oz (398 mL) can cannellini beans, drained and rinsed

14 oz (398 mL) can chopped tomatoes with herbs

2 sprigs of fresh thyme

**Each serving provides** • 346 cals • 26 g protein • 19 g fat of which 5 g saturates • 17 g carbohydrate

**1 Brown the meats** Heat 1 tbsp (15 mL) oil in a large flameproof casserole or heavy-based pan and brown the sausages all over for 5 minutes. Remove from the pan and add the duck pieces and bacon. Stir-fry until browned all over.

**2 Add the vegetables** Add the onion and garlic to the casserole or pan, and cook for 5 more minutes. Cut each sausage into four pieces and return to the casserole or pan, followed by the beans, the tomatoes, thyme and seasoning.

**3 Finish the cassoulet** Bring to the boil, then simmer gently, uncovered, for 15-20 minutes or until the liquid is slightly reduced. Serve.

**Cooking tip** You can give the cassoulet a traditional topping, if you have time. Preheat the grill to high, then scatter **4 tbsp (60 mL) dried bread crumbs** over the cassoulet at the end of step 3. Grill until the crumbs turn golden (if necessary, wrap a wooden handle with foil to protect it from the heat of the grill).

### Flageolet and monkfish cassoulet

Instead of the duck and sausages, use **14 oz (400 g) monkfish fillets** (black membrane removed), cut into 1¼-in. (3-cm) chunks. Lightly brown the monkfish at step 1 for 2-3 minutes. Increase the **bacon to 7 oz (200 g)** and use a **14-oz (398-mL) can of flageolet beans** instead of the cannellini beans. Cook the cassoulet for 15 minutes, adding the monkfish for the last 5-7 minutes of cooking. Serve with lightly steamed Swiss chard or spinach.

### Vegetarian cassoulet ⓥ

Omit all the meats and use **3 smoked garlic cloves** instead of fresh. Add **1 chopped fennel bulb** and **1 peeled and chopped carrot** to the onion at step 2, and use **2 cans each of the tomatoes and beans**. For a more substantial dish, add a **7-oz (200-g) package smoked or marinated tofu**, cubed. Make the bread-crumb topping (see Cooking tip), adding **3 tbsp (45 mL) grated Parmesan or Italian-style hard cheese**.

**...more ideas**

# Hot and Spicy Pepper, Rice and Beans

Rustle up a speedy version of the popular West Indian classic rice 'n' peas for a delicious, nourishing one-pot meal, and give it a real kick with hot chili peppers – if you're brave enough. Serve with a baby spinach and iceberg lettuce salad.

## Serves 4

- 2 tbsp (25 mL) vegetable oil
- 1 large onion, chopped
- 1 red pepper, chopped
- 2 large garlic cloves, crushed
- 1-2 red chili peppers, to taste, seeded and chopped (see Shopping tip)
- 5 oz (150 g) chorizo sausage, or other spicy cured sausage, cubed
- 1⅓ cups (325 mL) basmati rice, rinsed
- 14 oz (398 mL) can coconut milk
- 2½ cups (600 mL) boiling water, or chicken stock made with stock cubes
- 2 sprigs of fresh thyme, plus extra to garnish
- 1 bay leaf
- 14 oz (398 mL) can black-eyed peas, kidney beans or gunga peas, drained

**Each serving provides** • 645 cals • 18 g protein • 32 g fat of which 16 g saturates • 71 g carbohydrate

**1 Fry the vegetables** Heat the oil in a large, heavy-based pot, and cook the onion, pepper, garlic and chili peppers for 5 minutes or until just softened.

**2 Add the rice** Toss in the cubed sausage, then the rice, and stir-fry for 1-2 minutes. Pour in the coconut milk and water or stock. Season and bring to the boil. Stir in the herbs, then cover and simmer gently for 10 minutes.

**3 Add the beans** Stir in the beans, and cook for a further 5 minutes or until the rice is tender and the beans heated through. Serve, sprinkled with a little thyme.

**Shopping tip** Go as hot as you dare – try Scotch bonnet, habanero or bird's eye chili peppers.

**30** mins prep/cook time

# fish

# Salmon Puffs with Tzatziki

These scrumptious cut-and-fold pastries are irresistible dunked in tzatziki, the Greek-style cucumber and yogurt dip. Serve with boiled new potatoes and crunchy salad leaves.

**Serves 4**

¾ lb (375 g) pack pre-rolled puff pastry

5⅓ oz (160 g) skinless salmon fillet, cut into ½-in. (1-cm) squares

¼ lb (125 g) frozen fava beans

1 oz (30 g) fresh fennel or dill, chopped

1 oz (30 g) snipped fresh chives

1 egg, beaten

½ cup (125 mL) ricotta cheese

½ cucumber

1 cup (250 mL) Greek-style yogurt

1 garlic clove, crushed (optional)

**Each serving provides** • 548 cals • 22 g protein • 35 g fat of which 5 g saturates • 40 g carbohydrate

**10** mins prep time

**20** mins cook time

**1 Make the filling** Remove the pack of pastry from the fridge and, if time allows, leave it, still wrapped, at room temperature for 20 minutes. Preheat the oven to 460°F (240°C). Put the salmon squares in a bowl and add the frozen fava beans and herbs. Season and mix well.

**2 Fill the puffs** Unroll the pastry, leaving it on its paper, then cut it into four 7 x 3⅓-in. (17.5 x 8.5-cm) pieces. Brush the egg lightly all over the pastry. Divide the salmon mixture among the pastry pieces, mounding it in the centre and leaving a border of pastry at top and bottom and keeping the long ends clear on either side. Place the ricotta cheese in small dollops on each mound of filling. Fold the long ends of the pastry up to meet over the filling and pinch them together at the top. Press the sides together to seal in the filling.

**3 Bake the pastries** Transfer the pastries to a baking sheet and brush with egg. Bake for 20 minutes or until puffed and golden.

**4 Make the tzatziki** While the pastries are baking, grate the cucumber into a sieve and press out the excess moisture over the sink. Mix the cucumber into the yogurt with the garlic, if using. Transfer the tzatziki to a serving bowl and serve with the hot salmon puffs.

**Swaps** • For salmon, use **cooked, peeled jumbo shrimp or flaked, smoked mackerel**. • For broad beans, use frozen **peas or corn**. • For fennel or dill, use **watercress**.

● Line the baking sheet with parchment paper or foil to save cleaning time.
● Buy good-quality tzatziki instead of making your own.

**...speed it up**

# Aromatic Steamed Mullet
## with Young Vegetables

Bay, lime and olive oil create a delicately aromatic sauce for mullet cooked in parcels, topped with a sprinkling of sorrel. Serve with steamed vegetables for a stylish, no-fuss meal.

**Serves 4**

**1 lb (500 g) washed new potatoes**

**2 leeks, sliced**

**½ lb (250 g) baby carrots**

**1 lime**

**4 red mullet fillets, about 3½ oz (100 g) each**

**12 thin cucumber slices**

**4 bay leaves**

**8 tsp (40 mL) olive oil**

**4 small zucchini, halved lengthwise**

**1 oz (30 g) fresh sorrel leaves, finely shredded**

Each serving provides • 312 cals • 24 g protein • 11 g fat of which 1 g saturates • 30 g carbohydrate

**1 Boil the potatoes** Cook the potatoes in a pot of boiling water for 10 minutes or until tender. Drain. Meanwhile, prepare a large pot of boiling water with a large steamer on top. Cut four pieces of foil, each large enough to enclose a folded fish fillet.

**2 Prepare the vegetables** Arrange the leeks in the steamer with the carrots, in one layer if possible, then set aside. Grate the zest from the lime, or use a zester, and set aside in a small bowl. Cut the lime into quarters.

**3 Make the fish parcels** Lay a fish fillet skin side down on each piece of foil. Top the wide end of each fillet with 3 cucumber slices and a bay leaf. Season to taste. Lightly squeeze a little juice from a lime quarter over each fillet and fold the narrow end over. Top with the squeezed lime quarters. Drizzle 2 tsp (10 mL) olive oil over each. Bring the foil up to enclose the fillets in neat parcels that will fit inside the steamer. Set the parcels aside.

**4 Steam the vegetables** Cook the prepared vegetables in the steamer for 5 minutes. Put the zucchini on top of the partly-cooked vegetables, cut sides up. Add the foil parcels and steam for a further 10 minutes or until all the vegetables are tender and the fish is cooked.

**5 Add the flavourings** Open the foil parcels and sprinkle a little lime zest and shredded sorrel into each. Divide the vegetables among four plates. Transfer the fish to the plates using a slotted spatula, then pour the juices from the foil over. Serve immediately.

Swaps • For red mullet, use **Alaska pollock or Pacific sole fillets**. • For sorrel, use **parsley, or a mixture of parsley, dill and a little tarragon**. Alternatively, for a stronger flavour use **arugula or watercress**.

### Chinese-style striped bass

Follow the basic recipe but use **striped bass** fillets instead of red mullet and omit the lime. Add **1 shredded scallion** and **1 tsp (5 mL) grated fresh ginger** to each fillet instead of the cucumber and bay. Sprinkle them with **1 tsp (5 mL) each of toasted sesame oil, dry sherry and light soy sauce** mixed together, instead of the olive oil. Steam **7 oz (200 g) baby corn, baby carrots and snow peas** and **7 oz (200 g) asparagus stalks** (woody ends removed) as step 4, instead of the carrots and leeks. Add **7 oz (200 g) halved bok choy** in place of the zucchini 4 minutes before the end of the cooking time. Omit the sorrel and sprinkle with a little **chopped fresh coriander**, if you like.
Serve with plain cooked rice.

...another idea

# Grilled Lemon **Alaska Pollock**
## with Golden Couscous and Fennel

A bed of couscous spiced with turmeric and flavoured with fennel soaks up the buttery cooking juices from grilled Alaska pollock – an amazingly fast meal that looks and tastes terrific.

**10** mins prep time  **6** mins cook time

**Serves 4**

1¼ cups (300 mL) couscous

1 tsp (5 mL) turmeric

2 tbsp (25 mL) olive oil

4 white-skinned Alaska pollock fillets, about 5⅔ oz (160 g) each

2 fennel bulbs

2 scallions, sliced

2 tbsp (25 mL) capers

1 lemon

2½ tbsp (40 mL) butter

**Each serving provides** • 448 cals • 32 g protein • 16 g fat of which 6 g saturates • 42 g carbohydrate

**1** **Soak the couscous** Put the couscous in a heatproof bowl and stir in the turmeric. Pour in boiling water to cover the couscous by just under ½ in. (1 cm). Do not stir. Cover the bowl and set aside.

**2** **Prepare the Alaska pollock** Preheat the grill to high. Brush the grill pan lightly with a little of the olive oil. Lay the pollock fillets skin side up in the pan. Brush the skin lightly with olive oil. Set aside.

**3** **Slice the fennel** Prepare the fennel while the grill heats up: Reserve any fronds for garnish, cut the bulbs in half, discard any tough core and then slice them finely. Separate the slices into thin shreds and put them into a bowl. Add the scallions, capers and remaining olive oil. Mix well.

**4** **Cook the Alaska pollock** Grill the Alaska pollock for 3-4 minutes or until the skin is beginning to brown. Turn the fillets using a slotted spatula. Grate the zest from the lemon, or use a zester, and sprinkle it over the fish. Cut the lemon into eight wedges and arrange them in the grill pan. Dot the butter over the fillets and season. Grill for 1-2 minutes or until the fish is firm and just cooked.

**5** **Flavour the couscous** Toss the couscous with the fennel mixture and divide it among four warm plates. Add the Alaska pollock and hot lemon wedges. Pour over the cooking juices and serve immediately, garnished with fennel fronds.

**Swaps** • For Alaska pollock, try some of the following: **trout fillets**, (you will need 2 per portion if they are small); **hake steaks or fillet portions**, allowing 2-4 minutes cooking on the second side; portions of skinless **salmon fillet**, allowing 2-3 minutes cooking on the second side.

Make and freeze savoury butters to add instant flavour and a sauce to grilled, steamed or baked fish. Mix the butter with the flavouring, shape it into a roll about 1¼ in. (3 cm) in diameter, wrap in plastic wrap and chill until firm. Slice the roll into thin slices and freeze uncovered on a tray, then pack in a bag. To use, add one or two slices to each piece of cooked fish – the butter will melt to make a tasty sauce. With ½ lb (250 g) softened butter, try the following ideas:

• the grated **zest of 1 lemon, 1 tbsp (15 mL) lemon juice** and **6 tbsp (90 mL) chopped parsley**.

• **1 tbsp (15 mL) English mustard** and **4 tbsp (60 mL) chopped fresh tarragon**.

• **2 tbsp (25 mL) finely chopped fresh ginger, 2 chopped scallions** and the **grated zest of 1 lime**.

• **1 seeded and chopped fresh green chili pepper, 4 tbsp (60 mL) snipped fresh chives** and **4 tbsp (60 mL) chopped fresh coriander**.

**...flavoured butters for fish**

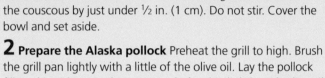

# Mustard-Mayo Pacific Halibut
## with Tarragon-Orange Zucchini

Make an easy, creamy mustard and mayonnaise topping for plain grilled halibut, then enjoy with grilled zucchini sprinkled with citrus zest and herbs, and crusty French bread.

**Serves 4**

1 tbsp (15 mL) olive oil

4 zucchini, halved

4 Pacific halibut fillets, about 3 oz (90 g) each

4 tbsp (60 mL) mayonnaise

2 tsp (10 mL) Dijon mustard

leaves from 2 sprigs of fresh tarragon

coarsely grated zest of 1 orange

orange wedges, to serve

**Each serving provides** • 227 cals • 18 g protein • 16 g fat of which 2 g saturates • 2 g carbohydrate

**1** **Grill the zucchini** Preheat the broiler to high. Brush an ovenproof dish with a little oil and lay the zucchini inside, cut side down. Brush with a little oil and broil for 3 minutes. Turn the zucchini, brush with oil and cook for a further 4-5 minutes or until browned and tender. Set aside in their dish.

**2** **Cook the halibut** While the zucchini are broiling, prepare the halibut. Brush the grill pan with a little oil and put the fillets in it, skin side down. Mix the mayonnaise and mustard, then spread this evenly over the fish. Put the pan under the broiler and cook for about 5 minutes. The topping should be golden and the fish firm and cooked through. If the fish begins to brown too quickly in the first 1-2 minutes of cooking, lower the pan so that it is farther away from the heat.

**3** **Serve** Sprinkle the tarragon and orange zest over the zucchini. Transfer the halibut to warm plates and add the zucchini. Garnish with orange wedges and serve.

**Swaps** • For Pacific halibut, use **Dover sole**. The skin is tough and the fillets thin, so they cook quickly, and the skin is not eaten. • Or use **whiting fillets**. If they are fairly thick, broil them skin side up for 2 minutes, then turn them over and spread with the mayonnaise mixture. Finish cooking as in the basic recipe.

**20 mins** prep/cook time

### Smoked haddock with mustard

Lay **4 portions of smoked haddock fillet** in a dish and pour over boiling water to cover them generously. Cover and leave to stand for 5 minutes or until the fish is part-cooked. Transfer the fillets to the lightly oiled grill pan using a slotted spatula, as step 2, and finish as for the basic recipe, using **3 tbsp (45 mL) ricotta cheese** instead of the mayonnaise, and **whole-grain mustard** instead of Dijon mustard. Serve with the tarragon-orange zucchini.

## ...another idea

# Honey and Mustard Salmon
## with Crushed Lima Beans and Spinach

Turn a fillet of salmon into something special with a super-fast sticky marinade and serve with wilted spinach, crushed lima beans from your pantry and bread or new potatoes.

**Serves 4**

1 tbsp (15 mL) canola oil

1 tbsp (15 mL) soy sauce

2 tsp (10 mL) clear honey

2 tsp (10 mL) whole-grain mustard

grated zest and juice of 1 lemon

4 skinless salmon fillets, about
4 oz (125 g) each

2 x 14-oz (398-mL) cans butter
beans, drained and rinsed

1 large garlic clove, crushed

2 tbsp (25 mL) extra virgin olive oil

pinch of crushed chili flakes

7 oz (200 g) fresh baby leaf spinach,
rinsed

12 vine-ripened cherry tomatoes

**Each serving provides** • 410 cals
• 32 g protein • 22 g fat of which
3.5 g saturates • 21 g carbohydrate

**Swap** For salmon, use **mackerel
fillets**.

**5** mins prep time **8** mins cook time

**1** **Make the marinade** In a shallow dish, mix together the vegetable oil, soy sauce, honey, mustard and 1 tbsp (15 mL) of the lemon juice. Add the salmon and coat with the marinade. Set aside.

**2** **Combine the beans and flavourings** Put the butter beans and garlic in a pan with the olive oil, remaining lemon juice, the zest and crushed chili flakes. Set aside.

**3** **Wilt the spinach and heat the beans** Heat a ridged griddle or frying pan until hot. Meanwhile, tip the spinach into a dry pan with only the water that clings to its leaves and stir over a low heat for 2 minutes or until wilted. Drain and set aside. Gently heat the beans.

**4** **Griddle the salmon** Cook the salmon in the heated ridged griddle or frying pan for 2-3 minutes on each side or until just firm and pink. Add the tomatoes for the last 1-2 minutes of the cooking time.

**5** **Crush the beans** Roughly crush the beans with a vegetable masher or fork. Stir in the spinach and seasoning. Divide the beans and spinach among four serving plates. Arrange a salmon fillet on top of each and scatter the tomatoes around the side. Serve at once.

**Cooking tips** • If you have time, leave the salmon to marinate overnight, ready to cook the next day. • Add frozen spinach if fresh is not available, and cook according to the package instructions.

## Baked salmon with avocado salsa

Preheat the oven to 425°F (220°C). Prepare the salmon and its marinade in a shallow ovenproof dish. Bake the salmon, uncovered, for 15 minutes or until it flakes easily and is browned in places. For the salsa, halve, pit and dice **2 avocados**. Add **2 tbsp (25 mL) white wine vinegar**, **2 tbsp (25 mL) chopped candied ginger** and **1 crushed garlic clove**. Snip **4 scallions** and the tender ends and leaves from **1 oz (30 g) fresh coriander** over the salsa. Mix lightly. Serve the salmon with the beans and spinach for the main recipe, with the salsa instead of the tomatoes.

# ...another idea

Wash baby spinach in a colander, then cook it by pouring boiling water over it in the sink and leaving it to wilt. It only takes a few minutes and there's no pan to wash up.

# ...speed it up

# 5 toppings and dressings for grilled and fried fish

Fish makes a perfect meal in a hurry because it cooks so quickly. You can transform it into something extra-special with very little effort by adding a simple topping or dressing. The selections here range from delicate to piquant, and all take just moments to make. Try them on plain baked or steamed fish, as well as grilled or fried. All recipes serve 4.

## buttery **garlic** and **herb** crumbs

In a food processor, whiz **4 slices whole-grain or white bread** into coarse crumbs (or grate a large chunk of bread on a coarse grater). Chop **1 oz (30 g) fresh parsley leaves, 4 large sprigs of fresh dill or fennel** and a **bunch of fresh chives.** Melt **3½ tbsp (50 mL) butter** in a pan, add **1 finely chopped garlic clove,** the crumbs and herbs. Mix well and remove from the heat.

**Each serving provides**
• 176 cals • 3 g protein • 11 g fat of which 7 g saturates • 17 g carbohydrate

**5** mins prep time

**2** mins cook time

● Good on white fish: broil thick fillets on one side, turn and pile on the crumbs for a thick crust, then broil slowly until golden. ● Sprinkle over white fish fillets, cutlets or steaks before baking. ● Fry the crumbs slowly until crisp and pale golden, then sprinkle over plain cooked fish before serving.

**...to use**

Spread out the mixture on a foil-covered baking tray and freeze uncovered, then pack in a freezer bag. Freeze for up to six months. To use, sprinkle the required amount of frozen mixture over the fish and cook as above.

**...keep it**

# simple **mustard** and **dill** dressing

Whisk **2 tsp (10 mL) white (superfine) sugar, 2 tbsp (25 mL) whole-grain mustard** and **3 tbsp (45 mL) cider vinegar** together. Whisk in **6 tbsp (90 mL) extra virgin olive oil** to make a thick dressing. Stir in **4 tbsp (60 mL) chopped dill** and **2 tbsp (25 mL) capers**.

**Each serving provides** • 170 cals • 1 g protein • 17 g fat of which 2 g saturates • 3 g carbohydrate

5 mins prep time

- Pan-fried, griddled or grilled salmon or trout fillets.
- Fish and seafood kebabs, especially chunks of salmon and white fish skewered and grilled until firm.
- Hot-smoked salmon on a mixed-leaf salad.
- Crispy battered calamari rings or filo-wrapped jumbo shrimp (buy chilled or frozen and cook according to the package instructions).

**...serve with**

# black **olive** tapenade

Put a **1.7-oz (48-g) can anchovy fillets** in olive oil (with the oil from the can) into a food processor or blender with **3½ oz (100 g) pitted black olives, 2 garlic cloves, 1 tbsp (15 mL) capers** and the **grated zest and juice of 1 small lemon**. Process until smooth, scraping down the sides of the bowl occasionally. Transfer to a serving dish and serve as a sauce for plain grilled or baked white fish fillets or steaks, or griddled tuna or swordfish.

**Each serving provides** • 52 cals • 3.5 g protein • 4 g fat of which 1 g saturates • 0.5 g carbohydrate

5 mins prep time

- Add the tapenade to the pan juices remaining after frying fish and stir for a few seconds, then spoon over or alongside the fish. • Spread the tapenade thinly over thick whitefish fillets or steaks before grilling. • Toss the tapenade with halved cherry or baby plum tomatoes and grill or fry briefly until just hot. Spoon over grilled or fried whitefish, tuna or mackerel. • Toast slices of baguette and spread with tapenade, then serve with grilled or fried fish, jumbo shrimp or mixed seafood. • Serve the tapenade with warm soft flour tortilla wraps, shredded crisp lettuce and scallions to season and wrap grilled or griddled jumbo shrimp, scallops or strips of tuna.

**...to use**

# quick **tartar** sauce

Finely slice **1 scallion** and mix into **⅔ cup (150 mL) plain low-fat yogurt** and **⅔ cup (150 mL) mayonnaise**. Add **3 tbsp (45 mL) snipped fresh chives, 2 tbsp (25 mL) chopped capers** and **1 chopped small gherkin**. Stir to combine.

**Each serving provides** • 282 cals • 2 g protein • 29 g fat of which 4.5 g saturates • 4 g carbohydrate

5 mins prep time

- Grilled sole, salmon or hake.
- Fish cakes, battered fish or fish fingers.
- Fried bread-crumb-coated fish fillets battered jumbo shrimp or calamari.

**...serve with**

# green sauce

Remove the hard, coarse stems from **1 oz (30 g) fresh parsley, 1 oz (30 g) fresh dill or fennel** and **1 oz (30 g) fresh chives**. Put into a food processor or blender with **2⅔ oz (75 g) watercress**. Use blender to finely chop, then add **1¼ cup (300 mL) Greek-style yogurt** and pulse very briefly to combine the ingredients into a bright green sauce. Stir in a squeeze of **lemon juice**, to taste. Add seasoning, if you like.

5 mins prep time

**Each serving provides** • 117 cals • 6 g protein • 9 g fat of which 5.5 g saturates • 4 g carbohydrate

- Serve with bread-crumb-coated fish, spooning a little over the top. • Grill fillets of hake, haddock or cod with spices or chopped, seeded chili pepper, then spoon over the green sauce – particularly good with lots of mashed or new potatoes. • Top grilled or fried salmon or trout fillets with a drizzle of table cream (optional) and spoon over some green sauce.

**...to use**

# Hasty **Haddock** with Tomato and Red Onion Salsa

A salad-style salsa provides punchy flavour for simply perfect grilled fish. Just add some baby new potatoes and peas for a refreshingly different meal.

**Serves 4**

1 red onion, halved and very thinly sliced

4 tomatoes, halved and cores removed

¼ tsp (1 mL) crushed chili flakes

1 tbsp (15 mL) chopped candied ginger

1 tsp (5 mL) sugar

1 tbsp (15 mL) tomato paste

1 tbsp (15 mL) red wine vinegar

3 tbsp (45 mL) olive oil

4 portions skinless haddock loin or thick fillet, about ¼ lb (125 g) each

mustard greens and garden cress, to garnish

**Each serving provides** • 216 cals
• 24 g protein • 9 g fat of which
1 g saturates • 10 g carbohydrate

**Swap** For haddock, use **hake or whiting**.

**1** **Prepare the salsa** Separate the onion slices into shreds and put them into a bowl. Thinly slice the tomatoes and add to the bowl. Sprinkle in the chili flakes, ginger and sugar, then stir in the tomato paste and vinegar with seasoning to taste. Stir in 2 tbsp (25 mL) of the olive oil and set aside.

**2** **Cook the haddock** Preheat the grill to high. Lightly oil the grill pan, then add the haddock portions, skin side up, and brush with a little of the remaining oil. Cook for 3 minutes. Turn the fish, brush with the remaining oil and cook for a further 3 minutes or until cooked through.

**3** **Serve** Divide the salsa among four plates and lay the haddock portions on top. Garnish with mustard and cress and serve immediately.

**Cooking tip** This recipe will also work with thin fillets; just reduce the cooking time slightly.

**10** mins prep time  **6** mins cook time

**Tuna with cucumber and watercress salsa**
For a green salsa, peel and dice **½ cucumber**, dice **2 celery sticks**, seed and chop **1 green chili pepper**, and shred **2 oz (60 g) watercress**. Mix with the **grated zest and juice of 1 lime** and **2 tbsp (25 mL) extra virgin olive oil**. Broil or griddle **4 tuna steaks** instead of the haddock. Serve with the salsa and with couscous and grilled or sautéed zucchini.

**...another idea**

# Crisp **Haddock** and **Jumbo Shrimp** **Gratin** with Baby Spinach

Frozen jumbo shrimp are a great standby and transform a modest amount of fish into a hearty dish. Serve with mashed potatoes, peas and green beans for irresistible comfort food made easy.

**12** mins prep time **15** mins cook time

**Serves 4**

⅔ lb (300 g) baby spinach leaves

½ lb (250 g) skinless haddock fillet

4 tbsp (60 mL) cornstarch

2½ cups (625 mL) 1% milk

¾ cup (175 mL) aged Cheddar cheese, grated

4 scallions, chopped

a little freshly grated nutmeg

7 oz (200 g) frozen cooked, peeled jumbo shrimp

1 oz (30 g) fresh parsley, chopped

6 bread sticks, plain or sesame flavoured

**Each serving provides** • 408 cals • 35 g protein • 12 g fat of which 7 g saturates • 44 g carbohydrate

**1 Prepare the haddock** Preheat the oven to 425°F (220°C). Spread out the spinach in a deep ovenproof dish large enough to hold the fish in one layer. Cut the haddock into four equal pieces and put them on top of the spinach.

**2 Prepare the sauce** Put the cornstarch in a pot and stir in a little of the milk to make a smooth, thin paste. Gradually stir in the remaining milk, then cook over a low heat, whisking continuously, until the sauce boils and thickens. (The sauce will seem too thick but it will thin down when baked with the cheese, fish and jumbo shrimp.)

**3 Add the flavourings and jumbo shrimp** Whisk in three quarters of the cheese and all the scallions with nutmeg and seasoning to taste. Remove from the heat and stir in the frozen jumbo shrimp and parsley. Immediately pour the sauce over the fish and spinach to cover evenly.

**4 Add the crunchy topping** Snap the bread sticks into short, coarsely crumbled pieces, and sprinkle all over the sauce. Press them in gently so that they are almost submerged. Sprinkle with the remaining cheese. Bake for 15 minutes or until bubbling hot and golden.

**Swaps** • For haddock, use virtually any skinless, boneless fish: **Pacific cod, pollock, whiting, smoked haddock or salmon**. • Or soften **frozen cod steaks** in the microwave for a few seconds, then cut them into chunks and distribute over the spinach. • Or use drained **canned tuna or salmon** instead of the fish or to replace the jumbo shrimp (use the liquid from salmon in the sauce). • For spinach, use **frozen mixed vegetables**. • Instead of mashed potato, **fresh pasta or couscous** are great accompaniments.

---

• To avoid grating and chopping, add 3-4 tbsp (45-60 mL) pesto to the sauce instead of the cheese and parsley.
• Cut up a bundle of scallions in one go, using scissors.
• Bake and serve the gratin in individual ovenproof dishes to cut down on dishes – the cooking time will be the same.

## ...speed it up

# Pacific Cod Parcels with Chorizo

Wrap spicy chorizo sausage in parcels with frozen cod loins and peppers, then leave to bake for a super-convenient, richly flavoured meal. Just serve with a tomato salad and a baguette to mop up the juices.

**10** mins prep time

**30** mins cook time

### Serves 4

**canola oil, for greasing**

**4 frozen thick-cut Pacific cod loins (skinless and boneless), about ¼ lb (125 g) each**

**1 chorizo sausage, about 2 oz (60 g), thinly sliced**

**1 red pepper, cut into strips**

**1 yellow pepper, cut into strips**

**2 tsp (10 mL) balsamic or sherry vinegar**

**1 tbsp (15 mL) chopped fresh parsley (optional)**

Each serving provides • 313 cals • 29 g protein • 12 g fat of which 6 g saturates • 23 g carbohydrate

Swap For cod, use **haddock or pollock**.

1 **Prepare the foil** Preheat the oven to 400°F (200°C). Cut out four 12-in. (30-cm) squares of foil and lightly grease with a little oil.

2 **Add the parcel ingredients** Put a cod loin in the centre of each square of foil. Scatter over the chorizo and pepper strips, and sprinkle each one with ½ tsp (2 mL) vinegar. Season with black pepper.

3 **Bake the parcels** Bring up the edges of the foil and fold together loosely to make four parcels. Put in a roasting pan or shallow ovenproof dish, then bake for 25-30 minutes or until the fish is tender and flakes easily.

4 **Open the parcels** Serve the foil parcels opened on serving plates and sprinkle with parsley, if you like.

Put a partly-baked garlic baguette into the oven 10-15 minutes before the fish is cooked and add 12 cherry tomatoes to the roasting pan or dish with the parcels for the last 5 minutes of cooking.

**...to serve**

Keep a package of frozen sliced mixed peppers in the freezer and use ⅔ lb (300 g) for this recipe.

**...speed it up**

### Pacific halibut parcels with lemon and thyme

Preheat the oven to 425°F (220°C). Make the foil squares as step 1 and lay a skinless **halibut fillet** on each. Top each fillet with 2 sprigs of **fresh thyme**, a little **grated lemon zest** and a knob of **butter**, then fold the tail end over onto the wide end. Close the parcels as step 3, place in a roasting pan and bake for 10 minutes. Cut a **French loaf** into ½-in. (1-cm) thick slices and put onto a baking sheet. Top with **tomato slices**, drizzle with a little **chili oil** and heat in the oven for the last 5 minutes. Sprinkle with **chopped fresh parsley** and serve with the fish.

**...another idea**

# Basque-Style Pacific Cod with Peppers

**Serves 4**

**30 mins** prep/cook time

2 tbsp (25 mL) olive oil

1 onion, halved and thinly sliced

2 large red peppers, thinly sliced into short strips

2 large green peppers thinly sliced into short strips

2 sprigs of fresh oregano

3 garlic cloves, crushed

14 oz (400 g) large ripe tomatoes, diced

2 oz (60 g) pitted black olives, halved

1 tsp (5 mL) sugar

good pinch of chili powder

1 tbsp (15 mL) wine vinegar

14 oz (400 g) skinless thick Pacific cod fillet

1 oz (30 g) flat-leaf parsley, chopped

**Each serving provides** • 224 cals • 22 g protein • 9 g fat of which 1 g saturates • 16 g carbohydrate

**To serve** For a more substantial meal, serve with boiled rice or crushed or mashed potatoes.

This one-pan wonder bursts with tempting colour and flavour from peppers, tomatoes and a hint of chili. Serve with country-style bread and crunchy chicory leaves.

**1 Fry the vegetables** Heat the olive oil in a large, deep frying pan or sauté pan. Add the onion, peppers, oregano and garlic. Cook, stirring occasionally, for 5 minutes or until the vegetables are slightly softened.

**2 Add the flavourings** Add the tomatoes and olives to the pan with the sugar, chili powder and vinegar. Cook over a medium-high heat, stirring frequently, for 3 minutes or until the tomatoes are slightly softened. Add seasoning to taste.

**3 Cook the cod** Cut the cod into four equal portions and add them to the pan, shuffling them down into the vegetables. Reduce the heat so that the vegetables bubble gently. Cover with a piece of foil, crumpling it inside the rim of the pan, and cook for about 5 minutes. The cod should be firm, succulent and opaque, with flakes that just separate. Sprinkle the parsley over the fish and vegetables, and serve in large pasta bowls or soup plates.

**Swaps** • For cod, use **hake**. • For a different flavour and texture, add a minimum of salt when seasoning and sprinkle slivered good-quality **salted almonds** over the cooked fish and vegetables before serving.

**Addition** Spread **7 oz (200 g) pre-cooked mussels** over the cod mixture for the last 3 minutes of cooking time to heat through completely.

• Frozen or bottled peppers, drained, save preparation and cooking time.

• Use a 14-oz (398-mL) can chopped tomatoes instead of diced fresh tomatoes.

**...speed it up**

# Baked Rosemary **Monkfish**
## with Tomatoes and Lime

Rosemary, garlic and lime add zip to monkfish fillets in this stylish and speedy bake. Great with boiled and crushed potatoes laced with a little olive oil, parsley and chives, and some steamed broccoli.

**10** mins prep time

**20** mins cook time

### Serves 4

1 tbsp (15 mL) olive oil

1 lb (500 g) monkfish fillet (black membrane removed), in two pieces

2 large garlic cloves, cut lengthwise into quarters

2 sprigs of fresh rosemary, broken into small sprigs

1 lime

2 tbsp (25 mL) butter

4 tomatoes, halved

**Each serving provides** • 170 cals • 20 g protein • 9 g fat of which 4 g saturates • 3 g carbohydrate

**Swap** For monkfish, use **hake or salmon**.

**1 Prepare the parcels** Preheat the oven to 400°F (200°C). Cut two pieces of foil, each large enough to enclose a piece of monkfish. Brush the foil with a little of the oil.

**2 Flavour the fish** If there is any black membrane remaining on the monkfish fillets, insert a sharp knife underneath it and cut it away. Put one fillet on each piece of foil. Make small cuts all over the fish. Push the pieces of garlic and small sprigs of rosemary into the slits in the fish.

**3 Add lime** Grate the zest from the lime over the fish. Trim off the ends of the lime, then cut it into four thick slices. Squeeze a few drops of juice from the lime slices over the fish, then lay the slices on top of the fillets. Dot with the butter and season to taste.

**4 Seal the parcels** Put the tomatoes, cut side up, alongside the fish. Fold up the foil to enclose the fish and tomatoes completely and seal the edges.

**5 Cook and serve** Put the parcels on a baking tray and bake for 10 minutes. Open the foil and bake for a further 10 minutes or until the fish is opaque and cooked through. Test with the point of a knife. Cut each piece of fish in half and transfer to plates with the tomatoes. Pour over the juices from the parcels and serve immediately.

### Monkfish and pepper kebabs

Cut **1 lb (500 g) monkfish** into bite-sized chunks. Cut **4 red peppers** into chunks. Thread the chunks of fish and pepper and **4 halved tomatoes** on to four metal skewers. Put on greased foil on a baking tray. Sprinkle with the garlic, rosemary, lime zest and seasoning as for the basic recipe. Top with the lime slices and dot with the butter. Fold up the edges of the foil to catch the juices but do not enclose the kebabs completely. Bake for 15-20 minutes, as for the basic recipe, or until the fish and peppers are cooked and lightly browned in places.

### Pacific halibut with ginger and paprika

Cut **1 lb (500 g) boneless Pacific halibut steak** into four equal portions, placing two on each piece of foil as the basic recipe (or wrap in individual foil parcels if you prefer). Soften **2 tbsp (25 mL) butter** and beat with **1 tsp (5 mL) grated fresh ginger**, a **good pinch of dried thyme** and **4 tbsp (60 mL) chopped fresh parsley**. Dot this flavoured butter over the fish, season to taste and sprinkle with a good pinch of **ground paprika**. Wrap and bake as for the basic recipe.

## ...more ideas

# Succulent Hake with
## Walnut, Garlic and Lemon Crust

This tender white fish is enhanced with this quick, herby, full-flavoured crust. Accompany with small pasta shells tossed with a little soft cheese, and a leaf and baby tomato salad.

**10** mins prep time

**15** mins cook time

### Serves 4

2 slices whole-grain bread with crusts, cut into small dice

3 tbsp (45 mL) 1% milk

1 tbsp (15 mL) olive oil

1 lemon

2 scallions, chopped

1-2 large garlic cloves, crushed

½ cup (125 mL) walnut pieces, chopped

1 oz (30 g) fresh flat-leaf parsley, chopped

4 portions skinless hake fillet, about 7 oz (120 g) each

**Each serving provides** • 272 cals • 26 g protein • 15 g fat of which 2 g saturates • 9 g carbohydrate

**1 Make the crust** Preheat the oven to 425°F (220°C). Put the bread into a bowl and pour the milk and oil evenly over. Grate the zest from the lemon, or use a zester, and add to the bread mixture. Add the scallions, garlic, walnuts and parsley. Stir the mixture, pressing it with the back of the spoon to moisten all the bread evenly.

**2 Cook the hake** Put the hake into a shallow ovenproof dish that holds the fillets fairly snugly. Season lightly. Divide the bread mix among the portions of fillet, piling it up and pressing it on firmly to keep it in place. Bake for 15 minutes or until the crust is well browned and crisp, and the hake is cooked through. Test the middle of one piece with the point of a knife – the fish flakes should part and look firm, but succulent, and white.

**3 Serve** Cut the lemon into wedges. Transfer the fish to plates and garnish with lemon wedges.

**Swap** For hake, use other white fish, such as **Pacific cod, haddock or pollock,** or try **salmon.**

Toss the bread, lemon zest, scallions, garlic, walnuts and parsley in a food processor, then add the milk and oil, and pulse for a few seconds to mix.

## ...speed it up

### Serves 4

4 mackerel fillets, about 3 oz (90 g) each

4 tsp (20 mL) olive oil

2 apples, peeled

leaves from 1 sprig of fresh rosemary

3 tbsp (45 mL) orange marmalade

3 tbsp (45 mL) cider vinegar

**Each serving provides** • 248 cals • 15 g protein • 14 g fat of which 3 g saturates • 16 g carbohydrate

**Swaps** • For mackerel, use **skinless salmon fillet,** but omit the apples and rosemary. • For marmalade, use **plum or damson jam** with **halved pitted plums** instead of apple.

**8** mins prep time

**5** mins cook time

Oily fish, such as mackerel, are particularly good for our health and doctors recommend we eat them once or twice a week. Mackerel is also one of the less expensive fish so it makes an economical as well as a healthy family meal.

## ...healthy plus

# Marmalade-Glazed Mackerel
## with Apples

**Fresh mackerel fillets take moments to cook and taste incredible with the contrasting flavours of tangy marmalade and apples in this ultra-simple dish. Serve with green beans, broccoli and potatoes or whole-grain rolls and salad.**

**1 Prepare the mackerel** Remove any fine bones that remain in the mackerel. Preheat the grill to high. Brush a shallow flameproof dish (such as a lasagna dish) with a little of the oil and put the mackerel fillets in it, skin side up. (The fish can be cooked in the grill pan but a dish is more convenient.) Make three cuts across each mackerel fillet, scoring the skin to prevent it from curling up during cooking.

**2 Add the apples** Cut the apples into quarters and remove the cores, then cut each quarter into three or four slices. Put these in the dish around the mackerel. Brush the apples and fish with the remaining oil. Sprinkle the rosemary leaves over the fish.

**3 Cook the mackerel** Grill the mackerel for 2-3 minutes or until the skin is browned in places. Meanwhile, stir the marmalade and vinegar together in a bowl. Turn over the mackerel fillets and apple slices. Brush a little of the marmalade mixture over the apples, then spoon the remainder evenly over the mackerel fillets. Grill for 2 minutes or until the fish and apples are well browned in places. The fish should be firm and cooked, with flakes that separate easily and look opaque. Serve immediately.

# 5 ways with canned tuna

Canned tuna is one of the most useful foods to have in the pantry. Most people use it straight from the can, but by adding some herbs, flavourings and vegetables, it can be magically transformed into a variety of irresistible dishes. All recipes serve 4.

## tuna and **corn hash**

Peel and cut **1½ lb (700 g) floury potatoes** into ¾-in. (2-cm) dice, then boil in lightly salted water for 10 minutes or until tender. Add **7 oz (200 g) frozen corn**, bring back to the boil, then drain. Return the potatoes and corn to the pot and lightly crush about half the potatoes with a fork. Drain a **6-oz (170-g) can tuna in oil**, adding half the oil to the potatoes and reserving the remainder. Add the tuna, **2 tbsp (25 mL) chopped fresh oregano or 1 tsp (5 mL) dried oregano**, and **4 finely chopped scallions**. Mix well. Preheat the grill to high. Heat the reserved olive oil in a frying pan. Turn the potato mixture into the pan and press it flat. Cook over a medium heat for about 5 minutes or until browned underneath. Put the pan under the grill to brown the top of the hash. Serve cut into wedges with a salad of mixed greens and sliced tomatoes.

**Each serving provides** • 354 cals • 15 g protein • 16 g fat of which 2 g saturates • 39 g carbohydrate

**10** mins prep time   **20** mins cook time

## quick tuna **bake**

Preheat the oven to 425°F (220°C). Cook **11 oz (350 g) fresh or dried tagliatelle** in boiling salted water according to the pack instructions. Meanwhile, heat **1 tbsp (15 mL) olive oil** in a large frying pan and cook **7 oz (200 g) halved small button mushrooms** and **1 sliced bunch of scallions** for 5 minutes or until tender. Stir in **7 oz (200 g) low-fat soft cheese with garlic and herbs**, **4 tbsp (60 mL) 1% milk**, **7 oz (200 g) frozen broccoli florets** and **5 oz (150 g) frozen peas**. Heat gently, stirring occasionally, until the cheese has melted and combined with the milk to make a sauce and the vegetables have thawed. Stir in a drained **6-oz (170-g) can tuna**. Drain the tagliatelle and mix with the tuna and vegetable sauce. Transfer to a baking dish and sprinkle with **¾ cup (175 mL) grated aged cheddar cheese**. Bake for 10 minutes or until lightly browned. (Or brown the top under the grill for 5 minutes.)

**Each serving provides** • 527 cals • 27.5 g protein • 20 g fat of which 8 g saturates • 55 g carbohydrate

**15** mins prep time   **10** mins cook time

## peppers with tuna and mushrooms

Heat **2 tbsp (25 mL) olive oil** in a frying pan and add **1 chopped onion**. Cook for 5 minutes or until softened. Add **½ lb (250 g) halved or quartered chestnut mushrooms**. Season and cook, stirring occasionally, until the mushrooms give up their juices. Add **1 tbsp (15 mL) whole-grain mustard**, the **grated zest of 1 lemon**, **1 crushed garlic clove** and **4 tbsp (60 mL) dry sherry**. Cook, stirring until the mushrooms are evenly coated with a little sauce. Meanwhile, drain and slice a **9-oz (280-g) jar of roasted red peppers**. Mix the peppers into the mushrooms and heat gently for 1 minute. Finally, stir in a **6-oz (170-g) can tuna**, drained, and **1 oz (30 g) chopped fresh parsley**. Serve immediately, with crisp salad leaves and plenty of hot crusty bread or boiled rice.

**Each serving provides** • 188 cals • 12 g protein • 11 g fat of which 2 g saturates • 5 g carbohydrate

**10** mins prep time    **10** mins cook time

## tomato and basil omelette with tuna

Dice **8 tomatoes**. Beat **6 eggs** with seasoning and stir in the tomatoes. Finely snip **10 large fresh basil leaves** (or 4-5 tender sprigs) and add them to the eggs. Preheat the grill to high. Heat **1 tbsp (15 mL) olive oil** in a nonstick frying pan (about 10-in/25-cm) that can go under the grill safely (wrap a wooden handle with foil) and pour in the egg mixture, spreading the tomatoes evenly. Cook over a medium heat, lifting the edges at first to allow the egg to run under the set omelette. Reduce the heat if the omelette starts to brown too quickly. When the omelette is three-quarters set, put it under the grill to finish cooking the top. Meanwhile, drain a **6-oz (170-g) can tuna** and mix it with **3 tbsp (45 mL) mayonnaise**, **3 tbsp (45 mL) plain yogurt** and **1 oz (30 g) snipped fresh chives**. Cut the omelette into quarters and divide among four plates. Spoon the tuna mixture over each portion and sprinkle with **ready-made croutons**. Add watercress, arugula or other salad leaves to the plates and serve with crusty bread.

**Each serving provides** • 346 cals • 24 g protein • 25 g fat of which 5 g saturates • 7 g carbohydrate

**10** mins prep time    **6** mins cook time

## warm salad with spicy tuna and feta

Cook **1¼ cup (300 mL) basmati rice** according to the pack instructions. Meanwhile, boil **4 eggs** for 10 minutes. Drain the eggs and put them into a bowl of cold water until cool enough to handle. Peel and cut into quarters, then set aside. Cut **8 baby plum or cherry tomatoes** in half and set aside. Drain a **6-oz (170-g) can tuna** and put into a bowl. Finely chop a ¾-in (2-cm) piece peeled **fresh ginger** and add to the tuna with **4 chopped scallions** and **2 tbsp (25 mL) chopped fresh coriander leaves**. Dice **7 oz (200 g) feta cheese** and add to the tuna. Add the tuna mixture to the cooked basmati rice and lightly fold the two together. Divide the mixture among serving bowls and top with the eggs and tomatoes. Sprinkle a **pinch of chili powder** over the eggs and serve immediately.

**Each serving provides** • 487 cals • 29 g protein • 20 g fat of which 9 g saturates • 47 g carbohydrate

**10** mins prep time    **12** mins cook time

# Tasty Tuna Fish Cakes

Take cans of tuna and corn from the pantry and add horseradish and scallions for fabulous fish cakes that all the family will enjoy. Serve with lemon mayonnaise and a leafy salad, or with steamed green beans and some quick-fried, halved tomatoes.

**30** mins prep/cook time

**Serves 4**

**1 lb (500 g) floury potatoes, peeled and cut into chunks**

**2 tbsp (25 mL) butter**

**1 tbsp (15 mL) creamed horseradish**

**2 tbsp (25 mL) chopped fresh parsley**

**3 scallions, chopped**

**¾ cup (175 mL) canned corn, drained**

**6 oz (170 g) can tuna chunks, drained**

**2 tbsp (25 mL) plain flour**

**2 tbsp (25 mL) vegetable oil**

**tartar sauce and lemon wedges, to serve**

Each serving provides • 360 cals • 16 g protein • 15.5 g fat of which 5 g saturates • 41 g carbohydrate

Additions • Add a chopped **green chili pepper, grated lime zest, garlic** and chopped **fresh coriander**. • Or, add grated **lemon zest**, chopped **parsley** and **capers**.

Swaps • For tuna, use a **can of pink salmon**. • For parsley, use **2 tbsp (25 mL) green pesto**. • Omit the herbs and use a **can of corn with added red and green peppers**.

**1 Make the mashed potatoes** Cook the potatoes in a pot of boiling water for 15-20 minutes or until tender. Drain thoroughly, then return to the pot with the butter and mash until very smooth.

**2 Add the flavourings** Add the horseradish, parsley, scallions and corn to the hot mashed potato and stir until thoroughly mixed, then add the tuna and season to taste. Allow the mixture to cool slightly.

**3 Make the fish cakes** Shape the mixture into eight thick flat cakes, each measuring about 2¾ in. (7 cm) in diameter. Dust them on both sides with the flour.

**4 Cook the fish cakes** Heat the oil in a large frying pan, preferably nonstick. Add the fish cakes and cook over a medium heat for 3-4 minutes on each side or until well browned, turning them carefully with a slotted spatula. If you don't have a large enough pan, cook the fish cakes in two batches, keeping the first batch warm while you cook the second. Serve hot with tartar sauce and lemon wedges.

Cooking tip If you have time, leave the fish cakes to chill in the fridge for 30 minutes before cooking, as this will make them easier to handle.

### Flash-baked fish burgers

Preheat the oven to 460°F (240°C). Grease a large, flat dish with a little **oil** (a lasagna dish is ideal). Cut **12½ oz (380 g) skinless boneless white fish fillet** into four large pieces. Put **4 roughly chopped scallions** and **3 slices whole-grain bread** in a food processor or blender and whiz to make coarse crumbs. Add the fish and pulse for a few seconds to chop roughly. Add **1 egg** and seasoning, then pulse briefly to mix – do not over-process. Turn the mixture into a bowl, mix it together by hand and divide into four. Shape into soft balls, put in the dish and press out into 4-in. (10-cm) round burgers. Brush with a little olive oil and bake for 15 minutes or until firm. Serve in warm buns, with crisp salad leaves and cucumber; or in split, warm English muffins, spread thinly with tomato ketchup and a dollop of mayonnaise, and topped with lettuce and sliced tomato.

## ...another idea

# Spicy Stir-Fried **Squid** with Sugar Snap Peas

**Basil and coriander bring a fabulous burst of flavour to crisp stir-fried vegetables topped with tender, chili-spiced squid. Serve with noodles for a memorable meal in minutes.**

**10** mins prep time

**9** mins cook time

**Serves 4**
⅔ **lb (300 g) squid rings**
¼-½ **tsp (1-2 mL) chili powder**
1 **tbsp (15 mL) ground coriander**
2 **tbsp (25 mL) canola oil**
½ **lb (250 g) sugar snap peas**
1¾ **oz (50 g) fresh ginger, peeled and chopped**
2 **garlic cloves, sliced**
2 **celery sticks, sliced**
1 **red pepper, sliced into short strips**
1 **oz (30 g) fresh basil leaves (or tender sprigs)**
1 **oz (30 g) fresh coriander leaves (or tender sprigs)**
6 **scallions, sliced**
6 **tbsp (90 mL) dry sherry**

**Each serving provides** • 186 cals
• 15 g protein • 7 g fat of which
1 g saturates • 9 g carbohydrate

**1 Season the squid** Put the squid in a bowl and season with the chili powder and coriander. Mix well and set aside.

**2 Stir-fry the vegetables** Heat a wok or large frying pan with 1 tbsp (15 mL) canola oil. Add the sugar snap peas and stir-fry over a high heat for 1 minute or until they are bright green. Add the ginger, garlic, celery and pepper strips, with seasoning to taste, and stir-fry for 3-4 minutes. Remove from the heat. Stir in the basil, coriander and scallions, then divide the vegetables among four large pasta bowls or deep plates.

**3 Cook the squid** Heat the remaining oil in the wok or pan. Stir-fry the squid for 2 minutes or until it is just firm (do not overcook the pieces or they will become rubbery). Season the squid, then arrange the rings on the vegetables. Pour the sherry into the pan and cook over a high heat for 1 minute, stirring to loosen any residue from the pan. Pour the cooking juices over the squid and vegetables, and serve immediately.

**Swaps** • For squid rings, use **peeled raw jumbo shrimp**. • Or use chunks of skinless firm, thick fish fillet – try **swordfish, hake, sablefish or salmon**. • For the vegetables, buy **sliced prepared vegetables or frozen stir-fry vegetable mixes** – just cook for an extra minute if frozen.

# Nippy Niçoise Salad

Create this classic main-meal salad from the simplest of ingredients. A can of anchovies, speedily blended with olive oil, lemon juice, mustard and garlic, makes an ideal dressing. Serve with crusty French bread.

**Serves 4**

¾ lb (375 g) pre-washed baby new potatoes

7 oz (200 g) green beans

3 eggs

1.7 oz (48 g) can anchovy fillets

1 garlic clove, crushed

1 tsp (5 mL) Dijon mustard

1 tbsp (15 mL) lemon juice

5 tbsp (75 mL) olive oil

6 oz (170 g) can tuna, drained

1 romaine lettuce, torn

8 baby plum tomatoes, or baby tomatoes, halved

12 pitted black olives

**Each serving provides** • 392 cals • 22 g protein • 25 g fat of which 4 g saturates • 20 g carbohydrate

**15** mins prep time **12** mins cook time

So that the potatoes cook as quickly as possible, cut any larger ones in half to make sure they are all roughly the same size.

## ...cooking tip

The dressing can be made the day before and stored in a covered jug or bowl in the fridge. Whisk with a fork before using.

## ...get ahead

**1 Cook the potatoes and beans** Cook the potatoes in a pot of lightly salted boiling water for 10-12 minutes or until tender. Add the green beans for the last 4 minutes of cooking. Drain, rinse under cold water and drain again.

**2 Boil the eggs** While the potatoes are cooking, add the eggs to a pot of boiling water and cook for 7-8 minutes, so that the yolks remain slightly soft and creamy. Drain the eggs and put them into a bowl of cold water. Peel and cut into quarters lengthwise.

**3 Make the dressing** Drain the can of anchovy fillets. Put the anchovies, garlic, mustard, lemon juice and olive oil into a blender or food processor and purée until smooth and creamy. Spoon half of this dressing over the cooked potatoes and beans, and gently toss together.

**4 Assemble the salad** Separate the tuna into chunks. Put the lettuce into a salad bowl. Top with the potatoes and beans followed by the eggs and tomatoes, then scatter over the tuna and olives. Serve drizzled with the remaining dressing.

**Swaps** • For tuna, use **7 oz (200 g) cooked, peeled jumbo shrimp**. • For green beans, use **7 oz (200 g) asparagus spears**. Snap off any woody ends from the asparagus stalks at the point where they break easily, then cut the spears into short pieces and steam over the potatoes for 4-5 minutes.

**Serves 4**

4 tuna steaks, about 3½ oz (100 g) each

4 tsp (20 mL) ras-el-hanout spice mix

10 oz (300 g) green beans

2 tbsp (25 mL) clear honey

grated zest and juice of 2 lemons

4 tomatoes, halved and sliced

14 oz (398 mL) can kidney beans, drained and rinsed

2 tbsp (25 mL) olive oil

1 small onion, halved and sliced

2 large red peppers, sliced

2 large garlic cloves, sliced

**Each serving provides** • 335 cals • 32 g protein • 11 g fat of which 2 g saturates • 28 g carbohydrate

**Swaps** • For tuna, use **swordfish steaks**. • For kidney beans, use **cannellini or borlotti beans**.

**15** mins prep time **7** mins cook time

• Make the salad in advance and leave it to cool, then cover. Chill if leaving for more than 2 hours (it can be made 4-5 hours ahead). • Sprinkle the fish with the spice; cover and chill in the fridge if leaving for more than 30 minutes.

## ...get ahead

• You will find ras-el-hanout spice mix among the standard spice mixes or speciality products in the supermarket.

• Frozen tuna can be used. Sprinkle it with the spice and set aside to thaw, preferably overnight in the fridge, before cooking.

## ...shopping tips

# Tuna with Moroccan Spices and Bean Salad

Moroccan ras-el-hanout spice mix is a terrific flavouring for rapidly seared tuna accompanied by a sweet-and-sour bean salad. Serve with flatbreads and a watercress and arugula salad tossed with fresh coriander.

**1 Prepare the tuna** Put the tuna steaks on a plate and sprinkle the ras-el-hanout over both sides to coat them in the spice. Set aside.

**2 Make the salad** Put the green beans in a small pot, with just enough boiling water to cover them, and bring to the boil. Boil for 2 minutes. Drain, rinse under cold water and drain again, then put into a heatproof bowl. Immediately add the honey, lemon zest and juice, then mix well. Add the tomatoes and kidney beans to the bowl.

**3 Cook the vegetables** Heat half the oil in a frying pan. Add the onion, peppers and garlic, and cook, stirring, over a high heat for 1 minute or until very lightly cooked. Add to the salad and mix well.

**4 Cook the tuna** Return the frying pan to the heat and pour in the remaining oil. Add the tuna, scraping any spice mix from the plate on to the fish. Cook over a high heat for 2 minutes. Turn and cook for a further 2-3 minutes, pressing the fish lightly with a slotted spatula. It should be just cooked through.

**5 Serve the salad** Divide the salad among four plates. Slice the tuna into strips and lay them on the salad. Scrape any juices and spices from the pan and pour over the tuna. Serve at once.

**Spice swaps** • For ras-el-hanout, use a mix of **4 tsp (20 mL) ground coriander, ½ tsp (2 mL) ground cinnamon, ¼ tsp (1 mL) ground mace or freshly grated nutmeg** and a good **pinch of chili powder**. • Or use any of the fiery African spice mixes – try **harissa paste**, for example. You will need 2-4 tsp (10-20 mL).

# Creamy **Seafood** Wraps
## with **Zucchini** and **Cucumber** Salad

You have to try these to believe how good they taste. The luscious filling is so quick and easy, and the tender zucchini and crisp cucumber salad, with its spiky chili and lime seasoning, is a perfect accompaniment.

**30 mins** prep/cook time

**Serves 4**

**4 scallions, finely sliced**

**4 large tomatoes, diced**

**5 oz (150 g) low-fat soft cheese (like ricotta) with garlic and herbs**

**½ lb (250 g) ready-to-eat seafood mix, including mussels, jumbo shrimp and squid**

**4 large soft flour tortillas**

**1 tbsp (15 mL) olive oil**

**½ cup (125 mL) aged cheddar cheese, grated**

**2 small zucchini, thinly sliced**

**½ cucumber, thinly sliced**

**5 oz (150 g) arugula**

**1 lime**

**a little chili oil**

**Each serving provides** • 358 cals • 24 g protein • 12 g fat of which 6 g saturates • 41 g carbohydrate

**1 Make the filling** Preheat the oven to 400°F (200°C). Put the scallions into a bowl and add the tomatoes, then mix in the soft cheese and season lightly with ground black pepper. Gently mix in the seafood, without breaking it up.

**2 Fill the tortillas** Lay out the tortillas and divide the seafood mixture among them, spreading it over the centre of each, then roll up tightly. Put in a large ovenproof dish or roasting pan. Brush with a little oil. Sprinkle the cheese over the top and cover loosely with foil. Bake for 20 minutes or until heated through. Uncover for the last 5 minutes to lightly brown the cheese.

**3 Make the salad** While the tortillas are heating through, toss the zucchini and cucumber together in a bowl with the arugula. Divide among four large plates. Grate the zest from the lime, or use a zester, and sprinkle it over the salads. Trickle a little chili oil over the top. Cut the lime into eight wedges and add two to each plate.

**4 Serve** Cut the wraps in half and arrange on or beside the salads. Serve immediately.

### Jumbo shrimp and avocado wraps

Instead of mixed seafood, use **cooked, peeled jumbo shrimp**, thawing and draining the jumbo shrimp if frozen. Add **2 peeled, pitted and diced avocados** instead of the tomatoes. Serve with **cherry tomatoes** and **arugula** instead of the zucchini salad.

## ...another idea

# Corn **Kedgeree**
## with Chili and Coriander

Smoked haddock is the basis of a classic Anglo-Indian fish kedgeree, given a twist with extra spice and the distinctive taste of coriander. A salad of peppery arugula, watercress, scallions and radishes is just right on the side.

**30** mins prep/cook time

**Serves 4**

**4 eggs**

**1 cup (250 mL) basmati rice**

**½ tsp (2 mL) turmeric**

**2½ cups (625 mL) boiling water**

**1 lemon**

**¼ cup (50 mL) frozen corn**

**¼ cup (50 mL) frozen peas**

**14 oz (400 g) skinless undyed smoked haddock fillet, cut into 1-in. (2.5-cm) chunks**

**2½ tbsp (40 mL) butter, cut into small pieces**

**1 fresh green chili pepper, seeded and cut into rings**

**1 oz (30 g) fresh coriander, leaves coarsely chopped**

**Each serving provides** • 485 cals • 34 g protein • 17 g fat of which 7 g saturates • 50 g carbohydrate

**1** **Hard-boil the eggs** Add the eggs to a pot of boiling water and cook for 10 minutes. Drain the eggs and put them into a bowl of cold water. Peel and coarsely chop.

**2** **Cook the rice** While the eggs are boiling, put the rice into a large pot and stir in the turmeric. Stir in the boiling water and bring to the boil. Stir once, reduce the heat to low and cover the pot. Simmer for 5 minutes. Meanwhile, grate the zest from the lemon, or use a zester, and put into a bowl. Cut the lemon into wedges.

**3** **Add the vegetables and fish** Sprinkle the corn and peas over the rice in the pot. Add the fish, spreading out the chunks evenly. Bring back to the boil but do not stir. When the water is bubbling steadily, reduce the heat, cover the pot tightly and leave to cook for 10 minutes. The chunks of fish should be opaque, firm and succulent, and the liquid should have been absorbed.

**4** **Assemble the dish** Scatter the butter over the fish, then fork all the ingredients together lightly. Divide among four warm pasta plates or large shallow bowls. Sprinkle with the chopped egg, chili rings, coriander and lemon zest. Garnish with lemon wedges and serve.

# Steamed Scallop Parcels

Pack delicate scallops in little parcels with vegetables and a fragrant dressing for great eating made easy. Serve with straight-to-wok noodles stir-fried in hot olive oil and chives.

**12** mins prep time  **10** mins cook time

**Serves 4**

8 scallions, sliced

⅔ lb (300 g) small scallops or queen scallops (without roes)

2 tbsp (25 mL) dry sherry

1 tbsp (15 mL) light soy sauce

1 tbsp (15 mL) toasted sesame oil

½ lb (250 g) snow peas

7 oz (200 g) asparagus tips

1 oz (30 g) fresh ginger, peeled and finely chopped

**Each serving provides** • 165 cals
• 21 g protein • 4 g fat of which
1 g saturates • 8 g carbohydrate

**1 Prepare the parcels and steamer** Cut four 12-in. (30-cm) squares of foil. Prepare a pot of boiling water with a steamer on top (see Cooking tips).

**2 Marinate the scallops** Put half the scallions into a bowl and add the scallops, sherry, soy sauce and toasted sesame oil. Mix well and set aside to marinate briefly.

**3 Prepare the vegetables** Divide the snow peas and asparagus among the squares of foil. Sprinkle with the ginger and remaining scallions. Fold up the foil to form deep nests around the vegetables, turning the edges in slightly to enclose them in open-topped bundles. Put them into the steamer and cook for 5 minutes.

**4 Cook the scallops** Add the scallops to the vegetables, dividing them evenly among the packages. Pour in all the seasoning mix. Re-cover the steamer and cook for a further 3-5 minutes or until the scallops are just firm. Serve.

**Swap** For scallops, cook strips of **skinless Alaska pollock or Pacific sole fillet**. Allow 4 fillets, and cut them crosswise into ½- or ¾-in. (1- or 2-cm) wide strips. Marinate as for the basic recipe, then criss-cross them fairly loosely on top of the vegetables at the end of step 3 and finish cooking as for the scallops.

• If you don't have a steamer, stand a heatproof bowl or soufflé dish in a large lidded pot. Pour boiling water into the pot until it comes to about ¾ in. (2 cm) below the rim of the dish. Bring the water to a simmer. Stand a heatproof plate on top of the bowl or dish and place the parcels on this to steam, covering the pot with a close-fitting lid. • Alternatively, the parcels can be steamed in a bamboo steamer over a wok. Pour in enough boiling water to come about ½ in. (1 cm) below the steamer or rack in the wok.

## ...cooking tips

### Marinated salmon with asparagus and sesame seeds

Take **4 portions of skinless salmon fillet**, about ¼ lb (125 g) each, and double the quantity of **asparagus** from the basic recipe; omit the snow peas. Marinate the salmon as for the scallops. Steam the asparagus in the foil as in step 3, then add the salmon and its marinade. Steam for 5-8 minutes or until just firm and pink. Dry-roast **2 tbsp (25 mL) sesame seeds** in a small frying pan, shaking the pan often, until they are lightly browned. Sprinkle these over the salmon when serving.

## ...another idea

# Sizzling **Scallops** with **Noodle** Stir-Fry and Wilted **Watercress**

**10** mins cook time

**8** mins prep time

Homely stir-fried vegetables and noodles set off sophisticated scallops, all boosted with a brilliant combination of flavours. The pan juices make a delicious sauce for the watercress.

**Serves 4**
7 oz (200 g) fine egg noodles
⅔ lb (300 g) scallops without roes
1 garlic clove, crushed
grated zest of 1 lemon
1 tsp (5 mL) English mustard
leaves from 4 sprigs of fresh
   tarragon
3 tbsp (45 mL) olive oil
2 x ⅔-lb (300-g) packages stir-fry
   vegetables (such as broccoli,
   peppers and cabbage)
5 oz (150 g) watercress

**Each serving provides** • 413 cals
• 28 g protein • 14 g fat of which
2 g saturates • 47 g carbohydrate

**1** **Soften the noodles** Put the noodles in a large bowl and cover them generously with boiling water. Cover and set aside for 5 minutes or until softened.

**2** **Marinate the scallops** Cut the scallops into thick slices and put them into a bowl. Add the garlic, lemon zest, mustard and tarragon, then stir in 2 tbsp (25 mL) oil. Mix well and set aside.

**3** **Stir-fry the vegetables** Heat a large frying pan or wok with the remaining oil. Add the vegetables and stir-fry for 5 minutes.

**4** **Mix with the noodles** Drain the noodles, wipe the bowl with a paper towel and return them to the warm bowl. Add the stir-fried vegetables and mix well. Set aside.

**5** **Cook the scallops** Add the scallops to the pan or wok, scraping in all the mustard mixture, and cook quickly for 2-3 minutes, turning the slices once. Divide the vegetable and noodle mixture among four large plates. Arrange the scallops on the plates. Add the watercress to one side.

**6** **Make a sauce** Add 4 tbsp (60 mL) boiling water to the pan or wok and bring it to the boil, stirring to loosen all the cooking residue. Boil hard for a few seconds. Spoon the boiling juices over the watercress and serve immediately.

**Swap** For scallops, use **sablefish fillet**. Buy an 11-oz (350-g) piece and slice it into ½-in. (1-cm) thick medallions.

Stir-fries are great for using up vegetables you have in your fridge such as carrots, celery, zucchini and peppers. Cut them into similar-sized sticks or slices so that they will cook in the same amount of time.

## ...use it up

# poultry

# Cashew and Chicken Stir-Fry

Chicken, nuts and apricots flavoured with tangy fresh basil make a refreshing summer-style stir-fry. Serve with rice noodles or fluffy white rice for a healthy meal in moments.

**15** mins prep time

**9** mins cook time

**Serves 4**

2 tbsp (25 mL) olive oil

1 lb (500 g) skinless chicken breast fillets, cut into strips

1¾ oz (50 g) cashews

1 large yellow pepper, sliced

4 celery sticks, thinly sliced

4 scallions, sliced

2 zucchinis, halved lengthwise and thinly sliced

1¾ oz (50 g) ready-to-eat dried apricots, sliced

4 tbsp (60 mL) dry sherry

grated zest and juice of 1 lime

1 tsp (5 mL) toasted sesame oil

½ bok choy, finely shredded

1 oz (30 g) fresh basil leaves

**Each serving provides** • 349 cals • 34 g protein • 16 g fat of which 3 g saturates • 12 g carbohydrate

**1** **Stir-fry the chicken and nuts** Heat a large frying pan, skillet or wok with the olive oil. Add the chicken and cashews, and stir-fry for 2-3 minutes or until the chicken strips are cooked and the nuts are lightly browned.

**2** **Stir-fry the vegetables** Add the pepper, celery and scallions, and stir-fry for 1-2 minutes to soften the vegetables slightly. Stir in the sliced zucchinis and apricots, and stir-fry for 1-2 minutes. The vegetables should be lightly cooked but still crisp.

**3** **Add the flavourings** Add the sherry, lime zest and juice to the vegetables, then the sesame oil. Season and boil, stirring, for 30-60 seconds to cook off the alcohol and coat all the ingredients. Finally, add the bok choy and basil, and mix briskly. Remove from the heat and serve immediately.

● Buy ingredients such as chicken and dried apricots ready chopped, to save cutting them up (and reduce the washing-up). ● There is a wide variety of prepared stir-fry vegetables, sold individually, in multi-vegetable packages or in prepared mixes, fresh or frozen, which can be used instead of the pepper, zucchini, celery and scallions. Check portion sizes on the package – allow about 1 lb (500 g) prepared vegetables for four people.

**...speed it up**

# Golden Kebabs
## with Zesty Mayonnaise

Full of contrasting flavours and textures from fruit, peppers and chicken, these fast-cooking kebabs are flavoured with garlic and turmeric and have a punchy dressing on the side. Serve with couscous or focaccia and a green salad.

**15** mins prep time

**10** mins cook time

**Serves 4**
2 tbsp (25 mL) olive oil
2 tsp (10 mL) turmeric
2 garlic cloves, crushed
4 skinless chicken breast fillets, about ¼ lb (125 g) each
3 nectarines, halved and stoned
12 baby peppers, halved
2 scallions, chopped
grated zest of ½ lemon
6¾ tbsp (100 mL) mayonnaise
⅓ cup (75 mL) plain low-fat yogurt
pinch of cayenne pepper or chili powder (optional)
lemon juice, to taste

**Each serving provides** • 463 cals • 31 g protein • 30 g fat of which 5 g saturates • 19 g carbohydrate

**1 Flavour the chicken** Put the olive oil in a bowl. Add the turmeric, garlic and plenty of seasoning. Cut each chicken breast into six chunks, then add these to the mixture and toss to coat them thoroughly. Set aside.

**2 Thread the kebabs** Preheat the broiler to high. Cut each nectarine half into four wedges, to give 24 pieces in total. Thread the chicken, nectarines and peppers onto eight metal skewers, nestling the wedges of nectarine inside (or close to) the pepper halves and alternating them with chunks of chicken. Put them into a large, shallow, ovenproof dish, or into a grill pan.

**3 Cook the kebabs** broil the kebabs for 5 minutes on each side. The chicken should be cooked through and the peppers and edges of the nectarines should be well browned, with a hint of charring in places.

**4 Make the zesty mayonnaise** In a small bowl, mix the scallions and lemon zest with the mayonnaise and yogurt. Season with a hint of cayenne or chili powder, if you like, and add lemon juice to taste. Serve dollops of the dressing beside the kebabs.

**Swaps** • For chicken, use **turkey or duck breast**. • For nectarines, use **papaya or mango**. Select fruit that is just ripe but firm; peel it, discard the seeds or stone, then cut into large chunks. • For baby peppers, use **large peppers** and cut them into quarters lengthwise.

### Thai kebabs
Coat the chicken with **2 tbsp (25 mL) Thai green curry paste** instead of the oil, turmeric and garlic. Thread the kebabs with the chicken, nectarines (or use peaches) and the peppers as step 2 and cook as step 3. Serve the kebabs with a quick peanut sauce instead of the mayonnaise: Mix **4 tbsp (60 mL) peanut butter** with **2 crushed garlic cloves, 4 chopped scallions, ¼-½ tsp (1-2 mL) crushed chili flakes**, the juice of **1 lemon** and **2 tbsp (25 mL) boiling water**.

## ...another idea

# Creamy Chicken Korma

Coconut and almonds give this mild korma its distinctive richness.
Take a few minutes to prepare it, then leave it in the oven to cook.
Serve with basmati rice or warm nan bread.

**15** mins prep time

**1** hour cook time

### Serves 4

1 tbsp (15 mL) canola oil

1 onion, chopped

1 tsp (5 mL) finely chopped fresh ginger

2 tbsp (25 mL) korma (mild) curry paste or powder

1 lb (500 g) skinless chicken breast fillets, thickly sliced

⅔ cup (150 mL) hot chicken stock, made with stock cubes

14 oz (398 mL) can coconut milk

½ cup (125 mL) ground almonds

2 tbsp (25 mL) chopped fresh coriander (optional)

### Each serving provides

- 475 cals • 40 g protein
- 32 g fat of which 14 g saturates
- 6 g carbohydrate

**1 Fry the flavourings** Preheat the oven to 350°F (180°C). Heat the oil in a flameproof casserole or heavy pot and lightly cook the onion and ginger for 4-5 minutes or until softened. Stir in the curry paste or powder and cook over a low heat for 1 minute, taking care that it does not burn.

**2 Cook the chicken** Add the chicken slices to the casserole or pot, stirring to coat them in the spicy onions. Add the stock and coconut milk, and bring to the boil. Season. If cooked in a pot, transfer to a warm casserole. Cover with a tight-fitting lid, then put in the oven and leave to cook for 45 minutes to 1 hour.

**3 Add the almonds** When ready to serve, remove the casserole from the oven, and stir in the ground almonds to thicken the sauce. Scatter coriander on top, if you like.

If you need this dish in a hurry, simmer it on the stovetop for 20 minutes at step 2 instead of transferring it to the oven, then continue with step 3.

**...speed it up**

# Chicken Tikka
## with Mushrooms and Peppers

Succulent mushrooms and refreshing green peppers complement spicy grilled chicken in a fusion of traditional spices that is just right for a speedy mid-week meal. Serve with nan or pita breads cut into strips.

**15** mins prep time

**15** mins cook time

### Serves 4

**8 skinless boneless chicken thighs,** about 1¼ lb (625 g) total weight

**3 tbsp (45 mL) tandoori spice mix**

**3 tbsp (45 mL) canola oil**

**1 lb (500 g) button mushrooms,** stalks discarded

**4 green peppers, cut into quarters** then into chunks

**4 tbsp (60 mL) chopped fresh** coriander

**lemon wedges, to garnish**

**Each serving provides** • 356 cals • 36 g protein • 21 g fat of which 5 g saturates • 5.5 g carbohydrate

**To serve** Make a simple **raita** to complete the meal (see To serve, page 140), or simply accompany with good-quality bought **tzatziki**.

**1** **Spice the chicken** Preheat the grill to high. Put the chicken in a large, shallow ovenproof dish or grill pan, keeping the pieces close together in the middle. Sprinkle the spice mix over the chicken. Drizzle 1 tbsp (15 mL) oil over and then use a spoon and fork to turn the chicken pieces over several times to coat them evenly in the spice and oil.

**2** **Cook the chicken and vegetables** Grill the chicken, skinned side up, for 5 minutes, then turn over. Add the mushrooms, gill side down, and the peppers, skin side up. Brush the vegetables lightly with 1 tbsp (15 mL) oil. Grill for 5 minutes or until lightly browned. Turn the chicken and vegetables over. Brush the remaining oil over the vegetables and cook for a further 4-5 minutes.

**3** **Serve** Transfer the chicken and vegetables to large plates, spooning all the cooking juices over them. Sprinkle with the coriander. Garnish with lemon wedges and serve.

**Teriyaki chicken**
Instead of tandoori spice mix, use **6-8 tbsp (90-125 mL) teriyaki sauce**. Swap the vegetables for **1-2 eggplants** cut into ¾-in. (1-cm) slices, **1 bunch whole, trimmed scallions** and ½ **lb (250 g) baby corn**. Serve with a salad of shredded **bok choy** and **rice noodles** (cooked according to the pack instructions) tossed with **1 tbsp (15 mL) rice vinegar**, **2 tbsp (25 mL) light soy sauce** and ½ **tsp (2 mL) sugar**.

## ...another idea

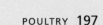

# Chicken Thai Green Curry

Fragrant Thai green curry paste transforms chicken and plump miniature eggplants and zucchini into an exotic meal, with the minimum of preparation. For a real treat, serve the curry with creamy coconut rice.

**Serves 4**

**4 skinless chicken breast fillets, about ¼ lb (125 g) each**

**4 tbsp (60 mL) Thai green curry paste**

**2-3 tbsp (25-45 mL) olive oil**

**2 onions, sliced**

**2 garlic cloves, crushed**

**1 red pepper, sliced**

**½ lb (250 g) baby eggplants, halved**

**2 cups (500 mL) boiling water**

**7 oz (200 g) baby zucchini, stalks trimmed**

**4 large tender fresh basil sprigs, coarsely shredded**

**4 large tender fresh coriander sprigs, coarsely shredded**

**Each serving provides** • 292 cals • 32 g protein • 13 g fat of which 2 g saturates • 12 g carbohydrate

1 **Spice the chicken** Put the chicken in a dish and add the curry paste. Turn the chicken breasts over several times to coat them with the paste.

2 **Brown the chicken** Heat 2 tbsp (25 mL) oil in a large, fairly deep frying pan (a skillet – a deep frying pan with a lid – is ideal) over a medium-high heat. Add the chicken and lightly brown the pieces for 1 minute on each side, then remove and set aside.

3 **Brown the vegetables** Add the remaining oil if necessary, then add the onions, garlic, pepper and eggplants to the pan. Cook, stirring, for 1 minute. Return the chicken pieces to the pan, shuffling them in among the vegetables, and scrape in any juices and curry paste from the dish.

4 **Simmer the curry** Season and pour in the boiling water. Heat until simmering, then reduce the heat so that the liquid bubbles steadily, and cover closely with a lid or foil. Simmer for 10 minutes.

5 **Cook the zucchini** Add the zucchini to the pan, re-cover and cook for a further 5 minutes. Taste for seasoning, remove from the heat and stir in the basil and coriander. Serve immediately.

Prepare some creamy coconut rice (similar in texture to a risotto) to accompany the curry. Simmer **1 cup (250 mL) long-grain rice** in plenty of boiling water for 7 minutes, then drain and return it to the pot. Stir in a **14-oz (398-mL) can coconut milk** and **1 cup (250 mL) boiling water** with a pinch of salt, and bring back to the boil. Reduce the heat to the minimum setting, cover tightly and cook for 12-15 minutes, stirring once or twice, until the rice is tender and the coconut milk is creamy. Season to taste before serving.

**...to serve**

# Chicken and Shrimp Jambalaya

This colourful dish of jumbo shrimp, chicken and spicy chorizo sausage looks and tastes spectacular, yet it is easy to make using a time-saving, pre-made salsa for flavour. Serve with a green salad.

**30** mins prep/cook time

### Serves 4

3½ oz (100 g) chorizo sausage, cut into small chunks

⅔ lb (300 g) skinless chicken breast fillets, cut into bite-sized pieces

2 cups (500 mL) long-grain rice

4 cups (1 L) hot chicken or vegetable stock, made with stock cubes

1 bay leaf

7 oz (200 g) bottle tomato salsa

7 oz (200 g) raw, peeled tiger jumbo shrimp

3 tbsp (45 mL) chopped fresh parsley

dash of Tabasco sauce (optional)

**Each serving provides** • 528 cals • 37 g protein • 9 g fat of which 3 g saturates • 78 g carbohydrate

**1 Fry the chorizo** Heat a large, deep frying pan over a medium heat. Add the chorizo and fry for 2-3 minutes or until just starting to brown. Remove from the pan using a slotted spoon and set aside. Add the chicken to the chorizo oil and cook for 1-2 minutes, stirring until lightly coloured. Remove and set aside.

**2 Add the rice and stock** Add the rice to the pan and cook, stirring, for 1 minute. Pour in the hot stock and add the bay leaf. Reduce the heat, then cover the pan with a lid or foil and simmer gently for 5 minutes.

**3 Add the meat to the rice** Stir the chorizo and chicken into the rice. Cover the pan and simmer for 10 minutes. Stir in the salsa, jumbo shrimp and parsley, and cook for a further 3-4 minutes or until the jumbo shrimp are just cooked, most of the liquid has been absorbed and the rice is tender.

**4 Serve** Remove the bay leaf, then season and sprinkle with a dash of Tabasco sauce, if you like. Serve immediately.

**Cooking tip** You can use **frozen raw jumbo shrimp**; add them at step 3 after the meat and rice have simmered for 8 minutes. If you want to use **cooked jumbo shrimp**, add them after the salsa has cooked for 1 minute at step 3.

### Seafood jambalaya
Leave out the chorizo and chicken, and stir in a **12-oz (375-g) skinned salmon fillet**, cut into bite-sized cubes, with the jumbo shrimp. Stir in **2 tbsp (25 mL) snipped fresh chives** instead of the parsley and squeeze a little **lime juice** over the jambalaya before serving.

**...another idea**

# Cinnamon-Mustard Chicken with Sweet Potatoes and Peppers

Apple juice gives this cinnamon-and-mustard dressing a delicious hint of sweetness. Wedges of sweet potato, pepper and onion are all prepared in minutes and baked with the chicken for a hassle-free family favourite.

**Serves 4**

2 tbsp (25 mL) wholegrain mustard

2 tsp (10 mL) ground cinnamon

1 cup (250 mL) apple juice

8 skinless, boneless chicken thighs, about 1¼ lb (625 g) total weight

4 sweet potatoes, about 2 lbs (1 kg), peeled and cut into chunky wedges

4 onions, quartered

2 red peppers, quartered lengthwise

2 yellow peppers, quartered lengthwise

2 tbsp (25 mL) olive oil

**Each serving provides** • 585 cals • 38 g protein • 19 g fat of which 5 g saturates • 69 g carbohydrate

**1 Flavour the chicken** Preheat the oven to 460°F (240°C). Mix the mustard, cinnamon and apple juice in a large ovenproof dish or roasting pan. Add the chicken, turning the pieces over several times to coat them in the apple dressing. Set aside.

**2 Parboil the sweet potatoes** Put the sweet potato wedges in a large pot. Pour in boiling water to cover and boil for 5 minutes.

**3 Combine the ingredients** Drain the sweet potatoes, then add them to the chicken together with the onions and peppers. Turn all the vegetables in the dressing to coat them evenly, then turn the chicken thighs once more and leave them skinned side up.

**4 Roast and serve** Season the ingredients to taste and drizzle over the oil. Roast for 20 minutes or until the chicken and vegetables are cooked and well browned. Test the chicken is cooked by piercing the thickest part with the point of a knife; the juices should run clear, not pink. Serve.

**Swap** For an extra-fruity flavour, use **mango juice** instead of apple juice and add a peeled, stoned and sliced firm **mango** to the roasting pan halfway through cooking.

# Tomato-baked Chicken
## with Potatoes

**Golden pieces of chicken, flavoured with oregano and tomato, and juicy cherry tomatoes top roasted potato slices in this simple "make-and-bake" dish. Toss some peppers and scallions in a garlicky dressing to serve.**

**Serves 4**

1½ lb (750 g) large potatoes, peeled and cut into ½-in (1-cm) thick slices

2 tbsp (25 mL) olive oil

8 skinless boneless chicken thighs, about 1¼ lb (625 g) total weight

8 tsp (40 mL) tomato paste

8 tender fresh oregano sprigs

10 oz (300 g) small cherry tomatoes

2 lettuce hearts, separated into leaves, to serve

**Each serving provides** • 453 cals • 37 g protein • 18 g fat of which 4 g saturates • 37 g carbohydrate

**Swaps** • For sliced potatoes, use whole **baby new potatoes** cooked in their skins. • For tomato paste, use **tomato paste with herbs and/or garlic, or tapenade**.

**1 Cook the potatoes** Preheat the oven to 460°F (240°C). Put the potato slices in a pot, add boiling water to cover and bring to the boil. Reduce the heat slightly and boil for 5 minutes or until just tender but still firm. Drain.

**2 Layer the potatoes** Pour 1 tsp (5 mL) oil into a large, shallow ovenproof dish. Add the potatoes in a single layer, overlapping them slightly if necessary. Slide the first few slices of potato around on the oil to grease the dish.

**3 Add the chicken and tomatoes** Open out the chicken thighs and spread with the tomato paste. Season well, then add an oregano sprig to each. (Pull off the leaves and discard the central stalks of the sprigs if they are tough.) Fold the chicken in half to enclose the oregano and put on top of the potatoes. Add the tomatoes, distributing them evenly.

**4 Bake** Sprinkle with seasoning and drizzle the remaining oil evenly over the ingredients. Bake for 15-20 minutes or until the chicken is well browned and cooked through, and the potatoes are beginning to turn golden and crisp at the edges. Serve immediately, with lots of little crisp lettuce leaves on the side.

### Spiced yogurt chicken

If you have any, sprinkle some **white cumin seeds** over the potatoes when you layer them in the dish. Mix **8 tbsp (125 mL) plain low-fat yogurt** with **2 tbsp (25 mL) tandoori spice mix, or 1 tbsp curry powder**, and **1 crushed garlic clove**. Spread half of this paste in the chicken, instead of the tomato paste, and sprinkle with chopped **scallion**. Add the chicken and tomatoes to the dish and spread the remaining yogurt mixture over the top.

**...another idea**

# 5 ways with chicken breasts

Skinless chicken breast fillet is one of the most versatile white meats. It lends itself to recipes from all around the world, which can be conjured up using other pantry ingredients. Keep chicken breasts in the freezer for healthy, super-quick meals any day of the week. All recipes serve 4.

## chicken with toasted almonds

Season **4 tbsp (60 mL) plain flour**, adding a generous pinch of **paprika and/or mace**. Roll **4 skinless chicken breast fillets, about ¼ lb (125 g) each**, in the flour until well coated. Heat a dry frying pan and toast **½ cup (125 mL) slivered almonds** until golden. Shake the pan and stir the almonds frequently so that they do not burn – they will brown in 2-3 minutes. Remove from the pan. Heat **2 tbsp (25 mL) olive oil or 2 tbsp (25 mL) unsalted butter** in the pan and cook the chicken over a medium heat for about 4 minutes on each side or until browned and cooked through. Serve sprinkled with the almonds, and with **lemon wedges** for their juice. Serve with thick fries and a crisp green salad.

**Each serving provides** • 327 cals • 35 g protein • 14 g fat of which 2 g saturates • 16 g carbohydrate

 **5** mins prep time  **11** mins cook time

## creamy leek and mushroom chicken

Heat **2 tbsp (25 mL) olive oil** in a large pan. Add **⅔ lb (300 g) skinless chicken breast fillets**, diced, and **½ lb (250 g) small button mushrooms**. Cook over a medium to medium-high heat, stirring, for 3-5 minutes or until the chicken is lightly cooked, browned in places and firm. Turn down the heat, stir in **½ lb (250 g) sliced leeks** and cook, stirring, for 3-5 minutes or until the leeks are softened and reduced. Stir in **3 tbsp (45 mL) plain flour** until well mixed with the leeks, then stir in **1 cup (250 mL) chicken stock**, made with a stock cube, and **1 cup (250 mL) milk** with seasoning to taste. Bring to the boil, stirring, and simmer gently for 5 minutes. For a herby result, stir in **4 tbsp (60 mL) chopped fresh parsley** and **2 tbsp (25 mL) chopped fresh tarragon** and the **grated zest of 1 lemon**. Serve with rice or pasta. (This mixture can also be used as a pie filling, with a mashed potato topping.)

**Each serving provides** • 226 cals • 23 g protein • 8 g fat of which 2 g saturates • 16 g carbohydrate

 **10** mins prep time **15** mins cook time

# baked chicken strips

Preheat the oven to 460°F (240°C). Line one or two large baking sheets with baking parchment. Cut **1 lb (500 g) skinless chicken breast fillets** lengthwise into thin strips. In a bowl, beat **1 egg** with **1 tbsp (15 mL) olive oil**, **1 tbsp (15 mL) milk** and seasoning. Add the chicken strips and mix well. Spread **6 oz (175 g) fine white bread crumbs** on a large plate or tray. Roll the chicken in the crumbs to coat evenly, then place them on the parchment-covered baking sheet. Sprinkle any remaining crumbs over and bake for 15 minutes or until crisp and golden. Serve with lemon wedges. Alternatively, heat oil for deep-frying to about 375°F (190°C) – a small cube of bread should brown in 20 seconds – and fry the chicken strips in batches, for 3-4 minutes or until they are crisp and golden. Serve with new potatoes and a salad.

For a super-fast version, roll the chicken strips in well-seasoned flour and bake without additional coating for 5-8 minutes.

...speed it up

**Each serving provides** • 284 cals • 36 g protein • 7 g fat of which 1 g saturates • 22 g carbohydrate

# barbecue-grilled chicken

Mix **1 tbsp (15 mL) canola oil**, **2 tbsp (25 mL) Dijon mustard**, **2 tbsp (25 mL) tomato paste**, **1 tbsp (15 mL) sugar** and **2 crushed garlic cloves**. Add a **good pinch of chili powder** (or more, to taste). Cut three slashes into each of **4 skinless chicken breast fillets, about ¼ lb (125 g) each**. Put in a shallow, ovenproof dish and coat both sides with the mustard mixture. Season well. Cook the fillets on a barbecue over a medium heat for 15-20 minutes, turning regularly. You may need to brush them with oil to keep them moist. Alternatively, cook under a medium grill for about 4 minutes on each side. Grill some whole **scallions** alongside to serve with the chicken. Serve with crusty bread or microwaved "baked" potatoes and salad. Also good cold.

**Each serving provides** • 203 cals • 31 g protein • 5 g fat of which 1 g saturates • 8 g carbohydrate

# chicken arrabbiata

Heat **2 tbsp (25 mL) olive oil** in a pan. Add **1 lb (500 g) skinless chicken breast fillets**, diced, with **1 chopped onion**, **2 crushed garlic cloves**, **2 diced celery sticks** and **2 seeded and chopped fresh green chili peppers or 1 tsp (5 mL) crushed chili flakes**. Cook for 5 minutes. Stir in **2 x 14-oz (398-mL) cans chopped tomatoes** and seasoning, then bring the mixture to the boil. Reduce the heat and half-cover the pan. Simmer gently for 15 minutes. Serve with cooked rigatoni or penne, offering a chunk of fresh Parmesan cheese for grating over, and freshly ground black pepper for a little extra heat.

**Each serving provides** • 231 cals • 33 g protein • 7 g fat of which 1 g saturates • 9 g carbohydrate

# Thyme **Chicken** with Roots

A great family meal that is so easy to prepare. Add a hint of thyme and orange to chicken and vegetables, then leave to roast. Serve with a green vegetable.

**15** mins prep time

**1** hour cook time

**Serves 4**

2 lbs (1 kg) floury potatoes, peeled and cut into large chunks

4 baby parsnips, peeled and cut into quarters lengthwise

4 carrots, peeled and cut in half lengthwise

1 red onion, quartered

4 tbsp (60 mL) olive oil

1 tbsp (15 mL) clear honey

1 orange, quartered

4 chicken breast fillets, with skin, about ¼ lb (125 g) each

a few sprigs of fresh thyme or rosemary, or ½ tsp (2 mL) dried

**Each serving provides** • 513 cals • 35 g protein • 19 g fat of which 4 g saturates • 55 g carbohydrate

**1** **Cook the potatoes** Preheat the oven to 375°F (190°C). Parboil the potatoes for 5 minutes, then drain. Return the potatoes to the pot, cover and shake vigorously to roughen the edges.

**2** **Prepare the vegetables and chicken** Lay the potatoes, parsnips, carrots and onion in a large roasting pan. In a small bowl, mix together the oil, honey and squeezed juice from the orange quarters. Drizzle over the vegetables and toss to coat evenly. Slash the skin on the chicken fillets several times with a sharp knife, then place among the vegetables with the squeezed orange quarters. Season and poke in the herb sprigs, or sprinkle with dried herbs.

**3** **Cook the dish** Roast the chicken and vegetables in the oven, turning the vegetables over from time to time, for 1 hour or until the chicken is golden and cooked through and all the vegetables are tender.

**To serve** If you have time, make a gravy to serve with the chicken. Transfer the chicken and vegetables to a warm plate and cover to keep warm. Sprinkle **1 tbsp (15 mL) flour** over the pan juices and stir on the stovetop for 2 minutes. Gradually add **1¼ cups (300 mL) chicken stock** and bring to a simmer, stirring until thickened.

# Paprika and Lemon Chicken
## with Halloumi Eggplants

Simply spiced chicken fillets are enhanced by speedily grilled baby eggplants stuffed with golden-crusted halloumi cheese. Fabulous with fava beans and chunks of crusty bread.

**10** mins prep time   **10** mins cook time

**Serves 4**

8 baby eggplants, about ¾ lb (375 g) total weight

5 oz (150 g) halloumi or feta cheese, cut into 8 slices

4 skinless chicken breast fillets, about ¼ lb (125 g) each

2 tsp (10 mL) paprika

grated zest of 1 lemon

2 tbsp (25 mL) olive oil

lemon wedges, to serve

**Each serving provides** • 342 cals • 39 g protein • 19 g fat of which 2 g saturates • 4 g carbohydrate

**1** **Prepare the eggplants** Leaving their stalks in place, slice the eggplants in half lengthwise. Slice each half horizontally into two layers, leaving the slices attached at the stalk end. Cut the halloumi slices in half crosswise to give pieces the right size for slipping into the eggplants later. Set aside.

**2** **Season the chicken** Preheat the grill to high. Put the chicken in a large, shallow ovenproof dish. Sprinkle with the paprika and add seasoning. Sprinkle with the lemon zest, then drizzle 1 tbsp (15 mL) oil evenly over the chicken. Turn the pieces over a few times to distribute the seasoning evenly.

**3** **Cook the chicken and eggplants** Put the eggplants in the dish, cut side up, and drizzle the remaining oil over them. Grill for 5 minutes or until the chicken is browned on one side. Turn the chicken and eggplants over and grill for a further 2 minutes.

**4** **Fill the eggplants with cheese** Slide a piece of halloumi or feta cheese between the layers of each eggplant half, then slip the top layer slightly to one side without breaking it off so that the cheese inside is exposed for grilling. Grill for a further 3 minutes or until the chicken and eggplants are cooked. Serve garnished with lemon wedges to squeeze over the chicken.

• Halloumi and feta are salty, so do not salt the eggplants.
• If baby eggplants are not available, slice 2 eggplants into 8 horizontal slices each, and lay the halloumi cheese on top of the slices. Then grill as before.

## ...cooking tips

### Jerk chicken with plantain and pickled chili peppers
Sprinkle with **jerk seasoning mix** instead of paprika and omit the lemon zest. Instead of the eggplants, slice **4 small plantains** (green bananas) in half lengthwise. Omit the halloumi. Drain a **1-lb (500-g) jar of pickled jalapeño chili peppers** and add them to the grill pan when turning the chicken and plantain over. Mix **4 tbsp (60 mL) snipped fresh chives** into **1 cup (250 mL) sour cream or Greek-style yogurt** and serve with the chicken. To accompany, crush **1 lb (500 g) boiled sweet potatoes** and toss with **½ lb (250 g) baby spinach leaves** and **3½ tbsp (45 mL) butter** over a low heat for 1-2 minutes.

## ...another idea

# One-Pot **Chicken** Casserole
## with Creamy Sherry Sauce

Take advantage of small, trimmed leeks, turnips and potatoes to speed up classic dishes with a "throw-it-all-in" approach. Brown everything briefly to add flavour, then bring it together with a creamy sauce.

**5** mins prep time

**25** mins cook time

### Serves 4

2 tbsp (25 mL) olive oil

8 skinless boneless chicken thighs, about 1¼ lb (625 g) total weight

½ lb (250 g) button mushrooms

6 oz (175 g) baby leeks

4 small turnips, peeled and quartered

1 lb (500 g) pre-washed small new potatoes

2⅓ cups (575 mL) chicken stock, made with a stock cube

4 tbsp (60 mL) medium or sweet sherry

7 oz (200 g) green beans

1 tbsp (15 mL) cornstarch

1 cup (250 mL) plain low-fat yogurt

grated zest of 1 lemon

**Each serving provides** • 477 cals • 40 g protein • 19 g fat of which 5 g saturates • 34 g carbohydrate

**1 Brown the chicken** Heat the oil in a large pot or flameproof casserole. Add the chicken, then season and cook over a high heat for 2 minutes, turning over to brown both sides. Remove from the pot and set aside on a plate.

**2 Cook the vegetables** Add the mushrooms to the pot and cook over a high heat, stirring, for 1 minute. Then reduce the heat and add the leeks, laying them across the middle of the pot and moving the mushrooms to the sides. Add the turnips and potatoes in an even layer.

**3 Add the stock and chicken** Pour in the stock and add the sherry. Bring to the boil. Put the chicken on top of the vegetables, adding any juices from the plate. Reduce the heat so that the stock bubbles steadily without boiling too fiercely. Cover and cook for 10 minutes.

**4 Cook the beans** Add the green beans, cover and continue to bubble for a further 5 minutes or until the chicken and vegetables are cooked. Using a slotted spoon, divide the ingredients among four warmed plates or transfer them to a serving dish. Keep warm while finishing the sauce.

**5 Reduce the stock** Boil the cooking stock hard, over a high heat, in the open pot for 5 minutes to reduce it slightly and concentrate the flavour. Meanwhile, mix the cornstarch to a smooth paste with the yogurt and lemon zest.

**6 Make the sauce** Gradually add a little and then most of the reduced stock to the yogurt mixture, stirring, and pour it back into the pot. Bring to the boil, stirring, to thicken the sauce slightly. (The cornstarch stabilizes the yogurt and prevents it from curdling.) Taste for seasoning. Pour a little of the sauce over the chicken and vegetables, and serve the remainder separately.

### Moroccan chicken stew

Add **2 crushed garlic cloves** and **1 tbsp (15 mL) Moroccan spice mix**, such as ras-el-hanout or harissa, with the mushrooms at step 2. Add **2 sliced red peppers** instead of turnips, and chunks of **butternut squash** instead of potatoes. Pour in **1¼ cup (300 mL) boiling water** instead of the stock and sherry, and **2 x 14-oz (398-mL) cans chopped tomatoes**. After putting the chicken thighs on the vegetables at step 3, sprinkle **2 x 14-oz (398-mL) cans chickpeas**, drained and rinsed, over the top; omit the green beans. Do not reduce the cooking juices at step 5. Omit the yogurt mixture and sprinkle with **chopped fresh coriander leaves** and **lemon zest** before serving.

**...another idea**

# Pan-fried Chicken
## with Mushrooms
## and Blueberries

A few good ingredients, cooked simply, make this dish a stylish supper. Blueberries add a hint of sweetness to the mushroom and mustard sauce, and it all goes perfectly with mashed potatoes and a salad.

**5** mins prep time

**18** mins cook time

**Serves 4**

1 tbsp (15 mL) all-purpose flour

4 skinless chicken breast fillets, about ¼ lb (125 g) each

2 tbsp (25 mL) olive oil

2 thick back (Canadian) bacon slices, cut into strips, or 3 strips bacon, chopped

½ lb (250 g) chestnut mushrooms, sliced

1 tbsp (15 mL) Dijon mustard

7 oz (200 g) blueberries

juice of ½ lemon

3 tbsp (45 mL) finely chopped fresh parsley

lemon wedges to garnish (optional)

**Each serving provides** • 274 cals • 35 g protein • 11 g fat of which 2 g saturates • 8 g carbohydrate

**To serve** If you like, crush some boiled new potatoes with a little chopped fresh parsley and seasoning, divide among the plates and serve the chicken on top.

**1** **Flour the chicken breasts** Put the flour into a shallow dish and season it well, then spread it out. Add the chicken breasts and turn them over to coat in the flour. Shake off the excess.

**2** **Cook the chicken** Heat the oil in a large frying pan over a medium-high heat. Add the chicken breasts, reduce the heat to medium and cook for 2-3 minutes or until well browned and crisp underneath. Turn over and cook for 4-5 minutes to brown and crisp the other side. Reduce the heat again, if necessary, to prevent the breasts from browning too quickly. Press them gently with the back of a spatula occasionally to help them to brown evenly. Pierce the middle of one breast with the point of a knife to check that the meat is cooked and not pink.

**3** **Cook the mushroom mixture** Transfer the chicken to a serving dish and keep warm. Add the bacon to the pan and cook, stirring, for 2 minutes or until the strips are cooked and the fat runs out. Add the mushrooms and continue to cook over a fairly high heat, stirring, for 2 minutes. Do not overcook them or they will become soggy.

**4** **Add the blueberries** Make a little space in the middle of the pan, add the mustard and quickly stir it with the mushrooms and bacon for a few seconds until well mixed. Gently stir in the blueberries. Add the lemon juice, stir and immediately remove the pan from the heat before the blueberries begin to soften.

**5** **Serve** Sprinkle in the parsley, then spoon the mushrooms and blueberries over the chicken without any more stirring. Serve immediately, garnished with lemon wedges for extra juice to sharpen the blueberries, and parsley, if you like.

**Swaps** • For chicken, use **pheasant or duck breasts, or turkey breast portions**. • Instead of using only chestnut mushrooms, use ⅔ lb (300 g) **mixed mushrooms**, such as chestnut, shiitake and oyster, halved, quartered or sliced. • For blueberries, use halved **seedless Concord or red grapes**.

# Sesame-Soy Chicken Livers
## on Crunchy Herb Salad

**Chicken livers are a wonderfully tasty and versatile basis for super-fast, healthy meals. Try this fusion of salad and Asian seasonings, served with crusty bread or rice.**

**15 mins prep time**

**10 mins cook time**

**Serves 4**
½ bok choy, shredded
2 red peppers, diced
5 oz (150 g) arugula
1 oz (30 g) fresh coriander leaves, chopped
10 scallions, thinly sliced or chopped
1 tbsp (15 mL) olive oil
1 tbsp (15 mL) toasted sesame oil
2 garlic cloves, crushed
½ lb (250 g) chicken livers, trimmed (if necessary) and each cut into 3-4 pieces
½ tsp (2 mL) five-spice powder
6 oz (175 g) thickly sliced lean cooked ham, cut into short strips
2 tbsp (25 mL) soy sauce
4 tbsp (60 mL) dry sherry
2 tbsp (25 mL) sesame seeds

**Each serving provides**
• 265 cals • 24 g protein • 13 g fat of which 3 g saturates • 9 g carbohydrate

**1** **Prepare the salad** Mix the bok choy, peppers, arugula and coriander leaves in a large bowl. Add half the scallions and mix well. Divide the salad among four plates or pasta bowls.

**2** **Cook the chicken livers** Heat the olive and sesame oils in a frying pan over a medium heat. Add the garlic, chicken livers and five-spice powder. Cook for 3 minutes, stirring and turning the livers until they are firm. Add the ham and cook for a further minute, turning and stirring gently.

**3** **Make the dressing** Add the soy sauce and sherry to the pan, and bring to the boil. Shake the pan and stir gently, taking care not to break up the livers. Let the mixture bubble for a few seconds so that the alcohol evaporates from the sherry. Add the remaining scallions and remove the pan from the heat.

**4** **Serve** Divide the chicken liver mixture among the salads and spoon over the juices as a dressing. Sprinkle with the sesame seeds and serve.

### Chicken livers with mustard and tarragon
Make the salad as for the basic recipe, but substitute **parsley** for the coriander, if you prefer. Omit the sesame oil and use **2 tbsp (25 mL) olive oil**. Add the garlic and chicken livers, with **¼ tsp (1 mL) ground mace**, or a **little freshly grated nutmeg**, instead of the five-spice powder. Add the ham with **1 tbsp (15 mL) whole-grain mustard**. Omit the soy sauce and stir in the dry sherry with the **grated zest of 1 lemon**. Add **2 tbsp (25 mL) chopped fresh tarragon** with the remaining scallions at step 3. Season and serve. This dish is also good served on chunky slices of whole-grain toast, for a hasty supper.

**...another idea**

# Orange Chicken and Rice Salad

Cooked chicken makes a healthy meal in minutes if you add rice and a little imagination. Perk it up with pistachios, crisp carrot, zesty orange and punchy chives.

**15** mins prep time

**12** mins cook time

**Serves 4**

1 cup (250 mL) long-grain rice

⅔ lb (300 g) carrots, peeled and grated

juice of 1 large orange

2 tsp (10 mL) English mustard

2 tbsp (25 mL) olive oil

6 tbsp (90 mL) snipped fresh chives

1 lb (500 g) ready-cooked skinless chicken breast fillets, cut into bite-sized chunks

4 tbsp (60 mL) pistachio nuts

7 oz (200 g) lamb's lettuce (mâche) or baby spinach

orange wedges, to garnish (optional)

**Each serving provides** • 464 cals • 38 g protein • 13 g fat of which 2 g saturates • 52 g carbohydrate

1 **Cook the rice** Put the rice into a large pot and add plenty of boiling water. Bring back to the boil and stir once, then lower the heat to a gentle simmer. Cover and cook for 10-12 minutes or until the grains are just tender. Drain.

2 **Prepare the salad** While the rice is cooking, put the carrots in a large bowl. Add the orange juice, mustard, oil and chives. Season. Add the chicken and mix into the salad with the pistachio nuts.

3 **Finish the salad** Add the rice to the salad and mix lightly. The cold ingredients and dressing will quickly cool the rice to make a deliciously warm salad. Toss in the lamb's lettuce leaves and serve garnished with orange wedges, if you like.

**Swaps** • For rice, use **orzo** (Greek rice-shaped pasta) **or small soup pasta shapes**. • For the chicken, use diced, cooked **turkey or ham** (or a mixture of both), **or smoked pork loin**. • For carrots, use **grated celeriac** with the **grated zest and juice of 1 lime** instead of the orange.

The salad can be made earlier in the day, a few hours before you want to eat. Cook the rice in advance, drain and leave it to cool. Prepare and mix the other ingredients but keep them separate until the rice has completely cooled. Mix, cover and chill the salad until required. Remove from the fridge about 20 minutes before serving.

**...get ahead**

Make the salad with brown rice if you have a little more time to spare – the rice takes about 30 minutes to cook.

**...healthy plus**

# Aromatic Chicken
## and Vegetable Steamboat

**In this super-quick version of a Mongolian firepot, morsels of spiced chicken and vegetables are cooked in a fragrant stock with rice noodles. The broth is served at the end of the meal.**

*Serves 4*

- **1 lb (500 g) skinless chicken breast fillets, cut into thin strips**
- **½ tsp (2 mL) five-spice powder**
- **2 tbsp (25 mL) light soy sauce**
- **1¼-in. (3-cm) piece fresh ginger, peeled and chopped**
- **1 celery stick, thinly sliced**
- **1 garlic clove, thinly sliced**
- **1 lemon grass stalk or strip of lemon peel**
- **6 cups (1.5 L) chicken stock, made with stock cubes**
- **1 large red pepper, cut into chunks**
- **½ lb (250 g) baby corn**
- **7 oz (200 g) broccoli florets**
- **2 scallions, thinly sliced**
- **½ lb (250 g) fresh rice noodles (or straight-to-wok noodles)**
- **½ lb (250 g) bok choy, quartered lengthwise**

**Each serving provides** • 315 cals • 37 g protein • 6 g fat of which 1 g saturates • 29 g carbohydrate

**30** mins prep/cook time

**1 Flavour the chicken** Put the chicken into a bowl. Add the five-spice powder and soy sauce, and mix well. Set aside.

**2 Prepare the stock** Put the ginger into a large pot with the celery, garlic, lemon grass or lemon peel and stock. Bring to the boil, then reduce the heat. Cover and simmer for 5 minutes.

**3 Cook the chicken and vegetables** Add the chicken to the stock, then add the red pepper, baby corn and broccoli. Bring back to the boil and simmer for 3 minutes or until the chicken is cooked and the vegetables are barely tender.

**4 Add the noodles** Add the scallions and noodles, and stir gently and briefly to combine, then bring back to the boil.

Lay the bok choy over the top and simmer for about 2 minutes or until the bok choy leaves are wilted and the noodles are hot and cooked.

**5 Serve** Take the pot to the table and serve, ladling the cooked ingredients into bowls with a little of the broth. Ladle out the last of the broth at the end of the meal.

**Swap** For noodles, use **Chinese dumplings or won ton**, found among dim sum selections (especially in Chinese and Asian supermarkets). There are several different types, with various fillings. Follow the pack instructions for serving portions and timing.

# Sizzling Chicken Salad
## with Dates and Minted Yogurt

Crunchy seeds with dates and garlic add texture and flavour to lightly spiced grilled chicken and a green salad simply dressed with minty yogurt. Serve with flatbread or crusty baguette.

**10** mins prep time  **10** mins cook time

**Serves 4**

**4 skinless chicken breast fillets,** about ¼ lb (125 g) each

**2 garlic cloves, crushed**

**1 tsp (5 mL) ground mace**

**3 tbsp (45 mL) olive oil**

**1 romaine or iceberg lettuce, torn** into pieces

**5 oz (150 g) arugula**

**4 scallions, sliced**

**14 oz (398 mL) can artichoke hearts,** drained and halved

**8 tender mint sprigs, chopped,** plus extra to garnish

**1 cup (250 mL) plain low-fat yogurt**

**4 tbsp (60 mL) mixed seeds (such as** sunflower, sesame, pumpkin and linseed)

**3½ oz (100 g) dried pitted dates,** sliced

**Each serving provides** • 407 cals • 38.5 g protein • 17 g fat of which 3 g saturates • 29 g carbohydrate

**Swaps** • For dates, use ready-to-eat **dried figs.** • For chicken, use **turkey or pheasant.**

---

● Choose a dish or pan that the chicken will fill snugly for grilling, and that will hold the juices and prevent them from evaporating and burning during cooking.

● Look out for packages of mixed seeds on the snack shelves in supermarkets and health-food shops. They are usually pre-roasted, so need only a few seconds to make them crisp and brown under the grill.

## ...cooking tips

**1 Season the chicken** Preheat the grill to high. Put the chicken breasts in a shallow ovenproof dish or pan. Sprinkle with a little salt and pepper, the garlic, mace and oil, then turn the chicken pieces over a few times to distribute the seasonings.

**2 Cook the chicken** Slide the dish or pan under the grill and cook the chicken for 10 minutes, turning once, until well browned on both sides and cooked through. Test by piercing the thickest part with the point of a knife; the juices should run clear and the flesh should be white, not pink. Leave the chicken in the dish or pan to add the topping.

**3 Assemble the salad** While the chicken is cooking, mix the lettuce, arugula, scallions and artichoke hearts. Divide the salad among four large plates. Mix the mint into the yogurt and set aside.

**4 Add the seeds and dates** Turn the chicken over and sprinkle with the seeds, pressing them on with a spoon. Grill for 10-20 seconds to heat and brown the seeds. Add the dates and stir them with the seeds and juices around the chicken.

**5 Serve** Slice the chicken and arrange it on the salads with the dates and seeds, spooning over all the cooking juices. Drizzle the mint and yogurt dressing over, and serve immediately, garnished with mint.

# Orange Turkey Sauté

A sauté is a French-style stir-fry, cooked over a high heat in a frying pan – great for pre-cut turkey strips cooked with mushrooms, orange and brandy. Accompany with buckwheat, rice or couscous.

**10** mins prep time

**8** mins cook time

**Serves 4**

2 tbsp (25 mL) olive oil
1 small onion, chopped
1 lb (500 g) turkey strips
¾ lb (375 g) mushrooms, sliced
4 tbsp (60 mL) brandy
grated zest and juice of
   2 oranges
1 tsp (5 mL) sugar
8 tbsp (125 mL) chopped fresh
   parsley
4 tbsp (60 mL) plain low-fat yogurt

**Each serving provides** • 268 cals • 32 g protein • 8 g fat of which 5 g saturates • 8 g carbohydrate

**Swaps** • For turkey, use **chicken strips**. • Instead of brandy, use **cider or dry sherry**.

**1 Fry the onion** Heat the oil in a large frying pan. Add the onion and cook over a high heat for 1 minute, stirring frequently.

**2 Cook the turkey** Add the turkey and cook, stirring and turning frequently over a high heat, for 2-4 minutes or until the strips are browned and just cooked.

**3 Add the mushrooms** Stir in the mushrooms and cook over a medium-high heat for 1 minute, so that the mushrooms begin to brown.

**4 Make the sauce** Add the brandy – it will sizzle and hiss – followed by the orange zest and juice, and the sugar. Boil, stirring, for about 1 minute, just long enough to coat everything with the sauce. Season and add the parsley. Serve immediately, drizzling yogurt over each portion.

## Turkey sauté with mascarpone

Add **2 crushed garlic cloves** with the onion at step 1 and **2 bottled marinated red peppers**, sliced into strips, with the turkey at step 2. Instead of brandy, orange zest and juice, add **¾ cup (175 mL) tomato paste** with the sugar. Omit the yogurt. Enrich the sauce by stirring in **3-4 tbsp (45-60 mL) mascarpone** and finish with **2 oz (60 g) sliced black olives** and **basil leaves** instead of parsley. Serve topped with shavings of **Parmesan cheese**. Serve with gnocchi, cooked according to the package instructions.

**...another idea**

• The turkey mixture is great for prepare-ahead pies (pastry-topped or shepherd's-pie-style with mashed potato), in lasagna (layered with a tomato sauce, lasagna and a cheese sauce topping) or for filling pancakes (buy unsweetened pre-made), or wraps. • Fill pancakes or wraps with the turkey mixture, then roll up and put into a greased ovenproof dish. Top with grated cheese, then cover with foil and bake for about 15 minutes at 400°F (200°C).

**...get ahead**

# 5 ways with leftover chicken or turkey

One of the joys of a roast chicken or turkey is the tender meat left over – perfect for rustling up a super-quick meal. Add pantry flavourings, some fresh ingredient basics and perhaps a few special extras, and you're ready to go. All recipes serve 4.

## coronation **turkey** with mixed-vegetable rice

Mix **4 finely chopped scallions** and **3½ oz (100 g) chopped ready-to-eat dried apricots** with **6¾ tbsp (100 mL) mayonnaise** and **6¾ tbsp (100 mL) plain low-fat yogurt**. Add **1-3 tsp (5-15 mL) curry paste** (your favourite strength), to taste, and seasoning. Stir in **⅔ lb (300 g) diced cooked turkey**. Cook a **24-oz (750-g) package frozen rice with vegetables** in a large frying pan according to the package instructions. Add the chicken or turkey mayonnaise mixture to the rice mixture and stir over a very low heat for 2-3 minutes to heat through, stirring frequently. Serve immediately.

**Each serving provides** • 511 cals
• 34 g protein • 22 g fat of which
4 g saturates • 45 g carbohydrate

**10** mins prep time    **10** mins cook time

## stuffed **peppers** with **chicken** and couscous

Put **1 cup (250 mL) couscous**, **2 tbsp (25mL) currants** and **1 chopped garlic clove** in a bowl and pour over **1¼ cup (300 mL) boiling vegetable stock**, made with a stock cube. Cover and leave to stand. Meanwhile, halve and seed **4 red or green peppers**, then cook in boiling water for 5 minutes. Drain well and put into a grill pan, cut side up. Stir **½ lb (250 g) diced cooked chicken** and **1 tbsp (15 mL) chopped fresh oregano** into the couscous. Season, then divide among the peppers. Top with **3½ oz (100 g) crumbled feta cheese** and broil slowly, under a medium heat, for 10 minutes or until hot and golden. Serve with salad.

**Each serving provides** • 322 cals • 27 g protein
• 8 g fat of which 4 g saturates • 37 g carbohydrate

**10** mins prep time    **15** mins cook time

# chicken, chickpea and pepper sauté

Heat **2 tbsp (25mL) olive oil** in a large pan. Add **1 large sliced onion**, **1 tbsp (15 mL) grated fresh ginger** and **1 chopped garlic clove**, and cook for 3 minutes. Add **1 each sliced red, green and yellow peppers** and cook for a further 3 minutes. Stir in about **7 oz (200 g) diced cooked chicken** and **2 x 14-oz (398-mL) cans chickpeas**, drained and rinsed. Season and cook gently for 2-3 minutes or until thoroughly heated. Add **2 tbsp (25mL) chopped fresh coriander leaves** and the **grated zest of 1 lemon**. Serve with warm crusty bread and a bowl of plain low-fat yogurt with snipped fresh chives stirred in.

**Each serving provides** • 318 cals • 26 g protein • 11 g fat of which 2 g saturates • 30 g carbohydrate

**15** mins prep time  **9** mins cook time

# chicken in chinese pancakes

Put **1 tbsp (15 mL) olive oil** in a small frying pan with **4 tbsp (60 mL) soy sauce** and **4 tbsp (60 mL) dry sherry**. Add **½ tsp (2 mL) five-spice powder**, **2 crushed garlic cloves** and **1 tbsp (15 mL) sugar**. Gently heat until the sugar dissolves, then bring to the boil and let the mixture bubble for a minute. Cut about **⅔ lb (300 g) cooked chicken** into strips and add to the pan. Cook, stirring, for 3-4 minutes or until the chicken is hot and sticky. Shred **1 bunch of scallions** and slice **1 cucumber**, then arrange on a plate with **½ bok choy**, shredded. Heat **2 packages of Chinese pancakes** according to the package instructions. Serve the chicken with the scallions, cucumber, bok choy and pancakes. Each diner places a little chicken and lots of vegetables in each pancake, then rolls it up.

**Each serving provides** • 409 cals • 32 g protein • 11 g fat of which 2 g saturates • 41 g carbohydrate

**15** mins prep time  **8** mins cook time

# turkey and pomegranate salad

Dice **7 oz (200 g) cooked turkey** and **3½ oz (100 g) cooked ham** and mix together. Whisk **2 tbsp (25mL) balsamic vinegar** and **1 tsp (5 mL) sugar** with **4 tbsp (60 mL) olive oil in a large bowl**. Halve and thinly slice **1 red onion** and add to the bowl with **3½ oz (100 g) watercress** and the torn leaves of **1 lettuce**. Toss with the dressing. Scatter with the **seeds of 1 pomegranate, or 7 oz (200 g) blueberries or halved, seedless red grapes**, then with **4 tbsp (60 mL) chopped pecan nuts or walnuts** and **¾ cup (175 mL) finely crumbled blue cheese**, such as Stilton. Divide among four plates or bowls. Add the turkey and ham. Serve with bread.

**Each serving provides** • 415 cals • 30 g protein • 27 g fat of which 7 g saturates • 5 g carbohydrate

**20** mins prep time

You can use either chicken or turkey in any of these recipes.

**...cooking tip**

# Mandarin Turkey
### with **Bean Sprout** and
### **Watercress** Salad

**Griddling is an ideal way to cook turkey steaks quickly. These have a punchy seasoning and are partnered with sweet and tangy mandarins. Serve with warm chapatis and a salad of bean sprouts and watercress.**

**15** mins prep time

**5** mins cook time

**Serves 4**

**4 turkey breast steaks, about ¼ lb (125 g) each**

**2 tbsp (25 mL) chopped fresh rosemary**

**1 tsp (5 mL) crushed chili flakes**

**1 tbsp (15 mL) coriander seeds, coarsely crushed**

**2 tbsp (25 mL) olive oil**

**4 mandarin oranges**

**14 oz (400 g) bean sprouts**

**2⅔ oz (75 g) watercress**

**8 scallions, sliced**

**4 tsp (20 mL) sugar**

**8 tbsp (125 mL) mayonnaise**

**cayenne pepper (optional)**

**Each serving provides** • 478 cals • 39 g protein • 30 g fat of which 5 g saturates • 14 g carbohydrate

**1 Prepare the turkey** Put the turkey steaks into a shallow dish. Sprinkle with the rosemary, crushed chili flakes, coriander seeds and 1 tbsp (15 mL) oil. Season and turn the steaks over a few times to distribute the seasonings.

**2 Prepare the mandarins** Peel the mandarins, then slice in half across the middle and discard any seeds.

**3 Make the salad** Mix the bean sprouts, watercress and scallions, and divide them among four plates.

**4 Cook the turkey** Heat a ridged griddle or frying pan over a high heat. Brush the turkey steaks with the remaining oil. Cook over a high heat for 1½-2 minutes on each side or until well browned and cooked through; when cut, the juices should run clear, not pink. Transfer to the plates.

**5 Cook the mandarins** Add the mandarin halves to the griddle or pan, cut side down, and cook for 30-60 seconds or until they are browned on the surface and hot. Transfer them to the plates, browned side up, and top each half with ½ tsp (2 mL) sugar. Add a dollop of mayonnaise to each plate and sprinkle with a little cayenne pepper, if you like. Serve.

**Swaps** • For turkey, use **duck**. Buy skinless, boneless breast fillets and beat them out thinly between two pieces of baking parchment or greaseproof paper. • Or use **thin pork loin steaks**.

If you have a vegetarian in the family, you can use the seasoning in step 1 for tofu instead of turkey. For one person, use **half a block of firm tofu** and slice it in half horizontally. Season with ½ **tbsp (7 mL) finely chopped rosemary**, a pinch of **crushed chili flakes, 1 tsp (5 mL) ground coriander** and **1 tsp (5 mL) olive oil**. (You will need two blocks of tofu for four people, using the full quantity of seasoning, but using ground coriander and finely chopped rosemary.) Put the tofu into an ovenproof dish and grill for 3-4 minutes on each side to brown both sides, turning the slices with a large slotted spatula. (They are less likely to stick and break if grilled rather than griddled or fried.)

...or try this

# Best Turkey Burgers

Made with ground turkey, these burgers are big on flavour and low in fat, for a satisfying dinner that's quick to make and a great favourite with children. Serve in English muffins or ciabatta rolls.

**15** mins prep time

**10** mins cook time

Serves 4

**1 lb (500 g) ground turkey**
**4 scallions, thinly sliced**
**2 tsp (10 mL) dried mixed herbs**
**1 tsp (5 mL) ground mace**
**1 tbsp (15 mL) tomato paste**
**1 tbsp (15 mL) canola oil**
**4 English muffins or ciabatta rolls**
**2 tbsp (25 mL) mayonnaise**
**8 lettuce leaves**
**½ onion, thinly sliced (optional)**
**about 20 cherry tomatoes, to serve**

Each serving provides • 453 cals
• 37 g protein • 15 g fat of which
3 g saturates • 45 g carbohydrate

**1 Flavour the turkey** Put the turkey into a bowl. Add the scallions, herbs, mace and tomato paste, with plenty of seasoning. Mix well until thoroughly combined, stirring and pressing the mixture firmly with the back of the mixing spoon.

**2 Shape the burgers** Divide the mixture into four portions. Roll one portion into a ball, then press it flat into a fairly thin burger, about 4 in. (10 cm) in diameter. Set aside on a plate or board. Repeat with the remaining mixture.

**3 Cook the burgers** Heat a very large frying pan over a high heat, then add the canola oil and tilt the pan to coat it evenly. Add the burgers, reduce the heat to medium and press them flat with a spatula. Cook for 4-5 minutes or until the burgers are well browned underneath. Turn over, press flat and cook for a further 4-5 minutes or until well browned on the second side.

**4 Finish and serve** While the burgers are cooking, slice the English muffins or rolls in half horizontally and spread the bottom layer with mayonnaise. Add a couple of lettuce leaves to each. When cooked, put a burger on each and add a little onion, if you like. Replace the top of the roll and serve with a little pile of cherry tomatoes.

**Swaps** • Make the burgers with **ground turkey breast** for a lighter flavour and softer texture. • Or try them with **ground chicken**.

**Cooking tip** The bread can be toasted until golden on the split side, if you prefer.

The turkey meatball mixture (see right) can be used to make sophisticated burgers. Try serving them on slices of grilled pre-made **polenta** (cooked according to the package instructions, or use homemade, see Cooking tip, page 151). Top the burgers with a bought tomato salsa or a hot tomato sauce, and serve with a salad, or with creamy mashed potatoes and stir-fried cabbage.

**...or try this**

## Turkey meatballs

Make meatballs with **ground turkey breast** and **2 tbsp (25 mL) chopped fresh tarragon or sage** (or a mixture) instead of the dried herbs. Omit the tomato paste and add **3½ oz (100 g) chopped cooked ham**, **1 beaten egg** and **4 tbsp (60 mL) rolled oats**. Mix, then roll into balls the size of small plums. Fry in the oil over a medium heat, rolling them around the pan with a spoon and fork to keep them in shape. When browned, add **2 x 14-oz (398-mL) cans chopped tomatoes**, **4 tbsp (60 mL) sherry** and seasoning. Bring to the boil, then reduce the heat and cover. Simmer for 20 minutes or until the meatballs are cooked and the sauce well flavoured. Stir occasionally. Serve with rice.

**...another idea**

# Blue-Brie Turkey Pockets
## with Quick Cabbage and Walnuts

For a smart meal in the minimum of time, stuff turkey breasts with rich, creamy blue brie and add a flavour kick of lively ginger and sweet apple. Serve with new potatoes and stir-fried cabbage with walnuts.

**Serves 4**

1 oz (30 g) fresh ginger, peeled and grated

1 dessert apple, peeled, cored and grated

4 thick turkey breast steaks, about ¼ lb (125 g) each

5 oz (150 g) blue brie, cut into 4 wedges

3 tbsp (45 mL) olive oil

1 lb (500 g) green cabbage, finely shredded

8 scallions, sliced

1¾ oz (50 g) walnuts, chopped

**Each serving provides** • 507 cals • 52 g protein • 30 g fat of which 9 g saturates • 9 g carbohydrate

**1 Stuff the turkey pockets** Preheat the oven to 460°F (240°C). Mix the ginger and apple. Cut horizontally through each turkey breast, slicing a pocket into the meat. Take care not to cut right through. Divide the ginger and apple mixture among the pockets, then push a wedge of cheese into each one. Press the meat together, moulding it back into shape and pushing the filling evenly into the pockets.

**2 Bake the turkey** Put the turkey pockets in a shallow ovenproof dish, large enough to hold them neatly in one layer. Brush with 1 tbsp (15 mL) oil and sprinkle with seasoning to taste. Bake for 15 minutes or until the turkey is browned on top and cooked through, and the filling is running out in places.

**3 Cook the cabbage and walnuts** While the turkey is cooking, heat the remaining oil in a large pan and add the cabbage, scallions and walnuts. Cook over a medium heat, stirring most of the time, for about 5 minutes or until the cabbage is reduced in volume and lightly cooked. Add seasoning to taste.

**4 Serve** Transfer the turkey pockets to plates using a large serving spoon, spooning over the escaping cheese and juices. Add some cabbage to each plate and serve immediately.

**15** mins prep time **15** mins cook time

### Breaded mozzarella and tomato escalopes
Lightly season **4 thin turkey breast steaks**, about 1 lb (500 g) total weight, and put them in a shallow ovenproof dish in a single layer. Top with **4 thinly sliced plum tomatoes** and sprinkle with **8 shredded fresh sage leaves**. Thinly slice **7 oz (200 g) mozzarella cheese** and arrange on top of the tomatoes. Brush with **1 tbsp (15 mL) olive oil**. Mix **1¾ oz (50 g) fresh bread crumbs** with **3 tbsp (45 mL) grated Parmesan cheese**, and press this onto the mozzarella to cover the tops of the steaks completely. Bake as the basic recipe for 15 minutes or until the topping is crisp and golden, with the mozzarella moist and runny.

## ...another idea

# Brandied Blackcurrant **Duck** with Sautéed Parsnips

Slightly sweet parsnips are superb with crisp-skinned duck fillets in a rich, fruity glaze that's simplicity itself to make. Serve with steamed green beans and warm French bread.

**10** mins prep time

**20** mins cook time

**Serves 4**

½ lb (250 g) small parsnips, peeled and cut into ¼-in. (5-mm) slices

2 onions, each cut into 8 wedges

4 duck breast fillets, about 7 oz (200 g) each

1 tbsp (15 mL) canola oil

8 tbsp (125 mL) brandy

4 tbsp (60 mL) blackcurrant liqueur

juice of 1 lemon

parsley sprigs, to garnish

**Each serving provides** • 768 cals • 29 g protein • 55 g fat of which 16 g saturates • 23 g carbohydrate

### Duck in orange and sherry sauce

Omit the parsnips and onion wedges. Instead of the blackcurrant glaze, add **1 thinly sliced red onion** to the frying pan for the final 5 minutes of cooking. Then remove the onion with the duck. Add the **grated zest and juice of 2 oranges**, **4 tbsp (60 mL) sherry**, **1 tbsp (15 mL) sherry vinegar or balsamic vinegar**, **1 tsp (5 mL) soft dark brown sugar** and the **juice of 1 lemon** to the pan. Boil, stirring in all the sediment from the pan, to thicken the sauce. Spoon over the duck. Serve with new potatoes.

## ...another idea

**1 Cook the vegetables** Put the parsnips and onions into a large pan and pour in boiling water to cover. Bring back to the boil, then cover and reduce the heat. Simmer for 5 minutes. The parsnips should be tender but firm. Drain thoroughly, then return the vegetables to the pan.

**2 Crisp the duck skin** While the vegetables are cooking, prick the duck skin all over without cutting into the meat. Heat the canola oil in a frying pan over a high heat and add the duck breasts, skin side down. Reduce the heat and cook, pressing the duck occasionally (but not turning the pieces), for 5 minutes or until the fat has run and the skin is crisp and very well browned.

**3 Brown the vegetables** Drizzle 2 tbsp (25 mL) of the duck fat over the parsnips and onions, and mix well, then set them over a low-medium heat to brown lightly and slowly while the duck finishes cooking. Stir and turn the parsnips and onions occasionally, adding seasoning to taste. The parsnips should remain firm and the pieces of onion should be tender but slightly crisp in places. Transfer to warm plates.

**4 Finish cooking the duck** Pour off the remaining excess fat from the frying pan and turn the duck breasts over. Cook them over a low-medium heat for 10-15 minutes, turning over once more. After 10 minutes, they will be very pink and juicy in the middle; after 15 minutes they should be cooked through but still pale pink in the middle and succulent. Season during the last minute or so. Arrange the duck over the vegetables, sliced if you prefer.

**5 Make the glaze** Add the brandy, blackcurrant liqueur and lemon juice to the frying pan. Bring to the boil over a high heat and boil for about 30 seconds, stirring in all the sediment from the pan, to reduce the mixture to a sticky, aromatic sauce. Spoon this over the duck, add parsley to garnish and serve immediately.

# Crispy Duck
## with Garlic and Rosemary Roasted Potatoes

**This has all the appeal of a fabulous Sunday roast but cooks in a fraction of the time. Enjoy the crispy duck and aromatic potatoes with steamed cauliflower florets and a leaf salad.**

**5** mins prep time

**25** mins cook time

Serves 4

1 lb (500 g) pre-washed baby new potatoes

8 garlic cloves, peeled

2 tbsp (25 mL) chopped fresh rosemary

4 duck breast fillets, about 7 oz (200 g) each

8 fresh bay leaves, plus extra to garnish

fruit jelly or preserve, such as crabapple or currant, to serve

**Each serving provides** • 686 cals • 30 g protein • 52 g fat of which 16 g saturates • 25 g carbohydrate

**1 Parboil the potatoes** Preheat the oven to 460°F (240°C). Put the potatoes and garlic in a pot, add boiling water to cover and boil for 5 minutes. Drain well and turn into a large, shallow ovenproof dish. Sprinkle with the rosemary, season and set aside.

**2 Roast the duck** While the potatoes are cooking, prick the skin on the duck breasts all over and put into a small roasting pan, skin side up. Scrunch the bay leaves to release their flavour, then rub them over the duck skin. Put two leaves under each duck breast. Season and roast for 5 minutes.

**3 Roast the potatoes** Spoon a little duck fat from the roasting pan over the potatoes and roll them around in the dish to coat them. Put them into the oven. Continue to roast the duck with the potatoes for 20 minutes or until both are well browned and cooked. Turn and baste the duck twice more. Add a little more duck fat to the potatoes, if necessary, and pour off any excess from the roasting pan

**4 Serve** Discard the bay leaves before serving and garnish with fresh leaves. Serve with a sweet and tangy fruit jelly or preserve.

**Swaps** • For garlic, use **sprigs of fresh thyme** with the rosemary. • Instead of (or as well as) bay leaves, cook the duck on a bed of **orange peel, pared thickly from 2 oranges**. Serve garnished with **orange wedges**, so that their juice can be squeezed over. • For duck, use **chicken breast fillets** with skin on, cooked the same way, but reduce the oven temperature to 425°F (220°C). Put **sprigs of fresh thyme** and pared **lemon peel** under the chicken and brush the skin with **olive oil**. Season the skin well.

# Sweet-and-Sour Duck

Crisp, stir-fried sugar snap peas make a fresh contrast with soft noodles and rich, roasted duck served with a quick-and-easy sauce of honey, soy sauce and lime juice.

**Serves 4**
4 duck breast fillets, about 7 oz (200 g) each
2 tbsp (25 mL) soy sauce
2 tbsp (25 mL) clear honey
1 tbsp (15 mL) fresh lime juice
1 tbsp (15 mL) peanut oil
7 oz (200 g) sugar snap peas
4 x 5-oz (150-g) packages straight-to-wok medium noodles
sweet chili sauce, to serve

**Each serving provides** • 872 cals • 38 g protein • 54 g fat of which 16 g saturates • 60 g carbohydrate

**Swaps** • For sugar snap peas, use **7 oz (200 g) broccoli, cut into ¾-1½-in. (2-3-cm) pieces,** or **5 oz (150 g) snow peas,** cut in half lengthwise, with **1 carrot,** peeled and cut into fine matchstick strips. • Frozen **soya beans** would also work well in this recipe, instead of the sugar snap peas.

**1 Prepare the duck** Preheat the oven to 400°F (200°C). Score a criss-cross pattern all over the duck skin and through the fat, without cutting into the meat. Heat a flameproof casserole or heavy-based frying pan over a medium heat and add the duck breasts skin side down.

**2 Brown the duck** Blend the soy sauce, honey and lime juice together, then brush a little over the meaty side of the duck. Fry for 3-4 minutes or until the skin is well browned, then turn over and cook for a further minute. Remove the duck to a plate and pour off the fat in the pan. If using a flameproof casserole, wipe it clean with a paper towel, then return the duck to the casserole, skin side up. Otherwise transfer the duck to a warmed ovenproof dish so that it is skin side up.

**3 Roast the duck** Stir 2 tbsp (25 mL) cold water into the remaining soy sauce mixture and drizzle over the duck. Transfer the casserole or dish to the oven and roast for 8-10 minutes or until the duck is cooked through and the sauce is thickened and reduced.

**4 Stir-fry the sugar snap peas** While the duck is roasting, heat a wok or large frying pan with the oil over a medium-high heat and stir-fry the sugar snap peas for 3-4 minutes or until almost tender. If not quite ready by this time, add 2 tbsp (25 mL) water, cover with a lid and steam for a further 1-2 minutes.

**5 Assemble the dish** Pour the sauce from the duck into the pan with the peas, add the noodles and stir-fry for 5 minutes. Carve the duck into thin slices, then add to the noodles and toss over a high heat for a final few seconds. Serve at once, with the sweet chili sauce separately.

**30** mins prep/cook time

---

The drained fat from the duck can be saved and used for roasting potatoes. Keep refrigerated and use within one week.

## ...keep it

---

**Serves 4**
3 tbsp (45 mL) fish sauce or soy sauce
2 tbsp (25 mL) toasted sesame oil
1 tbsp (15 mL) soft dark brown sugar
1¾ oz (50 g) fresh ginger, peeled and chopped
4 duck breast fillets, about 7 oz (200 g) each
½ lb (250 g) baby corn
7 oz (200 g) dried medium egg noodles
14 oz (400 g) bean sprouts
7 oz (200 g) bok choy, shredded
8 scallions, sliced
1 red chili pepper, halved, seeded and thinly sliced
2 tbsp (25 mL) smooth or crunchy peanut butter
grated zest and juice of 1 lime
1 garlic clove, crushed

**Each serving provides** • 980 cals • 42 g protein • 69 g fat of which 19 g saturates • 50 g carbohydrate

**10** mins prep time   **20** mins cook time

---

If entertaining, provide friends with a choice of toppings in addition to the duck, by cooking vegetarian or seafood options. Bake one or more blocks of tofu (about ½ lb/250 g each) in the marinade or use the marinade to coat thick portions of salmon fillet (about 4 oz/125 g each serving). Cook the duck, tofu and salmon in separate dishes.

## ...or try this

# Ginger Duck with Noodle Salad
## and Spicy Peanut Dressing

**Thai-style seasonings bring piquant flavours to this fast but elegant salad. Succulent roast duck tops a fabulous mix of soft noodles and crunchy bean sprouts, baby corn and bok choy, tossed with chili.**

**1 Prepare the seasoning** Preheat the oven to 460°F (240°C). Mix 2 tbsp (25 mL) of the fish or soy sauce with the sesame oil and sugar in a shallow ovenproof dish just large enough to hold the duck breasts snugly in a single layer. Stir in half the ginger.

**2 Cook the duck** Score a criss-cross pattern all over the duck skin and through the fat, without cutting into the meat. Put the breasts into the dish and turn them over several times to coat with the seasoning. Roast, skin side up, for 18-20 minutes or until the skin is crisp and very well browned (check after 15 minutes). The meat should be just cooked through, with a hint of pinkness in the middle.

**3 Prepare the salad** While the duck is roasting, put the baby corn into a large pot and pour in plenty of boiling water. Boil for 2 minutes. Add the noodles and boil for a further 2 minutes. Drain in a colander and rinse for a couple of seconds under cold water. Shake well to drain. Transfer to a large bowl. Add the bean sprouts, bok choy, most of the scallions (reserve a little for sprinkling over the duck) and half the chili pepper slices. Mix well and divide among four large plates or pasta bowls.

**4 Make the peanut dressing** Mix the peanut butter with the lime zest and juice, garlic and the remaining fish or soy sauce. Stir in 1 tbsp (15 mL) water.

**5 Assemble the dish** Transfer the duck breasts to a plate. Carefully spoon off the fat from the juices in the dish, then stir 1 tbsp (15 mL) boiling water into the juices. Slice the duck breasts, if you have time. Drizzle the peanut dressing over the salads. Top with the duck and spoon over the cooking juices (there will not be much, but it will have lots of flavour). Sprinkle with the remaining ginger, chili pepper slices and scallions, and serve at once.

# meat

# Pan-Fried Steaks
## with Italian Sauce

Lean, juicy steaks are quick to cook and taste delicious with a tomato sauce, jazzed up with a little wine, garlic, olives and capers. Serve with tagliatelle and a salad of leaves and thinly sliced green pepper.

**10** mins prep time  **20** mins cook time

**Serves 4**

4 rump or sirloin steaks, trimmed of fat, about ¼ lb (125 g) each

2 tbsp (25 mL) olive oil

1 onion, finely chopped

2 garlic cloves, crushed

14 oz (398 mL) can chopped tomatoes

6¾ tbsp (100 mL) white or red wine

⅔ lb (300 g) tagliatelle

1 tbsp (15 mL) capers, drained and rinsed

12 pitted black or green olives, halved

2 tbsp (25 mL) chopped fresh basil, plus basil leaves, to garnish (optional)

**Each serving provides** • 469 cals • 38 g protein • 14 g fat of which 3 g saturates • 48 g carbohydrate

**Addition** After frying the onion and garlic, add **7 oz (200 g) sliced mushrooms** to the sauce. Omit the capers and olives, if you like.

**1 Season and cook the steaks** Rub the steaks on both sides with 1 tbsp (15 mL) olive oil and a little black pepper. Heat a large frying pan, then cook the steaks, in two batches if necessary, for about 2½ minutes on each side for rare, 4 minutes each side for medium, and 7 minutes each side for well done. Remove to a plate using a slotted spoon and keep warm.

**2 Make the sauce** Add the remaining oil to the pan, then add the onion and garlic, and cook gently for 5 minutes or until softened. Stir in the tomatoes and wine. Cook gently for 5-10 minutes, stirring occasionally to break down the tomatoes, to make a sauce.

**3 Cook the pasta** While the sauce is cooking, cook the pasta in a pot of boiling water for 8 minutes, or according to the package instructions, until al dente. Drain. Stir the capers into the sauce with the olives and basil, and season to taste.

**4 Add the steaks** Return the steaks to the frying pan to heat through, spooning the sauce over the meat. Divide the pasta among four plates and add some basil leaves if you like. Serve the steak and sauce over the top.

**Swap** • For chopped tomatoes, use a **14-oz (398-mL) can chunky tomato sauce**.

You can give meat an exotic flavour by using a dry rub before grilling or pan-frying. Mix the ingredients together and rub over the steaks up to 30 minutes before cooking. Try these mixtures:

● For an Asian flavouring, combine **½ tsp (2 mL) salt**, **½ tsp (2 mL) sugar**, **2 tsp (10 mL) garam masala**, **1 tsp (5 mL) crushed chili flakes** and **1 crushed garlic clove**.

● For a Cajun flavouring, combine **1 tsp (5 mL) paprika**, **2 tsp (10 mL) cracked black peppercorns**, **½ tsp (2 mL) coarse sea salt**, **1 crushed garlic clove**, the **grated zest of 1 lemon**, **2 tsp (10 mL) dried sage** and a **pinch of cayenne**.

## ...cooking tips

The sauce also tastes great with grilled meats such as **pork steaks and chops or lamb chops and cutlets**, and also goes very well with **fish**, so it's worth making a double batch and freezing half. Cool quickly after cooking, pack into a freezer container and freeze for up to one month. To use, thaw, reheat and simmer for 3 minutes.

## ...keep it

# Stir-Fry Steak and Kidneys

Make short work of cooking traditional steak and kidneys by stir-frying with onion and pepper, perked up with wine and horseradish. Serve with green beans and noodles.

**10** mins prep time

**12** mins cook time

## Serves 4

- 7 oz (200 g) lamb's kidneys, cores removed
- 2 tbsp (25 mL) canola oil
- 1 onion, thinly sliced
- 1 large red pepper, thinly sliced
- 14 oz (400 g) round steak, trimmed of fat and sliced into thin strips
- 4 tbsp (60 mL) red wine
- 1-1½ tbsp (15-20 mL) grated horseradish from a jar, to taste
- 1 tbsp (15 mL) dark soy sauce

### Each serving provides

- 265 cals • 32 g protein
- 11 g fat of which 3 g saturates
- 7 g carbohydrate

**1 Cook the vegetables** Cut the kidneys into bite-sized chunks. Heat a wok or large frying pan with 1 tbsp (15 mL) oil and stir-fry the onion and pepper slices for 3-4 minutes to soften slightly. Remove from the pan and keep hot.

**2 Cook the meat** Heat the remaining oil in the wok or pan and add the steak strips and chunks of kidney. Stir-fry over a high heat for 4-5 minutes or until evenly coloured, allowing the excess liquid to reduce by boiling.

**3 Make the sauce** Add the red wine and boil rapidly, stirring, for 1-2 minutes to reduce the liquid slightly. Stir in the horseradish to taste and soy sauce, then season.

**4 Finish and serve** Return the onion and pepper to the pan, and bring back to the boil, then serve.

**Swaps** For red wine, use **Guinness or another strong brown ale**, and instead of soy sauce, use **Worcestershire sauce**.

---

## Serves 4

- 1 lb (500 g) lean round steak
- 2 tsp (10 mL) black peppercorns
- ¾ cup (175 mL) pecan halves
- 2 tbsp (25 mL) olive oil
- 2 tsp (10 mL) butter
- 1 onion, thinly sliced
- ¾ lb (375 g) button mushrooms, sliced
- 4 tbsp (60 mL) brandy
- ⅔ cup (150 mL) sour cream
- 3 oz (90 g) arugula

### Each serving provides

- 499 cals • 33 g protein
- 34 g fat of which 10 g saturates
- 6 g carbohydrate

**15** mins prep time

**15** mins cook time

---

Always keep the heat as high as possible when stir-frying and keep the ingredients on the move constantly, to cook everything quickly and retain as many nutrients as possible.

## ...cooking tip

**Pastry-topped steak and kidney**

Put one sheet of **pre-rolled puff pastry rounds** from a 1-lb (500-g) package on a baking sheet and mark into eight wedges (or cut a rectangular sheet into eight rectangles). Brush with beaten **egg**. Bake at 425°F (220°C) for 12-15 minutes or until golden and crisp. Meanwhile, cook the steak and kidney as the basic recipe, replacing the hot horseradish with **creamed horseradish**. Omit the soy sauce and add **2-3 tbsp (25-45 mL) heavy cream** at the end of cooking. Season to taste and serve each portion with two wedges or rectangles of pastry.

## ...another idea

# Peppered Beef with Pecans

This rich dish is great for an ultra-easy special dinner, any day of the week. Lightly crushed peppercorns give the steak a piquant flavour that complements the toasted pecans. Serve with garlicky mashed potatoes.

**1 Prepare the steak** Slice the steak into thin strips, trimming off any excess fat. Lightly crush the peppercorns using a mortar and pestle (or use a rolling pin) and put into a large bowl. Toss the steak strips with the peppercorns.

**2 Toast the nuts** Put the pecans in a large, dry pan or wok and toast over a medium-high heat, tossing regularly, for 2-3 minutes. Chop them roughly and set aside.

**3 Fry the vegetables** Heat 1 tbsp (15 mL) oil with the butter in the pan or wok and stir-fry the onion over a medium heat for 2-3 minutes to soften slightly. Add the mushrooms and cook over a high heat for 3-4 minutes or until lightly softened. Add a little salt to taste.

**4 Fry the steak** Remove the mushrooms and onions from the pan and put on to a plate. Add the remaining oil to the pan and stir-fry the steak strips over a fairly high heat for 2-3 minutes or until sealed.

**5 Make the sauce** Add the brandy and bring to the boil. Boil for about 30 seconds. Return the onions and mushrooms to the pan and stir in the sour cream. Heat until blended. Add the arugula leaves and stir until wilted, then sprinkle over the pecans and serve immediately.

**Swap** For brandy, use **beef stock**, made with a stock cube.

For garlicky mashed potatoes, boil peeled **potatoes**, cut into small chunks, and **1 unpeeled garlic clove** while you prepare and cook the steak. When tender, drain the potatoes. Peel the garlic clove and return to the pot. Mash the potatoes and garlic with **1 tbsp (15 mL) of butter** and enough milk to make a smooth mash. Season and add a few **snipped fresh chives**.

## ...to serve

### Mustard beef with walnuts

Omit the peppercorns from the basic recipe. Stir-fry the beef strips in the oil and butter, but use **1 thinly sliced red onion** and **2 thinly sliced celery sticks** instead of the mushrooms. Omit the brandy and sour cream. Add **6¾ tbsp (100 mL) red wine** at step 5 and simmer for 2-3 minutes to reduce slightly. Stir in **2 tbsp (25 mL) whole-grain mustard** and **⅔ cup (150 mL) heavy cream**. Bring to the boil, season and add the arugula, then sprinkle over **¾ cup (175 mL) roughly chopped walnuts** instead of the pecans.

## ...another idea

# Family Shepherd's Pie

This classic favourite makes a comforting meal, especially on a cold day. Lean ground beef is a healthy filling that takes minutes to cook, and the topping is quickly browned in the oven. Serve with peas or seasonal greens.

**30 mins** prep/cook time

### Serves 4
1 lb (500 g) lean ground beef
1 onion, finely chopped
1 large carrot, peeled and grated
1 celery stick, finely chopped
1 tbsp (15 mL) tomato paste
1 tsp (5 mL) Worcestershire sauce
1 tsp (5 mL) dried mixed herbs
1⅓ cups (325 mL) hot beef stock, made with a stock cube
1 tbsp (15 mL) all-purpose flour
2 lb (1 kg) floury potatoes, peeled and cut into small chunks
6¾ tbsp (100 mL) 1% milk, warmed
2 tbsp (25 mL) butter

**Each serving provides** • 489 cals • 35 g protein • 18 g fat of which 9 g saturates • 50 g carbohydrate

**1 Fry the meat and vegetables** Heat a large, heavy-based pot until hot, then add the ground beef and vegetables, and fry, stirring occasionally to break up any lumps, for 5 minutes or until lightly browned all over. Meanwhile, stir the tomato paste, Worcestershire sauce and mixed herbs into the stock. Sprinkle the flour over the beef and vegetables.

**2 Add the stock** Stir the flavoured stock into the ground meat. Bring to the boil, then reduce the heat, cover and cook gently for 15 minutes. Season to taste.

**3 Cook the potatoes** While the meat is cooking, cook the potatoes in a pot of boiling water for 10 minutes or until tender. Drain the potatoes, then mash with the warmed milk and the butter. Season. Preheat the broiler to medium.

**4 Brown the topping** Spoon the meat mixture into a large, warm ovenproof dish. Spread the mashed potato over the top and fluff up with a fork. Put under the broiler to brown lightly and crisp the top.

**Swaps** For a vegetable mash, replace some of the potatoes with **turnip, carrots or parsnips**, or add some **chopped scallions or lightly cooked sliced leeks** to the mashed potato.

**Cooking tip** If you prefer, you can bake the shepherd's pie at 400°F (200°C), for 20 minutes or until the topping is golden.

### Beefy stuffed tomatoes
Use a batch of the cooked meat, simmered for 5 minutes, to make this recipe. Slice the tops off **8 firm beefsteak tomatoes** and set aside. Cut a small slice from the base of any tomatoes that do not sit upright. Scoop out the seedy centres using a teaspoon, and discard. Leave the tomato shells upside down to drain. Stand the tomatoes in a roasting pan or a shallow ovenproof dish. Using a slotted spoon, fill the tomatoes with the meat mixture. Replace the tops and bake at 400°F (200°C) for 15 minutes. Remove the tops and sprinkle with ½ **cup (125 mL) grated Parmesan or aged cheddar cheese**. Bake uncovered for a further 5 minutes or until the tomatoes are tender. Serve hot with rice and a salad.

## ...another idea

● There is no need to add fat to the pan when frying ground meat, as there will be enough fat in the meat. ● When buying ground beef, choose a good-quality, lean meat, as cheap ground beef often has a high fat content and may contain offal. If in doubt, you can always choose a cut of beef and ask your butcher to grind it for you.

## ...healthy plus

● You can prepare the whole pie ahead (or just the meat mixture). Cool, then keep chilled in the fridge. Cover with foil and reheat thoroughly in the oven at 375°F (190°C) for 45 minutes, uncovering for the last 10-15 minutes to brown the top. ● Make up a triple batch of the meat mixture and use one third for the pie. Quickly cool and freeze the remainder, divided into two freezerproof containers. To use, thaw a batch in the fridge overnight, then use it to make another meal, such as Beefy Stuffed Tomatoes (left), or Bolognese Soufflés (page 102). Or add a few drops of Tabasco sauce and 2 tbsp (25 mL) chopped fresh basil or coriander to the mixture to make a quick version of the Spicy Beef Rolls (page 232).

## ...get ahead

# Spicy **Beef** Rolls

Serve simply spiced ground beef flavoured with tomato in soft floury rolls with shredded lettuce and a tomato salad on the side. It's a super-fast meal tailor-made for a busy family that often eats at different times.

**10**
mins prep
time

**20**
mins cook
time

**Serves 4**
1 lb (500 g) lean ground beef
1 onion, finely chopped
1 red or green pepper, finely chopped
7 oz (200 g) tomatoes, chopped
1 tbsp (15 mL) all-purpose flour
1 tbsp (15 mL) tomato paste
⅔ cup (150 mL) beef stock, made with a stock cube
a few drops of Tabasco sauce
2 tbsp (25 mL) chopped fresh basil or coriander
4 large whole-grain rolls
crisp shredded lettuce and hot chili sauce, to serve

**Each serving provides** • 498 cals
• 37 g protein • 17 g fat of which
6 g saturates • 53 g carbohydrate

**1 Fry the meat and vegetables** Heat a large, heavy-based pot until hot, then add the ground beef and onion. Fry over a medium heat for 7 minutes or until browned all over, stirring occasionally to break up any lumps. Add the pepper and tomatoes, and cook for 3 minutes, then sprinkle over the flour.

**2 Add the stock** Stir the tomato paste into the stock, then add the Tabasco sauce and basil or coriander. Stir ⅔ cup (150 mL) stock into the meat mixture. Bring to the boil, then reduce the heat, cover and cook gently for 10 minutes. Add a little extra stock if needed and season.

**3 Serve** When ready to serve, split the rolls in half and toast them lightly. Put some shredded lettuce on the base of each roll and spoon the meat sauce on top. Each person can add chili sauce to taste.

## Chili con carne

For a classic chili, fry the ground beef with the onion, as the basic recipe, and **1 crushed garlic clove**, **2 tsp (10 mL) chili powder** and **1 tsp (5 mL) ground cumin**. Simmer with the flavoured stock plus a **14-oz (398-mL) can chopped tomatoes or chunky tomato sauce** at step 2, then stir in a **14-oz (398-mL) can red kidney beans**, drained and rinsed. Heat through for 5 minutes. Season. Serve over rice with **sour cream and grated cheese**.

## ...another idea

Cooked ground meat is suitable for freezing. Cool quickly and transfer to a freezerproof container. Freeze for up to one month. To use, thaw overnight in the fridge. Reheat and simmer for 10-15 minutes.

## ...keep it

# Chili Beef and Taco Salad

This simple warm salad is full of crunchy textures, and handy to make when time is short. Serve with sour cream or Greek-style yogurt to balance the hot chili flakes.

**15** mins prep time
**14** mins cook time

### Serves 4

1 lb (500 g) lean minced steak
2 garlic cloves, crushed
1 tsp (5 mL) crushed chili flakes
2 tbsp (25 mL) sun-dried tomato paste
3 tbsp (45 mL) chopped fresh oregano, or 1 tsp (5 mL) dried
juice of 1 lemon
¼ iceberg lettuce, torn
2 ripe avocados, halved, pitted and sliced
1 red onion, thinly sliced
3 tomatoes, chopped
2⅔ oz (75 g) tortilla chips

### Each serving provides

• 479 cals • 32 g protein
• 31 g fat of which 9 g saturates
• 20 g carbohydrate

**1 Fry the meat** Heat a large, heavy-based frying pan until hot, then add the ground beef and fry for 2-3 minutes, stirring to break up any lumps.

**2 Add the flavourings** Add the garlic and chili flakes, then cook for a further 6-8 minutes or until lightly browned, stirring often. Stir in the tomato paste, oregano and lemon juice, then cook on a low heat for 2-3 minutes. Season.

**3 Make the salad** While the meat is cooking, put the iceberg lettuce, avocado slices, onion and tomatoes in a wide salad bowl. Add the meat mixture and toss well to mix evenly. Scatter some of the tortilla chips over and put the remainder in a separate bowl. Serve at once.

**Swaps** • For crushed chili flakes and sun-dried tomato paste, use **2-3 tbsp (25-45 mL) sweet chili dipping sauce**, and replace the oregano with **chopped fresh coriander**. • Instead of lemon juice, use **lime juice**.

**To serve** Add more tortilla chips or some **toasted chunks of pita bread** if feeding a hungry family.

To feed more people, stir in a **14-oz (398-mL) can red kidney beans, borlotti or pinto beans**, drained and rinsed, at the end of step 2 and heat the mixture through thoroughly.

## ...cooking tip

A ground steak is more expensive than normal ground beef as it is made from tender, lean cuts of meat, but it makes a less fatty dish.

## ...shopping tip

# 5 ways to spice up ground meat

Ground meat is an all-time useful standby – quick to cook and adaptable. Most types of meat are now available ground, including ultra low-fat versions such as lean ground steak and ground beef. Here's an international selection of fast, spicy ways to pep it up. All recipes serve 4.

## indian **lamb** or **beef** keema

Fry **1 large chopped onion** with **1 crushed garlic clove** in **2 tbsp (25 mL) peanut oil** over a medium heat for 3 minutes or until softened. Stir in **1 lb (500 g) lean ground lamb or beef** and a diced **potato**. Add **1 tsp (5 mL) each of ground coriander and cumin, chili powder and turmeric** and **1 tbsp (15 mL) of garam masala**, and cook, stirring, for 1 minute. Add **6¾ tbsp (100 mL) beef stock**, made with a stock cube, and a **14-oz (398-mL) can chopped tomatoes**. Season, cover and simmer for 13 minutes or until the potato is tender. Add **5 oz (150 g) frozen peas** and simmer for 3 minutes. Serve sprinkled with **chopped fresh coriander**, accompanied by warmed nan breads and a chunky tomato salad.

**Each serving provides** • 338 cals • 30 g protein
• 16 g fat of which 5.5 g saturates
• 19 g carbohydrate

**10** mins prep time   **20** mins cook time

## thai **beef** with **coconut**

Finely chop **3 shallots, 2 garlic cloves** and a **¾-in. (2-cm) piece of fresh ginger**. Heat **2 tbsp (25 mL) canola oil** in a wok or large frying pan, add the shallots, garlic and ginger, and stir-fry with **1 lb (500 g) lean ground steak** over a high heat until lightly browned. Stir in **1 tbsp (15 mL) red curry paste, 1 tbsp (15 mL) fish sauce** and **1 tbsp (15 mL) dark soy sauce**. Crumble in **2-3 dried kaffir lime leaves** and add **6¾ tbsp (100 mL) beef stock**, made with a stock cube, and **3 tbsp (45 mL) coconut cream**. Simmer for 6 minutes. Sprinkle with **grated coconut** and **chopped fresh coriander** and serve with Thai fragrant rice.

**Each serving provides** • 302 cals • 29 g protein
• 19 g fat of which 9.5 g saturates • 3 g carbohydrate

**10** mins prep time   **10** mins cook time

● If you enjoy cooking Thai meals, it's worth keeping **dried kaffir lime leaves** in the pantry. You can use fresh leaves if you prefer; shred them very finely before adding them. ● **Dried curry leaves** make a good alternative if you are having difficulty finding the kaffir lime leaves.

## ...shopping tips

# arabian **ground** lamb

In a large, wide pan, dry-fry **1 lb (500 g) lean ground lamb** with **2 crushed garlic cloves** and **1 large chopped onion** for 3 minutes or until lightly browned. Stir in **1 tbsp (15 mL) Baharat spice mix** and cook for 1 minute. Add **3½ oz (100 g) dried raisins or sultanas, 2 chopped tomatoes, 1 tbsp (15 mL) tomato paste** and **1 tbsp (15 mL) chopped fresh mint**. Season and cook, uncovered, over a medium heat for 5 minutes, stirring occasionally. Serve in warmed flatbreads with shredded crisp lettuce leaves and a spoonful of minted plain yogurt.

**Each serving provides** • 287 cals • 27 g protein • 10 g fat of which 4 g saturates • 24 g carbohydrate

**Swap** Baharat is a North African spice mix. It is now becoming easily available, but if you are unable to find it, you can use **1½ tsp (7 mL) harissa paste, or 1 tbsp (15 mL) Moroccan ras-el-hanout spice mix** or **Tunisian tabil spice**.

**10** mins prep time    **10** mins cook time

# szechuan spiced **pork** stir-fry

Toast **3½ oz (100 g) cashews** in a dry wok or large pan over a medium-high heat, tossing regularly, for 3 minutes or until golden brown. Set aside. Heat **1 tbsp (15 mL) peanut oil** in the wok or pan and stir-fry **1 lb (500 g) lean ground pork** for 3 minutes or until light golden brown. Stir in **1 crushed garlic clove** and **2-3 tsp (10-15mL) Szechuan spices**. Add a chopped **bunch of scallions** and stir-fry for 1 minute, then add **3½ oz (100 g) baby corn** and **3½ oz (100 g) snow peas**, and stir-fry for 6 minutes or until just tender. Add the squeezed juice of **1 lime** and **2 packages of straight-to-wok noodles**, and cook, stirring occasionally, for 2 minutes or until thoroughly heated through. Stir in the cashews and serve.

**Each serving provides** • 461 cals • 38 g protein • 21 g fat of which 5 g saturates • 31 g carbohydrate

**Swap** For Szechuan spices, use **five-spice powder**

**5** mins prep time    **15** mins cook time

For potato wedges, cut **2 lb (1 kg) unpeeled potatoes** lengthwise into same-size wedges. Put into a large bowl and pour over **2 tbsp (25 mL) olive oil**. Stir, or cover and shake, to coat in the oil, then transfer to a baking sheet in a single layer. Season. Put on the top shelf of the oven and bake at 425°F (220°C) for 20-25 minutes or until tender and golden brown.

## ...to serve

# cajun spiced **meatballs**

Fry **1 chopped onion** and ½ **chopped green pepper** in ½ **tbsp (7 mL) olive oil** for 5 minutes. Add to **1 lb (500 g) lean ground pork or beef** with **2 tsp (10 mL) Cajun spice blend, 1 tbsp (15 mL) chopped fresh mint** and ground black pepper. Mix, then roll into ping-pong-sized balls and toss in **fried bread crumbs** to coat. Arrange on a baking tray and bake in a preheated oven at 425°F (220°C) for 15 minutes or until golden brown. Serve with a fresh tomato and onion salsa and pasta or oven-baked potato wedges, if you have time. Put these on the top shelf of the oven before starting the meatballs, and they will be ready by the time the meatballs are cooked.

**10** mins prep time    **20** mins cook time

**Each serving provides** • 233 cals • 29 g protein • 7 g fat of which 2 g saturates • 14 g carbohydrate

# Creamy **Liver** with **Leeks** and **Pancetta**

Calf's liver has a delicate flavour and is exceptionally tender, needing the briefest cooking time. This update on the traditional combination of liver and onions is impressive yet speedy. Serve with new potatoes or diced sautéed potatoes.

**10** mins prep time

**15** mins cook time

**Serves 4**

5 oz (150 g) diced pancetta or
  6 strips bacon, chopped

1 lb (500 g) calf's liver, thinly sliced

⅔ lb (300 g) baby leeks, sliced
  diagonally

1 tbsp (15 mL) butter or 2 tsp
  (10 mL) oil, if needed

1⅓ cups (325 mL) beef stock, made
  with a stock cube

2 tbsp (25 mL) balsamic vinegar

4 tbsp (60 mL) heavy cream

**Each serving provides** • 307 cals
• 30 g protein • 20 g fat of which
8 g saturates • 3 g carbohydrate

**1 Fry the pancetta** Heat a wide,
heavy-based sauté pan and fry the
pancetta or bacon over a fairly high
heat for 4-5 minutes or until golden
brown. Lift out with a slotted spoon.

**2 Cook the liver** Add the liver to the
pan and fry quickly for about 2 minutes
on each side or until evenly coloured.
Remove and keep hot with the
pancetta or bacon.

**3 Cook the leeks** Add the leeks to the
pan, with the butter or oil if needed,
and fry for 30 seconds, stirring. Stir in
the stock and heat until boiling. Simmer
for 2-3 minutes or until the leeks are
just tender.

**4 Assemble the dish** Stir in the
balsamic vinegar and return the liver
and pancetta or bacon to the pan. Stir
in the heavy cream. Bring to the boil.
Adjust the seasoning to taste and serve.

**Swaps** • For calf's liver, use **lamb's
liver**. • For baby leeks, use **large leeks**,
thinly sliced.

# Lamb Rhogan Gosht

Warm up on a chilly winter's day with this aromatic, rich
and golden lamb curry. It's a no-fuss recipe that can be left
to simmer gently and needs just warmed garlic and
coriander nan breads to accompany.

**Serves 4**

**30** mins
prep/cook
time

2 tbsp (25 mL) peanut or canola oil

1 onion, roughly chopped

1 orange pepper, diced

1 sweet potato, peeled and diced

1 garlic clove, crushed

1 tbsp (15 mL) medium curry
  powder

1 lb (500 g) lamb neck fillet, cut into
  bite-sized chunks

¾ cup (175 mL) lamb or beef stock,
  made with a stock cube

2 tbsp (25 mL) tomato paste

4 tbsp (60 mL) plain yogurt

2 tbsp (25 mL) chopped fresh
  coriander

2 tbsp (25 mL) slivered almonds

**Each serving provides** • 433 cals
• 30 g protein • 28 g fat of which
10 g saturates • 18 g carbohydrate

**1 Fry the vegetables** Heat the oil in a large pot and add the onion, pepper,
sweet potato and garlic. Fry for 4-5 minutes, stirring occasionally, until
beginning to soften but not browned.

**2 Add the spices and lamb** Stir in the curry powder and cook for a further
minute, then add the lamb, stirring to coat evenly with the spicy mixture.

**3 Cook the curry** Add the stock and tomato paste, then bring to the boil.
Reduce the heat, cover and simmer for 15 minutes or until the lamb and
vegetables are tender. Adjust the seasoning if necessary. Stir in the yogurt and
coriander, sprinkle with the slivered almonds and serve.

**Swap** For sweet potato, use **pumpkin, or butternut or acorn squash**,
peeled and seeded, then diced.

For a vegetarian version, omit the lamb. Cook the vegetables as step 1.
Add the curry powder and stir for 1 minute, then add **1 small
cauliflower**, cut into small florets, **¾ cup (175 mL) vegetable stock**, and
**2 tbsp (25 mL) crunchy peanut butter**. Bring to the boil, then cover and
simmer for 10 minutes or until the cauliflower is tender. Stir in **3½ oz
(100 g) baby spinach leaves** and heat until wilted. Add **4 tbsp (60 mL)
heavy cream or ricotta cheese** instead of the yogurt and sprinkle with
**toasted cashews or peanuts**
instead of the almonds.

## ...or try this

# Lamb Steaks Provençale

A quick and colourful, chunky sauce of Mediterranean vegetables makes a delicious accompaniment to succulent steaks of griddled lamb. Serve with French baguettes to mop up the juices, or with chunks of garlic bread.

**10** mins prep time   **15** mins cook time

### Serves 4

**2 tbsp (25 mL) olive oil**
**1 large red onion, diced**
**1 large green pepper, diced**
**2 zucchini, diced**
**1 small fennel bulb, chopped**
**2 garlic cloves, chopped**
**4 tsp (20 mL) herbes de Provence**
**4 lean lamb leg steaks,**
   **about ¼ lb (125 g) each**
**4 large plum tomatoes, diced**
**2 tbsp (25 mL) black olive tapenade**

**Each serving provides** • 315 cals
• 29 g protein • 18 g fat of which
5 g saturates • 11 g carbohydrate

**1 Cook the vegetables** Heat the oil, reserving about 2 tsp (10 mL), in a deep frying pan and add the onion, pepper, zucchini, fennel, garlic and herbs. Cook over a medium heat, stirring occasionally, for 10 minutes or until softened and lightly browned.

**2 Cook the lamb** While the vegetables are cooking, brush the lamb steaks lightly with the remaining oil and season lightly. Cook, turning once, on a hot ridged griddle or heavy-based frying pan, or under the grill, for 5-8 minutes, depending on thickness, until slightly pink in the centre. Remove from the heat.

**3 Finish the sauce** Add the tomatoes and tapenade to the vegetables, then simmer for a further 3-4 minutes or until softened. Add the lamb steaks to the vegetables, then serve.

Swaps • For lamb leg steaks, use **lamb chops**. • For fresh plum tomatoes, use **ordinary tomatoes, or a 14-oz (398-mL) can chopped plum tomatoes**. • For herbes de Provence, use **2-3 tsp (10-15 mL) fennel seeds** to give the dish a warm, aniseed flavour. • For tapenade, use **6-8 pitted black olives**, roughly chopped, and stir into the dish, or add **2 tbsp (25 mL) green pesto** instead.

The vegetables can be cooked in advance, cooled and stored covered in the fridge. You'll find the flavours actually improve with a few hours' keeping. Eat within two days. They can be served cold or reheated gently until boiling.

## ...get ahead

**Moroccan lamb**
Cook the vegetables as step 1, but replace the herbs with **1 tsp (5 mL) harissa paste**. Cook the lamb as the basic recipe. Omit the tomatoes and tapenade for the sauce, and add **8 quartered ready-to-eat dried apricots** with **1 cup (250 mL) fresh orange juice**. Simmer for 3-4 minutes. Stir in **3 tbsp (45 mL) chopped fresh coriander**. Serve with couscous.

## ...another idea

# Rosemary-Glazed Lamb Chops

Accompany tender lamb chops, brushed with a delicately sweet, herb-scented glaze, with eggplant and ciabatta, all quickly cooked together on the grill. All they need is a crisp green salad to serve.

**10** mins prep time

**15** mins cook time

**Serves 4**

2 tbsp (25 mL) currant jelly

2 tsp (10 mL) Dijon mustard

4 tsp (20 mL) chopped fresh rosemary leaves

4 lean lamb loin chops, about ¼ lb (125 g) each

3-4 tbsp (45-60 mL) olive oil

1 eggplant, thickly sliced

8 slices ciabatta bread

fresh currants, to garnish (optional)

**Each serving provides** • 474 cals • 30 g protein • 21 g fat of which 6 g saturates • 43 g carbohydrate

**1 Prepare the glaze** In a small pot mix together the currant jelly, mustard and rosemary. Preheat the broiler to high.

**2 Grill the lamb and eggplant** Put the lamb chops on the grill rack, brush lightly with oil, then season. Arrange the eggplant slices on the grill rack, brushing with oil. Broil for 6-8 minutes, turning the lamb once and the eggplant slices occasionally, until golden.

**3 Add the glaze** Gently heat the glaze, then brush a little over the lamb. Broil for a further 2 minutes. Turn the lamb over and glaze the other side. Cook for 1-2 more minutes.

**4 Grill the ciabatta** While the lamb is finishing cooking, brush the ciabatta slices with a little oil and add to the grill rack. (Move the eggplant slices to make room or remove them from the rack and keep warm if already golden.) Broil the ciabatta until golden on both sides.

**5 Serve** Heat the remaining glaze until almost boiling. Put the lamb and eggplant on serving plates, then spoon the hot glaze over the lamb. Serve, garnished with currants if you like, accompanied by the ciabatta slices.

**Swaps** • For eggplants, use **4 large flat mushrooms**.
• For ciabatta slices, use split, toasted **plain English muffins**.

# Lamb, Potato
## and Sun-Dried Tomato Salad

Packed with flavour, this express salad makes an unusual all-in-one supper dish. Toss the warm ingredients in the dressing so that the richness of mint, balsamic vinegar and mustard will be absorbed and accentuated.

**15** mins prep time

**15** mins cook time

**Serves 4**

4 lamb steaks, about ¼ lb (125 g) each

olive oil, for brushing

1¼ lb (625 g) pre-washed baby new potatoes, halved

¾ lb (375 g) green beans, cut into 1¼-in. (3-cm) lengths

5 scallions, finely chopped

2 oz (60 g) sun-dried tomatoes, coarsely chopped

2 tbsp (25 mL) chopped fresh mint, plus extra to garnish

5 tbsp (75 mL) extra virgin olive oil

1 tbsp (15 mL) balsamic vinegar

1 tbsp (15 mL) lemon juice

1 tsp (5 mL) Dijon mustard

1 tsp (5 mL) clear honey

**Each serving provides** • 492 cals • 31 g protein • 25 g fat of which 7 g saturates • 37 g carbohydrate

**1 Cook the lamb** Brush the lamb steaks lightly with oil and season. Heat a heavy-based frying pan over a medium heat and add the lamb. Cook for 5-8 minutes depending on the thickness, turning once, until slightly pink in the centre. Remove from the heat, cover lightly with foil and leave to rest for about 5 minutes.

**2 Cook the potatoes and beans** While the lamb is frying and resting, cook the potatoes in a pot of lightly salted boiling water for 10-12 minutes or until tender. Add the beans to the potatoes for the final 4 minutes of cooking.

**3 Assemble the salad** Drain the vegetables and put in a large serving dish with the scallions and sun-dried tomatoes. Slice the lamb and add to the vegetables, reserving any meat juices.

**4 Make the dressing** Put the mint, olive oil and vinegar in a screw-top jar and add the lemon juice, mustard and honey. Shake together until well mixed. Add the meat juices, then pour over the meat and vegetables. Toss lightly to coat evenly, sprinkle with extra mint and serve warm.

**Swap** For potatoes, use ¾ lb (375 g) pasta shapes such as penne or fusilli, cooked according to the pack instructions. Toss in the dressing while still warm.

**Addition** Toast **2 tbsp (25 mL) sunflower seeds** in a dry pan over a medium-high heat, tossing regularly, for 1-2 minutes or until golden. Scatter over the salad.

**Minty mustard and honey-glazed lamb**
Mix together **2 tbsp (25 mL) clear honey, 2 tsp (10 mL) English mustard** and **1 tbsp (15 mL) finely chopped mint**. Grill **4 lamb chump chops** as for the basic recipe, brushing with the mustard and honey glaze during the final few minutes of cooking. Instead of the eggplant, grill **4 sprigs of cherry tomatoes** on the vine, brushed with a little **olive oil**, alongside the lamb. Serve them as an accompaniment to the lamb, with the ciabatta or with toasted rustic rolls.

## ...another idea

# Spiced **Kiwi Lamb** Brochettes

Kiwis add a lovely sweet-and-sour flavour to these fast-cooking kebabs, and the fruit juice contains an enzyme that tenderizes the meat. Serve with wraps or pita breads and tzatziki or raita (see To serve, page 140).

**20** mins prep time

**10** mins cook time

### Serves 4

1¼ lb (625 g) lean boned leg of lamb, cut into bite-sized chunks

1 ripe kiwi

1 garlic clove, crushed

1 tbsp (15 mL) grated fresh ginger

1 tsp (5 mL) coriander seeds, crushed

1 tsp (5 mL) cumin seeds, crushed

2 small onions, each cut into 8 wedges

1 lime, cut into wedges

**Each serving provides** • 243 cals • 36 g protein • 26 g fat of which 7.5 g saturates • 4 g carbohydrate

**1 Flavour the lamb** Put the lamb into a bowl. Peel, chop and mash the kiwi to a pulp. Stir into the lamb chunks with the garlic, ginger and spices. Toss well to coat evenly. Cover and leave to marinate for 5 minutes.

**2 Thread the skewers** Preheat the grill to hot. Thread the chunks of meat on to four long metal skewers, alternating with the wedges of onion. Spoon over any remaining marinade and sprinkle with a little seasoning.

**3 Cook the brochettes** Grill the brochettes, turning occasionally, for 8-10 minutes or until golden and evenly cooked. Thread a wedge of lime on to the end of each skewer, then serve.

Swaps • For lamb, use **beef or veal fillet**. • For the ginger, coriander and cumin, use **1 tsp (5 mL) each of dried thyme, tarragon and dill**. Omit the lime. Serve with **creamed horseradish**.

Prepare the lamb to the end of step 1 and leave in the fridge to marinate for up to 3 hours. This will improve the flavour of the meat as well as tenderizing it.

**...get ahead**

These brochettes are a great choice for a barbecue, as all the preparation can be done in advance and you can leave them to marinate and tenderize. Cook over hot coals as for the basic recipe.

**...or try this**

### Serves 4

1 tbsp (15 mL) butter

1 tbsp (15 mL) olive oil

2 ripe pears, quartered, cored and sliced lengthwise

2 shallots, finely chopped

2 pork fillets, about 1 lb (500 g) total weight, thinly sliced

⅔ cup (150 mL) dry white wine

2 tbsp (25 mL) chopped fresh tarragon

4 tbsp (60 mL) heavy cream

**Each serving provides** • 311 cals • 28 g protein • 16.5 g fat of which 7 g saturates • 7 g carbohydrate

Swaps • For pears and white wine, use **apple rings and dry cider**. • For pork fillet, use **lamb leg steaks, or medallions of lamb neck fillet** and simmer at step 3 for 15-20 minutes or until tender.

**5** mins prep time

**20** mins cook time

# Pork Fillet with Pears
## and Tarragon

Tender pork with pears is a classic combination. Add a light and creamy tarragon-scented sauce for a special main course dish – ideal for smart but simple entertaining. Serve with lemon rice and steamed asparagus or broccoli.

**1 Cook the pears** Melt half the butter with ½ tbsp (7 mL) oil in a frying pan and fry the pears quickly over a high heat, turning once, for 5 minutes or until golden all over. Remove from the pan to a warm plate, and cover.

**2 Fry the shallots** Add the remaining butter and oil to the pan, then stir in the chopped shallots and cook over a medium heat, stirring occasionally, for 3-4 minutes or until softened and golden.

**3 Add the pork** Push the shallots to one side of the pan, add the pork slices and fry for 5-6 minutes or until lightly browned, turning once.

**4 Make the sauce** Pour the wine into the pan, bring to the boil then boil for 1-2 minutes to reduce slightly. Stir in the tarragon and heavy cream, then boil for a further minute. Adjust the seasoning to taste. Serve the pork slices topped with the pears, and the sauce spooned over the top.

**To serve** While boiling rice to serve with the dish, you can cook **asparagus or broccoli** in a steamer basket on top of the pot to save on washing up. Stir the **grated zest of 1 lemon** into the cooked rice before serving.

### Veal fillet with Calvados cream sauce

Heat **1 tbsp (15 mL) olive oil** with **1 tbsp (15 mL) butter** in a frying pan and fry **1 lb (500 g) veal fillet**, thinly sliced, with **1 thinly sliced onion** and **7 oz (200 g) button mushrooms** for 5-6 minutes or until the onion is softened. Stir in **4 tbsp (60 mL) Calvados** and **1 tbsp (15 mL) chopped fresh thyme**, then simmer for 1-2 minutes. Add **4 tbsp (60 mL) heavy cream**. Adjust the seasoning, bring to the boil and serve.

## ...another idea

# 5 beautiful burgers

Burgers don't have to be junk food. Home-made with good ingredients, they are ideal for sizzling barbecues, quick and easy family meals or classy dishes for entertaining. They take so little time to prepare and you can jazz them up with different flavour combinations. All recipes serve 4.

Shape the burgers to equal-sized, round patties about 3½ in. (9 cm) in diameter and about ¾ in. (2 cm) thick. Beef or lamb burgers can be cooked until they are slightly pink inside, if you like, but pork needs to be cooked through.

## ...perfect burgers

## luscious **blue cheese** beefburgers

Put **1 lb (500 g) lean ground steak** into a bowl with **1 finely chopped onion, 2 tsp (10 mL) dried thyme** and **2 tsp (10 mL) Dijon mustard**. Season and divide into eight equal pieces. Shape each into a round and flatten slightly. Top four of the rounds with 1 tbsp (15 mL) crumbled **Roquefort or Stilton cheese**. Put the four remaining rounds of meat on top, pressing firmly to seal in the cheese completely. Brush the burgers with a little oil and cook in a hot pan or under a hot grill, turning once, for 10-12 minutes or until golden brown. Serve with a arugula and cherry tomato salad and chunky fries.

**Each serving provides** • 228 cals • 30 g protein • 10 g fat of which 4 g saturates • 4 g carbohydrate

**10** mins prep time  **12** mins cook time

For a great-tasting plain burger omit the cheese and divide the mixture into four burger shapes. Cook as above.

## ...or try this

## mediterranean burgers

Mix ½ **lb (250 g) each of lean ground pork and lean ground beef** with **2 crushed garlic cloves, 2 tbsp (25 mL) finely chopped pine nuts, 8 sun-dried tomatoes**, chopped, and **2 tbsp (25 mL) chopped fresh basil**. Season with black pepper. Divide the mixture into four and shape into burgers. Grill using a high heat, or barbecue, for 10-12 minutes or until golden brown, turning once. Serve with a pepper, onion and olive salad, or grilled corn on the cob, and toasted chunks of ciabatta.

**Each serving provides** • 270 cals • 30 g protein • 14 g fat of which 3 g saturates • 6.5 g carbohydrate

**15** mins prep time  **12** mins cook time

# greek **lamb** burgers

Mix together **1 lb (500 g) lean ground lamb**, **¼ cup (50 mL) fresh white bread crumbs**, **1 crushed garlic clove**, **1 tbsp (15 mL) chopped fresh oregano, or 1 tsp (5 mL) dried**, and **½ cup (125 mL) roughly crushed feta cheese**. Season and shape into ovals about 4 ¾ x 3 in. (12 x 8 cm). Brush with **olive oil** and grill using a high heat, or cook on the barbecue, for 10-12 minutes or until golden brown, turning once. Serve the burgers in large pita breads with red onion rings, chunky cucumber slices and Greek-style yogurt or tzatziki.

**Each serving provides** • 241 cals • 28 g protein • 13 g fat of which 2 g saturates • 4 g carbohydrate

**10** mins prep time  **12** mins cook time

Always buy lean meat when making burgers, to give the best flavour with less fat.

## ...shopping tip

# veal and **ham** chutney burgers

Combine **14 oz (400 g) ground veal**, **2⅔ oz (75 g) finely chopped cooked ham**, **2 tbsp (25 mL) fresh brown bread crumbs**, **1 egg yolk** and seasoning. Divide into eight and shape each into a round. Top four of the rounds with 1 tbsp (15 mL) of your favourite **fruit chutney**. Set the remaining rounds on top and press together to seal in the chutney, shaping into burgers. Stretch out **4 strips of bacon**, thinly on a board with the back of a knife, then wrap one around each burger. Brush with **oil** and pan-fry or grill on high with the bacon joint underneath for 10-12 minutes or until golden, turning once. Serve in whole-grain buns with extra pickles and crisp romaine lettuce leaves.

**Each serving provides**
• 380 cals • 30 g protein
• 15 g fat of which 5.5 g saturates
• 34 g carbohydrate

**10** mins prep time  **12** mins cook time

For a quicker version, combine all the burger ingredients, except the bacon, together in a bowl and mix well, then shape into four burgers. You will need to use a **finely chopped chutney** for this version. Wrap in bacon as before, if you like, and cook as above.

## ...speed it up

# pork, **sage** and **onion** burgers

Combine **11 oz (350 g) lean ground pork** with **5 oz (150 g) pork sausage meat**, **1 finely chopped onion**, **1 tbsp (15 mL) Worcestershire sauce** and **2 tbsp (25 mL) chopped fresh sage leaves**. Season and mix well, then shape into four burgers. Dust lightly with a little flour. Heat **1-2 tbsp (15-25 mL) canola oil** in a heavy-based frying pan and fry the burgers over a medium-high heat, turning once, for 10-12 minutes or until golden brown. Drain and serve in burger buns with coleslaw and apple slices.

**Each serving provides** • 288 cals • 24 g protein • 17 g fat of which 5 g saturates • 10 g carbohydrate

**10** mins prep time  **12** mins cook time

# Thai **Pork Patties** with **Bok Choy**

For a lively midweek meal, try these little meat patties and vegetables, with typical aromatic Thai flavourings of green curry and lemon grass. Serve with Thai fragrant rice or coconut rice (see To serve, page 198).

**15** mins prep time

**12** mins cook time

**Serves 4**
4 scallions, finely chopped
1 lb (500 g) lean ground pork
1½ tsp (7 mL) Thai green curry paste
2 tsp (10 mL) lemon grass in oil
1 egg white
2 tbsp (25 mL) peanut or Canola oil
7 oz (200 g) bok choy, sliced lengthwise
6 oz (175 g) oyster mushrooms, sliced
¾ cup (175 mL) coconut milk
1 tsp (5 mL) fish sauce
1 tbsp (15 mL) sesame seeds

**Each serving provides** • 322 cals
• 31 g protein • 21 g fat of which
7 g saturates • 2 g carbohydrate

**1** **Prepare the pork mixture** Mix together the scallions, minced pork, curry paste, lemon grass and egg white until evenly bound together, pressing the mixture firmly with the back of the mixing spoon.

**2** **Make the patties** Divide the mixture into 12 pieces, then shape each into a round, flattening with your fingers to make a patty shape.

**3** **Fry the patties** Heat 1 tbsp (15 mL) oil in a heavy-based frying pan and fry the patties, turning once, for 8-10 minutes or until golden brown and thoroughly cooked.

**4** **Cook the vegetables** While the patties are frying, heat a wide frying pan or wok with the remaining oil and add the bok choy and mushrooms. Stir-fry over a high heat for 2-3 minutes to soften.

**5** **Add flavourings** Stir the coconut milk and fish sauce into the vegetables, bring to the boil then simmer for a further minute. Serve the pork patties with the bok choy and coconut mixture, sprinkled with sesame seeds.

**Red Thai beef patties with vegetables**
Prepare **1 lb (500 g) lean ground steak** as step 1 using **3 finely chopped scallions, 1½ tsp (7 mL) red Thai curry paste**, a crushed **garlic clove** and **1 egg white**. Shape into 12 patties and fry as step 3. Stir-fry **11 oz (350 g) mixed vegetables**, such as broccoli florets, snow peas and baby corn, in **2 tbsp (25 mL) oil** until just tender, then add a **4-oz (125-g) can bamboo shoots**, drained, and ¾ cup (175 mL) **coconut milk**. Bring to the boil and stir in **2 tbsp (25 mL) chopped fresh coriander**.

## ...another idea

Unless you cook with lemon grass very frequently, buying fresh can be wasteful, so **lemon grass in oil**, which can be stored in the fridge, is a useful alternative. **Dried lemon grass sticks** are also convenient to use and store. They can be crumbled straight into Thai-style dishes. You will need 1 tsp (5 mL) dried lemon grass for this recipe.

## ...shopping tip

# Roquefort **Pork** Chops

These pan-fried chops have a surprise tucked inside: rich blue cheese with a touch of lemon. They taste great and take moments to prepare. Serve with pasta shapes and spinach.

**10** mins prep time

**15** mins cook time

Serves 4

**4 thick, rindless pork loin chops, about ½ lb (250 g) each**

**½ cup (125 mL) Roquefort cheese, crumbled**

**grated zest of ½ lemon**

**1 tbsp (15 mL) canola oil**

**2 tbsp (25 mL) chopped fresh rosemary**

**7½ oz (229 g) young spinach leaves**

**1 tsp (5 mL) freshly grated nutmeg**

**lemon wedges, to serve**

**Each serving provides** • 585 cals • 38 g protein • 47 g fat of which 18 g saturates • 1 g carbohydrate

1 **Prepare the chops** With a sharp knife, make a horizontal slit in the fat side of each pork chop without cutting all the way through. Gently open out into a pocket.

2 **Add the stuffing** Mix the cheese with the lemon zest, then tuck this into the pocket of each chop, pressing the meat back over firmly to enclose.

3 **Cook the chops** Brush the pork chops lightly with oil on both sides and season with salt and pepper. Heat a frying pan until hot, then reduce the heat to medium and add the chops. Fry over a medium heat for 6-7 minutes on each side or until golden and evenly cooked. Sprinkle the rosemary over the chops and turn them once or twice to coat.

4 **Cook the spinach** Remove the chops and keep them warm, then add the spinach to the pan and stir until just wilted. Divide the spinach among four serving plates.

5 **Serve** Add a pork chop to each serving, then sprinkle lightly with nutmeg. Serve immediately with lemon wedges.

**Swaps** • For Roquefort, use **Gorgonzola** or **dolcelatte**. • For pork, use **veal chops**. • For Roquefort and lemon, try other combinations such as: • **Brie or camembert** with **1 tbsp (15 mL) sweet chili dipping sauce**. • **Cheddar cheese** with **1 tbsp (15 mL) fruity relish**. • **Ricotta cheese** with **½ oz (15 g) chopped fresh basil leaves**. • Crumbled **feta cheese** with **1 tbsp (15 mL) chopped fresh thyme**.

# Maple **Ham**
## with Mango-Ginger Salsa

**Make a fast mango salsa with a gingery kick to complement ham glazed with sweet and sharp maple and lime. Serve with watercress and warmed flatbreads.**

**15** mins prep time

**8** mins cook time

**Serves 4**

**1 ripe mango**
**2 tomatoes, finely chopped**
**1 scallion, finely chopped**
**1 tbsp (15 mL) grated fresh ginger**
**juice of 1 lime**
**2 tbsp (25 mL) maple syrup**
**4 ham steaks, about 7 oz (200 g) each, trimmed of fat**
**bunch of watercress, to serve**

Each serving provides • 173 cals • 17 g protein • 7 g fat of which 2 g saturates • 12 g carbohydrate

1 **Make the salsa** Using a sharp knife, halve, pit and peel the mango. Chop the flesh finely, then mix with the tomatoes and scallion.

2 **Add the flavourings** Add the ginger and half the lime juice to the chopped ingredients, stirring to mix evenly.

3 **Make the glaze** Preheat a medium grill. Mix the remaining lime juice with the maple syrup and brush over the ham steaks.

4 **Cook the ham** Place the ham steaks in a grilling pan and cook for 3-4 minutes on each side, or until golden brown. Serve the ham on a bed of watercress with a spoonful of the salsa alongside.

# Hot Pepper Italian Sausage Popovers

Children love popovers, and here the popular dish has been livened up with hot pepper and with sweet cherry tomatoes for extra flavour. Serve with finely shredded stir-fried cabbage or broccoli.

**30 mins** prep/cook time

### Serves 4

2 tbsp (25 mL) canola oil

12 good-quality Italian sausages, halved

7 oz (200 g) cherry tomatoes, halved

4 oz (125 g) all-purpose flour

2 eggs

1¼ cups (300 mL) 1% milk

1½ tsp (7 mL) hot pepper sauce

**Each serving provides** • 344 cals • 17 g protein • 17 g fat of which 5 g saturates • 33 g carbohydrate

**1 Bake the Italian sausages and tomatoes** Preheat the oven to 425°F (220°C). Brush a 12-cup deep bun pan or muffin pan with the oil and heat in the oven until hot. Add the sausages, placing two halves in each cup. Bake for 5 minutes. Turn the sausages then divide the tomato halves among the cups and bake for a further 2 minutes.

**2 Make the batter** While the sausages are cooking, put the flour, eggs, milk, hot pepper sauce and seasoning in a bowl and beat until smooth and bubbly.

**3 Bake the popovers** Remove the bun pan from the oven and quickly pour a little of the batter into each cup. Return to the oven and bake for 20 minutes or until well risen and golden brown. Serve immediately.

**Cooking tips** • Try some of the unusual sausages available, such as a pack of mixed types. Or use smaller cocktail sausages instead of chipolatas. • For an extra-light batter, use **half milk and half water** instead of all milk.

### Beefy onion popovers

Omit the sausages and tomatoes from the basic recipe. Put ¾ lb (375 g) **lean ground beef** into a heavy-based pan and fry with **1 small sliced red onion** for 3-4 minutes or until lightly browned. Season and stir in **1 tsp (5 mL) mixed dried herbs**. Divide among the oiled bun-pan cups and bake in the preheated oven for 5 minutes. Make the batter as step 2, replacing the hot pepper sauce with **1 tbsp (15 mL) Worcestershire sauce**, then pour into the pan around the meat mixture. Bake for 20-25 minutes.

## ...another idea

### Serves 4

1 tbsp (15 mL) olive oil

1 red onion, thinly sliced

2 tsp (10 mL) soft brown sugar

2 lb (1 kg) floury potatoes, peeled and cut into small chunks

8 good-quality sausages

1 tbsp (15 mL) all-purpose flour

1¼ cups (300 mL) hot beef stock, made with a stock cube

6¾ tbsp (100 mL) red wine

1 tbsp (15 mL) Worcestershire sauce

6¾ tbsp (100 mL) milk, warmed

3½ tbsp (50 mL) butter

2-3 tsp (10-15 mL) whole-grain mustard

**Each serving provides** • 638 cals • 22 g protein • 36 g fat of which 15 g saturates • 57 g carbohydrate

**Swaps** • Try different sausages, such as spicy **merguez sausages**. • For mash, serve **couscous**. • For mustard, use **creamed horseradish**.

**30 mins** prep/cook time

If you need to keep mashed potatoes hot for a few minutes, cover the pan with a clean dish towel instead of a lid – the potatoes will stay light and fluffy.

## ...cooking tip

# Sausages with Mustard Mashed Potatoes and Red Onion Gravy

Buy any good-quality or specialty sausages for this quick and easy pub favourite. Whole-grain mustard gives piquancy to the creamy mashed potatoes, and red wine makes a robust onion gravy. Serve with green vegetables.

**1 Caramelize the onion** Heat the oil in a large frying pan. Add the onion and sprinkle with the sugar, then cook gently, stirring from time to time, for 12-15 minutes or until the onion is lightly caramelized. Preheat the grill.

**2 Cook the potatoes and sausages** While the onion is cooking, boil the potatoes in lightly salted water for 15 minutes or until tender, and grill the sausages, turning regularly, for about 15 minutes or until evenly browned.

**3 Make the gravy** Sprinkle the flour over the caramelized onion, stir and cook for 1 minute, then gradually stir in the stock, wine and Worcestershire sauce. Bring to the boil, then reduce the heat and leave to simmer gently.

**4 Mash the potatoes** Drain the potatoes and return to the pot. Mash with the warm milk, butter and mustard to taste.

**5 Serve** Spoon a mound of mashed potato on to each plate, lay a couple of sausages on top and spoon over the gravy.

## Sausages with mustardy lentils

Pork, leek and herb sausages are particularly good for this recipe. Caramelize the onion as step 1. Meanwhile, cook the potatoes and sausages as step 2. Omit the flour and Worcestershire sauce and stir in **6¾ tbsp (100 mL) dry cider** instead of the wine and stock at step 3. Simmer to reduce by about half. Add **⅔ cup (150 mL) chicken stock**, made with a stock cube, with a **14-oz (398-mL) can green lentils**, drained, and **2 tbsp (25 mL) whole-grain mustard**. Heat until boiling. Mash the potatoes as step 4, but omit the mustard, and stir in **2 tbsp (25 mL) chopped fresh parsley**. Serve the sausages and parsley mashed potatoes with the lentils.

## ...another idea

# Venison with Chunky Vegetable Braise

Delicious and lean venison has a fine flavour that goes perfectly with butternut squash, chickpeas and celery in this easy harvest-style recipe. Serve with bread, or pre-made polenta slices, brushed with oil and grilled with the steaks.

**30** mins prep/cook time

**Serves 4**

2 tbsp (25 mL) olive oil

3 shallots, roughly chopped

1 lb (500 g) butternut squash, peeled and diced

2 celery sticks, sliced

1 bay leaf

1¼ cup (300 mL) beef stock, made with a stock cube

2 tbsp (25 mL) Worcestershire sauce

4 venison steaks, about 1½ in. (3 cm) thick and 5 oz (150 g) each

14 oz (398 mL) can chickpeas, drained and rinsed

1 tsp (5 mL) smoked or regular paprika

**Each serving provides** • 329 cals • 40 g protein • 11 g fat of which 2 g saturates • 22 g carbohydrate

Venison steaks can also be pan-fried in 1 tbsp (15 mL) oil. Cook on a high heat to sear, then reduce to medium heat and cook for 10-12 minutes.

**...cooking tip**

**1 Fry the vegetables** Heat the oil in a large, heavy-based pot and fry the shallots, squash and celery over a fairly high heat, stirring occasionally, for 5 minutes or until beginning to brown. Preheat the broiler to high.

**2 Add the flavourings** Add the bay leaf, stock and 1 tbsp (15 mL) Worcestershire sauce, and bring to the boil. Reduce the heat, then cover and simmer for 10 minutes or until the vegetables are just tender. Adjust the seasoning if necessary.

**3 Broil the venison** While the vegetables are cooking, brush the venison steaks with the remaining Worcestershire sauce and cook for 4-5 minutes on each side. Cut into thick pieces, if you like.

**4 Add the chickpeas** Stir the chickpeas into the pot of vegetables and bring back to the boil. Spoon the vegetables onto serving plates and top with the venison. Sprinkle with the paprika and serve.

**Swaps** • You can vary the vegetables according to the season: for squash, use **kohlrabi, turnip, parsnip or sweet potato**; for celery, use **leeks**. • For chickpeas, use other canned beans such as **borlotti, wax beans or cannellini**.

The vegetables can be frozen. Cook up to the end of step 2, cool quickly and put into a freezerproof container. Freeze for up to two months. To use, thaw, reheat and simmer for 3 minutes. **...keep it**

# Veal Parcels
## with Apricot, Cheese and Sage

**The gentle flavours of mild cheese, apricots, sage and orange are a delightful complement to delicate veal in these effortlessly easy parcels. They go well with buttery fettuccine and a baby leaf salad.**

**5** mins prep time

**25** mins cook time

Serves 4
4 veal escalopes, about ¼ in. (5 mm) thick and about ¼ lb (125 g) each
2 tbsp (25 mL) chopped fresh sage
¼ lb (125 g) mild cheddar cheese, or other young cheese
12 ready-to-eat dried apricots
2 tsp (10 mL) olive oil
juice of 1 orange

**Each serving provides** • 401 cals • 46 g protein • 14 g fat of which 7 g saturates • 24 g carbohydrate

**1 Season the veal** Preheat the oven to 425°F (220°C). Lay the veal escalopes on a board, season and sprinkle with the sage.

**2 Make the parcels** Cut the cheese into four slices and lay one over the middle of each escalope. Top each with three apricots. Wrap the escalope over to enclose the cheese and apricots, slightly overlapping the joint.

**3 Bake the parcels** Put the veal parcels, with the joint underneath, into a shallow ovenproof dish and brush them with the oil. Pour over the orange juice. Bake for 20-25 minutes, basting with the juices halfway through, until the meat is thoroughly cooked.

**Swaps** • For cheddar cheese, use **Lancashire, Cheshire or feta**. • For dried apricots, use slices of **fresh apricot, peach or nectarine** when in season. • For orange juice, use **6¾ tbsp (100 mL) medium-dry white wine**.

Make the veal parcels earlier in the day or even the day before. Put them in the baking dish and cover with plastic wrap, then store in the fridge until you're ready to bake. It's a good idea to remove them from the fridge about 20 minutes before cooking, otherwise they will be very cold and may take longer to cook. **...get ahead**

# vegetables

# Italian Pan-Fried Mushrooms

Fresh exotic mushrooms are available in the fall, and they add a wonderfully concentrated flavour to this express mushroom dish. Serve with creamy pasta or griddled ciabatta and a plum tomato salad.

**15** mins prep time  **8** mins cook time

## Serves 4 Ⓥ

⅔ cup (150 mL) pine nuts

1 tbsp (15 mL) olive oil

1 shallot, finely chopped

1 garlic clove, crushed

1 tbsp (15 mL) unsalted butter

5 cups (1.25 L) chestnut mushrooms, thickly sliced

1½ cups (375 mL) mixed exotic mushrooms, thickly sliced

2 tsp (10 mL) balsamic vinegar

1 tsp (5 mL) chopped fresh thyme

**Each serving provides**
- 155 cals • 4 g protein
- 15 g fat of which 3 g saturates
- 1 g carbohydrate

Toss freshly cooked pasta with **2 tbsp (25 mL) ricotta cheese,** steamed **baby spinach leaves** (pierce a 1½-lb/250-g bag and cook on high in the microwave for 2 minutes) and **freshly grated nutmeg**. Spoon the mushrooms on top and scatter with grated **Parmesan or Italian-style hard cheese**. Or cut a slightly stale **ciabatta loaf or small baguette** into diagonal slices. Brush with olive oil on both sides. Cook on a heated ridged frying pan or under a hot broiler for 1 minute on each side or until lightly browned. Serve the mushrooms on top of the toasts.

## ...to serve

**1 Toast the pine nuts** Put the pine nuts in a large, dry nonstick frying pan and toast for 2-3 minutes over a medium heat, stirring frequently, until a light golden brown. Remove from the pan and set aside.

**2 Fry the shallot** Add the oil and chopped shallot to the pan, and cook for 2 minutes or until starting to soften. Stir in the garlic.

**3 Cook the mushrooms** Turn up the heat a little and add the butter and chestnut mushrooms. Cook for 2 minutes. Add the mixed mushrooms and continue cooking for 2-3 minutes, stirring occasionally, until the liquid evaporates and the mushrooms are tender. Sprinkle over the vinegar, thyme and seasoning. Heat for a few more seconds, then stir in the pine nuts and serve at once.

**Swap** For pine nuts, use a ½-lb (250-g) package smoked tofu (with almonds and sesame seeds, if available). Cut into small cubes and fry in **2 tsp (10 mL) olive oil** for 2-3 minutes. Tip into a bowl and sprinkle with **1 tsp (5 mL) dark soy sauce**. Stir into the cooked mushrooms.

**15** mins prep time  **15** mins cook time

## Makes 6 Ⓥ

¾ lb (375 g) package pre-rolled puff pastry

1¼ cups (300 mL) chopped walnuts

1 tbsp (15 mL) unsalted butter

2 tbsp (25 mL) heavy cream

1¾ cup (425 mL) baby button mushrooms, chopped

1¾ cups (425 mL) chestnut mushrooms, sliced

1 garlic clove, crushed

½ tsp (2 mL) dried mixed herbs

1 egg yolk, lightly beaten with 1 tsp (5 mL) water

1 tbsp (15 mL) sesame seeds

**Each turnover provides** • 501 cals
- 9 g protein • 42 g fat of which 6.5 g saturates • 24 g carbohydrate

# Mushroom
## and Walnut Turnovers

These pretty, sesame-sprinkled puff-pastry parcels are simplicity itself.
Serve hot with steamed vegetables such as green beans, or cold with a
leafy salad or chunky coleslaw as a special treat for a packed lunch.

**1 Prepare the pastry and walnuts** Preheat the oven to
425°F (220°C). Remove the pastry from the fridge and, if time
allows, leave it, still wrapped, at room temperature for up to
20 minutes. Put the walnuts onto a large freezerproof plate
and put in the freezer to chill.

**2 Make the mushroom filling** Melt the butter in a nonstick
frying pan. Add 1 tbsp (15 mL) cream, the mushrooms, garlic
and herbs. Cook over a fairly high heat for 6-7 minutes or
until the mushrooms are tender and all the juices have
evaporated. Tip the mushrooms onto the chilled plate. Drizzle
with the remaining cream and season. Stir to mix with the
walnuts, then spread out in a single layer to cool.

**3 Make the turnovers** Carefully unroll the pastry, then cut
into six squares. Lightly brush the edges with a little beaten
egg yolk. Spoon the filling on to one side of a diagonal centre
line, then fold over to make a triangular turnover. Press the
edges together firmly to seal, then mark a pattern on them

with a fork. Brush all over with beaten egg, sprinkle the
surface with sesame seeds and make a slit in the top to
allow steam to escape.

**4 Bake the turnovers** Transfer the turnovers to a nonstick
baking sheet (or a baking sheet lined with baking parchment)
and bake for 15 minutes or until risen and lightly browned.

**Sun-dried tomato and pine nut turnovers** ⓥ
Complete step 1 using **3 tbsp (45 mL) pine nuts** instead of
walnuts. Put **¼ cup (50 mL) long-grain rice** in a pot with
**1 small diced zucchini, 6 chopped sun-dried tomatoes,
a pinch of dried oregano** and **⅔ cup (150 mL) vegetable
stock**, made with a stock cube. Cover and cook for 10-12
minutes or until the rice is tender and all the stock has been
absorbed. Cool and mix with the pine nuts as step 2. Continue
as the basic recipe.

## ...another idea

# Roast Squash and Zucchini
## with Lima Beans

Quickly roasted squash, red onions and zucchini are tossed in an orange and cardamom glaze for extra sweetness, then mixed with lima beans and topped with plain yogurt. Serve with crusty bread.

**10** mins prep time

**20** mins cook time

Serves 4 Ⓥ

2 red onions

1 butternut squash, about 1½ lb (750 g), peeled and cut into 1¾-in. (1.5-cm) chunks

2 tbsp (25 mL) olive oil

2 zucchini, cut into ½-in. (1-cm) slices

4 small sprigs of fresh thyme

6 cardamom pods

½ tsp (2 mL) brown sugar

4 tbsp (60 mL) orange juice

2 tsp (10 mL) balsamic vinegar

14-oz (398-mL) can lima beans, drained and rinsed

3½ (100 g) plain yogurt

**Each serving provides** • 247 cals • 8 g protein • 10 g fat of which 3 g saturates • 33 g carbohydrate

**1 Prepare the vegetables** Preheat the oven to 445°F (230°C), and put in a large nonstick baking tray to heat. Cut each onion into eight wedges. Put the chunks of squash and the onions into a bowl and drizzle over 1½ tbsp (20 mL) oil. Add a little seasoning and toss the vegetables with your hands or a large spoon to coat.

**2 Roast the vegetables** Take the tray out of the oven and tip the vegetables onto it, spreading them out in a single layer. Roast for 10 minutes. Meanwhile, put the zucchini into the bowl, add the thyme and drizzle with the remaining oil. Toss with your hands to coat. Set aside.

**3 Make the glaze** Crush the cardamom pods using a mortar and pestle or the end of a rolling pin. Discard the pods and grind the seeds using the mortar and pestle, or in an electric grinder, until fairly fine. Mix the seeds in a small bowl with the sugar, orange juice and vinegar. Turn the vegetables, then add the thyme-coated zucchini and lima beans. Drizzle everything with the glaze mixture. Roast for 10 minutes more, or until the vegetables are tender and lightly charred.

**4 Complete the dish** Remove the vegetables from the oven and spoon into a warmed serving dish or onto individual plates. Top the hot vegetables and lima beans with small spoonfuls of yogurt before serving.

**Swaps** • For butternut squash, use **pumpkin or kabocha squash**. • For zucchini, use **green peppers**.

**Addition** Roast **7 oz (200 g) pre-washed baby new potatoes**, quartered, and an extra **½ tbsp (7 mL) olive oil** with the squash.

# Eggplant Parmigiana

**This typically Italian mixture of eggplants, tomatoes, peppers, mozzarella and Parmesan comes together in no time and has a rich and full flavour. Serve with focaccia and a green salad.**

15 mins prep time    15 mins cook time

**Serves 4** Ⓥ

2 large eggplants, about 1⅔ lb (800 g) total weight

2 tsp (10 mL) olive oil

2 garlic cloves, crushed

1⅓ cups (325 mL) bottled tomato sauce

7 oz (200 g) can pimentos, drained and sliced

1 tsp (5 mL) dried mixed herbs

¼ cup (50 mL) grated Parmesan or Italian-style hard cheese

¼ lb (125 g) mozzarella, thinly sliced

3 tbsp (45 mL) pine nuts (optional)

**Each serving provides** • 188 cals • 11 g protein • 11 g fat of which 6 g saturates • 12 g carbohydrate

**1 Prepare the eggplants** Preheat the broiler to medium-hot. Remove the stalks from the eggplants and cut into ½-in. (1-cm) slices, then arrange on a broiler rack. Broil for 10 minutes or until the slices are lightly browned and tender, turning once.

**2 Make the sauce** While the eggplant slices are cooking, preheat the oven to 425°F (220°C). Heat the oil in a pot and gently cook the garlic for 1 minute. Stir in the tomato sauce, pimentos and herbs, and bring the mixture to the boil.

**3 Layer the eggplants and sauce** Put a third of the grilled eggplant slices into a large ovenproof dish. Spoon over about a third of the hot tomato sauce and spread evenly, then sprinkle with a heaping teaspoon of Parmesan cheese. Repeat the layers twice, finishing with a layer of tomato sauce.

**4 Finish the dish** Sprinkle the remaining Parmesan cheese over the sauce, then arrange the slices of mozzarella on top. Sprinkle with the pine nuts, if using. Bake for 15 minutes or until the eggplants are very tender and the cheese is melted and bubbling. Serve immediately.

**Ratatouille and cheese bake** Ⓥ

Heat **3 tbsp (45 mL) olive oil** in a large pan and gently cook **1 crushed garlic clove** and **2 sliced onions** until softened. Cut an **eggplant** lengthwise in half, and thinly slice; add this to the onion with **2 sliced zucchini** and **1 sliced red pepper**. Cook for 3-4 minutes. Stir in a **14-oz (398-mL) can chopped tomatoes with basil, 1 tbsp sun-dried tomato paste, 2 tsp (10 mL) chopped fresh thyme** and seasoning. Cover and simmer for 15-20 minutes or until all the vegetables are tender. Stir in a **14-oz (398-mL) can pinto beans**, drained and rinsed, bring to the boil and spoon into an ovenproof dish. Scatter with **¾ cup (175 mL) coarsely grated hard mozzarella**. Cook under a preheated medium-hot broiler for 5 minutes or until the cheese is golden brown.

**...another idea**

Mediterranean Tomato Sauce (page 268) can be used instead of bottled tomato sauce, if you prefer.

**...or try this**

# 5 great ways with a **can** of **tomatoes**

A can of tomatoes is an essential pantry ingredient. Incredibly versatile, it can be used to create a simple soup or a speedy sauce – or it can be the basis of many spectacular supper dishes. All recipes serve 4.

## red **pepper**, chili and **tomato** soup with **sausages**

Broil or gently fry **6 sausages** until golden brown, then set aside. Meanwhile, put **1 tbsp (15 mL) olive oil** into a pot and gently cook **1 roughly chopped onion**, **1 seeded and sliced red chili pepper** and **2 seeded and diced red peppers**, covered, for 6-7 minutes or until tender. Stir in a **14-oz (398-mL) can plum tomatoes**, **1¼ cups (300 mL) vegetable stock**, made with a stock cube, and **1 tbsp (15 mL) sun-dried tomato paste**. Season. Bring to the boil and reduce the heat a little. Half-cover the pot with a lid and simmer for 10 minutes or until the vegetables are tender. Slice the sausages. Purée the soup in a food processor or blender until smooth. Tip back into the pot and add the sausage slices, then reheat until piping hot. Serve topped with a swirl of heavy cream and a light sprinkling of cayenne pepper, and accompany with rosemary or garlic focaccia. Ⓥ

**Each serving provides** • 173 cals • 14 g protein • 6 g fat of which 1 g saturates • 16 g carbohydrate

**12** mins prep time **17** mins cook time

## **chickpea** and **tomato** pasta sauce

Heat **1 tbsp (15 mL) olive oil** in a heavy-based pan and gently cook **1 finely chopped red onion** for 7-8 minutes or until softened. (If time allows, add a finely chopped carrot and a celery stick.) Stir in **1 large crushed garlic clove**, **1 tbsp (15 mL) sun-dried tomato paste**, ¼ tsp (1 mL) crushed chili flakes and 1 tsp (5 mL) dried herbes de Provence, then cook for a few seconds. Add a **14-oz (398-mL) can chopped tomatoes**, a **14-oz (398-mL) can chickpeas**, drained and rinsed, **6¾ tbsp (100 mL) dry red wine or vegetable stock**, made with a stock cube, and a **bay leaf**. Bring to the boil, then simmer for 10 minutes or until the sauce has thickened a little. Remove the bay leaf and stir in **2 tbsp (25 mL) torn basil leaves**. Season. Serve with pasta (penne is ideal) and some grated Parmesan or Gruyère. Ⓥ

**Each serving provides** • 145 cals • 6 g protein • 5 g fat of which 0.5 g saturates • 16.5 g carbohydrate

**10** mins prep time **18** mins cook time

Sun-dried tomato paste has a richer flavour than ordinary tomato paste because it also contains chilies, oregano, garlic and capers. It's particularly useful when you are cooking in a hurry and don't have time to add many flavourings.

**...shopping tip**

# fennel, flageolet and mushroom goulash

Heat **2 tbsp (25 mL) olive oil** in a large pot and gently cook **1 sliced onion** over a medium heat for 5 minutes or until softened. Meanwhile, cut **3 fennel bulbs**, about 1½ lb (700 g) total weight, into very thin slices. Add to the onions with **2½ tbsp (30 mL) paprika**. Stir for a few seconds, then add **4 cups (1 L) button mushrooms**, halved, a **14-oz (398-mL) can chopped tomatoes with herbs**, **2 tbsp (25 mL) sun-dried tomato paste** and **1¼ cups (300 mL) vegetable stock**, made with a stock cube. Stir in a **14-oz (398-mL) can flageolet beans**, drained and rinsed. Season, bring to the boil and stir. Cover and simmer for 20 minutes, until the vegetables are tender. Serve with plain yogurt and crusty bread or rice. Ⓥ

**Each serving provides** • 202 cals • 11 g protein • 8 g fat of which 1 g saturates • 22 g carbohydrate

**10** mins prep time   **20** mins cook time

# pea and cauliflower pilaf

Heat **2 tbsp (25 mL) ghee or canola oil** in a large heavy-based pot and add **2 finely chopped shallots**. Cook for 2 minutes or until beginning to soften. Stir in **1 crushed garlic clove** and **7 oz (200 g) small cauliflower florets**. Stir over a high heat for 2-3 minutes or until starting to colour. Add **½ tsp (2 mL) ground turmeric**, **1 tsp (5 mL) ground cumin**, **1 tsp (5 mL) ground coriander**, **a pinch of crushed chili flakes** and **2 cups (500 mL) rinsed and drained basmati rice**. Stir over a medium heat for 1 minute, then add a **14-oz (398-mL) can chopped tomatoes**, **2 cups (500 mL) boiling vegetable stock**, made with a stock cube, **1 cup (250 mL) frozen peas** and seasoning. Bring to the boil, then cover and simmer gently for 12-14 minutes or until the rice is tender and the liquid has been absorbed. Stir in **1 tbsp (15 mL) chopped fresh mint**, if you like, and garnish with **½ cup (125 mL) toasted slivered almonds**. Ⓥ

**Each serving provides** • 462 cals • 14 g protein • 14 g fat of which 1 g saturates • 69 g carbohydrate

**10** mins prep time   **20** mins cook time

---

This bean mixture is also good as a filling for warm tortillas or taco shells. Serve them with store-bought or homemade guacamole. (For guacamole, halve, stone and peel **2 large avocados**. Mash with **3 tbsp lemon juice**, then stir in **1 crushed garlic clove**, **3 tbsp/45 mL sour cream**, and seasoning. Add a large **pinch of crushed chili flakes or a dash of Tabasco sauce**, if you like. Serve immediately.)

## ...cooking tip

# chili beans and cheese

Cook **1 finely chopped onion** and **1 chopped celery stick** in **1½ tbsp (20 mL) olive oil** for 8 minutes. Stir in **2 crushed garlic cloves** and **1-2 tsp (5-10 mL) chili powder**, to taste, and cook for a further 2 minutes. Add a **14-oz (398-mL) can chopped tomatoes**, a **14-oz (398-mL) can red kidney beans**, drained and rinsed, **½ tsp (2 mL) dried oregano** and seasoning. Simmer, uncovered, for 5 minutes or until the vegetables are tender. Pour the mixture into an ovenproof dish and scatter with **½ cup (125 mL) coarsely grated Monterey Jack or cheddar cheese**. Cook under a preheated hot broiler for 3-4 minutes or until melted and bubbling. Serve with slices of cornbread. Ⓥ

**Each serving provides** • 180 cals • 9 g protein • 9 g fat of which 3 g saturates • 17 g carbohydrate

**10** mins prep time   **20** mins cook time

# Cowboy Casserole

**Tempt children to enjoy vegetables with this easy leave-to-cook dish of vegetables and baked beans, spiced up with barbecue sauce and with a top layer of melting smoked cheese and sliced potatoes.**

**10** mins prep time

**30** mins cook time

**Serves 4** ⓥ

1⅓ lb (600 g) unpeeled baking potatoes, scrubbed and thinly sliced

2 tbsp (25 mL) butter or 1½ tbsp (20 mL) olive oil

1 tsp (5 mL) sun-dried tomato paste

14 oz (398 mL) can baked beans

¼ lb (125 g) frozen peas

¼ lb (125 g) frozen green beans

7 oz (200 g) can corn, drained

2 tbsp (25 mL) barbecue sauce

3½ oz (100 g) smoked cheese, roughly chopped

**Each serving provides**
- 404 cals • 17 g protein • 13 g fat of which 7 g saturates
- 58 g carbohydrate

**1 Parboil the potatoes** Preheat the oven to 400°F (200°C). Put the potatoes into a pot of lightly salted boiling water. Bring back to the boil, then half-cover with a lid and simmer for 4 minutes (the potatoes should be just tender, but not breaking up). Drain the potatoes thoroughly, reserving 4 tbsp (60 mL) of the cooking water. Tip the potatoes into a bowl, add the butter or oil and toss them using two wooden spoons, to lightly coat all over. Set aside.

**2 Prepare the vegetables** Blend the sun-dried tomato paste with the reserved hot water in the pot. Tip in the baked beans, peas, green beans, corn and barbecue sauce. Heat gently, stirring to mix everything together, until the mixture is barely warm and the peas and green beans have thawed. Tip into a shallow casserole dish, spreading out into an even layer. Scatter over the cubes of smoked cheese.

**3 Add the potato topping** Arrange the potato slices over the top, overlapping them slightly so that they completely cover the bean and cheese mixture. Bake for 30 minutes or until the potatoes are tender and the top is golden brown.

**Swaps** • Any combination of prepared **frozen, blanched fresh, or leftover cooked vegetables** can be used for this casserole. • To add extra protein, use **frozen soya beans** instead of the peas or green beans. • For potatoes, use peeled **sweet potatoes**, blanching them for just 3 minutes and adding **1 tsp (5 mL) lemon juice** to the cooking water to prevent them from discolouring.

# Brazilian Peppers

Halved yellow and red peppers make bright containers for an ultra-easy stuffing of spicy rice and pinto beans, topped with crunchy nuts and well-flavoured cheese. All it needs is a crisp salad to accompany it.

**Serves 4** Ⓥ

4 red and/or yellow peppers, halved lengthwise and cored

2 tsp (10 mL) olive oil

1 garlic clove, crushed

1 red chili pepper, halved, seeded and finely chopped

½ tsp (2 mL) dried oregano

2 tbsp (25 mL) sun-dried tomato paste

1 cup (250 mL) easy-cook white rice

1⅔ cups (400 mL) boiling vegetable stock, made with a stock cube

14 oz (398 mL) can pinto beans, drained and rinsed

½ cup (125 mL) aged cheddar cheese, grated

½ cup (125 mL) Brazil nuts, roughly chopped

**Each serving provides** • 490 cals • 17 g protein • 17 g fat of which 6 g saturates • 70 g carbohydrate

**30 mins prep/cook time**

**1 Start cooking the peppers** Preheat the oven to 425°F (220°C). Season the insides of the pepper halves and put them cut side down on a lightly greased baking sheet. Put them in the oven and cook for 12 minutes.

**2 Prepare the filling** While the peppers are cooking, heat the oil in a large pot and gently cook the garlic and chili pepper for 30 seconds. Stir in the oregano, tomato paste and rice. Add the stock, stir and bring the mixture to the boil. Reduce the heat a little and cover the pot. Cook for 10 minutes or until the rice is barely tender and most of the stock has been absorbed (there should be no more than 2 tbsp/25 mL of liquid – if necessary, simmer uncovered for 1-2 minutes more). Stir in the pinto beans; season to taste.

**3 Fill the peppers** Remove the pepper halves from the oven and turn them cut side up. Divide the rice filling among them (they should be completely filled with a nicely rounded top). Mix together the cheese and Brazil nuts, then scatter the mixture over the filling.

**4 Bake and serve** Return the filled peppers to the oven and bake, uncovered, for 10 minutes or until they are tender and the top is golden brown and crisp. Serve at once.

## Spicy bean-stuffed mushrooms Ⓥ

Wipe **8 large, flat mushrooms**, remove the stalks and chop these finely. Brush the gill sides with **1 tbsp (15 mL) olive oil** and season. Cook gill side up under a medium-hot broiler for 6 minutes. Turn over, brush with **1 tbsp (15 mL) oil** and cook for 5 minutes or until softened. Meanwhile, cook the chopped stalks and **1 crushed garlic clove** in **1 tbsp (15 mL) olive oil** for 2 minutes. Stir in **1 coarsely grated carrot** and **½ tsp (2 mL) chili powder** and cook for 2-3 minutes or until tender. Add a **14-oz (398-mL) can kidney beans**, rinsed, and **2 tbsp (25 mL) vegetable stock**. Mash and stir the mixture with a fork. Season and divide among the mushrooms. Sprinkle with a mixture of **½ cup (125 mL) each fresh bread crumbs and grated cheddar cheese**. Broil for 3-4 minutes or until golden brown.

## Tomatoes stuffed with almonds and couscous Ⓥ

Heat **1 tbsp (15 mL) olive oil** in a pot and gently cook **6 thinly sliced scallions** for 2 minutes. Stir in **1 tsp (5 mL) ground cumin** and a **pinch of ground turmeric**. Add **1 cup (250 mL) hot vegetable stock** and bring to a boil. Pour in **¾ cup (175 mL) couscous** in a steady stream, stirring constantly. Remove from the heat, cover and leave to stand for 5 minutes. Meanwhile, cut the tops off **8 beefsteak tomatoes** (keep the tops), and scoop them out. Stir **½ cup (125 mL) chopped dried apricots**, **¾ cup (175 mL) toasted slivered almonds** and **1 cup (250 mL) crumbled feta cheese** into the couscous. Spoon into the tomato shells, replace the tops and put on a baking sheet. Bake for 10 minutes or until tender.

## ...more ideas

# Chargrilled Vegetable Feast

Make a simple pasta meal into a taste sensation in record time. Quickly grill some colourful Mediterranean vegetables and add tangy feta cheese and toasted nuts. Accompany with a leafy salad.

**30** mins prep/cook time

**Serves 4** (V)

**1 large or 2 medium zucchini, sliced into rings**

**1 eggplant, sliced into rings**

**1 red pepper, cut into wide strips**

**1 yellow pepper, cut into wide strips**

**1 red onion, cut into thin wedges**

**5 tbsp (75 mL) olive oil**

**2 garlic cloves, crushed**

**½ cup (125 mL) pine nuts or walnuts**

**14 oz (400 g) tagliatelle**

**4 tbsp (60 mL) pesto**

**7 oz (200 g) feta cheese, roughly cubed**

**Each serving provides** • 796 cals • 29 g protein • 47 g fat of which 13 g saturates • 68 g carbohydrate

**1 Broil the vegetables** Preheat the broiler to medium-high. Put the vegetables in a large bowl and drizzle with the oil. Add the garlic and season with pepper. Mix together well, then spread the vegetables out in a grill pan. Broil for 20-25 minutes or until softened and lightly charred, turning from time to time and removing any vegetables that are cooked before the rest.

**2 Toast the nuts** While the vegetables are cooking, put the nuts in a dry pan and toast over a medium heat, tossing regularly, for 2-3 minutes or until golden brown. Tip onto a plate and set aside.

**3 Cook the pasta** Towards the end of broiling, cook the pasta in a pot of salted boiling water for 8 minutes, or according to the package instructions, until al dente. Drain thoroughly and return to the pan.

**4 Mix everything together** Add the vegetables and pesto to the pasta. Add the feta cheese and the nuts. Gently toss everything together and serve immediately.

**Vegetable hash** (V)

Preheat the broiler to high. Cut **2 zucchini** into cubes, **2 red peppers** into chunky pieces and **1 red onion** into wedges. Put into a grill pan. Add **3¼ cups (800 mL) button mushrooms**, quartered. Drizzle **3 tbsp (45 mL) extra virgin olive oil** over the vegetables. Season and add **1 tbsp (15 mL) rosemary leaves**. Toss to mix then spread out evenly. Broil for 10 minutes, turning the vegetables occasionally. Add **1 can artichoke hearts**, drained and quartered, **3 cooked and cubed potatoes** (optional) and **½ lb (250 g) mozzarella or halloumi cheese**, cubed. Toss with the vegetables and cook for 10 minutes or until golden. Serve on a bed of rice or bulgur wheat.

## ...another idea

# Sweet and Spicy Chickpeas

Protein-packed canned chickpeas are ideal for nutritious vegetarian cuisine in a hurry. Toss them in a spicy mixture then add to colourful vegetables. Serve with couscous or warmed chapattis and plain yogurt.

**Serves 4**

**14 oz (398 mL) can chickpeas, drained and rinsed**

**finely grated zest and juice of 1 lime**

**1 tsp (5 mL) white (superfine) sugar**

**1 tsp (5 mL) garam masala**

**½ tsp (2 mL) ground cinnamon**

**1 tsp (5 mL) dried oregano**

**2 tbsp (25 mL) canola oil**

**2 small onions, halved and thickly sliced**

**2 peppers (1 red, yellow or orange and 1 green), halved and thickly sliced**

**12 baby plum or cherry tomatoes, halved**

**Each serving provides** • 163 cals • 6 g protein • 8 g fat of which 1 g saturates • 18 g carbohydrate

**1 Combine the chickpeas and spices** Tip the chickpeas into a bowl. Add the lime zest and juice, sugar, garam masala, cinnamon and oregano. Stir to coat the chickpeas in the spicy mixture. Set aside for a few minutes.

**2 Cook the onions and peppers** Heat a large frying pan or wok with the oil. When the oil is hot, add the onions and stir-fry for 4 minutes or until just beginning to colour. Reduce the heat and add the peppers. Cook for a further 3-4 minutes, stirring occasionally, until the vegetables are almost tender.

**3 Add the tomatoes and chickpeas** Stir in the tomatoes, then add the spicy chickpea mixture. Cook for 2 minutes or until the vegetables are tender and everything is hot.

**10** mins prep time

**10** mins cook time

# Avocado and Almond Gratin

For a speedy meal, layer creamy, ripe avocados with sun-dried tomatoes and smother them with a simple lemony sauce to offset their richness, then top with toasted almonds. Serve with crusty bread and a green salad.

**15** mins prep time   **15** mins cook time

**Serves 4** (V)

1⅔ cup (400 mL) 1% milk

1 thick slice of onion, unpeeled

1 lemon

1 bay leaf

4 large, or 6 medium, ripe avocados

1¾ oz (50 g) soft sun-dried tomatoes (vacuum packed without oil or salt), roughly chopped

2 tbsp (25 mL) plain white flour

1 tsp (5 mL) Dijon mustard

⅔ cup (150 mL) slivered almonds

½ cup (125 mL) grated aged cheddar cheese (optional)

¼ tsp (1 mL) paprika

**Each serving provides** • 591 cals • 13 g protein • 51 g fat of which 10 g saturates • 22 g carbohydrate

1 **Flavour the sauce** Preheat the oven to 350°F (180°C). Pour half the milk into a pot. Remove the outer layer of skin from the onion slice (but leave on the inner layers as they will colour the sauce). Pare two thin strips of zest from the lemon. Add the onion, lemon zest and bay leaf to the milk and heat to boiling point. Cover the pot with a lid and leave to infuse for a few minutes.

2 **Prepare the avocados** While the milk is infusing, halve and peel the avocados, and remove the pits. Thickly slice the flesh and put into a bowl. Sprinkle with 2 tsp (10 mL) lemon juice and some ground black pepper, and toss to coat. Arrange half the slices in a baking dish, then scatter with the chopped tomatoes. Top with the remaining avocado slices.

3 **Finish the sauce** Discard the onion slice from the infused milk (but leave in the lemon zest and bay leaf). Mix the flour with the remaining milk and the mustard, then whisk into the warm, infused milk. Bring to the boil, stirring until thickened and smooth. Discard the bay leaf and lemon zest, then season the sauce with a little salt.

4 **Bake the dish** Pour the sauce over the avocados, then sprinkle the top with the slivered almonds, cheese, if using, and paprika. Bake for 15 minutes or until the sauce is bubbling and the almonds are lightly browned. Warm some crusty bread for 5 minutes in the oven at the same time to serve with the dish.

**Swaps** • For slivered almonds, mix **¼ cup (50 mL) roughly chopped unsalted peanuts** with the cheddar cheese. • For sun-dried tomatoes, use a **16-oz (450-g) jar roasted red peppers**, drained. • For slivered almonds and cheddar, use **¼ cup (50 mL) grated Parmesan or Italian-style hard cheese** and **¼ cup (50 mL) crunchy seed mix**.

Don't be tempted to use under-ripe avocados, as they will have a slightly bitter taste. Perfectly ripe fruit will be just soft when pressed and have creamy flesh.

**...shopping tip**

# Gnocchi with Mediterranean Tomato Sauce

For a super-fast and delicious change from pasta, cook gnocchi – little Italian potato or semolina dumplings. Toss them in a fresh tomato sauce with some Mediterranean herbs, and top with nuts and Parmesan cheese.

**15** mins prep time   **15** mins cook time

### Serves 4 (V)

- **14 oz (400 g) large tomatoes**
- **1½ tbsp (20 mL) olive oil**
- **2 garlic cloves, crushed**
- **6 scallions, thinly sliced**
- **½ tsp (2 mL) white (superfine) sugar**
- **1 tsp (5 mL) balsamic vinegar**
- **2 sprigs of fresh herbs such as rosemary and oregano (optional)**
- **2 tbsp (25 mL) red pesto**
- **1 lb (500 g) package gnocchi**
- **½ cup (125 mL) pistachios, roughly chopped**
- **¼ cup (50 mL) grated Parmesan or Italian-style hard cheese**

**Each serving provides**
- 415 cals • 12 g protein
- 20 g fat of which 5 g saturates
- 47 g carbohydrate

This is a useful sauce to make in batches and freeze for other dishes such as Eggplant Parmigiana (page 259) and Pasta Sauce, Mushroom and Chard Topping (page 271). This recipe makes 1⅓ cup (325 mL). Double or triple the quantities made here and divide into single batches in freezerproof containers. Freeze for up to one month. To use, thaw, reheat and simmer for 3 minutes.

## ...keep it

**1 Peel the tomatoes** Put the tomatoes in a heatproof bowl and cover with boiling water. Leave for 1 minute, then remove with a slotted spoon, rinse briefly under cold water, and peel off the skins. Quarter the tomatoes and discard the seeds. Roughly chop the flesh. Set aside.

**2 Make the sauce** Heat 1 tbsp (15 mL) oil in a pot and add the crushed garlic and sliced scallions. Cook gently for 2-3 minutes or until tender. Sprinkle over the sugar and balsamic vinegar, then add the tomatoes and fresh herbs, if using. Cook the sauce uncovered for 10 minutes or until thick and pulpy. Season and stir in the pesto.

**3 Cook the gnocchi** When the sauce is almost ready, fill a large pot with boiling water, add a little salt and return to the boil. Add the remaining olive oil, then tip in the gnocchi. Bring back to the boil and simmer for 2-3 minutes, or according to the package instructions, stirring gently once or twice during cooking. The gnocchi are cooked when they rise to the surface. Drain thoroughly and stir into the sauce. Spoon the gnocchi onto warmed plates and serve scattered with pistachio nuts and Parmesan cheese.

Gnocchi are a great standby ingredient, as they will keep in the fridge (unopened) for up to one month (check the best-before date). They can also be frozen.

## ...shopping tip

### Serves 4 (V)

- **1½ lb (750 g) waxy potatoes, peeled and cut into 1-in. (2.5-cm) cubes**
- **½ lb (250 g) baby spinach leaves**
- **3½ tbsp (50 mL) peanut oil**
- **1 onion, finely sliced**
- **2-in. (5-cm) piece fresh ginger, peeled and finely chopped**
- **1 small green chili pepper, halved, seeded and finely sliced**
- **1 tsp (5 mL) ground coriander**
- **¼ tsp (1 mL) ground turmeric**
- **2 x ½-lb (250-g) packages cooked green lentils**
- **2 garlic cloves, cut into fine shreds**
- **½ tsp (2 mL) cumin seeds**
- **2 tbsp (25 mL) chopped fresh coriander**

**Each serving provides** • 630 cals
• 37 g protein • 13 g fat of which 2 g saturates • 97 g carbohydrate

**10** mins prep time   **20** mins cook time

# Indian Spicy Potatoes
## with Spinach and Lentils

**Throw together the popular combination of potatoes, spinach and Indian spices and add full-flavoured green lentils for a fast and filling meal. It just needs a cool cucumber raita to accompany (see To serve page 140).**

**1 Boil the potatoes** Cook the potatoes for 8-10 minutes or until just tender. Drain.

**2 Cook the spinach** While the potatoes are boiling, cook the spinach in a steamer over the potatoes for 3-4 minutes, or pierce the bag of spinach several times and cook in the microwave for 2-3 minutes or until wilted. Tip into a colander and drain, squeezing out most of the excess liquid by pressing with the back of a spoon.

**3 Fry the onion and spices** Heat a large frying pan or wok with 3 tbsp (45 mL) oil. Add the onion and cook over a medium heat for 2 minutes, then stir in the ginger, chili pepper, ground coriander and turmeric. Cook for a few seconds, then add the potato cubes and stir-fry for 3-4 minutes. Separate the spinach leaves with two forks, then stir into the spicy potato mixture together with the lentils. Season to taste with salt. Heat gently until piping hot.

**4 Complete the dish** While the potato mixture is warming through, heat the remaining oil in a small frying pan. Add the garlic shreds and cumin seeds, then cook for 1-2 minutes or until lightly browned. Stir in half the chopped coriander. Tip the potato and lentil mixture into a warmed serving dish and sprinkle with the garlic and cumin seed mixture and the remaining coriander.

### Spicy root vegetables and haricot beans Ⓥ

Buy **prepared root vegetables** such as carrots and parsnips, and omit the potatoes. Cut into bite-sized chunks and cook in salted boiling water for 5 minutes or until barely tender. Drain. Cook the onion and spices, and add the root vegetables as step 3, omitting the lentils, then stir in a **14-oz (398-mL) can navy beans**, drained and rinsed, and warm through. Add the spinach as before and serve with plain yogurt.

## ...another idea

# 5 great baked potato toppings

Nothing beats steaming-hot baked potatoes. They can be left to bake in the oven or quickly cooked in a microwave, so are great as a no-fuss accompaniment – but add a tasty topping and they become a delicious, filling and nutritious meal in their own right. All recipes serve 4.

## scallion and smoked cheese topping

Thickly slice a prepared **bunch of scallions** on the diagonal. Cut an unpeeled **garlic clove** in half. Heat **2 tbsp (25 mL) unsalted butter** in a small frying pan and gently cook the scallions and unpeeled garlic for 3-4 minutes or until the scallions are tender. Discard the garlic and season the scallions. Split open the baked potatoes and spoon in half the scallions and all the garlicky butter from the pan. Roughly chop **5 oz (150 g) smoked cheese** into small cubes and scatter over the baked potatoes. Sprinkle the remainder of the scallions on top. Serve with watercress. Ⓥ

**Each serving provides**
(including 2 potatoes) • 357 cals
• 14 g protein • 15 g fat of which
9 g saturates • 45 g carbohydrate

**10** mins prep time  **4** mins cook time

• To oven-bake potatoes, preheat the oven to 425°F (220°C). For four people, scrub eight 6-oz (175-g) potatoes with a brush and prick all over with a fork. Push a metal skewer through each potato (this conducts heat to the middle of the potato so that it cooks faster). Bake for 50 minutes-1 hour; the skewers will come out easily when the potatoes are cooked. Cut a deep cross in the top of each potato and squeeze it open, holding it with a clean dishcloth.
• For speed, you can "bake" potatoes in a microwave. Prick the skin in several places with a sharp knife (this stops them exploding). For a 6-oz (175-g) potato, microwave on high for 3½ minutes. Turn and microwave for another 1-2 minutes or until tender. Leave to rest for a couple of minutes before serving. Cooking more than one potato at a time will take longer: Four will take about 8 minutes.

## ...perfect baked potatoes

# chickpea **dhal** topping

Stir-fry tiny florets cut from **1 small cauliflower** in **2 tbsp (25 mL) ghee or canola oil** for 3 minutes. Add 3 tbsp (45 mL) water and continue cooking for 2-3 minutes or until the water has evaporated and the florets are just tender and beginning to colour. Add a **14-oz (398-mL) can chickpea dhal** and **3½ oz (100 g) frozen peas**. Gently heat until the peas are hot and the dhal is bubbling. Spoon the dhal into the split baked potatoes, and top each with a large spoonful of **thick plain or Greek-style yogurt**, blended with **2 tbsp (25 mL) chopped fresh coriander**.

Each serving provides (including 2 potatoes)
• 490 cals • 22 g protein • 13 g fat of which 6 g saturates • 76 g carbohydrate

**10** mins prep time  **10** mins cook time

# black **olive**, bean and **jalapeño** pepper topping

Drain and rinse a **14-oz (398-mL) can red kidney beans**. Tip half into a bowl and roughly crush with a fork with **2 tbsp (25 mL) extra-virgin olive oil**, **½ tsp (2 mL) ground cumin** and seasoning. Stir in the remaining beans, **⅓ cup (75 mL) drained and roughly chopped pitted black olives in oil** and **1 finely chopped jalapeño pepper**. Divide among the split baked potatoes, then spoon **⅔ cup (150 mL) sour cream** over the top, if you like. Serve with a sliced avocado and plum tomato salad (tossed in 1 tbsp/15 mL lime juice, then in 2 tsp/10 mL extra-virgin olive oil).

Each serving provides (including 2 potatoes)
• 476 cals • 12 g protein • 23.5 g fat of which 4 g saturates • 58 g carbohydrate

**15** mins prep time  **0** mins cook time

# pasta sauce, **mushroom** and chard topping

Gently cook **2½ cups (625 mL) baby button mushrooms** in **1 tbsp (15 mL) olive oil or 1 tbsp (15 mL) unsalted butter** over a medium-high heat for 2-3 minutes or until beginning to brown and soften. Turn down the heat a little and stir in **¾ cup (175 mL) good-quality pasta sauce** (a tomato-based one is good for this recipe or you can opt for a creamy version). Add **5 oz (150 g) shredded Swiss chard or torn baby spinach leaves**. Simmer gently for 3-4 minutes or until the chard is tender and wilted. Spoon on top of the split baked potatoes and top with **1½ cup (375 mL) grated hard mozzarella**.

Each serving provides (including 2 potatoes)
• 361 cals • 15.5 g protein • 12 g fat of which 6 g saturates • 51 g carbohydrate

**10** mins prep time  **7** mins cook time

# goat cheese, pine nut and **pesto** topping

Toast **¼ cup (50 mL) pine nuts** in a small nonstick frying pan over a medium-high heat for 2-3 minutes, stirring constantly, until golden. Tip the nuts onto a plate and set aside. Split open the baked potatoes and divide **1½ cup (375 mL) soft goat cheese** among them. Drizzle each with **½ tbsp (7 mL) green pesto**, then scatter over the toasted nuts. Serve with an arugula salad. Ⓥ

Each serving provides (including 2 potatoes)
• 493 cals • 20 g protein • 27.5 g fat of which 10 g saturates • 45 g carbohydrate

**10** mins prep time  **3** mins cook time

There are now many vegetarian versions of popular cheeses available. If you are serving cheese to vegetarians, check that the cheese you are using is suitable. Look out for a vegetarian symbol on the package.

**...shopping tip**

# Vegetable Dhal

Warm spices, creamy coconut milk, fresh tomatoes and zucchini combine to make this classic lentil dish that's ready to go in minutes. Serve with Indian breads and thick, plain yogurt.

**5** mins prep time   **25** mins cook time

**Serves 4** Ⓥ

1¼ cups (300 mL) split red lentils, rinsed and drained

2 tbsp (25 mL) peanut oil

1 onion, finely chopped

2 garlic cloves, crushed

1 in. (2.5 cm) piece fresh ginger, peeled and grated

2 tsp (10 mL) ground cumin

2 tsp (10 mL) ground turmeric

1⅔ cups (400 mL) half-fat coconut milk

1⅔ cups (400 mL) hot vegetable stock, made with stock cubes

4 tomatoes

juice of ½ lime or 1 tbsp (15 mL) lemon juice

2 zucchini, cut into ½-in. (1-cm) dice

3 tbsp (45 mL) chopped fresh coriander (optional)

**Each serving provides** • 365 cals • 16 g protein • 16 g fat of which 7 g saturates • 42 g carbohydrate

The dhal can be made up to 24 hours beforehand, stored in the fridge, or frozen for up to three months. Thaw if frozen, reheat with an extra 2 tbsp (25 mL) vegetable stock or water, and simmer for 1-2 minutes.

## ...get ahead

**1 Cook the onions and spices** Put the lentils into a bowl and pour over enough cold water to cover them by about ½ in. (1 cm). Leave to soak while cooking the onion and spices. Heat the oil in a large heavy-based pot, add the onion and gently cook for 5 minutes or until almost soft, stirring occasionally. Add the garlic, ginger, cumin and turmeric. Cook for 1 minute, stirring all the time.

**2 Add the lentils** Drain the lentils and add to the pot with the coconut milk, vegetable stock and seasoning. Bring to the boil, then reduce the heat, half-cover the pot with a lid and simmer for 5 minutes.

**3 Prepare the tomatoes** While the lentils are simmering, put the tomatoes into a heatproof bowl and pour over boiling water to cover. Leave for 1 minute, then remove with a slotted spoon and rinse briefly under cold water. Peel off the skins and dice the flesh.

**4 Complete the cooking** Add the tomatoes to the lentil mixture with the lime or lemon juice. Re-cover the pot and simmer for a further 10 minutes. Stir in the zucchini and cook, stirring occasionally, for a further 5 minutes or until the lentils are tender and the dhal thick and creamy. Taste and adjust the seasoning if necessary, then stir in the coriander before serving, if you like.

**Swaps** For lentils and zucchini, use **2 x 14-oz (398-mL) cans red kidney beans**, drained and rinsed. Purée one can with **½ cup (125 mL) vegetable stock**, made with a stock cube, and add to the spices with the coconut milk. Stir in the beans from the second can. Add **½ lb (250 g) shredded spinach leaves** with the tomatoes, then simmer uncovered for 8-10 minutes. Sprinkle with poppy seeds.

# Baby **Leek** and **Mushroom** Quinoa

The protein-rich seed quinoa teams beautifully with baby mushrooms, leeks and a hint of lemon to make a light and simple meal. Scatter with toasted seeds for extra crunch.

**10** mins prep time

**20** mins cook time

**Serves 4** Ⓥ

4 tbsp (60 mL) mixed seeds

2 tbsp (25 mL) unsalted butter

5 oz (150 g) baby leeks, sliced on the diagonal in 1¾-in. (2-cm) lengths

2½ cups (625 mL) baby button mushrooms

1 garlic clove, crushed

1¼ cups (300 mL) quinoa, rinsed

3 cups (750 mL) vegetable stock

½ tsp (2 mL) dried mixed herbs

grated zest and juice of 1 small lemon

3 tbsp (45 mL) chopped fresh parsley

**Each serving provides** • 333 cals • 13 g protein • 16 g fat of which 5 g saturates • 36 g carbohydrate

**1 Toast the seeds** Gently toast the pumpkin and sunflower seeds in a large, dry pot for 2-3 minutes over a medium heat. Tip on to a plate and set aside.

**2 Fry the leeks and mushrooms** Add the butter to the pot and, when melted, stir in the leeks, mushrooms and garlic. Stir over a medium-high heat for 1 minute.

**3 Cook the quinoa** Add the quinoa to the pot and stir, then pour in the stock and add the herbs. Bring to the boil, then turn down the heat. Stir and cover the pot with a lid. Simmer gently for 15 minutes or until most of the stock has been absorbed and the quinoa and vegetables are tender.

**4 Complete the dish** Stir the lemon zest and juice into the quinoa with the chopped parsley and seasoning to taste. Serve scattered with the toasted seeds.

Toasted seeds add a delicious crunch to all kinds of dishes, from rice and grains to toppings for breakfast cereals and desserts. You can buy them ready toasted or prepare your own. Once toasted, spread them out and allow to cool completely, then store in an airtight jar. They will keep their freshly toasted flavour for up to two weeks.

## ...get ahead

### Lentil bolognese Ⓥ

Pour **2 cups (500 mL) boiling vegetable stock**, made with stock cubes, over **1¼ cups (300 mL) split red lentils** and leave to soak. Heat **2 tbsp (25 mL) olive oil** in a large pot and gently cook **1 large chopped onion** for 5 minutes or until almost tender. Stir in **2 crushed garlic cloves** and a **pinch of ground cinnamon** and cook for a few seconds. Add the lentils and stock to the pot with a **14-oz (398-mL) can chopped tomatoes with basil**. Stir, then half-cover the pot with a lid and cook for 15 minutes or until the lentils are tender. Season to taste and serve on top of pasta or as the filling in a vegetarian shepherd's pie.

## ...another idea

# Peking Vegetable Stir-fry

Toss tofu pieces in a Chinese-style baste, then roast until deliciously browned and flavourful. Serve with an assortment of stir-fry vegetables and rice or noodles.

**Serves 4** Ⓥ

2 tbsp (25 mL) hoisin sauce

2 tbsp (25 mL) soy sauce

1 tbsp (15 mL) sherry vinegar

1 tbsp (15 mL) clear honey

2 tbsp (25 mL) peanut oil

⅔-lb (300-g) package plain tofu, drained and cut into 1-in. (2.5-cm) cubes

3 tbsp (45 mL) vegetable stock, made with bouillon powder, or water

1 in. (2.5 cm) fresh ginger, peeled and grated

1 red pepper, halved and sliced

1½ cups (375 mL) baby button mushrooms, halved

7 oz (200 g) napa cabbage, shredded

7 oz (200 g) bok choy, shredded

1 tbsp (15 mL) toasted sesame seeds

**Each serving provides**
- 186 cals • 9 g protein
- 11 g fat of which 2 g saturates
- 13 g carbohydrate

**1 Baste and cook the tofu** Preheat the oven to 425°F (220°C). To make the baste, combine the hoisin sauce, soy sauce, vinegar, honey and ½ tbsp (7 mL) peanut oil in a small jug. Put the tofu in a small, shallow nonstick roasting pan, pour over two-thirds of the baste and toss to coat the tofu thoroughly. Roast for 8 minutes, then turn the tofu over and cook for a further 6-8 minutes.

**2 Stir-fry the vegetables** Meanwhile, blend the remaining baste with the vegetable stock and set aside. Heat a wok or a large, heavy-based nonstick frying pan over a high heat. Add the remaining peanut oil and heat for a few seconds, then add the ginger. Cook for a few seconds, stirring, then add the red pepper and mushrooms, and stir-fry for 2 minutes. Add the napa cabbage and bok choy together with the baste and stock mixture. Stir-fry for 2-3 more minutes or until the greens are wilted.

**3 Combine the tofu and vegetables** Stir the tofu into the greens and cook for a few more seconds, then pile high onto bowls of rice or noodles. Sprinkle with toasted sesame seeds and serve.

**Swaps** • For napa cabbage, use **¼ lb (125 g) green beans**, cut into 1½-in. (3-cm) lengths. Add with the red pepper and mushrooms. • For button mushrooms, use thickly sliced **mixed mushrooms** such as oyster and shiitake.

**Serves 4** Ⓥ

½ cup (125 mL) long-grain rice

1 cup (250 mL) vegetable stock, made with a stock cube

1 orange

3 tbsp (45 mL) walnut oil, or peanut or canola oil

1 tsp (5 mL) soy sauce

¼ red cabbage, about ½ lb (250 g), finely shredded

1¼ cups (300 mL) walnut pieces, broken into smaller pieces if large

3 tbsp (45 mL) sesame seeds

1 egg, lightly beaten

2½ tbsp (30 mL) canola oil

½ head napa cabbage, about ⅔ lb (300 g), shredded

3½ oz (100 g) young, tender bok choy leaves, halved lengthwise if large

**Each serving provides** • 539 cals
• 12 g protein • 44 g fat of which 5 g saturates • 25 g carbohydrate

> Tofu is a great source of protein and calcium and is low in fat, but has little flavour of its own, so it is best when marinated or flavoured by tossing it in a tasty baste.
>
> **...cooking tip**

# Chinese **Salad**
## with Mini Rice and Sesame Pancakes

**Little rice and sesame pancakes make an unusual topping for a crunchy salad of walnuts, marinated red cabbage and Chinese greens – all brought together with a refreshing orange dressing.**

**1 Cook the rice** Put the rice and stock into a pot and bring to the boil. Stir, then cover and simmer gently for 10 minutes or until the rice is tender and has absorbed all the stock. Turn the heat to low and leave the rice for 1 minute, stirring occasionally, to dry it a little. Tip the rice into a bowl, spread out and leave to cool.

**2 Marinate the red cabbage** While the rice is cooking, grate ½ tsp (2 mL) orange zest and put it into a large bowl. Squeeze the orange and add the juice to the bowl with the walnut, peanut or canola oil and soy sauce. Add seasoning and whisk together. Add the red cabbage and toss together well, then leave to marinate to soften the cabbage a little, while you finish preparations.

**3 Toast the walnuts** Put the walnut pieces into a large, dry nonstick frying pan. Toast them over a medium heat for about 3 minutes, turning frequently until golden. Tip onto a plate and set aside.

**4 Make the mini pancakes** Add the sesame seeds and beaten egg to the cooked rice. Stir together and season. Heat the canola oil in the frying pan and drop in small teaspoonfuls of the egg and rice mixture to make little pancakes, about 1 in. (2.5 cm) in diameter (you will probably need to do this in two batches, depending on the size of the pan). Cook over a medium-high heat for 2 minutes or until lightly browned, then turn over and cook the other side for 1½ -2 minutes.

**5 Complete the salad** Add the napa cabbage, bok choy and walnuts to the marinated red cabbage and toss to coat in the dressing. Divide the salad among individual plates and serve each topped with the rice and sesame pancakes.

**Swap** Instead of pancakes, toss stir-fried tofu into the salad: Whisk together **1 tsp (5 mL) grated fresh ginger**, **1 tbsp (15 mL) soy sauce** and **2 tsp (10 mL) canola oil** in a bowl. Stir in a **8-oz (250-g) package plain tofu pieces** to coat. Heat a large frying pan until hot, add the tofu and marinade, and stir-fry for 3-4 minutes.

### Spinach and mushroom salad ⓥ
Whisk together **1 tsp (5 mL) grated fresh ginger**, **1 tbsp (15 bmL) clear honey**, **2 tsp (10 mL) red wine vinegar** and **3 tbsp (45 mL) hazelnut oil**. Add **1 cup (250 mL) sliced button mushrooms** and mix to coat in the dressing. Toss in **½ lb (250 g) washed baby spinach leaves** and **4 hot or cold cooked vegetarian sausages** cut into 1¾-in. (2-cm) slices on the diagonal. Serve with boiled baby new potatoes.

## ...another idea

Add a large pinch of **Chinese five-spice powder** to the cooked rice with the beaten egg at step 4, and add **1 tsp (5 mL) toasted sesame oil** to the canola oil when frying for a richer flavour.

## ...spice it up

# Thai **Vegetables** with **Coconut** and **cashews**

**Thai green curry paste, made from fresh green chili peppers and herbs, adds a delicate flavour to this lively multi-textured vegetable dish. Serve with Thai fragrant rice or noodles for a swift light meal.**

**15** mins prep time

**15** mins cook time

### Serves 4 Ⓥ

⅔ cup (150 mL) cashews

2 tbsp (25 mL) canola oil

1 onion, finely chopped

1½ cups (375 mL) button mushrooms, sliced

¼ lb (125 g) snow peas

¼ lb (125 g) baby corn, halved lengthwise

1 green pepper, halved and sliced

3 tsp (15 mL) Thai green curry paste

1⅔ cups (400 mL) coconut milk

3½ oz (100 g) bean sprouts

Each serving provides • 307 cals • 8 g protein • 25 g fat of which 8 g saturates • 14 g carbohydrate

**1 Toast the cashews** Heat a large frying pan over a medium heat for 1 minute. Add the cashews and toast, stirring frequently, for 2-3 minutes or until the nuts are golden brown. Tip onto a plate and set aside.

**2 Cook the vegetables** Add the oil to the pan and cook the onion for 2 minutes or until beginning to soften. Turn up the heat a little and add the mushrooms. Continue cooking for 2-3 minutes, stirring constantly, then add the snow peas, baby corn and green pepper. Cook for a further 2 minutes, stirring.

**3 Finish the dish** Stir in the Thai paste and 3 tbsp (45 mL) coconut milk. Cook, stirring, for 1 minute. Stir in the remaining coconut milk and the bean sprouts. Simmer, stirring occasionally, for 2 minutes or until all the vegetables are tender and the coconut milk has reduced a little. Stir in half the cashews, then pile onto warmed plates and scatter over the remaining nuts.

**Swaps** For Thai green curry paste, use **red curry paste**, which is much spicier and richer and goes well with more robust vegetables. Add **1 tbsp (15 mL)** in this dish. Cut **11 oz (350 g) sweet potatoes or parsnips** into small cubes and stir-fry with the mushrooms at step 2. For the snow peas, corn and green pepper, add **5 oz (150 g) broccoli florets** and cook for 2 minutes at step 2. After adding the coconut milk at step 3, simmer for 4 minutes before adding the bean sprouts.

**Cooking tip** The heat in the green curry paste is tempered with creamy coconut milk in this recipe, but if you like mildly spiced dishes, you can reduce the curry paste a little.

# Warm Egg and Potato Salad
## with Spicy Peanut Sauce

Baby new potatoes take so little time to cook that they are perfect for busy people. Hard-boiled eggs and crisp, steamed vegetables are great partners in a warm salad drizzled with a creamy peanut sauce.

**15** mins prep time

**10** mins cook time

### Serves 4 Ⓥ

1½ lb (750 g) pre-washed baby new potatoes

2 large carrots, peeled and cut into matchsticks

¼ lb (125 g) fine green beans, cut into 1-in. (2.5-cm) lengths

1 small cauliflower, divided into small florets

6 eggs, at room temperature

1 tbsp (15 mL) canola oil

1 garlic clove, crushed

1 in. (2.5 cm) piece fresh ginger, peeled and grated

¼ tsp (1 mL) crushed chili flakes

1 tbsp (15 mL) lime juice

1 tsp (5 mL) light brown sugar

4 tbsp (60 mL) crunchy peanut butter

1 tbsp (15 mL) olive oil

1 tsp (5 mL) red wine vinegar

**Each serving provides** • 526 cals • 25 g protein • 30 g fat of which 6 g saturates • 42 g carbohydrate

**1** **Cook the vegetables** Put the potatoes into a large pot of boiling water that has a steamer on top. Cook for 10-12 minutes or until they are just tender. Put the carrots, beans and cauliflower into the steamer and cook for the last 8 minutes of the cooking time.

**2** **Hard-boil the eggs** While the vegetables are cooking, add the eggs to a pot of boiling water and cook for 8 minutes. Drain the eggs and put them into a bowl of cold water to cool.

**3** **Make the peanut sauce** While the vegetables and eggs are cooking, heat the canola oil in a small pot and cook the garlic, ginger and crushed chili flakes for 1 minute. Add the lime juice, sugar, peanut butter and 8 tbsp (125 mL) water from the potatoes. Heat until steaming, stirring to mix everything together.

**4** **Assemble the salad** Drain the potatoes and return to the pot. Add the steamed vegetables. Drizzle the olive oil and vinegar over all the vegetables and gently toss to coat lightly. Cover the pot with a lid to keep the vegetables warm. Peel the eggs and cut them into quarters lengthwise. Tip the vegetables into a warmed serving dish and arrange the quartered hard-boiled eggs on top. Drizzle over the hot peanut sauce and serve at once.

**Chinese vegetables with peanut sauce** Ⓥ
Instead of potatoes and fresh vegetables stir-fry a **1 lb (500 g) bag of frozen stir-fry or wok vegetables**, according to the package instructions. Drizzle over the peanut sauce and scatter **2 tbsp (25 mL) store-bought crunchy spicy seeds** on top. Serve with rice.

## ...another idea

# Middle Eastern Salad

Lots of chopped fresh herbs give this quick and simple dish, called *fattoush*, its pronounced flavour, and bite-sized pieces of crisply grilled pita bread provide texture. Serve for a light meal with a hint of summer at any time of the year.

**15** mins prep time

**2** mins cook time

**Serves 4** ⓥ

2 large white or sesame seed pita breads

4 tbsp (60 mL) olive oil

juice of 1 lemon

2 tbsp (25 mL) chopped fresh coriander

2 tbsp (25 mL) chopped fresh mint, plus mint leaves, to garnish (optional)

½ cucumber, cut into ½-in. (1-cm) dice

4 large tomatoes, quartered, cored and chopped

4 scallions, thinly sliced on the diagonal

14 oz (398 mL) can black-eyed peas or chickpeas, drained and rinsed

**Each serving provides** • 321 cals • 10 g protein • 14 g fat of which 2 g saturates • 41 g carbohydrate

**1 Toast the pita breads** Warm the pita breads in the toaster for 1 minute to make them easier to open up, then split each in half using a knife. Toast the four halves for 1 minute or until crisp and lightly browned. Tear into bite-sized pieces.

**2 Make the dressing** Put the olive oil and lemon juice into a small jug and whisk together with a fork. Season and stir in the fresh herbs.

**3 Assemble the salad** Put the cucumber, tomatoes, scallions and beans or chickpeas in a bowl. Drizzle over the dressing, then toss together until well mixed. Immediately before serving, add the pita bread pieces and mix again. Garnish with mint leaves, if you like.

**Swaps** • For scallions, add a small finely chopped **red onion**. • For the black-eyed beans or chickpeas, use a **19 oz (540 mL) can green lentils, drained and rinsed, or a ½-lb (250-g) sachet cooked brown lentils**.

**Additions** Chopped, dried **ready-to-eat apricots, sunflower seeds** or crumbled firm **goat cheese**.

# desserts

# Tropical **Fruit** Trifle

Everyone loves a trifle. In this lavish, super-quick version, moist almond macaroons laced with sherry are topped with tropical fruit, smooth custard and thick cream.

**10**
mins prep
time

**Serves 6**

**8 oz (250 g) small soft almond macaroons (about 18)**

**9 tbsp (140 mL) sweet sherry**

**28-oz (796-mL) can tropical mixed fruit in syrup**

**15 oz (425 g) can low-fat custard**

**¾ cup (175 mL) heavy whipping cream**

**Each serving provides** • 471 cals
• 27 g fat of which 12 g saturates
• 47 g carbohydrate

**1 Moisten the biscuits** Divide the macaroons among six 6¾-oz (200-mL) dessert glasses or trifle dishes. Sprinkle 1½ tbsp (20 mL) sherry over the biscuits in each glass or dish.

**2 Add the fruit** Drain the fruit, reserving the syrup. Spoon 2 tbsp (25 mL) of the syrup into each glass or dish. Reserve four or five pieces of fruit for decoration, then divide the remainder among the glasses.

**3 Top with custard and cream** Spoon the custard over the fruit, then top each with a large spoonful of cream. Chop the reserved fruit into small pieces and scatter over the cream. Chill in the fridge until ready to serve.

**Swaps** • For canned fruit, use **14 oz (400 g) fresh strawberries**, halved or quartered if large, and tossed in **1 tbsp (15 mL) white (superfine) sugar**, and moisten the biscuits with **orange juice** instead of sherry. • For sweet sherry, use an **orange liqueur**.

### Sublime syllabub trifle

Warm **½ jar raspberry or strawberry jam** in a small pot for 1 minute or until just melted. Remove from the heat and mix in **1 lb (500 g) frozen raspberries**. Slice a **pound or fruit cake** and arrange in a trifle bowl. Sprinkle with **4 tbsp (60 mL) sherry** and **4 tbsp (60 mL) orange juice**, and top with the raspberries and jam. Whisk **1 cup (250 mL) heavy cream** with the **grated zest and juice of 1 orange**, **1 tbsp (15 mL) icing (confectioner's) sugar** and **2 tbsp (25 mL) sweet sherry** until thick and just standing in peaks. Spread evenly over the fruit. Put in the freezer for 10 minutes (this is not essential, but it allows the ingredients to settle).

### Mandarin and lemon meringue trifles

For four servings, cut **4 slices pound or fruit cake**, then spread with **lemon curd** and lay in four dishes. Drain a **10-oz (284-mL) can mandarin sections** and divide among the dishes. Stir **4 tbsp (60 mL) lemon curd** into **2 cups (500 mL) plain low-fat yogurt** and spread over the fruit. Top with **small meringues**.

## ...more ideas

# Magic **Tiramisu**

**Here is a simple, speedy yet utterly luxurious slant on the delectable Italian dessert of coffee and liqueur-flavoured sponge cake topped with a creamy mascarpone layer and dusted with chocolate.**

**10 mins prep time**

**Serves 8**

**4 tsp (20 mL) instant coffee granules**

**6¾ tbsp (100 mL) boiling water**

**4 tbsp (60 mL) grappa, Tia Maria, Marsala or sherry**

**7 oz (200 g) sponge fingers**

**2 tbsp (25 mL) white (superfine) sugar**

**8 tbsp (125 mL) plain yogurt**

**1 lb (500 g) mascarpone**

**2-2½ squares (2-2½ oz/60-70 g) baking chocolate, grated, or chopped chocolate bars**

**Each serving provides** • 461 cals
• 34 g fat of which 21 g saturates
• 30.5 g carbohydrate

**1 Combine the coffee and alcohol** Dissolve the coffee in the boiling water, then add 6¾ tbsp (100 mL) cold water and the grappa, Tia Maria, Marsala or sherry.

**2 Make the sponge layer** Arrange the sponge fingers in a 8-in. (20-cm) square shallow dish (or pan), making a double layer. Spoon the coffee mixture evenly over the biscuits.

**3 Prepare the topping** Beat the sugar and yogurt into the mascarpone, then spread this over the biscuits, pressing down well once they are all covered. Pile the grated chocolate on top, then spread it out and press down. Chill for 10 minutes in the freezer, if possible.

**Swaps** • For mascarpone, use **low-fat ricotta or cottage cheese**.
• For grappa, Tia Maria, Marsala or sherry, use **orange juice**.

To make individual desserts to serve four, halve the quantities and make the tiramisu in four individual dishes.

## ...cooking tip

This freezes well. Cover the dish with plastic wrap and freeze until hard, then place in a plastic bag. Eat within three months. You can also freeze individual portions uncovered, then pack in plastic wrap and a freezer bag.

## ...keep it

# Spiced Fruit and Nut
## Freezer Cake

This mix-and-chill take on an Italian panforte – a wonderful mix of baked fruit, nuts, honey and spice – is the fastest-ever way to make an uncooked cake, and is irresistible with coffee or liqueurs.

**20** mins prep time
**10** mins chill time

### Serves 6

3½ oz (100 g) dark chocolate, broken

1 cup (250 mL) toasted slivered almonds or chopped hazelnuts

7 oz (200 g) luxury mixed dried fruit

3½ oz (100 g) ready-to-eat dried figs, chopped

1 cup (250 mL) ground almonds

2 tsp (10 mL) ground coriander

2 tsp (10 mL) ground cinnamon

2 tbsp (25 mL) clear honey

icing (confectioner's) sugar, for sprinkling

**Each serving provides** • 425 cals
• 24 g fat of which 4 g saturates
• 46 g carbohydrate

1 **Melt the chocolate** Set a heatproof bowl over a pot of gently simmering water. Add the broken chocolate and leave to melt, stirring occasionally. Put a 9-in. (23-cm) shallow round cake pan in the freezer. In a large bowl, mix together the slivered almonds or hazelnuts, mixed dried fruit, figs, almonds, coriander and cinnamon.

2 **Combine the ingredients** Pour the melted chocolate over the fruit mixture. Add the honey and mix well until all the ingredients are thoroughly combined.

3 **Fill the pan** Lay a large piece of plastic wrap in the cake pan and press it in to line the pan, leaving the excess overhanging the rim. Turn the mixture into the pan and press it down a little, then cover with the overhanging plastic wrap and press it out evenly with the heel of your hand until fairly smooth on top.

4 **Chill and serve** Chill in the freezer for 10 minutes or until the mixture has firmed up a little. Uncover the cake and turn it out onto a platter. Remove the plastic wrap, sprinkle generously with icing (confectioner's) sugar and cut into 12 wedges to serve.

**Swaps** Instead of figs, ground almonds, coriander, cinnamon and honey, put **7 oz (200 g) petit beurre cookies** in a plastic bag and crush them with a rolling pin, then add them to the fruit and nut mixture with **3½ oz (100 g) roughly chopped candied cherries**. Stir in **2 tbsp (25 mL) orange juice** before mixing in the chocolate.

### Spiced fruit and nut cake with mascarpone and cherries
Make some mock maraschino cherries: Put **12 candied cherries** in a cup or mug. Pour on **4 tbsp (60 mL) vodka** and **¼ tsp (1 mL) almond extract**. Stir, cover and set aside while you make the cake. Shape and chill the cake mixture as for the basic recipe. To serve, drain the cherries, reserving the almond vodka. Stir the liquid into **7 oz (200 g) mascarpone** with **1 tsp (5 mL) icing (confectioner's) sugar**. Top each wedge with a dollop of mascarpone and a cherry.

## ...another idea

# Warm Pear and Mango Compote

Just two cans from the pantry will conjure up an exotic dessert.
A few cardamom pods and a twist of lime bring uplifting flavours to this
simple warm compote, which is refreshing and deliciously aromatic.

**5** mins prep time

**6** mins cook time

**Serves 4**

**14 oz (398 mL) can mango slices in syrup**

**14 oz (398 mL) can pear quarters in syrup**

**coarsely grated or finely pared zest and juice of 1 lime**

**9 green cardamom pods**

**2 tbsp (25 mL) chopped pistachios**

Each serving provides • 165 cals
• 3 g fat of which 0.4 g saturates
• 36 g carbohydrate

**1 Prepare the fruit** Drain the mango slices and pear quarters in a sieve over a pot. Shake the sieve well, then set it aside over a bowl. If the mango slices are rather large, cut them into thinner slices.

**2 Make the syrup** Add the lime zest and juice to the pot. Cut a slit in each cardamom pod as you add it to the pot. Bring the syrup to the boil and boil hard for 5-6 minutes or until it is reduced by about half and aromatic with cardamom.

**3 Assemble and serve** While the syrup is boiling, arrange the mango slices and pear quarters in four large, shallow dessert dishes. Spoon over the reduced syrup (remove the cardamoms, if you like), sprinkle with pistachio nuts and serve.

Swaps • For lime and cardamoms, use the **zest of 1 orange** (without the juice) and **1 cinnamon stick**. • For pistachio nuts, use **chopped walnuts or toasted slivered almonds**. • For the mangos and pears, use a **14-oz (398-mL) can peach slices or halves** and a **14-oz (398-mL) can lychees**.

This compote is a terrific make-ahead dessert. Arrange the fruit in a large bowl, pour over the syrup (with the cardamom) and chill for several hours or overnight.

**...get ahead**

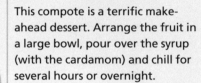

## Pear compote with rosewater and pistachio ricotta

Follow the main recipe but use **canned pear halves** instead of quarters. Mix **½ cup (125 mL) ricotta cheese** with **1 tsp (5 mL) icing (confectioner's) sugar** and **1 tbsp (15 mL) rosewater**. Spoon this into 4 pear halves and arrange them in the dishes, then press the pistachio nuts on top. Arrange the mango slices around the pears, slicing any remaining pear halves and adding them as well. Spoon over the reduced syrup and serve.

**...another idea**

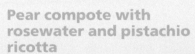

# 5 speedy fruit salads

These up-to-the-minute fruit salads are healthy, hassle-free, fast and fabulous. Take advantage of everyday pantry and exotic ingredients, and fruits in season, to make simple treats that are a step away from the ordinary. All recipes serve 4.

## spiced **orange** with **pomegranate**

Slice the tops and bottoms off **6 seedless oranges**. Using a sharp knife, cut off the peel and pith in one go, in wide strips down the side of the oranges. Slice the oranges and arrange on four plates. Sprinkle with a little **freshly grated nutmeg**. Cut a **pomegranate** into quarters. Remove the seeds with your fingers, over a bowl, discarding the membranes, peel and pith. Sprinkle the seeds over the oranges. Finely shred a few **mint leaves**, if you like, and sprinkle them over the salads.

**Each serving provides** • 85 cals • 0.2 g fat
of which 0 g saturates • 19.5 g carbohydrate

**10** mins prep time

## zesty **pineapple** and **kiwi** salad

Divide a **14-oz (398-mL) can pineapple pieces** in natural juice or syrup among four bowls. Peel and slice **4 kiwis** and arrange on the pineapple, then add a **14-oz (398-ml) can lychees**, with their syrup. Coarsely grate or zest **1 lime** over the salads, then squeeze over the juice before serving.

**Each serving provides** • 150 cals • 0.3 g fat
of which 0 g saturates • 38 g carbohydrate

**10** mins prep time

Make a **Breakfast Smoothie** with leftover fruit. For one person, whiz **1 cup (250 mL) fruit salad** in a blender with **1 cup (250 mL) plain low-fat yogurt**. Dilute as required with up to **½ cup (125 mL) unsweetened fruit juice**. **...use it up**

# peppered strawberries and blueberries

Hull **14 oz (400 g) strawberries**, halving any large ones, and arrange them on four plates. Divide **7½ oz (225 g) blueberries** among the plates. Grind some **black pepper** over the fruit and add **lemon wedges** to the plates for their juice. Serve with extra pepper and white (superfine) sugar.

**Each serving provides** • 44 cals • 0.2 g fat of which 0 g saturates • 10 g carbohydrate

# cardamom figs with dried cranberries and orange

Drain the syrup from **2 x 14-oz (398-mL) cans green figs** into a small pot. Split **4 green cardamom pods** and add them to the syrup with **2 tbsp (25 mL) dried cranberries** and the grated **zest and juice of 1 orange**. Put on a high heat and boil for 1 minute. Meanwhile, divide the figs among four bowls. Spoon the hot syrup over the figs and serve.

**Each serving provides** • 178 cals • 0.25 g fat of which 0 g saturates • 43 g carbohydrate

# guavas and plums with vanilla syrup and pistachios

Drain a **14-oz (398-mL) can plums**, pouring the syrup into a fairly large pan, then drain the syrup from a **14-oz (398-mL) can guava halves** into the same pan. Boil the syrup hard for 4-5 minutes or until reduced by about half. Meanwhile, pit the plums if necessary and divide them among four bowls. Add the guava halves. Add **1 tsp (5 mL) pure vanilla extract** to the syrup and spoon it over the fruit. Sprinkle with **½ cup (125 mL) chopped pistachios** and serve.

**Each serving provides** • 202 cals • 7 g fat of which 1 g saturates • 34 g carbohydrate

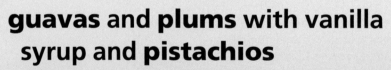

# Fresh Fig Puffs

A little rosewater and a few pistachios transform plain puff pastry into a crisp and fragrant base for luscious fresh figs. Super-easy to assemble, the dessert looks exquisite and tastes fabulous.

**5** mins prep time

**12** mins cook time

### Serves 6

¾ lb (375 g) package pre-rolled puff pastry (about 13⅓ x 9½ in./34 x 24 cm) (half used for this recipe)

2 tbsp (25 mL) rosewater

⅓ cup (75 mL) pistachios, chopped, plus extra to decorate (optional)

2 tbsp (25 mL) sugar

6 ripe fresh figs

6 tbsp (90 mL) thick Greek-style yogurt

3 tbsp (45 mL) clear honey

**Each serving provides** • 301 cals
• 16 g fat of which 4 g saturates
• 36 g carbohydrate

**1 Cut the pastry** Preheat the oven to 460°F (240°C). Remove the package of pastry from the fridge and, if time allows, leave it, still wrapped, at room temperature for up to 20 minutes. Unroll the pastry and halve it. Keep one half for another recipe. Cut the other half into six pieces, about 3⅓ x 3⅛ in. (8.5 x 8 cm) each. Put the pastry onto a baking sheet.

**2 Bake the puffs** Sprinkle the pastry with the rosewater and top with the pistachios and sugar. Bake for 10-12 minutes or until they are well puffed and browned.

**3 Assemble the desserts** While the pastry is cooking, trim the stalks off the figs and cut each one vertically into six wedges. Put a cooked puff pastry onto each plate and top with three fig wedges. Add a dollop of Greek-style yogurt at the side and arrange another three fig wedges around, and partly in, the yogurt. Drizzle honey over all the fig wedges, sprinkle with extra nuts, if you like, and serve at once.

**Swaps** • For fresh figs, use **drained canned green figs or fresh strawberries**, allowing three strawberry halves on top and three on the plate. • Or pile **4 or 5 fresh raspberries** on top of each pastry. • Or use **4 sliced fresh peaches or nectarines**, putting three slices on the pastry and three on the plate. Add **1 tsp (5 mL) apricot preserve** in a little pool on the fruit. • For yogurt, use **⅔ cup (150 mL) whipping cream**, whipped. • For honey, dust with **icing (confectioner's) sugar**.

## Puffy millefeuille

Take the **whole package of pastry** and make 12 pastry pieces. Omit the rosewater and use **slivered almonds** instead of the pistachios. Put the pastry pieces on the baking sheet and sprinkle the nuts and sugar over each piece. Bake as step 2. Cool on a wire rack for 5 minutes. Put half the pieces of pastry on plates, and top each one with **1 tbsp (15 mL) good-quality fruit conserve**, such as black cherry, damson or apricot. Add **1 tbsp (15 mL) thick Greek-style yogurt, sour cream or ricotta cheese**, to each and then spread the preserve and topping very lightly, marbling them together. Top with a second piece of pastry and dust with **icing (confectioner's) sugar**.

## ...another idea

# Sesame **Fruit Fritters**

Crisp and crunchy outside and fabulously juicy in the middle,
these fruit fritters are a quick treat for children, or remember them
for an impromptu dessert to follow a Chinese-style meal.

**5**
mins prep
time

**2**
mins cook
time

**Serves 4**
14 oz (398 mL) can pineapple slices
in light syrup (4 slices)
2 tbsp (25 mL) white (superfine)
sugar
2 tbsp (25 mL) toasted sesame seeds
⅔ cup (150 mL) all-purpose flour
canola oil, for frying

**Each serving provides** • 229 cals
• 12 g fat of which 1.5 g saturates
• 30 g carbohydrate

**1 Prepare the fruit** Drain the pineapple slices in
a sieve over a measuring cup, reserving the syrup.
Put a couple of layers of paper towels on a plate
and lay the pineapple slices on it. Cover with more
paper towels to dry the fruit.

**2 Make the coating** Mix the white (superfine)
sugar and sesame seeds and put them on a plate
ready for coating the cooked fritters.

**3 Make the batter** Increase the syrup from the
pineapple to 6¾ tbsp (100 mL), if necessary, with
a little cold water. Put the flour in a bowl and make
a well in the centre, then pour in about half the
syrup. Gradually mix the flour and syrup to make a
smooth, very thick batter. Add a little more syrup,
if necessary, beating to remove any lumps. Then
mix in the remaining liquid to make a smooth,
thick batter.

**4 Heat the frying oil** Heat about ½-in. (1-cm)
depth of canola oil in a frying pan. Drop a
teaspoonful of batter into the oil to check it is hot
enough: The batter should immediately sizzle, rise
and set, then it should brown in about 30 seconds.
Using a slotted spoon, remove and discard the
piece of batter, or it will burn.

**5 Cook the fritters** Put a pineapple slice in the
batter and use a spoon and fork to turn it so that it
is well coated all over. Carefully drop the pineapple
into the hot oil. Cook for 30-60 seconds, turning
the fritter when the bottom edge is bubbly and
crisp. If the batter is well browned on the second
side but the first side is a little pale, turn the fritter
a second time. Cook the fritters in pairs (or all four
at once if your pan is large enough).

**6 Add the coating** Drain the fritters using a
slotted spoon or slotted spatula, then put onto the
sesame sugar. Turn quickly to coat both sides and
serve at once.

**Swaps** • For pineapple, use other **canned fruits**,
such as peach halves. • Or use **fresh fruit**, and
use **apple or orange juice** to make the batter.
To prepare fresh fruit: Halve **4 bananas** widthwise;
quarter, peel and core **3 dessert apples**; halve and
pit **2 nectarines** (add them to the pan rounded
side down, first).

**Blueberry fritters**
Omit the sesame seeds and sugar. Make **half
the quantity of batter** with ⅓ cup (75 mL)
all-purpose flour and ¼ cup (50 mL) apple
juice (instead of the syrup). Add **7 oz (200 g)
blueberries** and stir very lightly. Cook spoonfuls
of the mixture, as steps 4 and 5, turning until
browned, risen and crisp. Drizzle with a little
**honey**.

## ...another idea

# Maple Creams

Raid the pantry to create a stylish dessert that's lighter than custard and creamier than a soufflé. Underneath the fluffy top is a surprise base of rich maple syrup.

**7** mins prep time   **10** mins cook time

## Serves 4

**6 tbsp (90 mL) maple syrup**
**¼ cup (50 mL) cornstarch**
**2 eggs, separated**
    **grated zest of 1 lemon**
**⅔ cup (150 mL) heavy whipping cream**

**Each serving provides**
• 266 cals • 14 g fat of which
7 g saturates • 33 g carbohydrate

**1 Prepare the ramekins** Preheat the oven to 445°F (230°C). Set four ⅔-cup (150-mL) ramekins on a baking tray and put 1 tbsp (15 mL) maple syrup in each dish. (Do not grease the dishes.)

**2 Blend the egg yolks and cream** Put the cornstarch in a bowl and add the egg yolks with the remaining maple syrup and the lemon zest. Stir the yolks and syrup into the cornstarch until smooth, then gradually stir in the cream until thoroughly combined.

**3 Prepare the egg whites** Put the egg whites into a separate, thoroughly clean and dry bowl. Whisk the whites using an electric mixer until stiff but not dry. Using a large metal spoon, fold the whites into the cream mixture until well combined. Take care not to stir out the air.

**4 Bake and serve** Divide the mixture among the ramekins and bake for about 10 minutes or until the mixture is puffed up, browned and just set. Have small plates or saucers ready for the hot dishes. Serve immediately.

**Swaps** • Instead of maple syrup, put a generous **1 tbsp (15 mL) fruit conserve**, such as black cherry or plum, into each dish and add **1 tbsp (15 mL) sugar** and **1 tsp (5 mL) pure vanilla extract** to the cream mixture.

## Soufflé-topped fruit
Put **7½ oz (225 g) frozen raspberries** into a 1-qt. (1-L) deep ovenproof dish or soufflé dish. Drizzle the 4 tbsp (60 mL) maple syrup over the fruit. Top with the maple cream mixture and bake at 425°F (220°C) for about 20 minutes or until the topping is well risen and browned, and the raspberries lightly cooked.

### ...another idea

## Serves 4

**14 oz (398 mL) can peach halves**
    **in syrup**
**4 slices brioche (about 1¾-in./**
    **2-cm thick)**
**6 tsp (30 mL) good-quality**
    **raspberry jam**
**4 tbsp (60 mL) mascarpone**
**1 tbsp (15 mL) sugar**
**2 tbsp (25 mL) unsalted butter**
**¼ cup (50 mL) slivered almonds**
**2 tbsp (25 mL) brandy**

**Each serving provides** • 466 cals
• 21 g fat of which 12.5 g saturates
• 65 g carbohydrate

**10** mins prep time   **7** mins cook time

### Mascarpone pears
Follow the basic recipe but use **canned pear halves** instead of peaches and trim the brioche to fit around them. Spread the brioche with **orange marmalade** at step 2. At step 6, add **2 tbsp (25 mL) marmalade** to the syrup when boiling down.

### ...another idea

For an impressive flambé dessert, cook and serve the peaches in a shallow ovenproof dish. Spoon the syrup over, without adding the brandy, then warm **3-4 tbsp (45-60 mL) brandy** in a pan for a few seconds. Pour the warm brandy over and set it alight, then take it to the table flaming.

### ...or try this

# Baked Peaches

**Create a sophisticated dessert in moments with a few simple, good-quality ingredients. Baked peaches stuffed with cool mascarpone rest on slices of vanilla brioche, spread with jam and soaked in brandy syrup.**

**1 Prepare the fruit** Preheat the oven to 460°F (240°C). Put a sieve over a pot and drain the peach halves into it. Set aside.

**2 Prepare the brioche** Trim off the edges of the brioche slices, removing the crust and rounding off the slices into circles that are slightly larger than the peaches. Spread the slices generously with jam, especially in the middle, and put them in a baking tray or shallow ovenproof dish. If you have more than 4 peach halves, chop the remainder and divide among the jam-covered brioche.

**3 Add the mascarpone** Put 1 tbsp (15 mL) mascarpone in the hollow of a peach half, leaving it in a dollop, then turn the peach upside down on to a slice of brioche and press it in place so that the mascarpone is concealed. (Don't worry if a little mascarpone shows – as long as most is inside the peach it will cook perfectly.) Repeat with the remaining peach halves and mascarpone.

**4 Add sugar and almonds** Sprinkle half the sugar over the domed tops of the peaches. Cut the butter into four slices and gently press one slice on top of each peach. Top with slivered almonds, pressing some on the butter so that a few will stay on top during cooking, then sprinkle with the remaining sugar.

**5 Bake the peaches** Bake for 7 minutes or until the butter has melted and the almonds are lightly browned. The edges of the brioche should be browned and crisp in places.

**6 Make the sauce** While the peaches are baking, boil the reserved peach syrup hard for about 3 minutes or until thickened. Transfer the peaches on brioche to warm serving plates. Add the brandy to the syrup and spoon it over the peaches. Serve immediately.

**Swaps** • For brandy, use **sweet sherry** or add **frozen raspberries** to the syrup and spoon alongside the brioche.
• For mascarpone, use **ricotta cheese**.

# 5 dream sauces for ice cream

You'll find a good choice of classy ice creams in larger supermarkets, which can be the basis of some wonderful desserts. Try these super sauces to transform ice cream into something extra-special. All recipes serve 4.

## melba purées

Purée a **14-oz (398-mL) can peach slices** with their syrup in a blender and transfer to a jug. Then purée **1¼ cups (300 mL) canned raspberries** with their syrup. (Sieve the raspberry purée if you have the time and really do not like the seeds.) The purées should be tangy and light to complement sweet ice cream, but if you prefer a sweeter flavour add **1 tsp (5 mL) icing (Confectioner's) sugar** to each. Divide the purées equally among four soup plates or dessert dishes, adding alternate amounts without mixing, peach first, then raspberry. Add ice cream to the centre and serve.

**Each serving provides** • 121 cals • 0.1 g fat of which 0 g saturates • 31 g carbohydrate

**10** mins prep time

## maple **walnut** cream sauce

Melt **1½ tbsp (20 mL) unsalted butter** in a small pot and add **1¾ cups (425 mL) walnut pieces**. Stir over a high heat for a few seconds, then reduce the heat and stir in **2 tbsp (25 mL) rum or brandy** and **6 tbsp (90 mL) maple syrup**. Bring to the boil, stirring, and bubble for about 2 minutes or until the syrup is reduced slightly. Stir in **⅔ cup (150 mL) heavy cream** and remove from the heat. Pour over ice cream – vanilla, chocolate or coffee – and serve immediately.

**Each serving provides** • 409 cals • 41 g fat of which 16.5 g saturates • 2 g carbohydrate

This sauce is also good with **pancakes** or **waffles**, warm cake, **rice pudding** or stewed apples.

...or try this

**5** mins prep time

**3** mins cook time

# rich **prune** and **port** sauce

In a blender, purée **3½ oz (100 g) ready-to-eat pitted prunes** with **1 cup (250 mL) orange juice** and **6 tbsp (90 mL) port** until smooth. Serve cold, or warm the sauce briefly in a small pot or in a suitable jug in the microwave. Serve the sauce with vanilla, coffee or chocolate ice cream.

**Each serving provides**
- 88 cals • 0.15 g fat
of which 0 g saturates
- 16 g carbohydrate

5 mins prep time

2 mins cook time

# hot **butterscotch** sauce

Put **2½ tbsp (35 mL) butter** into a small pot and add **½ cup (125 mL) packed light brown sugar** and **⅛ cup (30 mL) corn or table syrup**. Melt over a low-medium heat, stirring occasionally, until all the sugar has dissolved. Bring to the boil, then cook over a low heat, stirring occasionally, for 5 minutes. Remove from the heat and stir in **½ cup (125 mL) evaporated milk** (from a small can). Heat until gently bubbling, stirring. Transfer to a heatproof jug and serve immediately, poured over vanilla ice cream.

**Each serving provides**
- 257 cals • 12 g fat
of which 7 g saturates
- 38 g carbohydrate

5 mins prep time

15 mins cook time

# **chocolate** drizzle sauce

Heat **6 tbsp (90 mL) corn or table syrup** and **5 oz (150 g) broken dark chocolate** in a small pot over a medium heat, stirring until the chocolate has melted. Serve with ice cream, pancakes or fruit.

**Each serving provides**
- 312 cals • 10.5 g fat of which
6 g saturates • 56 g carbohydrate

3 mins prep time

3 mins cook time

> Stir in **1 cup (250 mL) heavy cream** and keep warm over a table warmer or fondue burner. Serve **biscuits, sponge fingers, marshmallows** and pieces of **fruit** to dip.
>
> **...or try this**

# Passion Fruit
## and Honey Zabaglione

Fragrant passion fruit and honey make a heavenly combination for a fruity version of the Italian dessert, zabaglione. It tastes wonderful when dunked with sponge finger biscuits or strawberries.

**5** mins prep time

**10** mins cook time

**Serves 4**
**4 ripe passion fruits**
**3 tbsp (45 mL) clear honey**
**4 large egg yolks**
**2 tsp (10 mL) lemon juice**

**Each serving provides** • 118 cals
• 5.5 g fat of which 2 g saturates
• 15 g carbohydrate

Serve the bowl of zabaglione as a dip, keeping it warm over a small pan of hot water at the table. Offer **strawberries**, **ground cherries**, **cherries**, chunks of **banana**, **chocolate finger biscuits** and **biscotti** to dip.

## ...or try this

**1 Prepare the passion fruits** Cut each fruit in half and scoop out all the pulp and seeds into a sieve set over a large heatproof bowl. Sieve the fruit thoroughly, then trickle 1 tbsp (15 mL) boiling water over the seed mixture in the sieve and scrape again with a spoon. Scrape any small amount of pulp from underneath the sieve into the bowl too. Discard the seeds.

**2 Whisk the zabaglione** Half-fill a pot with boiling water and heat to simmering point. Put the honey, egg yolks and lemon juice into the bowl with the passion fruit juice and whisk well with an electric mixer. Set the bowl over the pot of hot water and continue to whisk until the mixture is pale and thick and it holds a trail when the beaters are lifted out. This takes about 10 minutes and the mixture will look like a slightly soft, whisked sponge mixture when ready. Keep the water barely simmering – do not let it bubble too fiercely or the eggs will cook and separate.

**3 Serve the zabaglione** Remove the bowl from the pot and continue to whisk for 1 minute. Spoon, ladle or pour the mixture into four small glasses. Serve immediately.

**Swaps** • For passion fruits, honey and lemon juice, use **²⁄₃ cup (150 mL) good-quality fruit juice such as mango, or fruit purée such as raspberry**, and **3 tbsp (45 mL) sugar**. • To make a classic zabaglione, use **2 tbsp (25 mL) sugar** and **²⁄₃ cup (150 mL) Marsala wine** instead of the passion fruits, honey and lemon juice.

# Hot **Banana** and **Walnut** Sundae

**For a speedy, sweet treat to end a meal, serve bananas in a sticky and nutty sauce with ice cream. It's a fun, retro dessert given a modern zesty twist with orange, which balances the richness perfectly.**

**5 mins prep time**

**7 mins cook time**

**Serves 4**
3½ tbsp (50 mL) unsalted butter
1¾ cups (425 mL) walnut pieces
3 tbsp (45 mL) soft dark brown sugar
4 bananas, peeled
grated zest and juice of 1 orange
8 small scoops vanilla ice cream

**Each serving provides** • 497 cals
• 33 g fat of which 11 g saturates
• 47 g carbohydrate

**1 Begin the topping** Melt the butter in a frying pan, preferably nonstick, and add the walnuts. Fry the nuts over a medium heat for 1 minute. Add the sugar and cook, stirring, for 2 minutes.

**2 Add the bananas** Push the nuts to the side of the pan to make room for the bananas, then add them and cook for 30 seconds. Turn the bananas and cook for a further 30 seconds, shaking the pan gently.

**3 Make the sauce** Carefully pour the orange zest and juice into the pan – the mixture will bubble up and create a lot of steam, so take care. Shake the pan and stir the nuts and sugar, then bring to the boil. Allow to boil hard for 1 minute, moving the bananas a little with a spoon and fork so that the syrup boils evenly. The syrup should be reduced and just beginning to sizzle in places. It should form a sticky coating on and around the nuts. Remove the pan from the heat.

**4 Assemble and serve** Cut the bananas in half widthwise and put two halves on each plate. Spoon over the nut and toffee glaze. Top with two scoops of ice cream and serve.

### Hot chocolate pear sundae

Peel, core and halve **4 ripe dessert pears**. Cook the walnuts as the basic recipe and add the pear halves instead of the bananas. Instead of orange zest and juice, add **4 tbsp (60 mL) rum** to the nuts in the pan and stir for a few seconds, then remove the pan from the heat and stir in **4 tbsp (60 mL) heavy cream**. Top the pears with **chocolate ice cream** instead of vanilla and pour over the rum and walnut sauce. (Drained canned pear halves can be used instead of fresh fruit.)

**...another idea**

Any sugar will work well in this recipe. Soft dark brown sugar makes a dark, rich glaze, whereas light soft brown sugar is not quite as rich. Ordinary granulated sugar also works well, making a light, fruity glaze.

**...cooking tip**

# Fruity Yogurt
## with Chocolate Chip and Nut Crunch

**Plain yogurt makes the perfect instant dessert – it just needs a little imagination. Add some fruit and a crunchy nut topping and it will round off a meal perfectly.**

**Serves 4**

**4 chocolate chip shortbread cookies**

**½ cup (125 mL) toasted hazelnuts, chopped**

**2 tbsp (25 mL) clear honey**

**2 small bananas, sliced**

**4 ready-to-eat dried apricots, chopped**

**2½ cups (600 mL) plain yogurt**

**Each serving provides** • 409 cals
• 16 g fat of which 5 g saturates
• 57 g carbohydrate

**5 mins prep time**

**1 Make the topping** Put the shortbread biscuits in a plastic bag and crush coarsely using a rolling pin. Tip into a bowl and mix with the toasted hazelnuts and honey.

**2 Flavour the yogurt** Mix the bananas and apricots into the yogurt and divide among four bowls. Top with the biscuit, nut and honey mixture. Serve at once.

# Fabulous Fruity
## Cream of Wheat

**Don't be put off by school-day breakfast memories – properly cooked, cream of wheat is a smooth and creamy pudding that tastes delicious with added fruit. It's easy and full of goodness, and all the family will love it.**

**3** mins prep time

**10** mins cook time

**Serves 4**
⅓ cup (75 mL) cream of wheat
2 cups (500 mL) 3.25% milk
2 tbsp (25 mL) sugar
grated zest of 1 orange
5 oz (150 g) blueberries

**Each serving provides** • 180 cals
• 5 g fat of which 3 g saturates
• 29 g carbohydrate

**1** **Cook the cream of wheat** Put the cream of wheat in a pot and gradually stir in the milk. Bring to the boil over a medium heat, stirring continuously. This should take about 5 minutes. Simmer, stirring, for 5 minutes or until the cream of wheat is thick, creamy and smooth.

**2** **Sweeten and serve** Remove the pot from the heat and stir in the sugar and orange zest. Add the blueberries and fold them through gently, then divide the cream of wheat among four bowls and serve immediately.

**Swaps** For blueberries, use any **drained canned, frozen or prepared fresh fruit**. • To make chocolate cream of wheat, instead of blueberries or other fruit, stir in **3½ chopped dark or milk baking chocolate squares** with **1 tsp (5 mL) pure vanilla extract**. It's good hot or chilled (with cream). • To make chocolate banana cream of wheat, use **2 sliced bananas** and **2 tbsp (25 mL) chocolate chips**, with **raw sugar** instead of white sugar. • To make pina colada cream of wheat, use **13 tbsp (200 mL) coconut milk** and **1¼ cup (300 mL) 3.25% milk** to cook the cream of wheat. Fold in a **14-oz (398-mL) can pineapple pieces**, drained, and serve sprinkled with **toasted dried coconut**.

---

**Topping swaps** Try these other toppings with the plain yogurt.
• To make praline, brush a baking tray or a piece of foil with oil. Put **4 tbsp (60 mL) white (superfine) sugar** in a frying pan with ½ **cup (125 mL) slivered almonds**, then heat until the sugar melts. Heat on high for 1½-2 minutes, watching carefully, as the sugar caramelizes quickly once it melts. Have a slotted spatula ready and scrape all the nuts and caramel out onto the tray or foil as soon as they are brown – they will quickly burn if left in the pan. Leave to set, then break up and sprinkle over the yogurt (or ice cream, rice pudding or cream of wheat). • To make a sherried apricot sauce, mix **4 tbsp (60 mL) apricot jam** with **4 tbsp (60 mL) sweet sherry**. Drizzle over the yogurt and sprinkle with toasted slivered almonds. • To make a fresh ginger and blackcurrant topping for Greek-style yogurt, peel and finely chop ¾ **oz (20 g) fresh ginger**. Mix with **6 tbsp (90 mL) blackcurrant liqueur or syrup** and swirl it through the yogurt.

---

For the best result, take time to bring the cream of wheat and milk to the boil slowly. Stir all the time to avoid lumps.

## ...cooking tip

# Cinnamon **Strawberry** Pancake

This simple pancake is similar to drop scones but made in a fraction of the time and with the most fabulous, rich strawberry topping. Serve with ice cream if you are feeling decadent.

**10** mins prep time

**8** mins cook time

**Serves 4**

¾ cup (175 mL) all-purpose flour

1 tsp (5 mL) baking powder

1 tsp (5 mL) white (superfine) sugar

1 egg

1 tsp (5 mL) pure vanilla extract (optional)

6¾ tbsp (100 mL) 1% milk

1½ tbsp (20 mL) unsalted butter

14 oz (400 g) strawberries, hulled and halved

½ tsp (2 mL) ground cinnamon

3 tbsp (45 mL) granulated sugar

mint sprigs, to decorate (optional)

**Each serving provides** • 245 cals
• 7 g fat of which 4 g saturates
• 43 g carbohydrate

**1 Make the batter** Mix the flour, baking powder and white (superfine) sugar in a bowl. Make a well in the middle and add the egg and vanilla extract, if using. Pour in a little of the milk, then beat the egg lightly until it is mixed with the milk and vanilla. Gradually stir in the flour mixture and pour in the remaining milk a little at a time. Before all the milk is added and while the mixture is quite thick, beat well to remove all the lumps, then gradually beat in the remaining milk to make a smooth batter.

**2 Cook the pancake** Preheat the broiler to the hottest setting. On the stovetop, melt the butter in a 8-8½-in. (20-22-cm) frying pan that can safely be used in the oven (cover a wooden handle with foil). Swirl the butter around the pan, then pour in the batter and cook over a medium heat until the pancake is golden underneath. The batter should have risen and almost set on top. The surface will break into little bubbles.

**3 Finish under the broiler** Slide the frying pan under the broiler and cook for 1 minute. Scatter the strawberries evenly over the pancake. Sprinkle with the cinnamon and sugar, then grill for 3 minutes or until the sugar has melted. Cut into four wedges, decorate with mint, if you like, and serve immediately.

**Swaps** • Instead of making batter, use store-bought pancakes. Heat **4 large pancakes**, one at a time, in a little melted **unsalted butter** in the frying pan  for about 30 seconds each or according to the pack instructions, then fold each one into four. Put all 4 pancakes back in the pan, add the strawberries, cinnamon and sugar for the basic recipe (use white (superfine) sugar, as it melts quickly) and grill for about 1 minute. • For strawberries, use **raspberries, blueberries or blackberries**.

## Ricotta and raspberry pancake stack

Preheat the oven to 400°F (200°C). Cover a baking tray with foil and grease it with a little butter. Beat **1 cup (250 mL) ricotta cheese** with **3 tbsp (45 mL) icing (confectioner's) sugar** and the **grated zest of 1 lemon**. Have **12 oz (375 g) frozen raspberries** ready. From a **package of bought pancakes,** lay one pancake on the foil and spread with a third of the ricotta, then sprinkle with a third of the raspberries. Repeat twice more, then top with a pancake. Dot the top with **unsalted butter** and dust with a little **icing (confectioner's) sugar**. Bake for 15 minutes or until the sugar and butter have glazed the top and the raspberries have thawed. Cut into wedges to serve.

## Banana pancakes with fudge sauce

Roughly chop **2 x 2-oz (58-g) Mars Bars (or chocolate-caramel bars**), then put into a heatproof bowl with **6¾ tbsp (100 mL) table cream**. Set over a pot of gently simmering water and stir until melted into a smooth sauce. Heat **4 large store-bought pancakes** in a frying pan (see Swaps opposite). Slice **4 bananas** and divide among the pancakes. Fold into quarters and drizzle over the sauce. (Thinly sliced apple also works well in this recipe.)

# ...speedy desserts with bought pancakes

# 5 comforting rice puddings

**Canned rice pudding is a great pantry standby for dessert, and it just needs some fruit, nuts or spices for extra goodness and variety. Here's how to make a fast pudding as well as some occasional treats. All recipes serve 4.**

## quick rice pudding

Put **½ cup (125 mL) long-grain rice** (not easy-cook) in a heavy-based pot, preferably nonstick, and add **2 cups (500 mL) 1% milk**. Bring to the boil, stirring occasionally. Turn the heat to the lowest setting and stir until the milk sinks back, then cover and cook gently for 15 minutes, giving the pot a shake occasionally. Stir in an extra **1¼ cups (300 mL) 1% milk** and bring back to the boil, stirring all the time. Boil, stirring constantly, for 7 minutes. Remove from the heat and stir for 1 minute, then stir in **4-5 tsp (20-25 mL) sugar**. This is creamy, with soft grains of rice, like a traditional baked pudding.

**Each serving provides** • 205 cals • 4 g fat of which 2 g saturates • 37 g carbohydrate

**1** min prep time  **26** mins cook time

Put **⅔ cup (150 mL) rice flakes (beaten rice)** in a pan with 3 cups (750 mL) 1% milk. Bring to the boil, stirring often, then reduce the heat to low. Simmer, stirringoccasionally, for 10 minutes. Stir well, then stir in **4-5 tsp (20-25 mL) sugar**. The pudding should be smooth, with a slightly grainy texture.

### ...or try this

## indian-style rice pudding

Empty **2 x 15-oz (425-g) cans rice pudding** into a bowl. Grind the **seeds from 4 green cardamom pods** to a powder using a mortar and pestle. Add to the rice pudding with **4 tbsp (60 mL) chopped pistachios or toasted slivered almonds**, **1-3 tsp (5-15 mL) rosewater**, to taste, and **3 tbsp (45 mL) sultana raisins or chopped dried apricots**. Serve cold.

**Each serving provides** • 278 cals • 8 g fat of which 2 g saturates • 44 g carbohydrate

**4** mins prep time

# caramelized rice pudding

Preheat the grill to high. Divide the contents of a **15-oz (425-g) can rice pudding** among four small ramekins or bowls that will go under the grill. Sprinkle **1-2 tbsp (15-25 mL) raw cane sugar** over each pudding and grill until melted and bubbling. Can be eaten at once, or chilled.

**Each serving provides** • 166 cals
• 6 g fat of which 3.5 g saturates
• 25 g carbohydrate

**3** mins prep time  **4** mins cook time

# cinnamon rice with hot plums

Heat the contents of **2 x 15-oz (425-g) cans rice pudding**. Empty a **14-oz (398-mL) can halved plums in syrup** into a separate pot and heat, adding **¼ tsp (1 mL) ground cinnamon** to the plums. Divide the rice among four bowls and top with the plums. Sprinkle with extra cinnamon, if you like. Serve at once.

**Each serving provides** • 243 cals • 3 g fat of which 2 g saturates • 51 g carbohydrate

**5** mins prep time  **3** mins cook time

# rice condé

Whip **6¾ tbsp (100 mL) whipping cream** with **1 tsp (5 mL) pure vanilla extract** and fold it into a **15-oz (425-g) can rice pudding**. Layer the rice in glass dishes with a **14-oz (398-mL) can fruit pie filling**. Chill for 10 minutes in the freezer, if you have time.

**Each serving provides** • 287 cals • 15 g fat of which 9 g saturates • 37 g carbohydrate

**5** mins prep time

# Cheesecake Pairs

These delicious, zesty little lemon curd cheesecakes on a crumbly shortbread base make a simple but attractive no-cook dessert. Topped with strawberries, they look almost too good to eat.

**20 mins prep time**

**Serves 4**

**8 good-quality round butter shortbread cookies**

**grated zest and juice of 1 small lemon**

**3 tbsp (45 mL) lemon curd**

**½ lb (250 g) low-fat cream cheese, chilled**

**4 tsp (20 mL) icing (confectioner's) sugar**

**8 strawberries, hulled and sliced**

**Each serving provides** • 292 cals
• 13 g fat of which 8 g saturates
• 37 g carbohydrate

**1 Prepare the bases** Put the shortbread cookies on a board. Brush the tops generously with some of the lemon juice, then spread them with about half the lemon curd, keeping it in the centre of the cookies.

**2 Mix the cheese topping** Stir the remaining lemon juice and the zest into the cream cheese together with the icing (confectioner's) sugar. Divide the cheese mixture among the cookies, piling it on with a teaspoon.

**3 Add the topping** Spread the remaining lemon curd over the tops of the cheesecakes – there should be just enough to cover the centres thinly. Top each cheesecake with a sliced strawberry.

**Swaps** • For cream cheese, use **mascarpone, curd cheese or quark**. • Try different biscuit bases, such as **chocolate chip shortbread or cookies, or crunchy oat cookies**.

**Black Forest cheesecakes**
Cut a bought **plain chocolate cake** into slices about ½-¾ in. (1-2 cm) thick and stamp out eight circles using a 2-3-in. (5-7.5-cm) cutter. Moisten with a little **kirsch** and top with a little **black cherry conserve**. Make the cheesecake mixture as step 2, using **1 tbsp (15 mL) lemon juice** and the **zest**. Spread over the cake circles and top with more conserve. Decorate with bought **chocolate sprinkles** and serve with heavy cream to pour over.

## ...another idea

# Triple **Chocolate** Roulade

Treat everyone to this warm and light chocolate Swiss roll with its rich filling of chocolate spread. It's so quick and easy – just add a scoop of vanilla ice cream for the perfect balance.

**10** mins prep time  **10** mins cook time

**Serves 6**

**3 eggs**

**¾ cup (175 mL) white (superfine) sugar**

**⅔ cup (150 mL) plain flour**

**6 tbsp (90 mL) cocoa powder**

**1 tbsp (15 mL) brandy**

**½ tsp (2 mL) pure vanilla extract**

**1½ tbsp (20 mL) unsalted butter**

**1 tbsp (15 mL) icing (confectioner's) sugar**

**9 tbsp (140 mL) chocolate spread**

**Each serving provides** • 450 cals
• 21 g fat of which 3.5 g saturates
• 60 g carbohydrate

### Raspberry cake pudding

Make the cake without the cocoa. Sprinkle **10 oz (300 g) frozen raspberries** over the cake just before putting it in the oven. Bake for 10-15 minutes. Heat **6 tbsp (90 mL) raspberry jam** with **6 tbsp (90 mL) dry sherry or cider, or apple juice**, until melted. Serve the hot cake cut into squares, overlapping two squares on each plate. Drizzle the raspberry sauce over and serve with cream or ice cream.

## ...another idea

**1 Whisk the eggs and sugar** Preheat the oven to 425°F (220°C) and cover a large baking sheet with a sheet of baking parchment. In a large mixing bowl use an electric mixer to whisk the eggs with half the white (superfine) sugar until pale and very thick; the mixture will hold its shape. This takes about 3 minutes on high speed.

**2 Add the flour** Sift the flour and 2 tbsp (25 mL) cocoa evenly over the mixture, then use a large metal spoon to fold it in, turning the mixture over in big scoops rather than stirring it.

**3 Bake the cake** Pour the mixture on to the parchment and spread it out lightly into a rectangle about 9 x 13 in. (23 x 33 cm). Do not press heavily – it does not matter if the edges are not quite square. Bake for 8-10 minutes or until risen, set and springy in the middle.

**4 Make the syrup** While the cake is baking, put the remaining white (superfine) sugar into a pot with 2 tbsp (25 mL) of the remaining cocoa and ⅔ cup (150 mL) water. Bring to the boil, stirring, and boil for 2 minutes. Remove from the heat and stir in the brandy, vanilla extract and butter. Set aside over a low heat to keep warm.

**5 Turn out the cake** Dampen a clean dish towel with hot water, then lay it on a clean surface. Lay a sheet of baking parchment on top and sift the remaining cocoa and the icing (confectioner's) sugar over to about the size of the cake. Take the cake from the oven and invert it on to the cocoa on the paper.

**6 Roll the cake** Peel off the lining paper and trim off the crisp edges. Make a shallow cut about ½ in. (1 cm) in from a long edge but not right through the cake. Dollop the chocolate spread over the cake and spread it out thickly – no need to be too fussy. Roll up the cake and filling from the long edge with the cut, using the cut to start the roll tightly. Hold the paper and damp cloth to guide the roll, then hold the roll firmly in the damp cloth for a minute, so that it sets in place.

**7 Serve** Take off the towel and paper, sprinkling the cocoa mixture over the cake. Don't worry if the roll is slightly cracked. Cut six slices of roll, using a serrated knife, and arrange them on serving plates, then spoon the hot syrup over the top.

**Cooking tip** For an alcohol-free version, omit the brandy.

# Dark **Chocolate** Pots
## with White Chocolate Cream

Keep this unbelievably easy recipe a secret, never revealing that the silky, rich dessert of dark and white chocolate was created in minutes, not hours. Dark chocolate with 70 per cent cocoa solids will give the dessert the best flavour.

**10** mins prep time

**20** mins chill time

**Serves 6**

7 oz (200 g) dark chocolate

15 oz (425 g) low-fat custard (at room temperature)

1 tbsp (15 mL) brandy

½ cup (125 mL) light whipping cream

1 square (1 oz/28 g) white baking chocolate, finely grated

**Each serving provides**

• 376 cals • 24 g fat of which 13 g saturates • 37 g carbohydrate

**1** **Melt the chocolate** Put six ramekins, small glass dishes or shallow tumblers in the freezer to chill. Break the chocolate into small pieces and put into a heatproof bowl set over a pot of gently simmering water. Stir until the chocolate has melted – this will take about 3 minutes. Remove the bowl from the pot as soon as the chocolate has melted and stir until smooth.

**2** **Add the custard** Pour in about a third of the custard and stir lightly. The chocolate will begin to thicken and become glossy, so do not overmix – a couple of large scooping stirs are enough. Pour in all the remaining custard and stir to combine it with the chocolate. The mixture will thicken as the chocolate cools. Stir in the brandy.

**3** **Fill the dishes** Spoon the mixture into the chilled ramekins, adding it to the middle in dollops. Put in the freezer to chill for 20 minutes or until set.

**4** **Prepare the cream** Put the cream into a bowl and whip until it just begins to thicken and hold its shape. Stir in the grated white chocolate and chill in the fridge until you need it. Spoon the cream on to the chocolate pots and serve at once.

**Swaps** • Instead of light whipping cream, use ⅔ cup (150 mL) heavy whipping cream without whipping, chilled in the freezer for 5 minutes. • Or top the desserts with a dollop of **mascarpone** (with or without the grated white chocolate).

**Addition** Serve with **fresh soft fruits or sliced fresh nectarines, peaches, mango or pineapple** on the side.

## Soft chocolate orange creams

Melt **5 oz (150 g) chocolate** instead of 7 oz (200 g). Omit the brandy and add the **grated zest of 1 orange** and **2 tbsp (25 mL) orange juice**. Chill the pots in the freezer for 20 minutes. These are lighter and more softly set.

# ...another idea

• If using a chocolate bar, break it up quickly by slapping it in its wrapping on the countertop. Do this three or four times, holding the bar by different sides, then open the wrapping over a large bowl. The chocolate will be broken into very small pieces.

• If you want the sauce to be less rich you can omit the cream topping and grate a little white chocolate over the mousse.

# ...cooking tips

This versatile chocolate custard mixture can be used as a filling for **sponge** or **Madeira cake**, in **pastry tartlets** topped with **hulled and sliced strawberries** and **whipped cream**, or as a **warm chocolate dip** for **fruit** or **biscuits, sponge fingers or Italian biscotti**.

# ...or try this

# 5 fabulous ten-minute desserts

Take some fresh fruit and jazz up waffles, bought meringues or simple doughnuts – or just open some canned fruit and custard – to whip up the quickest-ever desserts when you fancy something sweet to follow a meal. All recipes serve 4.

## eton mess

Whip **1 cup (250 mL) whipping cream** until it just holds soft peaks. Break **4 meringue nests** into pieces and add them to the cream with **12 oz (375 g) raspberries**. Fold in lightly with a metal spoon, then divide the mixture among four dishes or glasses and serve.

**Each serving provides** • 390 cals • 33 g fat of which 21 g saturates • 20 g carbohydrate

**5** mins prep time

## lazy **gooseberry** fool

Drain a **12-oz (375-g) jar gooseberries or ground cherries**. Blend the fruit to a smooth purée. Turn a **15-oz (425-g) can low-fat custard** into a bowl and stir in the berry purée. Divide among four small ramekins or glasses and chill in the freezer for 5-15 minutes. Serve plain or top each dessert with **1 tbsp (15 mL) heavy whipping cream or Greek-style yogurt** and sprinkle with a few **toasted slivered almonds**, if you like.

**Each serving provides** • 119 cals • 1 g fat of which 0.6 g saturates • 22 g carbohydrate

**5** mins prep time    **15** mins chill time

# doughnut babas

Prick **4 doughnuts** in a few places around the top and put them on to plates. Spoon 1 tbsp (15 mL) **rum or orange juice** over each doughnut. Pile ½ **lb (250 g) raspberries** and **2 oz (60 g) black grapes** inside the doughnut rings, saving some for decoration. Add a dollop of **ricotta cheese or yogurt** to each. Sprinkle with **icing (confectioner's) sugar** and decorate with the reserved fruit.

**Each serving provides** • 464 cals • 30 g fat of which 13.5 g saturates • 39 g carbohydrate

5 mins prep time

# waffles with **grapes** and **almonds**

Heat **4 waffles** in a toaster or under the grill according to the package instructions. Meanwhile, melt **1½ tbsp (20 mL) unsalted butter** in a frying pan and add **2 tbsp (25 mL) slivered almonds**. Stir for a few seconds, then add **7 oz (200 g) seedless green grapes**. Cook, stirring, for 2 minutes or until the almonds smell nutty and are lightly browned. Add **1 tbsp (15 mL) sugar** and a **squeeze of lemon juice** and stir for a few seconds or until the sugar dissolves to glaze the grapes. Serve the fruit and nuts on the waffles.

**Each serving provides** • 242 cals • 14 g fat of which 3 g saturates • 26 g carbohydrate

5 mins prep time    3 mins cook time

# banana and **peach** stir-fry

Melt **1½ tbsp (20 mL) unsalted butter** in a frying pan and add **2 sliced bananas**, a **14-oz (398-mL) can peach slices**, drained, and the grated **zest of 1 orange**. Stir-fry for about 2 minutes over a high heat until the fruit is hot and beginning to brown. Stir in **2 tbsp (25 mL) maraschino cherry juice or or apple or black currant liqueur** and serve at once, with plain yogurt or ice cream.

**Each serving provides** • 129 cals • 4 g fat of which 3 g saturates • 23 g carbohydrate

5 mins prep time    2 mins cook time

# Oat-Topped **Nectarines**

Stir up a golden oaty topping to cover sticky cooked nectarines, for a dish that tastes like fruit crumble but without the effort. Serve with custard or ice cream.

**6** mins prep time   **12** mins cook time

**Serves 4**

⅔ cup (150 mL) rolled oats

2 tbsp (25 mL) brown sugar

3½ tbsp (50 mL) unsalted butter

4 firm, ripe nectarines, halved, pitted and sliced

2 tbsp (25 mL) granulated sugar

**Each serving provides** • 305 cals
• 13 g fat of which 7 g saturates
• 46 g carbohydrate

**1** **Cook the oats** Mix the oats and brown sugar in a bowl. Melt the butter in a large frying pan over a medium heat. Reduce the heat slightly. Add the oats and stir well, then spread them out evenly in the pan and leave to cook gently for 3 minutes.

**2** **Cook the nectarines** While the oats are cooking, put the nectarines in a pot and add the granulated sugar. Pour in 1 tbsp (15 mL) water and cook over a medium-high heat, stirring all the time, for 2-3 minutes or until the fruit is juicy, sticky and slightly softened around the edges. It should be sizzling in the pot. Remove the pot from the heat, cover and set aside.

**3** **Finish cooking the oats** Increase the heat under the oats to medium and cook them, stirring and turning all the time, for 5-6 minutes or until they are lightly browned. Keep an eye on the temperature, turning it down if the oats begin to brown noticeably quickly, or up if they are still pale and floury.

**4** **Assemble and serve** Turn the nectarines into a serving dish, spreading them evenly, and top with the oats. Spread out the oats and press them down gently with the back of a spoon. Serve at once – or leave to stand for a while, if you prefer.

**Swaps** • For nectarines, use **1 lb (500 g) cooking apples**, peeled, cored and thinly sliced, cooked with **4 tbsp (60 mL) sugar** and 1 tbsp (15 mL) water for 5 minutes or until tender.
• Or use **6 stalks of rhubarb**, trimmed and cut into ¾-in. (2-cm) lengths, and cooked with **4 tbsp (60 mL) sugar** and 1 tbsp (15 mL) water for 5 minutes.

## Brown betty

Omit the oats. Trim the crusts off **1 small white loaf** and reduce it to coarse crumbs in a food processor or blender, adding **3 tbsp (45 mL) white (superfine) sugar** instead of the brown. Melt **5½ tbsp (80 mL) butter** and stir-fry the bread crumbs until they are golden. Prepare and cook **8 nectarines** as step 2. Pour half of them into a soufflé dish, then add half the crumbs. Repeat with the remaining fruit and crumbs, then press down firmly with the back of a spoon. Leave to stand for 10 minutes before serving. Serves 4-6.

**...another idea**

# Apricot Almond Torte

For a fast finish to a special mid-week meal, take advantage of the excellent Italian biscotti that are available in larger supermarkets to make this divine dessert. It's easy, impressive and completely delectable.

**15** mins prep time

**30** secs cook time

### Serves 4

3 long almond and chocolate-chip biscotti, about 4 oz (125 g) total weight

3 tbsp (45 mL) medium sherry

grated zest and juice of 1 lemon

7 oz (200 g) ricotta cheese

3½ oz (100 g) marzipan, coarsely grated

14 oz (398 g) can apricot halves, drained

**Each serving provides** • 331 cals
• 13 g fat of which 5 g saturates
• 44 g carbohydrate

**1 Moisten the biscotti** Preheat the grill to high. Lay a piece of baking parchment on a baking tray or in the grill pan. Lay the biscotti on the paper, side by side and flat side down. Mix the sherry and lemon juice and use a teaspoon to spoon it evenly over the biscotti, allowing time for it to soak into the hard biscuits.

**2 Coat the biscotti** Mix the ricotta with the lemon zest and two thirds of the marzipan. Spread this all over the biscotti, covering them completely, with most of the mixture on top and a thin covering over the sides.

**3 Add the apricots** Arrange the apricot halves on top of the ricotta mixture, hollow sides up, and sprinkle with the remaining marzipan. Put under the grill for 25-30 seconds, which is all it takes for the marzipan to brown. Cut into slices to serve.

**Swaps** • For sherry, use **orange juice**. • For apricots, use drained **canned sliced peaches, halved pineapple slices or mandarin oranges**.

Once browned at step 3, the torte can be cooled and kept in the fridge until ready to serve. It keeps well for several hours or overnight, and it improves as the biscotti soften and the flavours mingle.

## ...get ahead

# Easiest-Ever Menus

**Entertaining can be easy, whether it's a weeknight or relaxed weekend meal, so there's no need to panic when you want to invite friends or family to share some good food with you. Try these simple menus and shortcut ideas.**

Sometimes the thought of entertaining can be daunting, but it becomes more manageable if you choose the right dishes. You don't always have to offer three complicated courses; most guests would be more than happy with two, especially if you serve olives or chips to nibble on first. Or you could serve a virtually no-prep first course, such as smoked salmon, melon or steamed asparagus, and for dessert, ice cream jazzed up with a simple sauce. Then you can concentrate on cooking

just the main course from any of the 30-minute recipes in this book. If you do have more time, one of the simpler first courses or dessert recipes will make the meal a little more special. The following menus are all stress-free, giving you time to relax and chat rather than slave away over the oven. You could substitute no-cook starters and the like for some of the recipes, or swap some of the courses between the menus – just experiment and enjoy. All menus serve 4.

### Easy summer supper

½ cantaloupe, sliced thinly, with scrunched Parma ham

Basque-Style Pacific Cod with Peppers (page 177), bread and salad

Doughnut Babas (page 307)

### Impromptu meal with friends

Roasted Artichoke and Pepper Bruschetta (half quantity) (page 64)

Garlic Seafood Pasta (page 126)

Zesty Pineapple and Kiwi Salad (page 286)

### Chilled-out dinner party

Greek Salad with Tahini Dressing (half quantity) (page 78)

Pan-Fried Chicken with Mushrooms and Blueberries (page 208), crushed potatoes and salad

Apricot Almond Torte (page 309)

### Vegetarian supper

Spinach and Parmesan Soufflés (page 103)

Sweet and Spicy Chickpeas (page 266), chapattis and yogurt

Ice cream with Melba Purées (page 292)

## Special mid-week get-together

Steamed asparagus with melted butter

Oriental Noodles with Plum and
Ginger Duck (page 134)

Passion Fruit and Honey Zabaglione (page 294)

## Relaxed celebration dinner

Hot-smoked salmon on a mixed-leaf salad with
Simple Mustard and Dill Dressing (page 173)

Peppered Beef with Pecans (page 229),
garlic mashed potatoes and snow peas

Eton Mess (page 306)

## Fresh-and-healthy lunch

Sliced avocado with vinaigrette (page 31)

Middle Eastern Salad (page 279)

Warm Pear and Mango Compote (page 285)

## Fuss-free informal supper

Deli spread - olives, thinly sliced salami, dips
served with crudites and pita bread

Creamy Chicken Korma (page 196),
nan bread and salad

Peppered Strawberries and Blueberries (page 287)

## Kids' favourite

Grapefruit halves

Cowboy Casserole (page 262)

Mint ice cream with Chocolate Drizzle Sauce
(page 293)

## Family picnic

Picnic Omelette with Feta and Peppers (page 97)

Moroccan Wraps (page 70)

Nectarines, strawberries and shortbread cookies

# Index

Recipes titles in *italic* refer to
...another idea or ...more ideas

# Acknowledgments

**PROJECT STAFF**
**For Reader's Digest Canada**
**Consulting Editor** Jesse Corbeil
**Proofreaders** John David Gravenor, Peter Deslauriers
**Designers** Andrée Payette, Ann Devoe
**Manager, Book Editorial** Pamela Johnson
**Production Manager** Gordon Howlett
**Production Coordinator** Gillian Sylvain

**The Reader's Digest Association (Canada) ULC**
**Vice-President, Book Editorial** Robert Goyette

**UK Project Team**
**Editor** Lisa Thomas
**Editorial Director** Julian Browne
**Art Director** Anne-Marie Bulat
**Head of Book Development** Sarah Bloxham
**Managing Editor** Nina Hathway
**Picture Resource Manager** Sarah Stewart-Richardson

**The Reader's Digest Association, Inc.**
**President and Chief Executive Officer** Mary Berner

**Created by Amazon Publishing Limited**
**7 Old Lodge Place, Twickenham TW1 1RQ**
**Editor** Jan Cutler
**Consultant Editors** Roz Denny, Norma Macmillan
**Editorial Assistant** Kate Eddison
**Recipe Writers** Catherine Atkinson, Linda Collister, Roz Denny, Christine France, Bridget Jones, Maggie Pannell, Gina Steer
**Recipe Testers** Catherine Atkinson, Anna Brandenburger, Linda Collister, Christine France, Maggie Pannell, Gina Steer, Susanna Tee
**Editorial Writer, Quick and Easy Cooking** Maggie Pannell
**Nutritionist** Jane Griffin
**Designers** Colin Goody, Murdo Culver
**Indexer** Hilary Bird
**Proofreaders** Barry Gage, Jill Steed

## Weeknight Meals Made Easy

Library and Archives Canada Cataloguing in Publication

Weeknight Meals Made Easy : 365 Sensationally Simple Meals Ready in Just 30 Minutes / the editors of Reader's Digest. -- 1st Canadian ed.

Includes index.

ISBN 978-1-55475-022-1 (bound).

We are committed to both the quality of our products and the service we provide to our customers. If you have any comments about the content of this book, please write to:
*in Canada:* The Book Editor, Reader's Digest Association (Canada) ULC, 1100 René-Lévesque Blvd. W., Montreal, QC H3B 5H5; and
*in the U.S.:* The Reader's Digest Association, Inc., Adult Trade Publishing, Reader's Digest Road, Pleasantville, NY 10570-7000

For more Reader's Digest products and information, visit our website:
in Canada at **rd.ca**
in the United States at **rd.com**

**Photography**
All images RD copyright © 2008 except pages 13, 30, 73, 74, 95, 96, 100, 130, 145, 176, 189, 284, 297, 308 Istock; pages 36, 46, 57, 80, 120, 150, 168, 194, 213, 253, 267, 273, 278 Shutterstock
**Art director** Luis Peral
**Photographers** David Munns, William Shaw, Kate Whitaker, Rob White
**Cover photograph** David Munns
**Food stylists** Valerie Berry, Georgina Footit, Lisa Harrison, Bridget Sargeson, Stella Sargeson, Joy Skipper, Sarah Tildesley
**Props stylists** Victoria Allen, Rob Merrett

Printed in United States
1 3 5 7 9 10 8 6 4 2